ATL Developer's Guide, 2nd Edition

ATL Developer's Guide, 2nd Edition

Tom Armstrong, with Ron Patton

M&T Books
An imprint of IDG Books Worldwide, Inc.
An International Data Group Company

Foster City, CA ◆ Chicago, IL ◆ Indianapolis, IN ◆ New York, NY

ATL Developer's Guide, 2nd Edition

Published by
M&T Books
An imprint of IDG Books Worldwide, Inc.
An International Data Group Company
919 E. Hillsdale Blvd., Suite 400
Foster City, CA 94404
www.idgbooks.com (IDG Books Worldwide Web site)

Library of Congress Catalog Card Number: 00-103921

ISBN: 0-7645-4683-X

Printed in the United States of America

10 9 8 7 6 5 4 3 2 1

10/RT/QW/QQ/FC

Distributed in the United States by IDG Books Worldwide, Inc.

Distributed by CDG Books Canada Inc. for Canada; by Transworld Publishers Limited in the United Kingdom; by IDG Norge Books for Norway; by IDG Sweden Books for Sweden; by IDG Books Australia Publishing Corporation Pty. Ltd. for Australia and New Zealand; by TransQuest Publishers Pte Ltd. for Singapore, Malaysia, Thailand, Indonesia, and Hong Kong; by Gotop Information Inc. for Taiwan; by ICG Muse, Inc. for Japan; by Intersoft for South Africa; by Eyrolles for France; by International Thomson Publishing for Germany, Austria and Switzerland; by Distribuidora Cuspide for Argentina; by LR International for Brazil; by Galileo Libros for Chile; by Ediciones ZETA S.C.R. Ltda. for Peru; by WS Computer Publishing Corporation, Inc., for the Philippines; by Contemporanea de Ediciones for Venezuela; by Express Computer Distributors for the Caribbean and West Indies; by Micronesia Media Distributor, Inc. for Micronesia; by Chips Computadoras S.A. de C.V. for Mexico; by Editorial Norma de Panama S.A. for Panama; by American Bookshops for Finland.

For general information on IDG Books Worldwide's books in the U.S., please call our Consumer Customer Service department at 800-762-2974. For reseller information, including discounts and premium sales, please call our Reseller Customer Service department at 800-434-3422.

For information on where to purchase IDG Books Worldwide's books outside the U.S., please contact our International Sales department at 317-596-5530 or fax 317-596-5692.

For consumer information on foreign language translations, please contact our Customer Service department at 800-434-3422, fax 317-596-5692, or e-mail rights@idgbooks.com.

For information on licensing foreign or domestic rights, please phone +1-650-655-3109.

For sales inquiries and special prices for bulk quantities, please contact our Sales department at 650-655-3200 or write to the address above.

For information on using IDG Books Worldwide's books in the classroom or for ordering examination copies, please contact our Educational Sales department at 800-434-2086 or fax 317-596-5499.

For press review copies, author interviews, or other publicity information, please contact our Public Relations department at 650-655-3000 or fax 650-655-3299.

For authorization to photocopy items for corporate, personal, or educational use, please contact Copyright Clearance Center, 222 Rosewood Drive, Danvers, MA 01923, or fax 978-750-4470.

is a registered trademark or trademark under exclusive license to IDG Books Worldwide, Inc. from International Data Group, Inc. in the United States and/or other countries.

is a trademark of IDG Books Worldwide, Inc.

ABOUT IDG BOOKS WORLDWIDE

Welcome to the world of IDG Books Worldwide.

IDG Books Worldwide, Inc., is a subsidiary of International Data Group, the world's largest publisher of computer-related information and the leading global provider of information services on information technology. IDG was founded more than 30 years ago by Patrick J. McGovern and now employs more than 9,000 people worldwide. IDG publishes more than 290 computer publications in over 75 countries. More than 90 million people read one or more IDG publications each month.

Launched in 1990, IDG Books Worldwide is today the #1 publisher of best-selling computer books in the United States. We are proud to have received eight awards from the Computer Press Association in recognition of editorial excellence and three from Computer Currents' First Annual Readers' Choice Awards. Our best-selling ...*For Dummies*® series has more than 50 million copies in print with translations in 31 languages. IDG Books Worldwide, through a joint venture with IDG's Hi-Tech Beijing, became the first U.S. publisher to publish a computer book in the People's Republic of China. In record time, IDG Books Worldwide has become the first choice for millions of readers around the world who want to learn how to better manage their businesses.

Our mission is simple: Every one of our books is designed to bring extra value and skill-building instructions to the reader. Our books are written by experts who understand and care about our readers. The knowledge base of our editorial staff comes from years of experience in publishing, education, and journalism — experience we use to produce books to carry us into the new millennium. In short, we care about books, so we attract the best people. We devote special attention to details such as audience, interior design, use of icons, and illustrations. And because we use an efficient process of authoring, editing, and desktop publishing our books electronically, we can spend more time ensuring superior content and less time on the technicalities of making books.

You can count on our commitment to deliver high-quality books at competitive prices on topics you want to read about. At IDG Books Worldwide, we continue in the IDG tradition of delivering quality for more than 30 years. You'll find no better book on a subject than one from IDG Books Worldwide.

John J. Kilcullen
John Kilcullen
Chairman and CEO
IDG Books Worldwide, Inc.

VIII
WINNER
*Eighth Annual
Computer Press
Awards ≥1992*

IX
WINNER
*Ninth Annual
Computer Press
Awards ≥1993*

X
WINNER
*Tenth Annual
Computer Press
Awards ≥1994*

XI
WINNER
*Eleventh Annual
Computer Press
Awards ≥1995*

IDG is the world's leading IT media, research and exposition company. Founded in 1964, IDG had 1997 revenues of $2.05 billion and has more than 9,000 employees worldwide. IDG offers the widest range of media options that reach IT buyers in 75 countries representing 95% of worldwide IT spending. IDG's diverse product and services portfolio spans six key areas including print publishing, online publishing, expositions and conferences, market research, education and training, and global marketing services. More than 90 million people read one or more of IDG's 290 magazines and newspapers, including IDG's leading global brands — Computerworld, PC World, Network World, Macworld and the Channel World family of publications. IDG Books Worldwide is one of the fastest-growing computer book publishers in the world, with more than 700 titles in 36 languages. The "...For Dummies®" series alone has more than 50 million copies in print. IDG offers online users the largest network of technology-specific Web sites around the world through IDG.net (http://www.idg.net), which comprises more than 225 targeted Web sites in 55 countries worldwide. International Data Corporation (IDC) is the world's largest provider of information technology data, analysis and consulting, with research centers in over 41 countries and more than 400 research analysts worldwide. IDG World Expo is a leading producer of more than 168 globally branded conferences and expositions in 35 countries including E3 (Electronic Entertainment Expo), Macworld Expo, ComNet, Windows World Expo, ICE (Internet Commerce Expo), Agenda, DEMO, and Spotlight. IDG's training subsidiary, ExecuTrain, is the world's largest computer training company, with more than 230 locations worldwide and 785 training courses. IDG Marketing Services helps industry-leading IT companies build international brand recognition by developing global integrated marketing programs via IDG's print, online and exposition products worldwide. Further information about the company can be found at www.idg.com.   1/26/00

Credits

ACQUISITIONS EDITORS
John Osborn
Greg Croy

PROJECT EDITOR
Michael Koch

TECHNICAL EDITOR
Allan Wyatt

COPY EDITORS
Victoria Lee
Mildred Sanchez

PROJECT COORDINATORS
Linda Marousek
Danette Nurse
Marcos Vergara

BOOK DESIGNER
Jim Donohue

GRAPHICS AND PRODUCTION SPECIALISTS
Robert Bihlmayer
Jude Levinson
Michael Lewis
Victor Pérez-Varela
Ramses Ramirez
Dina F Quan

DESIGN SPECIALISTS
Kurt Krames
Kippy Thomsen

ILLUSTRATORS
Gabriele McCann
Rashell Smith

PROOFREADING AND INDEXING
York Production Services

About the Author

Tom Armstrong is an independent author and consultant with over ten years of Microsoft-related development experience. Tom is currently working as chief technologist for Tradebot Systems and director of software architecture for BizSpace Inc., both in Kansas City, Missouri. Tom also instructs courses on C++, Windows DNA, and other COM+-related topics. He has written several books including *Designing and Using ActiveX Controls* (M&T Books, 1997) and *ActiveXpert* (McGraw-Hill, 1997). Tom also writes technical articles for publications such as *Dr. Dobb's Journal*, *Visual C++ Developer's Journal*, and *Component Builder*. You can reach him at Tom@WidgetWare.com.

Ron Patton is a consultant and trainer with over ten years of development experience in Microsoft and UNIX-related technologies. Ron works from his home in Gainesville, Florida, as a software engineer for Digital Archaeology based in Lenexa, Kansas. Ron also develops and instructs courseware on a variety of topics, including C++, MFC, COM and OLE DB. You can reach him at rpatton@fdt.net.

To Nicole, Jessica, Eric, and Shady with love.

Preface

This book is about one of Microsoft's most important new development tools: the Active Template Library (ATL). ATL is a C++-based framework that facilitates the development of small and efficient software components based on Microsoft's Component Object Model (COM). ATL is similar to the Microsoft Foundation Class (MFC) libraries, the most popular C++-based framework on the Windows platform. MFC has been around for about six years and has grown to be the dominant framework for developing Windows applications. In many cases, ATL is now the preferred framework to use when developing Windows-based software.

MFC will not go away overnight; in fact, you can use MFC with the ATL but existing MFC features probably will merge with ATL over time. Microsoft developed the new ATL framework primarily for one reason: a new application development architecture called the Component Object Model (COM).

COM is Microsoft's system-level, object-oriented technology that is used extensively within its products and tools. COM provides several features that software developers need. COM provides language independence, which enables developers to reuse their C++ modules in Visual Basic, Delphi, or virtually any other development environment. COM also provides location transparency, which enables a software module to execute anywhere in a distributed network environment. In addition, COM provides the standard object-oriented characteristics of encapsulation, polymorphism, and inheritance. COM is the future of all Microsoft-based development, and ATL is one of the most important tools that developers can use to take advantage of this shift in technology.

The primary focus of ATL is to enable the creation of small COM-based software modules. Then these modules are assembled to create larger applications. As developers move to this new component-based development model, they will use ATL. Microsoft also is committed to delivering COM on non-Windows platforms such as UNIX, Sun's Solaris, and Digital's VMS – ATL is one approach to providing a cross-platform COM development tool.

The history of ATL began in the fall of 1996 when Microsoft released version 1.0 as a freely downloadable add-on for Visual C++ (Version 4.2 at the time); version 1.1 followed shortly thereafter. ATL version 2.1, which added a significant amount of new functionality, was released as part of Visual C++ 5.0. The latest version, 3.0 included with Visual C++ 6.0, again significantly upgrades the functionality provided by ATL. Future versions eventually will provide nearly all of the functionality provided today by MFC.

The purpose of this book is to help you understand and adopt one of the most important developments in Windows-based development: the move to COM-based application development. ATL is a powerful tool in this new environment, and this book provides in-depth coverage of what you need to know.

Chapter Organization

I suggest you read the chapters in succession, although you can skim the first two chapters if you are familiar with C++ templates and COM. Chapter 1 covers C++ template-based development. Chapter 2 provides an in-depth introduction to the Component Object Model (COM) and introduces the examples that I use throughout the book.

With the exception of Chapters 1, 7, and 13, each chapter is divided into two primary sections. The first section provides a conceptual, code-based discussion of the topic, while the second section walks you through developing one or more sample applications that demonstrate the techniques described. This enables you to read the book for the concepts; when you actually need to use them in your projects, you can go back and read the explicit implementation section.

Here are brief introductions to each chapter:

Chapter 1, Developing with C++ Templates: ATL uses templates throughout its implementation. Chapter 1 provides an introduction to this new approach to building reusable C++ classes.

Chapter 2, Introducing the Component Object Model: A general overview and detailed discussion of COM. The example is a simple C++ (COM) COM client and server. In later chapters, I reimplement and enhance this example using ATL with various COM techniques.

Chapter 3, The Active Template Library: ATL is about building COM-based applications. This chapter introduces ATL with a discussion of its template-based implementation and its wizards. The chapter also includes coverage of ATL's classes and idioms.

Chapter 4, Interfaces, IDL, and Marshaling: Chapter 4 goes a bit deeper into the various interface mechanisms provided by COM. In particular, I cover the Interface Definition Language (IDL) and something called marshaling. After that, I cover some miscellaneous COM details such as error handling, memory management, and basic data types. Of course, all topics are discussed in the context of ATL.

Chapter 5, Containment and Aggregation: One important feature of COM is its support for software module reuse at a binary level. In this chapter, I look at COM's binary reuse techniques: containment and aggregation. After a quick introduction to the two techniques, I examine how ATL provides support for developing components that support and/or use containment and aggregation.

Chapter 6, Automation: Automation is the COM-based technology that almost all Windows developers are familiar with, at least from a user's perspective. Visual Basic uses automation extensively and ActiveX controls expose their functionality through automation. This chapter covers automation in detail, including a discussion of early and late binding, dual interfaces, and how ATL handles support for automation.

Chapter 7, Events and Connection Points: Chapter 7 covers two very important topics for those developers using COM in their development projects: events and connection points. Today, COM interface calls are synchronous by nature. However, by using various techniques, COM components can provide pseudo-asynchronous behavior through support for interface callbacks and connection points. This chapter covers these techniques along with the ATL implementation.

Chapter 8, ActiveX Controls: ActiveX controls play a major role in Microsoft's component-based future. ActiveX controls are COM-based components that implement a number of standard, Microsoft-defined interfaces. It actually is quite hard to articulate what an ActiveX control is, primarily because the definition has changed frequently over the years. But in this chapter, I cover what is called a full control. A full control is one that works in the popular development environments (such as Visual Basic), and implements at least 20 different COM interfaces.

Chapter 9, COM Enumerators and Collections: Managing a list of related items is a common aspect of software development. COM provides a standard technique for inserting and iterating a list of items through its concept of an enumerator object. Certain languages and tools, such as Visual Basic, expand this idea to include the concept of a collection, which exposes an enumerator object in a standard way. This chapter covers both of these techniques.

Chapter 10, COM Threading: COM threading is one of the most misunderstood (and feared) COM topics. There's no doubt that multithreading is a difficult topic in itself; by introducing COM into the equation, it becomes even more difficult. This chapter first covers the basics of COM threading and then moves into a discussion of ATL's support for the various COM threading models. The chapter ends with an example of a multithreaded math component that supports asynchronous method calls.

Chapter 11, OLE DB and ATL: One of the more powerful Microsoft technologies supported by the latest version of ATL is OLE DB. With the overwhelming success of Web-based e-commerce applications, OLE DB (with the help of ADO) has become the standard on which Microsoft developers have based their data access future. The latest version of ATL provides a plethora of new classes that enable developers to implement a generalized data access method to a proprietary data source based on OLE DB. This chapter covers all the gory details.

Chapter 12, Dialog Boxes and Windows: Initially, the ATL framework focused mostly on providing non-GUI support for building COM components. If, as a developer, you were interested in building an application that required extensive windowing support, you most likely would use the Microsoft Foundation Class (MFC) library or Visual Basic. However, with each new version of ATL, Microsoft continues to add MFC-like GUI functionality. In this chapter, I briefly discuss the window and dialog box support provided by ATL.

Chapter 13, COM+ Fundamentals: COM was created long ago as a workstation-level component technology. Then came a distributed version call DCOM in Windows NT 4. The technology was expanded again with Microsoft Transaction Server (MTS) to provide server-side component services and to fix many of the deficiencies of DCOM. COM+ was developed, and integrated into Windows 2000, to unify COM, DCOM, and MTS into a coherent, enterprise-worthy component technology. This chapter provides you with an overview of these new technologies.

The Examples

Because of the ubiquity and low cost of the World Wide Web, technical books no longer come with (or need) a CD-ROM containing example code. Instead, you can download all the examples along with other supporting material from my Web site. The majority of the examples use C++ and ATL and they are combined into one large Visual C++ workspace (`ATL_Examples.dsw`). There also are a number of Visual Basic examples, which are combined into one Visual Basic workspace (`VB_Projects.vbg`). Visit the following URL for complete details:

`http://www.widgetware.com`

Comments and Bug Reports

I welcome and encourage comments, suggestions, and bug reports at the following e-mail address. You can contact me via e-mail or through my Web site. The site contains examples, FAQs, pointers to other COM(+)/OLE/ActiveX sites, discussions, and other material concerning COM(+), ATL, and ActiveX technology.

`tom@WidgetWare.com`

Acknowledgments

I first have to thank the gang at IDG Books for doing most of the work required to publish this book. All of my editors, John Osborn, Matt Lusher, Michael Koch, Victoria Lee, Allan Wyatt, and Mildred Sanchez, kept me focused and provided needed encouragement – all without pushing too hard.

A very special thank you goes to Ron Patton, who graciously took the time to write a great chapter on ATL's OLE DB capabilities. Ron provided technical editing support for the other chapters as well. Thanks Ron, I owe you one.

Finally, I'm most thankful for my beautiful wife, Nicole, and my two children, Jessica and Eric. They add love, inspiration, hope, and especially joy to everything I do.

Contents at a Glance

Contents

Chapter 1

Developing with C++ Templates

IN THIS CHAPTER

- ◆ An introduction to C++ templates
- ◆ Demonstrating templates using a generic stack class
- ◆ The C++ syntax for template member functions
- ◆ Specifying template parameters in your classes
- ◆ Reusability as the primary goal of C++ templates
- ◆ Template use within the ATL framework

AS ITS NAME IMPLIES, the *Active Template Library (ATL)* uses C++ templates as a principal feature of its implementation. For that reason, this chapter takes a quick look at C++ templates and discusses how developing with templates differs a bit from what you may be accustomed to using.

Introducing Templates

Templates are a fairly new addition to the C++ language. They provide a generic way of developing reusable code by enabling you to build parameterized C++ types. There are two distinct types of templates: function templates and class templates. Using function templates is similar to using the C++ preprocessor in that they provide capabilities to substitute text at compile time, but in a type-safe way. Class templates enable you to write generic, type-safe classes.

Function Templates

To demonstrate function templates, lets examine a typical use of the C++ preprocessor to implement a generic MAX function. Without templates, a type-safe MAX function might be implemented this way:

```
long MAX( long a, long b )
{
```

```
    if ( a > b )
        return a;
    else
        return b;
}
double MAX( double a, double b )
{
    if ( a > b )
        return a;
    else
        return b;
}
```

For each type that is passed to the MAX function, you must provide an explicit implementation. Using a function template, however, you can do this instead:

```
template <class Type>
Type MAX( Type a, Type b )
{
    if ( a > b )
        return a;
    else
        return b;
}
```

If this is the first template you have seen, it may look a little strange. The template keyword identifies this as a template. The values between the less-than and greater-than characters specify the parameterized type, which is indicated by the class keyword. Then the Type parameter is replaced at compile time with a type specified by the template user. Here's what it looks like:

```
int main( int argc, char *argv[] )
{
    int    iMax = MAX<int>( 10, 12 );
    long   lMax = MAX<long>( 10, 12 );
    double dMax = MAX<double>( 10.0, 12.0 );
    return 0;
}
```

Again, the syntax is a bit arcane, but after inspection it should make sense. When calling the function, provide the type as a parameter to the function. Templates are compile-time constructs and basically expand for each specified type—just as an older C preprocessor macro might work. For example, the preceding code expands to something like this:

```
int main( int argc, char *argv[] )
```

```
{
  int MAXint( int a, int b )
  {
      if ( a > b )
          return a;
      else
          return b;
  }
  int iMax = MAXint( 10, 12 );
  ...
}
```

This is the expansion for only one function type, but you should get the idea. Function templates give you the flexibility of the C preprocessor and the type safety of writing a specific function for every possible type. You write the function once and use it over and over again by specifying the required specific type. Class templates provide the same flexibility at the class level.

Class Templates

Class templates are similar to function templates in that they enable the user of a class to specify a type at instantiation time. You can develop a generic type that operates on a user-defined type provided at compile time. This provides complete type safety for your class implementation. The most difficult aspect of template-based development is figuring out the syntax.

A Template-Based Stack Class

To demonstrate the basic features of template-based programming, I'll show you how to build an example class that implements a stack. I know this has been done before, but the example is short and it enables you to focus on how templates work.

To begin, a stack provides a LIFO (first last -in, -last first -out) structure in which to store elements of the same type. Stacks are used extensively at the hardware level, but they also are useful in software. What we want to do is design a stack class that can store any data type. Without C++ templates, this is impossible to do — at least in a straightforward way. Without templates, we would have to write code for each data type. Here's what an integer stack might look like:

```
class StackInt
{
public:
   StackInt()
   {
      m_sPos = 0;
   }
```

```
    ~StackInt() {}

    void      Push( int iValue );
    int       Pop();

    bool IsEmpty()
    {
        return( m_sPos == 0 );
    }

    bool IsFull()
    {
        return( m_sPos == 100 );
    }

    bool HasElements()
    {
        return( m_sPos != 0 );
    }

private:
    int   m_data[100];
    short m_sPos;
};

void StackInt::Push( int iValue )
{
    m_data[ sPos++ ] = iValue;
}

int StackInt::Pop()
{
    return m_data[ --sPos ];
}
```

There we have it — a nice, simple class that implements a stack. It has the typical Push and Pop methods, as well as a few others that enable the user to determine the state of the stack (whether the stack is empty, full, and so on). Here's how you might use the class:

```
int MAIN( int argc, char *argv[] )
{
    StackInt stack;
    stack.Push( 100 );
    stack.Push( 200 );
```

```
    stack.Push( 300 );
    while( stack.HasElements() )
    {
        cout << stack.Pop() << endl;
    }
    return 0;
}
```

The class is easy to use; however, it has a few problems. First, there isn't much error checking, but this is by design so as to keep the code small and easy to follow. Second, the stack supports only integers. Third, the size of the stack is set explicitly to 100. What if the user needs a larger stack? Well, you can use a parameterized constructor such as this one:

```
class StackInt
{
public:
    StackInt()
    {
        m_sSize = 100;
        m_data = new int[ m_sSize ];
        m_sPos = 0;
    }
    StackInt( short sSize )
    {
        m_sSize = sSize;
        m_data = new int[ m_sSize ];
        m_sPos = 0;
    }
    ~StackInt() {}
    void      Push( int iValue );
    int       Pop();
    bool IsEmpty()
    {
        return( m_sPos == 0 );
    };
    bool HasElements()
    {
        return( m_sPos != 0 );
    }
    bool IsFull()
    {
        return( m_sPos == m_sSize );
    }
private:
```

```
    short m_sSize;
    int* m_data;
    short m_sPos;
};

void StackInt::Push( int iValue )
{
    m_data[ m_sPos++ ] = iValue;
}

int StackInt::Pop()
{
    return m_data[ --m_sPos ];
}
```

The parameterized constructor makes the class more general because the user can specify the size of the stack now. However, we still have the problem of it only supporting integers. What if the user of the class wants a stack that manages doubles or strings or some other class, such as *MFC*'s (Microsoft Foundation Classes) CWnd, or a user-defined class such as CBankAccount? You would have to rewrite the class completely. It wouldn't be hard, and with a bit of cut and paste you would have the class built in no time.

For example, to build a class for doubles, you can do something like this:

```
class StackDouble
{
public:
    StackDouble()
    {
        m_sSize = 100;
        m_data = new double[ m_sSize ];
        m_sPos = 0;
    }
    StackDouble( short sSize )
    {
        m_sSize = sSize;
        m_data = new double[ m_sSize ];
        m_sPos = 0;
    }
    ~StackDouble() {}

    void    Push( double dValue );
    double  Pop();

    bool IsEmpty()
    {
```

```
       return( m_sPos == 0 );
   }
   bool HasElements()
   {
       return( m_sPos != 0 );
   }
   bool IsFull()
   {
       return( m_sPos == m_sSize );
   }

private:
   short m_sSize;
   double* m_data;
   short m_sPos;
};
```

Now you have a class that implements a stack for doubles. I've highlighted the changed code (in boldface type) and, as you can see, I've changed only three items: the name of the class, the parameter type of the Push method, and the actual type stored in the array. This seems simple. Is it something the compiler can do for us? Yes, and that's exactly what C++ templates do. Templates give you a compile-time substitution mechanism at the class level.

By providing substitution of types (and constants) at compile time, templates enable you to build generic classes that do not operate on a specific data type. Instead, the class user can provide the data type when an instance of the class is instantiated. At compile time, the template is "expanded" with the user-specified type and that generates a completely new and type-safe class. Let's look at the stack example again. This time, though, I use C++ templates:

```
template <class T>
class Stack
{
public:
   Stack()
   {
       m_sPos = 0;
   }
   ~Stack() {}

   void Push( T value );
   T    Pop();

   bool IsEmpty()
   {
```

```
        return( m_sPos == 0 );
    }
    bool HasElements()
    {
        return( m_sPos != 0 );
    }
    bool IsFull()
    {
        return( m_sPos == 100 );
    }

private:
    T m_data[100];
    short m_sPos;
};
```

The syntax for class templates is very similar to that of function templates. I use the `template` keyword to indicate that the class is a template class. Next, I provide one or more template parameters. Each parameter can be a `type` indicated by the class keyword, or a `constant` indicated by an existing, valid type. (I cover parameterized constants in the next example.)

The syntax within the class declaration uses the "type" (in this case, T) wherever you want it substituted at compile time. In the preceding example, you need to substitute the type of the array as well as the parameter and return types for the `Push` and `Pop` methods.

Implementing Member Functions

The syntax for implementing member functions (methods) outside the class declaration is a bit different. Following are the definitions for the `Push` and `Pop` methods; you must use the template keyword and the type name when defining the methods.

```
template <class T>
void Stack<T>::Push( T value )
{
    m_data[m_sPos++] = value;
}

template <class T>
T Stack<T>::Pop()
{
    return m_data[--m_sPos];
}
```

The syntax for constructors and destructors of templated classes also is different. Here's what the Stack constructor and destructor should look like when defined outside the class declaration:

```
Template <class T>
Stack<T>::Stack()
{
    sPos = 0;
}


Template <class T>
Stack<T>::~Stack()
{
}
```

Non-Type Template Parameters

Templates also enable you to provide parameterized constants when building generic classes. In the stack example, I can specify the size of the stack as part of the template. Again, this gives both the implementer and the user of the class more freedom. Here's what the stack class looks like with a short keyword that specifies the stack size:

```
template <class T, short sSize = 100>
class Stack
{
public:
    Stack()
    {
        m_sPos = 0;
    }
    ~Stack() {}

    void Push( T value );
    T    Pop();

    bool IsEmpty()
    {
        return( m_sPos == 0 );
    }
    bool HasElements()
    {
        return( m_sPos != 0 );
    }
```

```cpp
    bool IsFull()
    {
       return( m_sPos == sSize );
    }
    long GetSize()
    {
       return sSize;
    }

private:
   T m_data[ sSize ];
   short m_sPos;
};

template <class T, short sSize = 100>
void Stack<T>::Push( T value )
{
   m_data[ m_sPos++ ] = value;
}

template <class T, short sSize = 100>
T Stack<T>::Pop()
{
   return m_data[ --m_sPos ];
}
```

One difference in this implementation is that you need not create your array dynamically when the class is instantiated as you do with a version that doesn't use templates. Non-type template parameters are constants that are evaluated at compile time. That makes things a bit more efficient because you don't have to maintain a member to hold the actual size of the array.

Here's how you can use the new class:

```cpp
int main( int argc, char *argv[] )
{
   // Create a stack of doubles with a max size of
   // 20 elements
   Stack< double, 20 > doubleStack;

   cout << "doubleStack size is " << doubleStack.GetSize() << endl;
   doubleStack.Push( 1.1 );
   doubleStack.Push( 2.2 );
   doubleStack.Push( 3.3 );

   while( doubleStack.HasElements() )
   {
```

```
        cout << doubleStack.Pop() << endl;
    }

    // A dynamically created stack
    Stack<long>* plongStack = new Stack<long, 10>;

    plongStack->Push( 1000 );
    plongStack->Push( 2000 );

    delete plongStack;
    return 0;
}
```

As you can see, I provide a parameter for both the stack type and its size. Both techniques are employed extensively within ATL. The last part of the preceding example demonstrates the syntax for creating template-based objects using the new operator. Again, it's a bit different from what you may be used to, but the syntax is consistent in most circumstances.

Template-Based Reuse

Template-based reuse is different from *inheritance-based reuse.* If you are a C++ developer, you no doubt understand the concept of reuse by inheritance. With inheritance-based reuse, you reuse a class's implementation by deriving a new class and modifying its behavior by overriding the base class's methods, and so on. The key is to inherit as much functionality as possible.

With templates, you reuse a class by generating a new class implementation based on parameterized types. You achieve reuse by letting the compiler generate code for you. In the early days of templates, developers criticized templates because they increased compile times and bloated the resulting code; every new class produced its own object code. Today's compilers handle these issues much more efficiently and templates have become an effective way of developing generic, reusable code. Of course, you don't have to pick just one technique (for example, inheritance or templates) to create reusable classes, as they work fine together.

How ATL Uses Templates

This section takes a quick look at how ATL uses C++ templates in its implementation. I do not cover the actual ATL classes used in this example because I cover them in detail later. Instead, I focus on how ATL uses template techniques to access member functions in base classes. ATL's use of templates is quite unique in this regard because ATL does not make use of virtual functions when overriding behavior in a base class.

To begin, examine these two classes:

```
class CBase
{
public:
    CBase() {}
    ~CBase() {}

    void BaseMethod()
    {
        cout << "BaseMethod in Base" << endl;
    }
};

class CMath : public CBase
{
public:
    CMath() {}
    ~CMath() {}
};
```

Simple enough, you have a base class that has a single method called BaseMethod and another class that derives from CBase. The CMath class does not have any methods of its own, but does expose the behavior from the BaseMethod method inherited from CBase.

Next, take a look at the CComObject class that is modeled after an ATL implementation class:

```
template<class T>
class CComObject : public T
{
public:
    CComObject() {}
    ~CComObject() {}

    void CallBaseMethod()
    {
        T* pT = static_cast<T*>(this);
        pT->BaseMethod();
    }
};
```

The CComObject class is templated and requires a class parameter. However, as you can see, the parameter is used as the base class for CComObject. This means that CComObject ultimately derives from the class provided via the template parameter.

CComObject, then, is a generic class that calls specific methods in the base class. The other interesting aspect involves how the base class method is called. By passing the base class as a template parameter and using this type to cast the instance pointer, you get a direct pointer to the base class implementation.

This technique of accessing base class members allows the CMath implementation to override the BaseMethod implementation like this:

```
class CMath : public CBase
{
public:
   CMath() {}
   ~CMath() {}

   void BaseMethod()
   {
      cout << "BaseMethod in CMath" << endl;
   }
};
```

The important point here is that we are not using virtual functions to override behavior of upper-level classes. The ATL team went to great lengths to make the ATL as fast and efficient as possible. Virtual function calls in a large class hierarchy can be expensive (in terms of speed and code size) and this technique provides the same capability without them. You will see code like this throughout the implementation of ATL, so get used to it. In particular, you will see this constantly:

```
template<class T>
class XXXX : public T
{
...
   void SomeMethod()
   {
      T* pT = static_cast<T*>(this);
      pT->BaseClassMethod();
   }
...
}
```

This code simply is looking back up the inheritance hierarchy to find the most recent implementation of the called method. This lookup is performed during the compile process so as to provide very efficient calling. To complete this example, here's how you can create an instance of the resulting class:

```
void main(int argc, char* argv[])
{
```

```
CComObject<CMath>* pMath = new CComObject<CMath>;

pMath->CallBaseMethod();

delete pMath;
}
```

Summary

In this chapter, you learned the basics of C++ templates. In particular, you learned:

- ◆ C++ template technology is a recent addition to the C++ language.
- ◆ Function templates provide a good mechanism for writing type-safe, reusable functions .
- ◆ Class templates allow you to write reusable, type-safe classes by providing a preprocessor-like substitution technique.
- ◆ The Active Template Library (ATL) uses template technology throughout its implementation.

Now that you have a good understanding of C++ templates, let's move on to understanding what Microsoft's *Component Object Model (COM)* is all about. COM is an important new technology for Windows developers. Chapter 2 provides a detailed introduction.

Chapter 2

Introducing the Component Object Model (COM)

IN THIS CHAPTER

- Why software components are so important to today's developer

- Microsoft's Component Object Model (COM)

- The Essence of COM: The interface

- GUIDs, class factories, and other COM details

- The important COM APIs

- Developing a COM client and server application without the help of any C++ framework

BEFORE YOU START developing software with ATL, first you need to understand the details of the Microsoft Component Object Model. If you've done much Windows development, you know that COM is at the center of every new technology that Microsoft generates. Microsoft uses COM extensively within its own applications, tools, and operating systems and most new Windows functionality is delivered as a set of COM components instead of a series of API calls.

If you develop Windows software, you must have a solid understanding of COM. The focus of this chapter is to provide you with all the brutal details of low-level COM. ATL is a tool for developing COM-based software modules, or components. After exploring this chapter and its examples, you will be ready to dig into the details of the ATL framework.

Software Components and Their Attributes

COM deals with designing, building, and using software components. COM is a system-level technology provided in all of Microsoft's current 32-bit operating systems. By developing software using the COM programming model, a developer gets a significant amount of built-in functionality. In particular, COM endows a software module with the following attributes: language independence, robust versioning, location transparency, and object orientation. The following sections explain these attributes.

Language Independence: A Binary Standard

Although this book focuses primarily on building COM-based components with C++, COM components need not be written in any specific language. In fact, other languages, such as Visual Basic and Java, make it easy to develop and use COM-based components. The kicker here, though, is that the client (or user) of a COM-based component is oblivious to how or in what language the component actually was implemented.

In other words, COM-based software modules are *language independent.* You can write a component using C++ and use it from Visual Basic. You also can write a component in Visual Basic and use it from Java, C++, or Visual FoxPro. It doesn't matter.

One of COM's most important features is that it gives you a technique to write object-oriented code in any language you choose and deliver this functionality to users of any other language. COM supports what is called a *binary standard*: You can deliver a component housed within a DLL or EXE (a binary) and the component's functionality can be used from Visual Basic, Java, C++, or even COBOL. Of course, the language implementation must support COM and nearly every language used in the Windows environment does support COM.

Because this book is about ATL, I use the C++ language to implement components. I write most of the client applications (a software entity that uses a component) using C++, but I also demonstrate COM-based client development using Visual Basic.

Robust Versioning

Another important feature of COM is its support for *component versioning.* One difficult aspect of delivering software modules – especially in environments that are shared among multivendor applications – is the problem of upgrading functionality in deployed software modules. COM addresses this problem by providing a robust versioning technique based on COM's most fundamental entity: the component's interfaces.

COM enables robust versioning via its support for multiple interfaces on the same component. In other words, a component's functionality can be partitioned into small, distinct areas – each of them a specific COM interface. Then, versioning support is provided by allowing a component to expose slight variations of the same interface, which allows older applications to run unchanged and newer applications to take advantage of a component's new features.

Location Transparency

Another important COM feature is *location transparency*. It means that a component user – the client – need not know where a component is located. A client application employs the same COM services to instantiate and use a component regardless of where the component resides.

The component may reside directly within the client's process space (a DLL), in another process on the same machine (an executable), or on a machine located hundreds of miles away (a distributed object). COM and *Distributed COM (DCOM)* provide this location transparency. I'll discuss the process of providing location transparency in Chapter 4.

The client interacts with a COM-based component in exactly the same way despite where the component resides. The client interface does not change. Location transparency enables developers to build scalable, distributed, multitier applications without changing the programming model used by client applications.

Object-Oriented Characteristics

COM enables a software module to deliver its functionality in an object-oriented way. A majority of older software interoperability techniques (such as DLL exports and DDE) do not provide the typical object-oriented characteristics that C++ developers use daily. COM provides the three fundamental object-oriented characteristics of encapsulation, inheritance, and polymorphism and does so in a language-independent way. I discuss each of these characteristics in more detail later in this chapter.

Where Is COM Implemented?

COM is a model for implementing object-oriented, language-independent, location-transparent components or software modules. The model is described in Microsoft's *Component Object Model Specification*. Anyone can provide an implementation of COM's model. However, because Microsoft specifies it and has ultimate control over it, Microsoft has provided the initial implementation through its 32-bit operating systems (such as Windows 95, Windows 98, Windows NT, and Windows 2000). Support for COM is built into the operating system. There is no need to distribute additional software to use COM within your Windows applications.

Microsoft's implementation of COM is a small set of Win32 API functions and a large number of COM *interface declarations* (language-independent header files). This chapter focuses on the use of these APIs and interfaces – and I revisit this topic throughout the book – because ATL primarily is concerned with developing COM-based software.

Clients and Servers

It is important to understand the relationship between a component and the software entity using its services. A COM component typically provides functionality to some other software entity and so is viewed as a *server*. A software entity using a component's functionality is deemed the *client*. This seems straightforward, but there are many cases in which a server is also a client and a client routinely is a server. It has to do with interfaces. COM is about interfaces.

A software module that *implements* an interface is said to be the server or component. In other words, it provides a set of services through the implemented interface. A software module that uses, or *consumes*, an interface is said to be a client of that interface. It employs the services implemented by the server. In many cases, a component is both an implementer and a consumer of a number of COM interfaces.

OLE and ActiveX

There is a lot of confusion about COM, OLE, and ActiveX and how they differ. COM is a *system*-level standard that provides basic object model services on which to build higher-level functionality. Basically, it is a software-interoperability standard. OLE and ActiveX are examples of higher-level services built on top of this standard. OLE and ActiveX provide application-level features, but they are built using COM's services. So the terms COM, OLE, and ActiveX are interchangeable somewhat in that their capabilities and features are closely related. However, each term describes a separate set of high-level technologies despite a lot of crossover. Here's a quick history of OLE and ActiveX.

When *OLE* was introduced (circa 1991), the term was an acronym for object linking and embedding. Its primary purpose was to provide object linking and embedding support for Windows applications. This compound document functionality enabled users to embed Excel spreadsheets directly within Word documents.

Then, with the release of OLE 2.0 (circa 1993), OLE no longer was used as an acronym; instead, it was an umbrella term for several technologies based on COM. Many of the new capabilities that OLE 2.0 provided had nothing to do with linking and embedding. A good example of this is OLE automation (simply called *automation* now), whose primary purpose is to promote component and application interoperability through language and tool independence. It has nothing to do with compound documents.

In April 1996, Microsoft embraced the Web wholeheartedly and coined the term ActiveX to indicate a new direction in its product line. However, the majority of the new ActiveX technologies existed long before April 1996; they were categorized under a different name: OLE. In general, ActiveX replaced OLE to describe the majority of Microsoft's COM-based technologies. As a result, OLE again was used to describe only those technologies related to compound documents and object linking and embedding. Thus, it has reverted to its former status as an acronym.

Microsoft Transaction Server (MTS)

The COM programming model was developed in the early 1990s. It focused solely on providing component services on the Windows platform. During the 1990s, the Windows operating system was used mostly as a workstation operating system. This changed with the release of the Windows NT 4.0 Server in that Microsoft now focuses on building Windows into a scalable server platform.

Microsoft Transaction Server (MTS) is an add-on for Windows NT 4.0 that provides an execution environment for middle-tier components. In other words, it moves the COM programming model from the workstation to the back-end or middle-tier server. MTS managed to solve many of the deficiencies in COM with regards to enterprise-level development; however, it was not integrated directly into the operating system. With the release of Windows 2000, the COM and MTS programming model were merged together to produce COM+. Other enhancements to COM+ include a functional administrative environment and more component support code provided in the operating system. (In-depth coverage of MTS is beyond the scope of this book. See Chapter 13 for a full discussion of COM+.)

The Essence of COM: Interfaces

COM's implementation contains a handful of Win32 APIs, but the purpose of these APIs basically is to bootstrap the COM environment. After that, COM deals with implementing and using *interfaces*.

As a C++ developer, you implement and use interfaces all the time. As the implementer of a C++ class, a developer encapsulates the details of the class's implementation by using the `public`, `protected`, and `private` keywords. A user of the C++ class interacts with a class instance only through its public interface. This interface acts as a contract between the developer and the user of the class. The class implementer can change the internal implementation of the class because it is encapsulated. However, if the public interface is changed, it forces the user of the class to recompile his or her application. For this reason, the public interface should not change. Following is a simple C++ class declaration that demonstrates a public interface with four methods:

```
class Math
{
public:
    long Add( long, long );
    long Subtract( long, long );
    long Multiply( long, long );
    long Divide( long, long );
private:
    // Implementation here...
};
```

A COM interface closely resembles a C++ class's public interface. It enables you to describe methods and properties (data members) and fully encapsulate the details of the underlying implementation. However, unlike C++, COM does this in a language-independent, location-transparent fashion.

C++ Virtual Function Tables

COM interfaces are built using a C++ *Vtable*, which is short for *virtual function table*. A virtual function table in C++ provides late binding of an instance's functionality. Before I move into describing the implementation of a COM interface, let's review virtual functions.

Virtual functions enable C++ programs to resolve function calls dynamically at run time, instead of statically at compile time. This powerful feature of C++ provides for many of its object-oriented capabilities.

In early-binding languages, such as C, the specific function address to call in any particular instance is determined at compile time. C programs can support run-time binding, but the developer must do all the work (by using pointers to functions). C++ makes it much easier. Virtual functions allow the implementation of *polymorphism*, or the ability of an object to respond differently to the same method or member function at run time depending on the object's type.

These virtual functions don't do much if you declare them in only one class. The strength of virtual functions is manifested only as you augment existing base classes by creating subclasses. The following example demonstrates the power of using virtual functions:

```
class Fruit {
public:
   void    put_Color( string str )
   {
      m_strColor = str;
   }
   string  get_Color()
   {
      return m_strColor;
   }
   virtual void  Draw() {};
private:
   string   m_strColor;
};
```

The Fruit class contains a virtual method, Draw, which returns void and does nothing. The base Fruit class does not have an implementation for Draw because each particular type of fruit should implement its own Draw method. For example, use this code if you want to derive some fruit from the Fruit class:

```cpp
class Apple : public Fruit
{
    virtual void  Draw()
    {
      cout << "I'm an Apple" << endl;
    }
};
class GrannySmith : public Apple
{
    virtual void  Draw()
    {
      cout << "I'm a Granny Smith Apple" << endl;
    }
};
class Orange : public Fruit
{
    virtual void  Draw()
    {
       cout << "I'm an Orange" << endl;
    }
};
class Grape : public Fruit
{
    virtual void  Draw()
    {
       cout << "I'm a Grape" << endl;
    }
};
```

Each class derived directly or indirectly from Fruit implements its own Draw function that prints that particular fruit's type. In itself, this isn't anything spectacular. But look at the following code:

```cpp
int main()
{
    Fruit* pFruitList[4];
    pFruitList[0] = new Apple;
    pFruitList[1] = new Orange;
    pFruitList[2] = new Grape;
    pFruitList[3] = new GrannySmith;
    for( int i = 0; i < 4; i++ )
      pFruitList[i]->Draw();
}
// Produces this output
>
```

```
> I'm an Apple
> I'm an Orange
> I'm a Grape
> I'm a Granny Smith Apple
>
```

The preceding code illustrates the power of virtual functions. I declared an array of pointers of type Fruit, the base class, and assigned to each element the address of an instance of a particular derived fruit type. As the line pFruitList[i]->Draw() executes, the program determines dynamically at run time which member function to invoke. This dynamic binding is implemented with a virtual function table.

PURE VIRTUAL FUNCTIONS AND ABSTRACT CLASSES

An *abstract* class provides a model, or template, for all classes that derive from it. In the Fruit example, the base class Fruit is a good abstract class candidate. A "fruit" is itself an abstract thing. In real life, we cannot instantiate a general fruit object — something that has the broad characteristics of a fruit but isn't a specific kind of fruit. Developers use abstract classes to categorize and classify things that have similar characteristics. The base Fruit class contains the essence of all fruits, but nothing specific:

```
class Fruit
{
public:
   void put_Color( string str )
   {
      m_strColor = str;
   }
   string  get_Color()
   {
      return m_strColor;
   }
   virtual void Draw() = 0;
private:
   string m_strColor;
};
```

Abstract classes provide those properties and actions shared by all deriving classes. Abstract classes can choose not to implement specific member functions, requiring instead that deriving classes implement those functions. In the example, the Draw function is declared pure virtual by using the notation = 0. This indicates that all deriving classes must implement some form of the Draw function.

By declaring a pure virtual function within a class, the class designer also makes the class abstract — meaning that the class cannot be instantiated directly. Although the class itself cannot be instantiated, you can use pointers to the class; this proves to be an important characteristic. Recall the example with the array of `Fruit` pointers:

```
int main()
{
   // Now we can't do this
   Fruit fruit;
   // But we can still do this, and it produces the same output
   // as the earlier example.
   Fruit* pFruitList[4];
   pFruitList[0] = new Apple;
   pFruitList[1] = new Orange;
   pFruitList[2] = new Grape;
   pFruitList[3] = new GrannySmith;
   for( int i = 0; i < 4; i++ )
     pFruitList[i]->Draw();
}
```

The ability to determine object behavior at run time – instead of only at compile time – is a major improvement over C and provides the polymorphic behavior required by object-oriented development.

UNDERSTANDING VTABLES

As I described earlier, virtual functions enable C++ programs to invoke functions dynamically instead of statically. Other terms for dynamic and static function invocation are *late* and *early binding*, which refer to binding the function address either at run time or at compile time. Whenever you declare a function as virtual, the compiler adds a pointer to your class structure called the *vptr*, or virtual pointer. The vptr points to a Vtable structure that contains the addresses of any virtual functions in your class, as well as any base classes. Figure 2-1 depicts the vptr and Vtable entries for the following class definition:

```
class Fruit {
public:
   void     put_Color( string str )
    {
       m_strColor = str;
    }
   string   get_Color()
    {
       return m_strColor;
    }
   virtual void     Draw() {};
private:
   string   m_strColor;
```

```
}
class Apple : public Fruit
{
public:
    void Draw()
    {
        cout << "I'm an Apple" << endl;
    }
}
class GrannySmith : public Apple
{
public:
    void Draw()
    {
        cout << "I'm a Granny Smith Apple" << endl;
    }
}
```

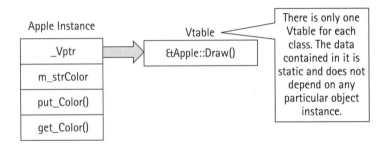

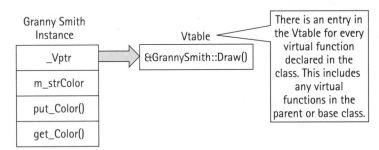

Figure 2-1: Vtable for fruit classes

This late binding of function addresses at run time is important to object-oriented languages. Some object-oriented languages — Smalltalk and Java in particular — bind all functions late. Others, including C++, leave it to the developer to decide which functions should bind late. C++ does this for performance reasons. There is overhead in providing the late binding necessary for polymorphic behavior. For every class that has at least one virtual function, a Vtable is needed for the class and a vptr is needed for each instance. The vptr must be initialized for each instance, and run-time overhead of function lookup is incurred every time a virtual function is called.

HOW COM USES VTABLES

C++ uses Vtables for implementing polymorphic behavior. COM, however, uses the C++ Vtable structure to build a COM interface. Because a Vtable is a table that holds function addresses, it is a good candidate for such an application. A COM interface actually is a pointer to a Vtable structure. This arrangement provides a convenient way to encapsulate the functionality of a component class.

A user of a COM interface has access only to the public methods of a component. Because COM uses a Vtable pointer, this also means that a component's interface can contain only methods. Figure 2-2 demonstrates this relationship. A component implementer cannot expose data members directly, although COM provides a way to simulate data members through its concept of properties.

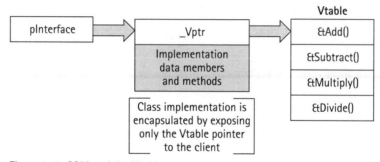

Figure 2-2: COM and the Vtable

The COM designers probably chose to use this C++ construct because most of them were C++ developers and because it would allow C++ compilers to produce components efficiently based on COM. It doesn't really matter. They had to choose some technique, and by picking the C++ Vtable they made it easier for C++ developers to understand. Other development tools, such as Visual Basic, hide these details from the developer anyway.

In the next few sections, I show you how to convert the C++ Math class into a COM component that exposes a basic interface with its public methods. To demonstrate COM's support for multiple interfaces, I also add another math-based interface:

```
class Math
{
public:
    long Add( long, long );
    long Subtract( long, long );
```

```
    long Multiply( long, long );
    long Divide( long, long );
private:
    // Implementation here...
};
```

COM Interfaces

Now that you understand that COM uses Vtables to implement its interfaces, let's go through the details by implementing a simple Math class as a COM component. The first step is to build a Vtable that exposes the component's public interface. Here's the declaration:

```
class IMath
{
public:
    virtual long    Add( long Op1, long Op2 ) = 0;
    virtual long    Subtract( long Op1, long Op2 ) = 0;
    virtual long    Multiply( long Op1, long Op2 ) = 0;
    virtual long    Divide( long Op1, Op2 ) = 0;
};
```

Next, you derive from this abstract class and provide the implementation just as you did before:

```
class Math : public IMath
{
public:
    long    Add( long Op1, long Op2 );
    long    Subtract( long Op1, long Op2 );
    long    Multiply( long Op1, long Op2 );
    long    Divide( long Op1, Op2 );
};
```

This is the first step in making your class available to non-C++ users. COM-based technologies, such as OLE and ActiveX, are composed primarily of interfaces such as the IMath class. The new class is abstract, so it contains at least one pure virtual function and contains only the public methods of the component class. In other words, its purpose is to describe the layout of a C++ Vtable completely.

In IMath, the "I" indicates that it is an interface declaration. COM uses this nomenclature throughout its implementation. The IMath class provides an external interface declaration for the math component. The most important aspect of the new IMath class is that it forces the creation of a C++ Vtable in any derived classes.

The use of virtual functions in a base class is central to the design of COM. The abstract class definition provides a Vtable that contains only the public methods (the interface) of the class. The `IMath` class contains no data members and no implementation functions. Its only purpose is to force the derived class (`Math`) to implement virtually the methods of the component's interface.

COM provides access to its components only through a Vtable pointer, so access to the component's implementation is impossible. Study this example. It is simple, but it contains the core concept of COM – the use of Vtables to provide the interface to a component's functionality. In the end, a COM interface is just a pointer to a pointer to a C++-style interface (or Vtable). Figure 2-3 depicts the relationship of the math component.

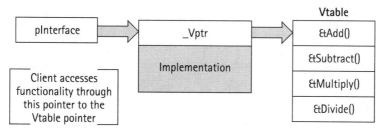

Figure 2-3: COM interfaces and the Vtable

In this example, you need to understand several concepts. First, all COM-based technologies, such as ActiveX and OLE, contain a number of abstract interface definitions just as the `IMath` class does. Ultimately, your job as the developer is to provide an *implementation* for those interfaces. That's one reason ActiveX is a standard. ActiveX provides the interface declarations and you provide the implementation. Several developers can provide different implementations for a standard ActiveX component by providing their own unique implementations. This is the concept behind ActiveX controls and all Active(X) technologies. The COM, OLE, and ActiveX specifications define the abstract classes that you must implement to create a COM-based component.

For example, if you put your abstract `IMath` class in a header file and then distribute it with various Windows development tools, you can call it a math component standard. Then any developer can build a component based on your `IMath` interface. Also, because it is a standard, other developers can develop software to use the `IMath` interface. In this way, you produce an environment in which anyone can implement a component that provides functionality via `IMath` and anyone can use a component that implements `IMath`. Without writing one line of executable code, you produce a standard. This is basically what COM does.

Accessing a COM Interface

Now that you know how a COM interface is described, let's take a look at how a client application can access and use the interface. We haven't yet covered all the details, but getting a look at both sides of the equation is important at the beginning. One of the most crucial COM API functions is `CoCreateInstance`. As its name implies, `CoCreateInstance` is used by a client application to create an instance of a component. The client provides some basic information about the component that it wants to create and COM handles all the details of finding the component, launching it, and returning the requested interface pointer. Here's a quick example of how a client application can create an instance of the math component and use its `IMath` interface:

```
// Create an instance and return the IMath interface
IMath* pMath;
HRESULT hr = CoCreateInstance( CLSID_Math,
                    NULL,
                    CLSCTX_INPROC,
                    IID_IMath,
                    (void**) &pMath );
// Use IMath
long lResult = pMath->Multiply( 44, 33 );
```

You declare a pointer to the abstract `IMath` class and then ask COM to create an instance of a component identified by its class identifier of `CLSID_Math`. I haven't covered the details yet, but the important point here is that COM creates the component instance and returns a pointer to a pointer to a Vtable structure described by your abstract `IMath` class. Once you have the pointer, you can access all functions exposed through the `IMath` interface.

The other technique of accessing a component's interface is through a standard interface that I will discuss shortly. As the next section describes, most components have more than one interface and a mechanism is needed to enable clients to access a specific one. Briefly, here's what it looks like:

```
IMath* pMath;
hr = pUnk->QueryInterface( IID_IMath, (void**) &pMath );
pUnk->Release();
if ( FAILED( hr ))
{
    cout << "QueryInterface() for IMath failed" << endl;
    CoUninitialize();
    return -1;
}
```

Understanding Multiple Interfaces per Component

One of COM's most important features gives a component the capability to implement multiple interfaces. This feature is key to COM's support for robust component versioning. For developers new to COM, this feature is also one of the most difficult aspects to understand.

To begin, take a look at the following C++ class declaration. It declares a math component with a few new features:

```
class Math
{
public:
    long Add( long lOp1, long lOp2 );
    long Subtract(long lOp1, long lOp2 );
    long Multiply(long lOp1, long lOp2 );
    long Divide( long lOp1, long lOp2 );

    long Factorial( short sOp );
    long Fibonacci( short sOp );

    void Draw();
private:
    // Implementation here...
};
```

The class now sports the capability to do advanced math functions, such as the factorial or Fibonacci of a given number, and it also has a new `Draw` method. A user of the class interacts with an instance via its public interface, which contains seven methods.

However, there is a certain implied grouping of the interface methods. The first four methods do simple math operations, the next two methods provide advanced math operations, and the `Draw` method provides some visual representation of the operation.

One of the drawbacks of C++ is that it can expose only one large interface to its users. This is where COM adds significantly to the design of components. COM provides the ability to partition a component's functionality into multiple interfaces, each one exposing a small, well-defined set of functionality. The client of the component then can interact directly with the piece of functionality that it needs. For example, here's what the component might look like as a COM-based component:

```
class IMath
{
public:
    virtual long   Add( long Op1, long Op2 ) = 0;
```

```
   virtual long    Subtract( long Op1, long Op2 ) = 0;
   virtual long    Multiply( long Op1, long Op2 ) = 0;
   virtual long    Divide( long Op2, Op2 ) = 0;
};

class IAdvancedMath
{
public:
   virtual long    Factorial( short sOp ) = 0;
   virtual long    Fibonacci( short sOp ) = 0;
};

class IDraw
{
public:
   virtual void Draw() = 0;
};

class Math : public IMath, public IAdvancedMath, public IDraw
{
public:
   // Implementation of each interface here

   ...
}
```

The Math class multiply inherits from three interface classes. Remember, because the classes are pure abstract classes, they don't provide any implementation (that is, code) to the Math class, which is responsible for providing the complete implementation.

C++ implements multiple inheritance by building several Vtables for the class. That is exactly what you want. Your C++ class now has three distinct Vtables. In other words, it now contains three COM-based interfaces. I'm getting a bit ahead of myself, but this example can help with your understanding of multiple interfaces. The important point is that your class now can expose its functionality in a more useful way. If a client wants only to draw the math component, then it needs to access and understand only the component's IDraw interface.

COM's support for multiple interfaces is also useful from a component implementer's view. As you will see, a COM component typically implements a number of interfaces already defined by Microsoft. By choosing from a large number of small, well-defined interfaces, a component can expose only the important functionality. There is no need to implement methods that do not pertain to the functionality it supports.

There are several ways to provide a C++ class with multiple Vtables. ATL uses the multiple inheritance technique. However, other Microsoft frameworks, such as MFC, use a concept called C++ *class nesting*. A third option is to use something called *interface implementations*, which is similar to C++ class nesting. In both cases, an additional C++ class implements each COM interface. Then these implementation classes are instantiated or embedded within an outer class through which their Vtables are exposed.

Multiple interfaces also provide COM's robust support for component versioning. Continuing with the math component example, let's say you want to add a new method to the IAdvancedMath interface to calculate the circumference of a circle. At first glance, it's easy — you just add the method to your IAdvancedMath interface. But wait — you can't do this because it will break any existing client application that uses IAdvancedMath. Why? The client has bound, at compile time, the structure of the IAdvancedMath Vtable.

COM requires you to implement a new interface — let's call it IAdvanced MathEx — whenever you change an existing interface. Any change to the interface, be it a new method or a new parameter added to an existing method, requires a new interface. Here's your new IAdvancedMathEx interface:

```
class IAdvancedMathEx : public IAdvancedMath
{
public:
    virtual long   Circumference( short sRadius ) = 0;
};
```

You derive the new interface from the old one and add the new method. The most important point is that your component now exposes both interfaces. In this way, you can distribute a newer version of the component without breaking any existing clients that use the older IAdvancedMath interface. New clients can take advantage of the new functionality by using the newer IAdvancedMathEx interface. The trick is to provide both implementations within one component and supply a mechanism whereby the client can "ask" for a specific interface. COM provides this functionality through the most important interface of all: IUnknown.

Standard COM Interfaces

The math component that I've been describing is not yet an actual COM component. All COM components are required to implement a standard COM interface (pulled in by WINDOWS.H) called IUnknown. IUnknown serves two purposes. The first is to provide a standard way for the component user (or client) to ask for a specific interface within a given component. QueryInterface, a method of IUnknown, provides this capability. The second purpose of IUnknown is to help in the management of the component's lifetime. The IUnknown interface provides two methods — AddRef and Release—which implement lifetime management of a component instance. I discuss this in more detail shortly. Following is the definition of IUnknown:

```
class IUnknown
{
    virtual  HRESULT   QueryInterface( REFIID riid, void** ppv ) = 0;
    virtual  ULONG     AddRef() = 0;
    virtual  ULONG     Release() = 0;
};
```

As you can see, IUnknown is an abstract class that provides the requirements for all classes that derive from it. It mandates that the three methods be implemented in the deriving class. It also ensures that the deriving class has a Vtable, just as in the IMath interfaces you examined earlier.

QueryInterface returns a pointer to a specific interface (such as IUnknown, IMath, and IDraw) contained within a component. The first parameter (REFIID) is a reference to the specific interface ID, which is a unique identifier for the particular interface we are querying. The second parameter, void**, is where the interface pointer is returned. The return value, HRESULT, is the handle to a COM-specific error structure that contains any error information.

HRESULTs

Most COM interface methods and API functions return an HRESULT (the exceptions are AddRef and Release). An HRESULT in Win32 is defined as a DWORD (32 bits) that contains information about the result of a function or method call. The high-order bit indicates the success or failure of the function. The next 15 bits indicate the facility and provide a way to group related return codes according to the Windows subsystem that generated the error. The lowest 16 bits provide specific information on what occurred. The structure of HRESULT is identical to the status values used by the Win32 API (see Figure 2-4).

HRESULT structure

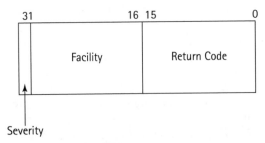

Severity

Figure 2-4: HRESULT **structure**

Nearly all COM method calls return HRESULTs because this provides a way for the COM run time to pass back error information beyond that of your application. In many cases, the COM run time must make low-level calls to the operating system as part of its implementation. An example is when COM marshals interface pointers to another process. (Chapter 4 discusses this *marshaling* process.) If an error occurs at this system level, COM returns an indication of the problem via the method's HRESULT return value. Only non-remotable or local interface methods may disregard the HRESULT return value requirement. These interfaces also must be marked with the *local* attribute.

COM provides several macros to help in determining the success or failure of a method call. The SUCCEEDED macro evaluates to TRUE if the function call is successful, and the FAILED macro evaluates to TRUE if the function fails. These macros aren't specific to COM and ActiveX, but are used throughout the Win32 environment and are defined in WINERROR.H. Return values in Win32 are prefixed with S_ when they indicate success and E_ when they indicate failure. Here's a look at WINERROR.H:

```
// From WINERROR.H
...
// Generic test for success on any status value (non-negative
numbers
// indicate success).
//
#define SUCCEEDED(Status) ((HRESULT)(Status) >= 0)
//
// and the inverse
//
#define FAILED(Status) ((HRESULT)(Status)<0)
...
//
// Create an HRESULT value from component pieces
//
#define MAKE_HRESULT(sev,fac,code) \
    ((HRESULT) (((unsigned long)(sev)<<31) |
            ((unsigned long)(fac)<<16) | ((unsigned long)(code)))
)
```

Throughout this chapter, you can see these macros used extensively. I discuss HRESULTs and COM error handling in more detail in Chapter 4.

Implementing IUnknown

In the math example, users who require the services of your component request one of the component's interfaces. This request can be made either through an existing IUnknown interface (on an existing math component) or during the component's instantiation (which I discuss shortly). COM requires the presence of the IUnknown interface in any COM object and that all COM interfaces also contain the IUnknown interface. In this way, a component user can obtain an interface pointer to any interface within the component by querying any existing interface on that component. Here's the math example with the IUnknown interface added to its implementation:

```cpp
// public interface definition
// An abstract class that derives from IUnknown
class IMath : public IUnknown
{
public:
    virtual long    Add( long Op1, long Op2 ) = 0;
    virtual long    Subtract( long Op1, long Op2 ) = 0;
    virtual long    Multiply( long Op1, long Op2 ) = 0;
    virtual long    Divide( long Op1, Op2 ) = 0;
};

class IAdvancedMath : public IUnknown
{
public:
    virtual long    Factorial( short sOp ) = 0;
    virtual long    Fibonacci( short sOp ) = 0;
};

// The actual implementation
class Math : public IMath, public IAdvancedMath
{
// We also have to implement IUnknown's methods
public:
    HRESULT    QueryInterface( REFIID riid, void** ppv );
    ULONG      Release();
    ULONG      AddRef();

    // IMath
    long    Add( long Op1, long Op2 );
    long    Subtract( long Op1, long Op2 );
    long    Multiply( long Op1, long Op2 );
    long    Divide( long Op1, Op2 );

    // IAdvancedMath
    long    Factorial( short sOp );
```

```
long    Fibonacci( short sOp );
};
```

The addition of deriving IMath from IUnknown requires that you implement seven methods: three from IUnknown and the four original IMath class methods. Every COM interface requires an implementation of IUnknown. Your IAdvanced Math interface also derives from it. Because of the way C++ implements multiple inheritance, you need to implement your IUnknown methods only once.

Figure 2-5 shows the Vtable layout for the IMath interface. Your component actually has two Vtables; the IAdvancedMath Vtable looks similar to that of Figure 2-5.

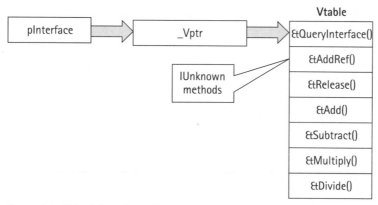

Figure 2-5: IMath **interface with** IUnknown **added**

Here is the implementation of IUnknown::QueryInterface for the math component:

```
HRESULT Math::QueryInterface( REFIID riid, void** ppv )
{
    *ppv = 0;
    if ( riid == IID_IUnknown )
        *ppv = (IMath*) this;
    else  if ( riid == IID_IMath )
        *ppv = (IMath*) this;
    else  if ( riid == IID_IAdvancedMath )
        *ppv = (IAdvancedMath*) this;
    if ( *ppv )
    {
        (IUnknown*)(*ppv)->AddRef();
        return( S_OK );
    }
    return( E_NOINTERFACE );
}
```

The basic purpose of QueryInterface is to return a Vtable pointer for the requested interface. One interesting aspect of the preceding code is the way a request for the IUnknown interface is handled. Both IMath and IAdvancedMath implement IUnknown, but you must choose only one implementation to return. This is because one of COM's rules states that an IUnknown interface pointer can identify a specific component instance. So QueryInterface must always return the same address in response to a request for an IUnknown interface. This arrangement enables client applications to determine whether they are working with the same instance of a component by comparing IUnknown* addresses.

Again, here is an example of a client instantiating and accessing a component's functionality through its COM interfaces. I create the component and ask for its IUnknown interface. After this call succeeds, I query through the IUnknown pointer for the IMath interface and subsequently use its functionality:

```
// Create an instance and retrieve its IUnknown interface
IUnknown* pUnk;
HRESULT hr = CoCreateInstance( CLSID_Math,
                   NULL,
                   CLSCTX_INPROC,
                   IID_IUnknown,
                   (void**) &pUnk );

// Query for IMath
IMath* pMath;
pUnk->QueryInterface( IID_IMath, (void**) &pMath );

// Use IMath
long lResult = pMath->Multiply( 44, 33 );
```

There is a standard way of depicting COM objects and their interfaces. Figure 2-6 depicts the Math class with its interfaces. IUnknown appears on the upper-right corner because it is required and so is present in any COM object. Other interfaces usually are shown on the lefthand side of the component. Remember, though, that every interface on the left also contains an IUnknown interface because every COM interface also implements IUnknown.

Component Lifetimes

You now know that access to a component's interface is obtained through IUnknown::QueryInterface. Lifetime management of components is handled with the other two methods provided by IUnknown: AddRef and Release. A typical COM component has several interfaces, and each one can be connected to multiple external clients. In the example, the component is a C++ class; what you will learn is how to manage the lifetime of a specific C++ class instance.

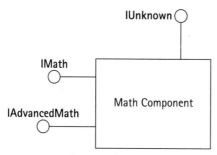

Figure 2-6: COM object representation

The user creates the instance through a mechanism provided by COM and employs the capabilities of that instance through its COM-based interfaces. Because you're using C++ to implement your example component, the instance is created with the C++ new operator. First, I describe how and when the instance is deleted; then I discuss how it's created.

Because an instance of a COM component can have multiple interfaces connected to multiple clients, you need reference-counting capability. Each time a client requests an interface, you increment a counter; when the client is finished with the interface, you decrement the counter. Eventually, when the outstanding interface reference count reaches zero, the COM object instance can go away. IUnknown::AddRef and IUnknown::Release provide a way for a client to increment and decrement the instance's internal counter.

In the Math class example, you need to maintain an internal reference counter. When you return an interface, you increment the counter. The client application must decrement the counter by calling IUnknown::Release when finished with the interface.

The component user cannot delete our C++ instance directly because the user has only a pointer to our C++ Vtable. In reality, the client shouldn't try to delete the object anyway because other clients (such as a C++ instance) could be accessing the same component object. Only the component itself, based on its internal reference count, can determine when it can or should be deleted. Following is the implementation of AddRef and Release in our math component:

```
Math::Math()
{
    // Initialize our reference counter
    m_lRef = 0;
}
ULONG Math::AddRef()
{
    return InterlockedIncrement( &m_lRef );
}
ULONG Math::Release()
```

```
{
   if ( InterlockedDecrement( &m_lRef ) == 0 )
   {
      delete this;
      return 0;
   }
   return m_lRef;
}
```

 The example uses the Win32 API functions `InterlockedIncrement` and `InterlockedDecrement`. These functions provide atomic access to our internal counter and make our component's reference counting thread-safe. I discuss other details about thread safety in Chapter 10.

To support the `AddRef` and `Release` methods of `IUnknown`, I added a member variable (`m_lRef`) that keeps a count of the current references, or outstanding interface pointers, to our object. The `AddRef` and `Release` methods directly affect a COM interface, but an interface is not an instance of the object itself. This object can have any number of users of its interfaces at a given time and must maintain an internal count of its active interfaces. When this count reaches zero, it is free to delete itself.

It is important that component users diligently call `AddRef` and `Release` to increment and decrement the component's reference count when appropriate. The `AddRef/Release` pair is similar to the `new/delete` pair used to manage memory in C++. Whenever a user obtains a new interface pointer or assigns its value to another variable, that user should call `AddRef` through the new pointer. You have to be careful, though. Some COM interface functions return pointers to interfaces and, in these cases, the functions themselves call `AddRef` through the returned pointer. The most obvious example is `QueryInterface`. It always calls `AddRef` prior to returning an interface pointer, so it isn't necessary to call `AddRef` again. Another important example is the COM API function `CoCreateInstance`. It always returns an interface pointer and, before doing so, ensures `AddRef` is called.

Globally Unique Identifiers

In distributed-object and component-based environments, unique identification of components and their interfaces is paramount. COM uses a technique described in the *Distributed Computing Environment (DCE)* standard for *remote procedure calls (RPC)*. The standard describes something called a *universally unique identifier (UUID)*. The Win32 RPC implementation is based on the *OSF (Open Software Foundation)* RPC standard and souses this concept extensively.

A UUID is a unique, 128-bit value with a very high probability. It combines a unique network address (48 bits) with a very granular time stamp (100 nanoseconds).

COM's implementation of the UUID is called a *globally unique identifier (GUID)* and basically is identical to a UUID. COM uses GUIDs to identify component classes (CLSID), interfaces (IID), type libraries, and component categories (CATID), to name a few. Here are the GUIDs used by the math component example:

```
// {A888F560-58E4-11d0-A68A-0000837E3100}
DEFINE_GUID( CLSID_Math,
             0xa888f560, 0x58e4, 0x11d0, 0xa6, 0x8a, 0x0,
             0x0, 0x83, 0x7e, 0x31, 0x0);
// {A888F561-58E4-11d0-A68A-0000837E3100}
DEFINE_GUID( IID_IMath,
             0xa888f561, 0x58e4, 0x11d0, 0xa6, 0x8a, 0x0,
             0x0, 0x83, 0x7e, 0x31, 0x0);
// {A888F562-58E4-11d0-A68A-0000837E3100}
DEFINE_GUID( IID_IAdvancedMath,
             0xa888f562, 0x58e4, 0x11d0, 0xa6, 0x8a, 0x0,
             0x0, 0x83, 0x7e, 0x31, 0x0);
```

The DEFINE_GUID macro creates a global constant that you can use throughout your programs, both on the client side and the server side. However, you can define the value only once. COM provides a set of macros to make management of this process easy. At the point in your programs where you want to define a GUID structure, you must include INITGUID.H before the header file that includes the declarations. Here's how it works in the math example:

```
//
// imath.h
//
// {A888F560-58E4-11d0-A68A-0000837E3100}
DEFINE_GUID( CLSID_Math,
             0xa888f560, 0x58e4, 0x11d0, 0xa6, 0x8a, 0x0,
             0x0, 0x83, 0x7e, 0x31, 0x0);
// {A888F561-58E4-11d0-A68A-0000837E3100}
DEFINE_GUID( IID_IMath,
             0xa888f561, 0x58e4, 0x11d0, 0xa6, 0x8a, 0x0,
             0x0, 0x83, 0x7e, 0x31, 0x0);
// {A888F562-58E4-11d0-A68A-0000837E3100}
DEFINE_GUID( IID_IAdvancedMath,
             0xa888f562, 0x58e4, 0x11d0, 0xa6, 0x8a, 0x0,
             0x0, 0x83, 0x7e, 0x31, 0x0);

class IMath : public IUnknown
{
public:
   ...
};
```

```
class IAdvancedMath : public IUnknown
{
    ...
};

//
// Client.cpp
//
#include <windows.h>
// Define the included GUIDs
#include <initguid.h>
#include "imath.h"
...
```

By including INITGUID.H, you change the meaning of the DEFINE_GUID macro. It not only declares the GUID's variable, but also defines and initializes it.

In the math example, you need three GUIDs. The CLSID identifies your component's class or type, and the two IIDs uniquely identify our COM Vtable interfaces: IMath and IAdvancedMath. There are a number of ways to generate GUIDs for your components. When you use Visual C++'s AppWizard and ATL Object Wizard, the GUIDs are generated automatically for you. You can generate them programmatically using COM's CoCreateGuid function. You also can generate them using two programs provided with Visual C++. UUIDGEN is a command-line utility that you can use if you need to generate a sequence of GUIDs for your projects. The following command line generates a list of 50 GUIDs and writes them to the specified file:

```
c:\devstudio\vc\bin\uuidgen -n50 > Project_Guids.txt
```

The other program, GUIDGEN, is graphical and provides several formatting methods for the created GUIDs. In our case, we need the DEFINE_GUID format. By using the Copy to clipboard option, you can paste the GUID definition directly into your source. Figure 2-7 shows the GUIDGEN program.

Figure 2-7: GUIDGEN utility

The COM API provides several functions for comparing GUIDs, creating GUIDs, and converting GUID types. Table 2-1 shows some of the more useful ones.

TABLE 2-1 USEFUL GUID HELPER FUNCTIONS

Function	Purpose
`CoCreateGuid( GUID* pGuid )`	Programmatic way of generating one unique GUID
`IsEqualGUID( REFGUID, REFGUID )`	Compares two GUIDs
`IsEqualIID( REFIID, REFIID )`	Compares two IIDs
`IsEqualCLSID( REFCLSID, REFCLSID )`	Compares two CLSIDs
`CLSIDFromProgID( LPCOLESTR, LPCLSID )`	Returns the CLSID for the given ProgID
`ProgIDFromCLSID( REFCLSID, LPOLESTR*)`	Returns the ProgID from the CLSID

Programmatic Identifiers

A component is uniquely identified by its CLSID, but remembering a component's CLSID can be difficult. COM provides another mechanism for naming a component: the *programmatic identifier*, or *ProgID*. A ProgID is a simple character string that is associated through the registry with the component's CLSID.

For example, I've chosen a ProgID of "Chapter2.Math" for the math component. Using the ProgID, you easily can specify an understandable component name as in this Visual Basic code:

```
Dim objMath as Object
Set objMath = CreateObject( "Chapter2.Math" )
objMath.Add( 100, 100 )
Set objMath = Nothing
```

The Visual Basic `CreateObject` statement takes as a parameter the component's ProgID. Internally, the statement uses the COM `CLSIDFromProgID` function to convert the ProgID into the component's actual CLSID. `CreateObject` then uses `CoCreateInstance` to create an instance of the component.

The Registry

Information needed by COM and client applications to locate and instantiate components is stored in the Windows *registry*. The registry provides nonvolatile storage for component information. Browser applications can determine the number and type of components installed on a system.

The registry orders information in a hierarchical manner and has several predefined, top-level keys. The one that pertains to this chapter is HKEY_CLASSES_ROOT. This section of the registry stores component information.

 On Windows 2000 systems, COM+ component information is stored in a second location called the *class store* or RegDB. See Chapter 13 for more details.

An important HKEY_CLASSES_ROOT subkey is CLSID (class identifier). It describes every component installed on the system. For example, our math component requires several registry entries before it can work.

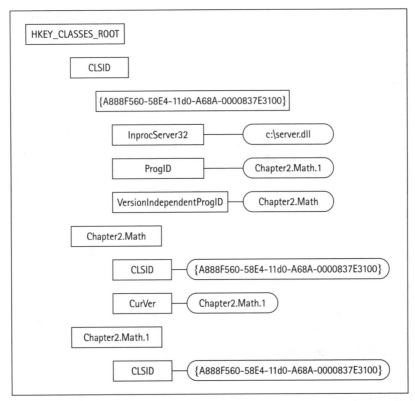

Figure 2-8: COM registry entries

Figure 2-8 shows the important COM registry entries that components must register. There are entries that provide a mapping of the ProgID to the underlying CLSID, and so on. The `LocalServer32` or `InprocServer32` entries provide a way for COM to locate the actual housing code in which the component is located. I discuss this in more detail in the next few sections. Table 2-2 describes each item in more detail.

TABLE 2-2 IMPORTANT REGISTRY KEY ENTRIES

Entry	Purpose
ProgID	Identifies the ProgID string for the COM class. It must contain no more than 39 characters and can contain periods.
InprocServer32	Contains the path and filename of the 32-bit DLL. It does not have to contain the path; if it does not, it can be loaded only if it resides within the Windows PATH. 16-bit versions do not include the "32" extension.
VersionIndependentProgID	Indicates the latest version of a component
LocalServer32	Contains the path and filename of the 32-bit EXE
CurVer	The ProgID of the latest version of the component class

Component Categories

Basic registry entries provide only limited information about a component. In the early days of COM-based technologies, you only needed a few registry entries to specify gross functionality of a component. The absence or existence of a subkey provided a lot of information. However, the large number of COM-based components now installed on a typical machine call for a more granular and useful approach to categorizing the capabilities of components.

Microsoft has responded to this need by providing a new mechanism for describing a component's functionality. The new specification, called *component categories*, provides system-defined and user-defined categories for various components. The information is still stored in the registry, but a new component makes it easy to add and remove entries without any knowledge of the registry itself.

THE CATID

Component categories are uniquely identified using a *category ID (CATID)*. Along with the CATID there is a *locale ID*, which is specified by a string of hexadecimal digits and a human-readable string. The known CATIDs are stored in the registry under the `HKEY_CLASSES_ROOT\Component Categories` key. Figure 2-9 shows some of the registry entries under this key. The `OLEVIEW` utility can display components by their component categories.

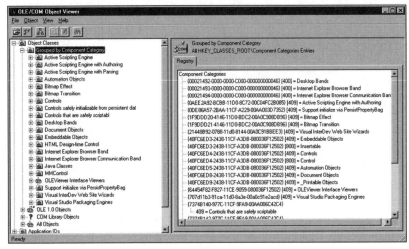

Figure 2-9: OLEVIEW and component categories

For backward compatibility, older registry entries that previously were used to categorize components are supported. As you can see from Figure 2-9, some registry entries have an `OldKey` entry. This provides a way to map the older registry mechanism to component categories. Table 2-3 lists the CATIDs associated with the old registry entries.

TABLE 2-3 CATEGORY IDS FOR OLD REGISTRY ENTRIES

Old Registry Entry	CATID Symbol From COMCAT.H	GUID
Control	CATID_Control	40FC6ED4-2438-11cf-A3DB-080036F12502
Insertable	CATID_Insertable	40FC6ED3-2438-11cf-A3DB-080036F12502
Programmable	CATID_Programmable	40FC6ED5-2438-11cf-A3DB-080036F12502
DocObject	CATID_DocObject	40FC6ED8-2438-11cf-A3DB-080036F12502
Printable	CATID_Printable	40FC6ED9-2438-11cf-A3DB-080036F12502

CATEGORIZING YOUR COMPONENTS

You categorize components in two different ways: by the component's capabilities and by the capabilities required by its potential clients. Two new registry entries communicate this information. The `Implemented Categories` entry lists those category capabilities that your component provides, and the `Required Categories` entry lists those categories that your component requires from its client. These subkeys are added below the CLSID of a component.

Currently, the Component Categories specification describes a few standard categories. Additional categories will be added as the technologies require them. For example, the ActiveX scripting model uses two component categories to indicate scripting support within controls. Table 2-4 shows some of the currently defined categories.

 Microsoft does not have to predefine component categories. You are welcome to create your own categories for your own components. Throughout this book, I use a unique component category to group the chapter examples.

TABLE 2-4 COMPONENT CATEGORIES

CATID Symbol from COMCAT.H	Purpose
CATID_PersistsToMoniker, CATID_PersistsToStreamInit, CATID_PersistsToStream, CATID_PersistsToStorage, CATID_PersistsToMemory, CATID_PersistsToFile, CATID_PersistsToPropertyBag	Used by Internet-aware controls to indicate which persistence methods they support. These categories can indicate that an interface is required if the control supports only one persistence method.
CATID_SimpleFrameControl	The control implements or requires the container to provide ISimpleFrameSite interface support.
CATID_PropertyNotifyControl	The control supports simple data binding.
CATID_WindowlessObject	The control implements the new windowless feature of the Controls '96 specification.
CATID_VBFormat, CATID_VBGet Control	The control uses one or both of these Visual Basic-specific interfaces.

Continued

TABLE 2-4 COMPONENT CATEGORIES *(Continued)*

CATID Symbol from COMCAT.H	Purpose
`CATID_VBDataBound`	The control supports the advanced data binding interfaces.
`CATID_RequiresDataPathHost`	The control expects help from the container with its data path properties. The container must support `IBindHost`.
`CATID_InternetAware`	The control implements or requires some of the Internet-specific functionality, in particular the new persistence mechanisms for Web-based controls. The control also handles large property values with the new data path property type. This includes support for asynchronous downloads.
`CATID_SafeForScripting`	The control is safe for use within scripting environments.
`CATID_SafeForInitializing`	The control can be initialized safely.

To support component categories, Microsoft has defined two new COM interfaces — `ICatRegister` and `ICatInformation` — which make working with component categories easier because there is no need to muck with the registry directly. Also, Microsoft has provided a system-level component that implements these interfaces; it's called Component Categories Manager.

THE COMPONENT CATEGORIES MANAGER

The *Component Categories Manager (CCM)* is a simple COM component that implements the `ICatRegister` and `ICatInformation` interfaces. Component categories are defined registry entries, and the CCM provides a simple way to maintain these entries within the registry. To create an instance of CCM, you use the COM `CoCreate Instance` function and pass the Microsoft-defined CCM CLSID: `CLSID_StdComponent CategoriesMgr`. You can request either interface it implements.

ICATREGISTER

The `ICatRegister` interface provides methods for registering and unregistering categories at both the system and the component level. Here's its definition:

```
interface ICatRegister : IUnknown
{
    HRESULT RegisterCategories(
```

```
        ULONG cCategories,
        CATEGORYINFO rgCategoryInfo[]);
    HRESULT UnRegisterCategories(
        ULONG cCategories,
        CATID rgcatid[]);
    HRESULT RegisterClassImplCategories(
        REFCLSID rclsid,
        ULONG cCategories,
        CATID rgcatid[]);
    HRESULT UnRegisterClassImplCategories(
        REFCLSID rclsid,
        ULONG cCategories,
        CATID rgcatid[]);
    HRESULT RegisterClassReqCategories(
        REFCLSID rclsid,
        ULONG cCategories,
        CATID rgcatid[]);
    HRESULT UnRegisterClassReqCategories(
        REFCLSID rclsid,
        ULONG cCategories,
        CATID rgcatid[]);
};
```

There are six registration methods, but three reverse the registration process. The RegisterCategory method takes the count and an array of CATEGORYINFO entries and ensures that they are registered on the system as valid component categories. This means placing them below the HKEY_CLASSES_ROOT\Component Categories key. In most cases, the category already is in the registry – but it doesn't hurt to make sure. Here's the definition of the CATEGORYINFO structure and some simple code that shows how to use the RegisterCategory method:

```
typedef struct  tagCATEGORYINFO
{
    CATID catid;
    LCID lcid;
    OLECHAR szDescription[ 128 ];
} CATEGORYINFO;

// Include the component category interfaces and symbols
#include "comcat.h"
...
HRESULT CreateComponentCategory( CATID catid, WCHAR* catDescription
)
{
    ICatRegister* pcr = NULL;
    HRESULT hr = S_OK;
```

```
// Create an instance of the category manager.
hr = CoCreateInstance( CLSID_StdComponentCategoriesMgr,
                       NULL,
                       CLSCTX_INPROC_SERVER,
                       IID_ICatRegister,
                       (void**) &pcr );
if (FAILED(hr))
   return hr;

CATEGORYINFO catinfo;
catinfo.catid = catid;

// English locale ID in hex
catinfo.lcid = 0x0409;

// Make sure the description isn't too large.
int len = wcslen(catDescription);
if ( len > 127 )
   len = 127;
wcsncpy( catinfo.szDescription, catDescription, len );
catinfo.szDescription[len] = '\0';
hr = pcr->RegisterCategories( 1, &catinfo );

pcr->Release();
return hr;
}
```

The preceding code creates an instance of the CCM and asks for `ICatRegister`. If everything works, a `CATEGORYINFO` structure is filled with the component information and the `RegisterCategory` method is called.

To add `\Implemented Categories` registry entries for a specific component, you use the `RegisterClassImplCategories` method. This method takes three parameters: the CLSID of the component, a count of the number of CATIDs, and an array of CATIDs to place under the `\Implemented Categories` key. The following code marks an ActiveX control as implementing the `Control` category:

```
ICatRegister* pcr = NULL ;
HRESULT hr = S_OK ;

// Create an instance of the category manager.
hr = CoCreateInstance( CLSID_StdComponentCategoriesMgr,
                       NULL,
                       CLSCTX_INPROC_SERVER,
                       IID_ICatRegister,
                       (void**)&pcr );
```

```
if (SUCCEEDED(hr))
{
    // Register that we support the  "Control" category
    CATID rgcatid[1];
    rgcatid[0] = CATID_Control;
    hr = pcr->RegisterClassImplCategories(clsid, 1, rgcatid);
}
if (pcr != NULL)
    pcr->Release();
```

To add "Category Required" entries for a component, you use the Register ClassReqCategories method. This method takes the same parameters as RegisterClassImplCategories so the code is nearly identical to that just shown.

OLEVIEW

A good tool for inspecting the registry from a COM perspective is the OLEVIEW utility provided with Visual C++ (and the Platform SDK). OLEVIEW provides several different views of the components on your system, as well as a number of other useful capabilities. Figure 2-9 shows OLEVIEW in action.

Component Housings

So far I've discussed the requirements for a COM-based component. Once a component is designed and implemented with a specific language (C++ in our case), it then must execute within the context of an operating system process. COM-based components are housed within either an *executable (EXE)* or a Windows *dynamic link library (DLL)*. Each housing type has its own characteristics. Component developers must implement certain functions differently depending on the particular housing in which their components execute.

The term *local server* describes an executable component housing. The executable may contain functionality in addition to supporting COM-based components. For example, Microsoft Word is a local server. It provides word-processing capabilities for users, but it also exposes a number of COM components that other applications can access.

An *in-process server* is a Windows DLL that houses COM-based components. A DLL executes in the context of the calling process, so the client process has direct memory access to any DLL-based components. This concept will become important when I discuss COM-based custom interfaces and marshaling in Chapter 4. In short, marshaling is the process of moving method parameters from one process to another. Marshaling can impact performance of your applications so it is important that you understand when and where it is used.

A *remote server* is housing that loads and executes on a remote machine. Typically, a remote server is implemented within an executable although this is not a requirement. You only have remote access to components housed within DLLs. COM provides a surrogate process in which the remote DLL can execute.

One of COM's benefits is that it provides location transparency for client processes (the user of the component). As I described earlier, COM-based services can be implemented in three different configurations: in-process via a DLL on the local machine, across-process on the same machine (local server), or on a remote machine via a DLL or executable. The client process, however, requires no knowledge of how the component is implemented or where it is located. The client creates an instance of a component; COM is responsible for locating and launching the housing. This makes COM-based components inherently multitier.

You should consider two primary factors when determining how to implement your components. The first is performance. Because in-process components execute in the address space of the client process, they provide the best performance. No marshaling of method parameters is required. (Chapter 4 discusses marshaling in detail .) The second factor is client robustness. By implementing your component using in-process housing, you potentially can crash the client. Major errors in an out-of-process component do not bring down the client application.

Class Factories

Because COM objects can reside outside the client's process space and must be accessed from various languages, a language-independent way of instantiating a component is required. In C++, the new operator creates an instance of an object. COM supplies a standard interface, IClassFactory, which a special creator component must implement in order to enable external clients to create instances of your components:

```
class IClassFactory : public IUnknown
{
    virtual HRESULT CreateInstance( LPUNKNOWN pUnk,
                                    REFIID riid, void** ppv ) = 0;
    virtual HRESULT LockServer( BOOL fLock ) = 0;
};
```

A *class factory* is a COM object whose sole purpose is to facilitate the creation of other, more useful COM objects. The CreateInstance method does what it says — it creates an instance of the specified component class and returns the requested interface on that instance. The LockServer method provides a way for a client to lock a server in memory. By locking a server in memory, the client ensures its future availability even when there are no instantiated components within the server. It typically is done for performance reasons. Listing 2-1 shows the class factory implementation for the math component.

Listing 2-1: Class Factory Code

```
MathClassFactory::MathClassFactory()
{
    m_lRef = 0;
```

```
}

MathClassFactory::~MathClassFactory()
{
}

STDMETHODIMP MathClassFactory::QueryInterface( REFIID riid, void**
ppv )
{
   *ppv = 0;
   if ( riid == IID_IUnknown || riid == IID_IClassFactory )
      *ppv = this;
   if ( *ppv )
   {
      AddRef();
      return S_OK;
   }
   return( E_NOINTERFACE );
}

STDMETHODIMP_(ULONG) MathClassFactory::AddRef()
{
   return InterlockedIncrement( &m_lRef );
}

STDMETHODIMP_(ULONG) MathClassFactory::Release()
{
   if ( InterlockedDecrement( &m_lRef ) == 0 )
   {
      delete this;
      return 0;
   }
   return m_lRef;
}

STDMETHODIMP MathClassFactory::CreateInstance
     ( LPUNKNOWN pUnkOuter, REFIID riid, void** ppvObj )
{
   Math*      pMath;
   HRESULT    hr;
   *ppvObj = 0;

   // Create our component instance
   pMath = new Math;
```

```
      if ( pMath == 0 )
         return( E_OUTOFMEMORY );

      hr = pMath->QueryInterface( riid, ppvObj );
      if ( FAILED( hr ) )
         delete pMath;

      return hr;
}
STDMETHODIMP MathClassFactory::LockServer( BOOL fLock )
{
   if ( fLock )
      InterlockedIncrement( &g_lLocks );
   else
      InterlockedDecrement( &g_lLocks );
    return S_OK;
}
```

COM typically handles the details of creating a component instance when the client uses the CoCreateInstance API call. However, a client can gain direct access to a component's class factory by using COM's CoGetClassObject function. In most cases, the CoGetClassObject function returns a pointer to the component's IClassFactory interface. Here's an example:

```
int main()
{
   IClassFactory* pCF;
   IMath* pMath;
   HRESULT hr;

   // Get the class factory for the Math class
   hr = CoGetClassObject( CLSID_Math,
                          CLSCTX_INPROC,
                          NULL,
                          IID_IClassFactory,
                          &pCF );

   // using the class factory interface create an instance of the
   // component and return the IMath interface.
   pCF->CreateInstance( NULL, IID_IMath, &pMath );

   // Release the class factory
   pCF->Release();
```

```
    // Use the component to do some work
    long lResult = pMath->Add( 100, 433 );

    // Release it when we're finished
    pMath->Release();
}
```

CoGetClassObject is a COM API function that returns the class factory of the requested component (identified by the CLSID). CoGetClassObject then returns the class factory interface so that you can create an instance of the math component class. Once you use the class factory, call Release, which deletes the class factory instance. This three-step process is performed often, so COM provides a helper function (CoCreateInstance) that encapsulates the steps. By using CoCreate Instance, you don't have to deal with the class factory interface; you just call CoCreateInstance with the specific component interface that you require.

Figure 2-10 depicts what you've built so far. You have two components, each with a number of interfaces. What you need now is a way of delivering or housing this functionality. COM provides mechanisms for this as well.

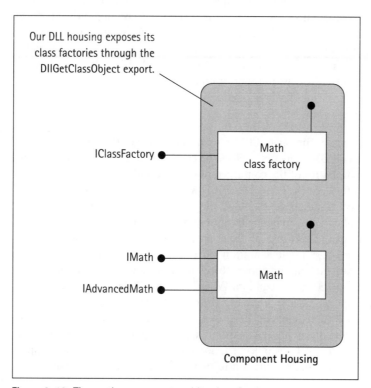

Figure 2-10: The math component and its class factory

COM-Based Reuse

COM provides two methods for reusing component class objects: containment and aggregation. They are similar to C++ reuse techniques, but COM provides *binary* reuse as opposed to the compile-time or source-code-dependent reuse provided by C++. For more details on these methods see Chapter 5; here I provide a brief description because you will encounter the terms in almost every chapter.

Containment

COM *containment* is similar to the C++ technique of class composition. *Class composition* is a technique in which you embed a class instance inside your own class. For example, you can implement a stack component by using an array object inside your stack class. In this way, you "contain" the array class. A user of the class does not have direct access to the array's methods unless you explicitly expose them through your stack class's public interface.

Containment and composition achieve reuse by using the services of a COM object or C++ class internally. The interface of the contained component is exposed only indirectly (if at all) via methods provided by the containing (or *outer*) component. The outer COM object uses the internal (or *inner*) COM component's interfaces in the implementation of its interfaces. The outer object can, if it chooses, expose the inner object's interfaces as well. The lifetime of the inner object is controlled completely by the outer component, just as in C++. A COM object does not have to do anything to support its use as an inner or contained object.

Aggregation

COM object *aggregation* is similar to COM containment except that the interface of the inner or contained COM object is exposed directly. The aggregate object doesn't need or use the functionality of the contained object internally, but instead exposes the inner object's interfaces as if they were its own. The IUnknown interface of the outer aggregate object provides access to all the interfaces of the inner object. This detail makes it complicated to implement aggregation at times.

The management of the lifetimes of the outer and inner objects must be coordinated through the IUnknown implementation. Successful lifetime management of the aggregate object requires that the inner object provide support for a *controlling unknown*: the outer object in aggregation. When an inner COM object is created as part of an aggregate, it is passed a pointer to the outer object's IUnknown implementation. The inner object then defers its IUnknown implementation to that of the outer object's. This arrangement provides a consistent approach to the management of the aggregate object's lifetime. A COM object supports aggregation if it includes support for deferring its IUnknown implementation to that of a controlling unknown.

COM APIs

Microsoft provides a number of Win32 API functions specific to COM, ActiveX, and OLE. There are more than 100 COM-specific calls and I can't cover them all here. By studying the major COM API functions, however, you can garner a good understanding of how COM works. The COM API functions provide the basis of higher-level services such as OLE and ActiveX. Remember that COM is a bunch of interface definitions that you must implement, and these API calls get things started. Table 2-5 shows the API functions that I introduce in this chapter.

TABLE 2-5 BASIC COM FUNCTIONS

Function	Purpose
CoInitialize, CoInitializeEx	Initializes the COM libraries for use by a process.
CoUninitialize (client and server)	Releases the COM libraries when their services are no longer needed. Not used by in-process servers.
CoGetClassObject (client)	Gets an instance of a class factory for a specific COM object.
CoCreateGUID (client and server)	Creates a new, unique GUID.
CoCreateInstance (client), CoCreateInstanceEx (client)	Creates an instance of a specific COM object, which may be on a remote machine.
CoRegisterClass (server)	Registers the existence of a class factory for a particular COM object.
DllCanUnloadNow (in-process server)	Called periodically by COM to determine whether the DLL can be unloaded (when there are no objects instantiated within the DLL housing). Implemented by in-process servers.
DllGetClassObject (server)	Entry point implemented by in-process servers so that client processes can obtain its class factory interfaces.

CoInitialize and CoInitializeEx

CoInitialize initializes the COM libraries and DLLs so that you can use the other APIs. CoInitialize takes one parameter, which currently is reserved and should be NULL.

CoInitializeEx was added to support the various COM threading models. Before NT 4.0, COM supported only the *apartment* threading model, which is the default threading model for CoInitialize. CoInitializeEx takes two parameters. The first parameter is reserved and should be NULL, and the second parameter specifies one of the threading models from the COINIT enumeration. I discuss COM threading in detail in Chapter 10.

```
typedef enum tagCOINIT{
  COINIT_APARTMENTTHREADED = 0x2,   // Apartment model
  COINIT_MULTITHREADED     = 0x0,   // OLE calls objects on any
thread.
  COINIT_DISABLE_OLE1DDE   = 0x4,   // Don't use DDE for Ole1
support.
  COINIT_SPEED_OVER_MEMORY = 0x8,   // Trade memory for speed.
} COINIT;
```

CoUninitialize

CoUninitialize is called to free the use of the COM libraries and DLLs. CoUninitialize should be called only if CoInitialize has been called successfully. Also, you should balance every call to CoInitialize with a corresponding call to CoUninitialize.

CoRegisterClassObject

An out-of-process server calls CoRegisterClassObject to register its class factories as available. CoRegisterClassObject must be called for every class factory provided by an executable. This should be done as soon as possible before processing the Windows message loop. Only executables use CoRegisterClassObject. In-process servers export the DllGetClassObject function to expose its component's class factories. Table 2-6 describes the parameters required by CoRegister ClassObject.

TABLE 2-6 COREGISTERCLASSOBJECT PARAMETERS

Parameter	Description
REFCLSID rclsid	The CLSID for the component class being registered.

Parameter	Description
LPUNKNOWN pUnk	The IUnknown pointer for the component class being registered.
DWORD dwClsContext	The requested context for the executable. This can be one of the following: CLSCTX_INPROC_SERVER CLSCTX_INPROC_HANDLER CLSCTX_LOCAL_SERVER CLSCTX_REMOTE_SERVER
DWORD flags	-REGCLS flags specify how to create multiple instances of the component. One of the following: REGCLS_SINGLEUSE REGCLS_MULTIPLEUSE REGCLS_MULTI_SEPARATE
LPDWORD lpdwRegister	A value returned that must be used when deregistering the class object using the CoRevokeClassObject function.

CoGetClassObject

A COM client uses CoGetClassObject to obtain a pointer to the class object interface of the specified component class. As you've seen, the standard IClassFactory interface usually is requested, but other options (for example, a custom class factory interface) are possible.

COM ensures that the server either is loaded (DLL) or running (EXE). If the component is housed within a DLL, COM loads the DLL and retrieves the requested interface by calling its exported DllGetClassObject function. If the component is contained within an executable that is not running, COM launches the executable (either locally or remotely), waits for the server to register its class factories with CoRegisterClassObject, and then returns the requested interface to the client.

For NT 4.0 and later, the COSERVERINFO parameter permits instantiation on remote systems. The COSERVERINFO structure allows specification of the server name as a UNC name (for example, \\twa_nt), DNS name (such as www.WidgetWare.com), or IP address (such as 191.51.33.1).

```
typedef struct _COSERVERINFO
{
```

```
    DWORD dwReserved1;
    LPWSTR pwszName;
    COAUTHINFO *pAuthInfo;
    DWORD dwReserved2;
}   COSERVERINFO;
```

In most cases, the client should use the shorthand `CoCreateInstance` function described next. There are three cases in which a client application might use `CoGetClassObject`. First, suppose that the client application intends to create several instances of the component object. In this case, it is efficient to retrieve only one copy of the class factory for the creation of these components. The second case occurs when the client application requires access to the `IClassFactory::LockServer` method to lock the component housing in memory, typically for performance reasons. The third case happens when the client application uses a creation technique that does not use the standard `IClassFactory` interface. Table 2-7 lists the `CoGetClassObject` parameters.

TABLE **2-7** COGETCLASSOBJECT PARAMETERS

Parameter	Description
REFCLSID rclsid	A reference to the CLSID for the specific component.
DWORD dwClsContext	The requested context for the server housing. This can be one, two, or all of the following:
	CLSCTX_INPROC_SERVER
	CLSCTX_INPROC_HANDLER
	CLSCTX_LOCAL_SERVER
	CLSCTX_REMOTE_SERVER
COSERVERINFO pServerInfo	Pointer to the COSERVERINFO structure.
REFIID riid	A reference to an IID for the specific interface to be returned from the created class object. This normally is IClassFactory so that the client can create an instance of the required component.
VOID** ppvObj	A void pointer to return the specified interface.

CoCreateInstance

The client application uses `CoCreateInstance` to create an instance of the specified component class. It is a helper function that calls `CoGetClassObject` to get a class factory for the component and then uses the `IClassFactory::Create`

Instance method to create the component instance. You should use CoCreate Instance instead of performing the three-step process shown next, unless your requirements match those discussed previously.

```
// What CoCreateInstance does internally
CoGetClassObject(..., &pCF );
pCF->CreateInstance(..., &pInt );
pCF->Release();
```

The parameters of CoCreateInstance are similar to those required by CoGetClassObject. The only difference is that the client using CoCreateInstance asks for the specific interface on the component (such as IDispatch) instead of an IClassFactory pointer.

To support distributed COM, the CoGetClassObject method uses a parameter that was reserved in previous COM versions to pass the COSERVERINFO structure. However, CoCreateInstance did not have any reserved parameter available for use, so a new method (CoCreateInstanceEx) is required. CoCreateInstanceEx creates an instance of the COM object on a remote machine. The fourth CoCreateInstance parameter supports the new COSERVERINFO parameter. The format is the same as described earlier with the CoGetClassObject function.

To improve performance when creating a component instance, the MULTI_QI structure was added to enable the client to query the interface for multiple interfaces in one call:

```
typedef struct _MULTI_QI
{
    const IID*     pIID;
    IUnknown *     pItf;
    HRESULT        hr;
} MULTI_QI;
```

The MULTI_QI structure enables you to provide an array of IIDs. This array is returned with the array of interfaces. Tables 2-8 and 2-9 show the parameters for CoCreateInstance and CoCreateInstanceEx.

TABLE 2-8 COCREATEINSTANCE PARAMETERS

Parameter	Description
REFCLSID rclsid	A reference to the CLSID for the specific component.
IUnknown* pUnkOuter	The controlling outer unknown when aggregation is used.

Continued

TABLE 2-8 COCREATEINSTANCE PARAMETERS *(Continued)*

Parameter	Description
DWORD dwClsContext	The requested context for the server housing. This can be one, two, or all of the following: CLSCTX_INPROC_SERVER CLSCTX_INPROC_HANDLER CLSCTX_LOCAL_SERVER CLSCTX_REMOTE_SERVER
REFIID riid	A reference to an IID for the specific interface to be returned from the created component object.
VOID** ppvObj	A void pointer to return the specified interface.

TABLE 2-9 COCREATEINSTANCEEX PARAMETERS

Parameter	Description
REFCLSID rclsid	A reference to the CLSID for the specific component.
IUnknown* pUnkOuter	The controlling outer unknown when aggregation is used.
DWORD dwClsContext	The requested context for the server housing. This can be one, two, or all of the following: CLSCTX_INPROC_SERVER CLSCTX_INPROC_HANDLER CLSCTX_LOCAL_SERVER CLSCTX_REMOTE_SERVER
COSERVERINFO* pServerInfo	Information about the remote server machine.
ULONG	Number of QueryInterfaces to perform for the MULTI_QI structure.
MULTI_QI	An array of MULTI_QI structures. This makes it more efficient to retrieve a series of interface pointers from the created component.

DllCanUnloadNow

Only in-process servers implement `DllCanUnloadNow`. Its purpose is to allow COM periodically to check whether the DLL can be unloaded. `DllCanUnloadNow` takes no parameters and returns either `S_FALSE`, indicating that the DLL cannot be unloaded or `S_OK`, indicating that the DLL can be unloaded.

DllGetClassObject

In-process servers implement `DllGetClassObject` to expose the class factories for its component objects. When a client application requests a component housed within an in-process server, COM calls the `DllGetClassObject` entry point within the DLL with the parameters shown in Table 2-10.

TABLE **2-10** DLLGETCLASSOBJECT PARAMETERS

Parameter	Description
`REFCLSID rclsid`	A reference to the CLSID for the specific component.

`DWORD dwClsContext`	The requested context for the DLL. This can be one of the following:
	
	`CLSCTX_INPROC_SERVER`
	`CLSCTX_INPROC_HANDLER`
	`CLSCTX_LOCAL_SERVER`
	`CLSCTX_REMOTE_SERVER`

`LPVOID pvReserved`	Reserved. Must be `NULL`.
`REFIID riid`	A reference to an IID for the specific interface to be returned from the created COM object. This normally is `IClassFactory` so that the client can create an instance of the requested component.
`VOID** ppvObj`	A void pointer to return the specified interface.

Miscellaneous COM Details

The purpose of this chapter is to give you an effective introduction to COM. It's hard to cover such a large topic in one chapter, so I will continue to build on the concepts presented here in the later chapters. However, there are a few more details that I need to clear up before we move on.

COM C++ Macros: STDMETHOD and STDMETHODIMP

To this point, I haven't used the standard COM and OLE macros when declaring interfaces because they get in the way of understanding what's going on in terms of instruction. COM and ATL use C/C++ macros extensively to hide the implementation details of the various platforms. You're getting ready to write some real code, so it's time I explain the macros that you will use. There are four macros for COM interface declarations and definitions: STDMETHOD, STDMETHODIMP, STDMETHOD_, and STDMETHODIMP_. You will use the first two macros nearly all of the time because they indicate an HRESULT return from a method. Those that end with an underscore are used only with IUnknown's AddRef and Release and they indicate a user-specified return value. In an earlier example of IMath, I declared it this way:

```
// public interface definition of our Math component
// An abstract class
class IMath
{
public:
    virtual long   Add( long Op1, long Op2 ) = 0;
    virtual long   Subtract( long Op1, long Op2 ) = 0;
    virtual long   Multiply( long Op1, long Op2 ) = 0;
    virtual long   Divide( long Op1, Op2 ) = 0;
};
```

Before you convert the preceding code to use the macros, you need to understand one more thing about COM. As I described earlier, every COM interface method should return an HRESULT with only two exceptions. But so far, you have been returning longs from the IMath methods. Now, you must move the result of your computation from a return value to a pass-by-pointer parameter. This step is important and is required because you must return an HRESULT.

Requiring all interface methods to return HRESULTs seems strange and restrictive at first, especially if you like the idea of using application-specific return values as part of your implementation. However, it isn't a big issue because there are ways to enable a client application to treat a method parameter as a return value. I discuss this in detail in Chapter 4.

Using COM's macros and moving the return value to the end as a pointer, the interface is declared as follows:

```
class IMath : public IUnknown
{
public:
    STDMETHOD(Add)( long, long, long* )        PURE;
    STDMETHOD(Subtract)( long, long, long* ) PURE;
    STDMETHOD(Multiply)( long, long, long* ) PURE;
    STDMETHOD(Divide)( long, long, long* )   PURE;
};
```

The actual expansion of STDMETHOD depends on the target platform and whether you use C or C++. The expansion for Win32 using C++ is as follows:

```
// OBJBASE.H
#define STDMETHODCALLTYPE          __stdcall
...
#define STDMETHOD(method)          virtual HRESULT STDMETHODCALLTYPE
method
#define STDMETHOD_(type,method) virtual type STDMETHODCALLTYPE
method
#define PURE                       = 0
#define STDMETHODIMP               HRESULT STDMETHODCALLTYPE
#define STDMETHODIMP_(type)        type STDMETHODCALLTYPE
```

As you can see, the earlier example is very similar to the expanded macro version except for the additional return type __stdcall. The Win32 API functions use this Microsoft-specific calling convention. It specifies that the caller should clean up the stack after the call. It isn't crucial to our understanding, but it makes for interesting reading.

The STDMETHOD macro also is used in the declaration of interface methods within the implementing class. The only difference is that you don't need the PURE qualifier. The STDMETHODIMP macros are employed when you actually implement the interface function, usually in your .CPP file. Following are the declarations of the IMath methods within the Math class.

```
Math : public IMath, public IAdvancedMath
{
    // IMath
    STDMETHOD(Add) ( long, long, long* );
    STDMETHOD(Subtract) ( long, long, long* );
    STDMETHOD(Multiply) ( long, long, long* );
    STDMETHOD(Divide) ( long, long, long* );
};
```

When you implement the functions in your `.CPP` file, use the `STDMETHODIMP` macros:

```
STDMETHODIMP Math::Add( long lOp1, long lOp2, long* pResult )
{
    *pResult = lOp1 + lOp2;
    return S_OK;
}
STDMETHODIMP Math::Subtract( long lOp1, long lOp2, long* pResult )
{
    *pResult = lOp1 - lOp2;
    return S_OK;
}
...
```

The primary purpose of the `STDMETHODIMP` macro is to prepend the `HRESULT` return type to the method implementation.

COM and Unicode

All COM functions and standard interface methods require Unicode strings. *Unicode strings*, also referred to as *wide character strings*, store characters as two bytes primarily to enable support for international character sets such as Kanji. The Windows NT operating system also implements its APIs using native Unicode strings. When you build a Visual C++ application, you have the option of building an ANSI- or Unicode-based application.

Windows 95 and Windows 98 provide native ANSI support, so if you want your application or component to run on Windows 95 and Windows NT (or even Window 2000) you must use the ANSI build. If you always run your applications on Windows NT, however, you can build your applications in straight Unicode and gain a slight performance improvement.

Most of us must target both operating systems and so we comply with ANSI, or *multibyte*, strings. As a result, we must convert our strings from ANSI to Unicode whenever we pass them to a COM function or through a COM interface method. There are several techniques that you can use to perform this conversion.

First, if you are passing a literal, you simply can add an "L" to the front of the string. The C++ compiler supports wide strings indicated in this manner. Here's an example:

```
// Get the unique CLSID from the ProgID
HRESULT hr = ::CLSIDFromProgID( L"Chapter2.Math.1", &clsid );
```

Second, you can use the native Win32 APIs to convert from Unicode to ANSI and back. Here's an example of converting an ANSI string (multibyte) to Unicode (wide):

```
// Convert the ProgID to Unicode
char* szProgID = "Chapter2.Math.1";
WCHAR  szWideProgID[128];
CLSID  clsid;
long lLen = MultiByteToWideChar( CP_ACP,
                         0,
                         szProgID,
                         strlen( szProgID ),
                         szWideProgID,
                         sizeof( szWideProgID ) );
// Terminate the returned string
szWideProgID[ lLen ] = '\0';
```

Third, you can use one of the many macros supplied by MFC or ATL. I haven't explained either of these frameworks yet, but you might as well take a quick look at an example:

```
USES_CONVERSION;

// Get the unique CLSID from the ProgID
char* szProgID = "Chapter2.Math.1";
HRESULT hr = ::CLSIDFromProgID( A2W( szProgID ), &clsid );
```

The USES_CONVERSION macro supplies temporary variables for the conversion and, as you can see, the A2W macro converts from ANSI to Unicode in place. There is a corresponding W2A and a number of macros for converting other string types.

COM and Polymorphism

COM supports the object-oriented concept of polymorphism, but most new students are unconvinced. Typically, what they need is a concrete example. Earlier in this chapter, I demonstrated the use of Vtables using a simple C++ Fruit class. To refresh your memory, here it is:

```
int main()
{
   Fruit* pFruitList[4];
   pFruitList[0] = new Apple;
   pFruitList[1] = new Orange;
   pFruitList[2] = new Grape;
   pFruitList[3] = new GrannySmith;
   for( int i = 0; i < 4; i++ )
      pFruitList[i]->Draw();
}
// Produces this output
```

```
>
> I'm an Apple
> I'm an Orange
> I'm a Grape
> I'm a Granny Smith Apple
>
```

Polymorphism is the ability of an object to respond differently to the same message (in C++, a message basically is a method). Another way to look at it is to say that the user of an object uses the same methods independent of the object's underlying implementation.

In the example, each of the four different objects (such as Apple and Orange) has implemented the Draw method described in the base Fruit class. A client application then can interact with each object using exactly the same methods. However, each object is free to implement its Draw in any way it deems necessary and also can respond differently to the Draw method. Here's an example:

```
class IFruit {
   virtual void Draw() = 0;
   ...
};

IFruit* pFruit[4];
CoCreateInstance( CLSID_Apple, IID_IFruit, ..., (void**)
&(pFruit[0]));
CoCreateInstance( CLSID_Orange, IID_IFruit, ..., (void**)
&(pFruit[1]));
CoCreateInstance( CLSID_Grape, IID_IFruit, ..., (void**)
&(pFruit[2]));
CoCreateInstance( CLSID_GrannySmith, IID_IFruit,
                  ..., (void**) &(pFruit[3]));
for( I = 0; I < 3; I++ )
   pFruit->Draw();
```

There we have it: four different COM objects, each possibly implemented by a different vendor, and all of them supporting the IFruit interface. Client applications, however, interact with each instance in exactly the same way.

Example: Building a Simple COM Client and Server

I have discussed a number of COM's features and attributes. Most of the demonstration code from this chapter comes from the example that I describe next. What follows are the step-by-step details of creating a C++ COM client and server application. Although the math component is simple, building the infrastructure to support the component takes quite a bit of code. Much of the support code is the same for every COM component you build. That is why frameworks such as ATL are popular. They encapsulate the tedious, routine code and enable you to focus on providing your components with unique functionality.

To get a solid understanding of how COM is implemented, I recommend that you download the code for this example (see the Preface for details) and step through it in debug mode. You also can follow along and type all the code by hand; that is what my students do. They complain at first, but are quite appreciative when everything finally works. The understanding gained by typing the code and getting it to work can help you as you read the forthcoming chapters.

Step 1: Create the Visual C++ Project

Start Visual C++ and create a new project, selecting Win32 Dynamic-Link Library. Give it the name "Server."

The initial project does not contain any files. You must build each of them yourself. Remember that it's tedious at first.

Step 2: Create IMATH.H

The next step is to declare the component's interfaces as abstract classes. Before you do that, however, you need three new GUIDs: one to uniquely identify the component and the other two to uniquely identify the component's custom interfaces. Use the GUIDGEN utility (shown in Figure 2-11) to create three GUIDs. Copy each one to the clipboard and then paste it into your IMATH.H file (described next). Be sure to use the DEFINE_GUID format.

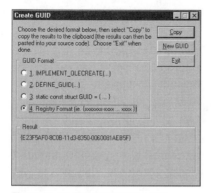

Figure 2-11: The GUIDGEN utility

Type the following code and save it in a file called IMATH.H; you should replace the GUIDs shown with those that you create using GUIDGEN:

```
//
// imath.h
//
// {A888F560-58E4-11d0-A68A-0000837E3100}
DEFINE_GUID( CLSID_Math,
          0xa888f560, 0x58e4, 0x11d0, 0xa6, 0x8a, 0x0, 0x0, 0x83,
          0x7e, 0x31, 0x0);
// {A888F561-58E4-11d0-A68A-0000837E3100}
DEFINE_GUID( IID_IMath,
          0xa888f561, 0x58e4, 0x11d0, 0xa6, 0x8a, 0x0, 0x0, 0x83,
          0x7e, 0x31, 0x0);
// {A888F562-58E4-11d0-A68A-0000837E3100}
DEFINE_GUID( IID_IAdvancedMath,
          0xa888f562, 0x58e4, 0x11d0, 0xa6, 0x8a, 0x0, 0x0, 0x83,
          0x7e, 0x31, 0x0);

class IMath : public IUnknown
{
public:
   STDMETHOD(Add)( long, long, long* )      PURE;
   STDMETHOD(Subtract)( long, long, long* ) PURE;
   STDMETHOD(Multiply)( long, long, long* ) PURE;
   STDMETHOD(Divide)( long, long, long* )   PURE;
};

class IAdvancedMath : public IUnknown
{
public:
   STDMETHOD(Factorial)( short, long* ) PURE;
   STDMETHOD(Fibonacci)( short, long* )  PURE;
};
```

Separate your interface definition, CLSID, and IIDs from the actual implementation so that you can provide just this information to the client program. With only this information, the client can access your component's functionality. Remember that the primary purpose of the preceding declarations is to provide potential clients with the correct Vtable layout and parameter types so that they can access the component's interfaces.

The client doesn't need the CLSID – you access the component through its ProgID – but it doesn't hurt to put it here. The PURE macro equates to = 0 to make the methods abstract.

Step 3: Declare the Component and Class Factory

Next, you declare your component class and a class factory for the component. Create a new file called MATH.H and enter the following code:

```
//
// math.h
//
#include "imath.h"

extern long g_lObjs;
extern long g_lLocks;

class Math : public IMath, public IAdvancedMath
{
protected:
    // Reference count
    long        m_lRef;

public:
    Math();
    ~Math();

public:
    // IUnknown
    STDMETHOD(QueryInterface( REFIID, void** ));
    STDMETHOD_(ULONG, AddRef());
    STDMETHOD_(ULONG, Release());

    // IMath
    STDMETHOD(Add)( long, long, long* );
    STDMETHOD(Subtract)( long, long, long* );
    STDMETHOD(Multiply)( long, long, long* );
    STDMETHOD(Divide)( long, long, long* );

    // IAdvancedMath
    STDMETHOD(Factorial)( short, long* );
    STDMETHOD(Fibonacci)( short, long* );
};

class MathClassFactory : public IClassFactory
{
protected:
    long        m_lRef;
```

```
public:
   MathClassFactory();
   ~MathClassFactory();

   // IUnknown
   STDMETHOD( QueryInterface(REFIID, void** ));
   STDMETHOD_(ULONG, AddRef());
   STDMETHOD_(ULONG, Release());

   // IClassFactory
   STDMETHOD(CreateInstance)(LPUNKNOWN, REFIID, void**);
   STDMETHOD(LockServer)(BOOL);
};
```

You derive your math class from both of your abstract interface classes — IMath and IAdvancedMath, which also derive from IUnknown. You then provide non-abstract declarations for the interface methods. The two global variables keep track of the total number of component instances within the DLL and the number of calls made to IClassFactory::LockServer.

Step 4: Implement the Component and Class Factory Classes

Create a MATH.CPP file for the component's implementation and add the following:

```
//
// Math.cpp
//
#include <windows.h>
#include "math.h"

//
// Math class implementation
//
Math::Math()
{
   m_lRef = 0;
   // Increment the global object count
   InterlockedIncrement( &g_lObjs );
}

// The destructor
Math::~Math()
{
   // Decrement the global object count
```

```
    InterlockedDecrement( &g_lObjs );
}
```

In your constructor, initialize the internal reference counter to zero and increment the global instance count for the DLL. Your destructor then decrements the global count.

Next, add the following:

```
STDMETHODIMP Math::QueryInterface( REFIID riid, void** ppv )
{
    *ppv = 0;
    if ( riid == IID_IUnknown )
        *ppv = (IMath*) this;
    else  if ( riid == IID_IMath )
        *ppv = (IMath*) this;
    else  if ( riid == IID_IAdvancedMath )
        *ppv = (IAdvancedMath*) this;
    if ( *ppv )
    {
        AddRef();
        return( S_OK );
    }
    return( E_NOINTERFACE );
}

STDMETHODIMP_(ULONG) Math::AddRef()
{
    return InterlockedIncrement( &m_lRef );
}

STDMETHODIMP_(ULONG) Math::Release()
{
    if ( InterlockedDecrement( &m_lRef ) == 0 )
    {
        delete this;
        return 0;
    }
    return m_lRef;
}
```

This code provides the implementation of your three IUnknown methods. Your component supports three interfaces: the required IUnknown and your two custom interfaces. QueryInterface checks to see that the client has requested a supported one and returns a pointer to a pointer to the appropriate Vtable. Remember, when using multiple inheritance you must cast the instance explicitly to get the correct Vtable. Before returning, increment the internal reference count by calling AddRef.

Next, add the implementations for each exposed interface method:

```
STDMETHODIMP Math::Add( long lOp1, long lOp2, long* pResult )
{
    *pResult = lOp1 + lOp2;
    return S_OK;
}


STDMETHODIMP Math::Subtract( long lOp1, long lOp2, long* pResult )
{
    *pResult = lOp1 - lOp2;
    return S_OK;
}


STDMETHODIMP Math::Multiply( long lOp1, long lOp2, long* pResult )
{
    *pResult = lOp1 * lOp2;
    return S_OK;
}


STDMETHODIMP Math::Divide( long lOp1, long lOp2, long* pResult )
{
    *pResult = lOp1 / lOp2;
    return S_OK;
}


// IAdvancedMath interface
static long calcFactorial( short n )
{
    // The factorial of 0 is 1
    if ( n <= 1 )
        return 1;
    return n * calcFactorial( n - 1 );
}


STDMETHODIMP Math::Factorial( short sOp, long* pResult )
{
    *pResult = calcFactorial( sOp );
    return S_OK;
}


static long calcFibonacci( short n )
{
    if ( n <= 1 )
        return 1;
```

```
    return calcFibonacci( n - 1 ) + calcFibonacci( n - 2 );
}


STDMETHODIMP Math::Fibonacci( short sOp, long* pResult )
{
    *pResult = calcFibonacci( sOp );
    return S_OK;
}
```

The preceding code is your no-brainer implementation, but at least it doesn't get in the way of your understanding of COM at this point.

Next, you have the implementation of the class factory class:

```
MathClassFactory::MathClassFactory()
{
    m_lRef = 0;
}


MathClassFactory::~MathClassFactory()
{
}


STDMETHODIMP MathClassFactory::QueryInterface( REFIID riid,
                                               void** ppv )
{
    *ppv = 0;
    if ( riid == IID_IUnknown || riid == IID_IClassFactory )
        *ppv = this;
    if ( *ppv )
    {
        AddRef();
        return S_OK;
    }
    return( E_NOINTERFACE );
}


STDMETHODIMP_(ULONG) MathClassFactory::AddRef()
{
    return InterlockedIncrement( &m_lRef );
}


STDMETHODIMP_(ULONG) MathClassFactory::Release()
{
    if ( InterlockedDecrement( &m_lRef ) == 0 )
    {
```

```
        delete this;
        return 0;
    }
    return m_lRef;
}

STDMETHODIMP MathClassFactory::CreateInstance
        ( LPUNKNOWN pUnkOuter, REFIID riid, void** ppvObj )
{
    Math*      pMath;
    HRESULT    hr;
    *ppvObj = 0;

    pMath = new Math;
    if ( pMath == 0 )
        return( E_OUTOFMEMORY );

    hr = pMath->QueryInterface( riid, ppvObj );
    if ( FAILED( hr ) )
        delete pMath;

    return hr;
}

STDMETHODIMP MathClassFactory::LockServer( BOOL fLock )
{
    if ( fLock )
        InterlockedIncrement( &g_lLocks );
    else
        InterlockedDecrement( &g_lLocks );
    return S_OK;
}
```

You've covered most of this already. The only exception is the implementation of the LockServer method. Your server housing (the DLL implementation) maintains a count of calls to lock the server. In the next section, you use this counter in your housing implementation.

Step 5: Create the Component's Housing (SERVER.CPP)

After saving MATH.CPP, create a new file and call it SERVER.CPP. It provides the housing code for your component. IMATH.H, MATH.H, and MATH.CPP constitute your component implementation. You now need housing code to wrap the component. Here it is:

```cpp
//
// server.cpp -
//      Implements the external entry points for our DLL housing
//

#include <windows.h>
#include <initguid.h>
#include "math.h"

long    g_lObjs = 0;
long    g_lLocks = 0;

// This entry point provides COM a standard way of accessing
// the housing's class factories.
STDAPI DllGetClassObject( REFCLSID rclsid, REFIID riid, void** ppv )
{
    HRESULT             hr;
    MathClassFactory    *pCF;

    // Make sure the CLSID is for our Math component
    if ( rclsid != CLSID_Math )
        return( E_FAIL );

    pCF = new MathClassFactory;
    if ( pCF == 0 )
        return( E_OUTOFMEMORY );

    hr = pCF->QueryInterface( riid, ppv );
    // Check for failure of QueryInterface
    if ( FAILED( hr ) )
        delete pCF;

    return hr;
}
STDAPI DllCanUnloadNow(void)
{
    if ( g_lObjs || g_lLocks )
        return( S_FALSE );
    else
        return( S_OK );
}
```

First, you include INITGUID.H to define the GUIDs used by the DLL. Next, you define the two global variables that maintain your housing reference counts. Remember, COM requires that a DLL export two functions to be a true component housing. (Actually, there are four functions, but I discuss them in Chapters 3 and 4.) Then, implement DllGetClassObject. COM calls this entry point on behalf of a client to access a component's class factory.

Check to make sure that the client is requesting a component that your housing supports. If you recognize it, create an instance of your Math class factory and call QueryInterface on the interface requested by the client. Your Math class factory supports only IUnknown and IClassFactory. If the client, or COM, requests anything else, you return an error.

Thanks to your two global variables, your implementation of DllCanUnloadNow is easy. Check whether there are any outstanding instances of the math component and determine the number of calls made to LockServer. If either value is nonzero, the DLL cannot be unloaded.

Step 6: Add Support for Self-Registration and Component Categories

An important requirement for COM components is to provide built-in support for self-registration. Self-registration simply is the ability to add the required COM component registry entries programmatically. I discussed these earlier in the chapter. In this section, I write the actual code to add the registry entries for the math component.

In a DLL-based component, the DLL must expose both the DllRegisterServer and DllUnregisterServer entry points. Utilities such as REGSVR32.EXE then load the DLL, locate these entry points via the GetProcAddress API, and call it. This adds or removes the items from the local registry. Listing 2-2 shows the actual implementation. The boldface code represents changes or additions to the original code shown in Step 5.

Listing 2-2: Housing Entry Points

```
//
// server.cpp -
//       Implements the external entry points for our DLL housing
//

#include <windows.h>

// Component category support
#include <comcat.h>

#include <initguid.h>
#include "math.h"
```

```
// Our component category GUID
#include "ATLDevGuide.h"

// Used to store the instance handle
// We need this to call the GetModuleFileName API
HINSTANCE g_hinstDLL = 0;

// Global instance and lock counts
long    g_lObjs = 0;
long    g_lLocks = 0;

//
// DllMain -
//      Called by Windows when important events happen
//      to the DLL. In particular, we are interested when
//      the DLL is initially loaded. When this occurs, we
//      save the instance handle for later use.
//
BOOL WINAPI DllMain( HINSTANCE hinstDLL, DWORD fdwReason,
                     LPVOID lpvReserved )
{
  if ( fdwReason == DLL_PROCESS_ATTACH )
     g_hinstDLL = hinstDLL;

  return TRUE;
}
...
//
// SetRegKeyValue - Private function that updates the registry
//
static BOOL SetRegKeyValue(
       LPTSTR pszKey,
       LPTSTR pszSubkey,
       LPTSTR pszValue )
{
  BOOL bOk = FALSE;
  LONG ec;
  HKEY hKey;
  TCHAR szKey[128];

  lstrcpy(szKey, pszKey);

  if (NULL != pszSubkey)
  {
    lstrcat( szKey, "\\" );
```

```
        lstrcat( szKey, pszSubkey );
    }

  ec = RegCreateKeyEx(
          HKEY_CLASSES_ROOT,
          szKey,
          0,
          NULL,
          REG_OPTION_NON_VOLATILE,
          KEY_ALL_ACCESS,
          NULL,
          &hKey,
          NULL);

  if (ERROR_SUCCESS == ec)
  {
    if (NULL != pszValue)
    {
      ec = RegSetValueEx(
              hKey,
              NULL,
              0,
              REG_SZ,
              (BYTE *)pszValue,
              (lstrlen(pszValue)+1)*sizeof(TCHAR));
    }
    if (ERROR_SUCCESS == ec)
      bOk = TRUE;
    RegCloseKey(hKey);
  }

  return bOk;
}


//
// DllRegisterServer - Entry point called by utilities such as
// REGSVR32.EXE to update the registry with the appropriate
// values for each component type in this DLL housing.
//
STDAPI DllRegisterServer(void)
{
    HRESULT  hr = NOERROR;
    CHAR     szModulePath[MAX_PATH];
    CHAR     szID[128];
    CHAR     szCLSID[128];
```

```
WCHAR    wszID[128];
WCHAR    wszCLSID[128];

GetModuleFileName(
  g_hinstDLL,
  szModulePath,
  sizeof( szModulePath ) / sizeof( CHAR ));

StringFromGUID2(CLSID_Math, wszID, sizeof( wszID ));
wcscpy( wszCLSID, L"CLSID\\" );
wcscat( wszCLSID, wszID );
wcstombs( szID, wszID, sizeof( szID ));
wcstombs( szCLSID, wszCLSID, sizeof( szID ));

// Create the ProgID keys.
SetRegKeyValue(
  "Chapter2.Math.1",
  NULL,
  "Chapter2 Math Component" );
SetRegKeyValue(
  "Chapter2.Math.1",
  "CLSID",
  szID );

// Create version independent ProgID keys.
SetRegKeyValue(
  "Chapter2.Math",
  NULL,
  "Chapter2 Math Component");
SetRegKeyValue(
  "Chapter2.Math",
  "CurVer",
  "Chapter2.Math.1");
SetRegKeyValue(
  "Chapter2.Math",
  "CLSID",
  szID);

// Create entries under CLSID.
SetRegKeyValue(
  szCLSID,
  NULL,
  "Chapter 2 Math Component");
SetRegKeyValue(
  szCLSID,
```

```
        "ProgID",
        "Chapter2.Math.1");
    SetRegKeyValue(
        szCLSID,
        "VersionIndependentProgID",
        "Chapter2.Math");
    SetRegKeyValue(
        szCLSID,
        "InprocServer32",
        szModulePath);

    // Register our component category
    CreateComponentCategory( CATID_ATLDevGuide,
                             L"ATL Developer's Guide Examples" );
    RegisterCLSIDInCategory( CLSID_Math, CATID_ATLDevGuide );

    return S_OK;
}
```

The preceding code also includes support to register your component's component categories. As I discussed previously in this chapter, components can advertise their functionality by using the component category support provided by COM. Throughout the rest of this book, I use a special component category to signify that the components are book examples. This makes it easy to identify all of the example components in OLEVIEW because you can view them grouped by component category.

In the previous code, I included a file called ATLDEVGUIDE.H. This is a small file that includes the definition of the unique category ID. You either can use the file provided in the downloadable examples or create your own ATLDEVGUIDE.H file like this one:

```
//
// ATLDevGuide.h - The component category used for all of the
//                 examples in the ATL: Developer's Guide
//

// {73038960-8306-11d3-A3ED-00203586EF11}
DEFINE_GUID( CATID_ATLDevGuide,
             0x73038960, 0x8306, 0x11d3, 0xa3, 0xed, 0x0, 0x20,
0x35, 0x86, 0xef, 0x11);
```

Step 7: Export Your Standard Entry Points

There is one remaining step to complete. To export your four external functions in
SERVER.CPP, you need a SERVER.DEF file. Create this file and add the following:

```
;
; Server.def : Declares the module parameters for the DLL.
;
LIBRARY       "SERVER"
DESCRIPTION   'SERVER Windows Dynamic Link Library'
EXPORTS
    ; Explicit exports can go here
    DllGetClassObject   PRIVATE
    DllCanUnloadNow     PRIVATE
    DllRegisterServer   PRIVATE
    DllUnregisterServer PRIVATE
```

Step 8: Insert the Files into the Project and Build It

Before building the project, use Insert → Files into project menu item to insert the
MATH.CPP, SERVER.CPP, and SERVER.DEF files into the project. If it compiles cleanly
on the first try, great. Once you have a DLL, you must register the component. The
Visual Studio IDE provides a Tools → Register Control option that calls your DLL
component's DllRegisterServer method. Make sure you do this before moving
on to test your component using OLEVIEW.

Step 9: Test the Math Component with OLEVIEW

Before you build a real client program, give your server a quick test. Start OLEVIEW,
make sure the Expert Mode is on, and click the ATL Developer's Guide Examples
node. You should find your component under Chapter2 Math Component. Once you
find it, try to expand it. If all succeeds, you see something like Figure 2-12.
Otherwise, some debugging is in order.

Step 10: Build a Simple COM Client

The client application is a simple Win32 console application. Using AppWizard,
create a Win32 Console Application and name it Client. Because AppWizard supplies only the project's make file, you must create the actual code files.

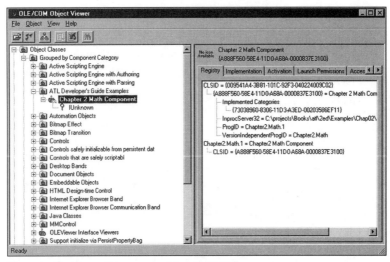

Figure 2-12: The math component in OLEVIEW

Next, create a file called CLIENT.CPP and add the code shown in Listing 2-3.

Listing 2-3: Com Client Code

```cpp
//
// Client.cpp
//

#include <windows.h>
#include <tchar.h>
#include <iostream.h>
#include <initguid.h>

#include "..\server\imath.h"

int main( int argc, char *argv[] )
{
   cout << "Initializing COM" << endl;
   if ( FAILED( CoInitialize( NULL )))
   {
      cout << "Unable to initialize COM" << endl;
      return -1;
   }

   // Get the unique CLSID from the ProgID
   HRESULT hr = ::CLSIDFromProgID( L"Chapter2.Math.1", &clsid );
   if ( FAILED( hr ))
   {
```

```
   cout.setf( ios::hex, ios::basefield );
   cout << "Unable to get CLSID from ProgID. HR = " << hr <<
                                                    endl;
   return -1;
}

// Get the class factory for the Math class
IClassFactory* pCF;
hr = CoGetClassObject( clsid,
                       CLSCTX_INPROC,
                       NULL,
                       IID_IClassFactory,
                       (void**) &pCF );
if ( FAILED( hr ))
{
   cout.setf( ios::hex, ios::basefield );
   cout << "Failed to GetClassObject server instance. HR = "
       << hr << endl;
   return -1;
}

// Using the class factory interface create an instance of the
// component and return the IUnknown interface.
IUnknown* pUnk;
hr = pCF->CreateInstance( NULL, IID_IUnknown, (void**) &pUnk );

// Release the class factory
pCF->Release();

if ( FAILED( hr ))
{
   cout.setf( ios::hex, ios::basefield );
   cout << "Failed to create server instance. HR = " << hr <<
                                                    endl;
   return -1;
}

cout << "Instance created" << endl;

IMath* pMath = NULL;
hr = pUnk->QueryInterface( IID_IMath, (void**) &pMath );
pUnk->Release();
if ( FAILED( hr ))
{
   cout << "QueryInterface() for IMath failed" << endl;
```

```
        CoUninitialize();
        return -1;
    }

    long result;
    pMath->Multiply( 100, 8, &result );
    cout << "100 * 8 is " << result << endl;
    pMath->Subtract( 1000, 333, &result );
    cout << "1000 - 333 is " << result << endl;

    // Try IAdvancedMath, QI through IMath
    IAdvancedMath* pAdvMath = NULL;
    hr = pMath->QueryInterface( IID_IAdvancedMath,
                                (void**) &pAdvMath );
    if ( FAILED( hr ))
    {
        cout << "QueryInterface() for IAdvancedMath failed" << endl;
        pMath->Release();
        CoUninitialize();
        return -1;
    }

    pAdvMath->Factorial( 10, &result );
    cout << "10! is " << result << endl;

    pAdvMath->Fibonacci( 10, &result );
    cout << "The Fibonacci of 10 is " << result << endl;

    cout << "Releasing IMath interface" << endl;
    pMath->Release();

    cout << "Releasing IAdvancedMath interface" << endl;
    pAdvMath->Release();

    cout << "Shutting down COM" << endl;
    CoUninitialize();

    return 0;
}
```

You start by including the IMATH.H header file from the server project. Before doing so, include INITGUID.H so that the component's GUIDs are defined. In main, you first initialize the COM libraries. Our example uses the component's ProgID to determine the correct CLSID. Before you can call CLSIDFromProgID, however, you must convert the ANSI ProgID into a Unicode string. All COM, OLE, and ActiveX calls have native Unicode implementations so you must convert all strings to Unicode before they are passed to any COM API functions.

After retrieving the CLSID for the component, call `CoGetClassObject` and request a pointer to the class factory interface for the math component. Then create an instance of the math component by calling `CreateInstance`. After you create the instance, release the class factory interface. `CreateInstance` returns an `IUnknown` pointer, through which you finally query for `IMath`. Once you have an `IMath` pointer, use the component's services to do some simple calculations.

When you're finished, release your `IMath` and `IAdvancedMath` interface pointers and call `CoUninitialize` before the application terminates.

Step 11: Build the Client Project

After entering the preceding code, insert `CLIENT.CPP` into the client project and build it. By running the client in debug mode, you can step into your server code. Take your time to really understand this simple COM-based client/server example. It contains the essence of COM-based development.

Debugging the Server

Debugging the client and server applications is easy. First, load the server project. Select the menu item Build → Start Debug → Go. The first time you attempt to debug the DLL, you are asked to specify the Executable for Debug Session. Enter the path to `CLIENT.EXE` and you're ready to debug. You also can specify the executable through the Project/Settings menu item.

If you get errors, they probably will be in the form of `HRESULT`s. To look them up, start Visual C++'s Error Lookup component (Tools → Error Lookup) and type the `HRESULT` in hex as shown in Figure 2-13.

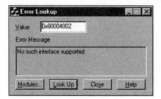

Figure 2-13: Visual C++ Error Lookup

What the Example Is Missing

The math example in this chapter implements a true COM component and shows how a client program might access its functionality. However, it is missing a few items that most COM-based components should provide: good error handling, support for interface marshaling, and self-description through a type library. In Chapters 3 and 4, I add these elements to the math example. Here's a list of what you have yet to do:

◆ Cover COM error handling so that you can handle divide by zero and similar errors

◆ Add marshaling support so that you can use the component in cross-thread, cross-process, and cross-machine environments. Right now, you can use the math component only in-process.

◆ Add a type library so that COM client applications (for example, Visual Basic) can investigate and display the component's capabilities programmatically

You add most of these capabilities in Chapter 3, although you use ATL. ATL provides most of these elements by default, and so you type less.

Summary

In this chapter, you learned the low-level basics of COM development. In particular, you learned:

◆ COM is a standard that enables communication between independent software modules.

◆ The COM run time is implemented by the Windows operating system.

◆ COM depends heavily on the concept of an abstract interface.

◆ COM's IUnknown interface provides support for lifetime management, run time discovery of functionality, and robust versioning for your components.

◆ COM uses the Windows registry to store information about your components

◆ Components must execute within a windows process and that means that your component code will be housed in either a Windows DLL or executable (EXE)

◆ The COM run time is accessed by a series of Windows APIs such as CoCreateInstance and CoInitialize.

With this introduction to the Component Object Model, we are now ready to delve into developing COM-based modules using the Active Template Library (ATL) in Chapter 3.

Chapter 3

The Active Template Library

IN THIS CHAPTER

- ◆ Basic ATL features
- ◆ The ATL development philosophy
- ◆ ATL's Wizards
- ◆ The structure of an ATL project
- ◆ ATL's support for basic COM services
- ◆ Building the math component using ATL

THE DEVELOPERS AT MICROSOFT initially had one goal in mind when they came up with the Active Template Library: to develop a framework that makes it easy to build small, fast COM-based components. The aim was to give software developers the flexibility to implement their components without any dependencies on secondary DLLs, including the standard C run-time DLL. Today, ATL is growing into the future C++ framework for all Windows development. ATL uses the new template-based features of C++ and is provided with source code as part of the Visual C++ development environment. Visual C++'s Developer Studio IDE also includes a number of Visual C++ wizards that make it easier to implement ATL in your projects.

This chapter covers the basics of ATL by showing you how to implement the math component of the previous chapter using ATL's features.

Basic ATL Features

ATL provides support for implementing the core aspects of a COM-based component. The ATL template classes take care of many of the tedious implementation details that you dealt with in Chapter 2. Here's a quick list of what ATL provides:

- ◆ AppWizard, which creates the initial ATL project
- ◆ Object wizard, which produces code for basic COM components

87

- ◆ Built-in support for low-level COM functionality such as IUnknown, class factories, and self-registration

- ◆ Support for Microsoft's *Interface Definition Language (IDL)*, which provides marshaling support for custom Vtable interfaces as well as component self-description through type libraries

- ◆ Support for IDispatch (automation) and dual interfaces

- ◆ Support for developing efficient ActiveX controls

- ◆ Basic windowing support

Many of these terms may sound foreign to you, but they will make more sense as you move through the chapters.

ATL versus MFC

The purpose of ATL is to facilitate the creation of small, COM-based components. The purpose of the Microsoft Foundation Class (MFC) is to speed development of larger, Windows-based applications, which generally have large GUIs. There is some overlap in functionality, primarily in the area of OLE and ActiveX support.

For example, you can create ActiveX controls with both ATL and MFC. By using MFC and its Control wizard, you can create a fully functional ActiveX control by adding just a few lines of code to the thousands already provided by MFC. However, the controls that you develop depend on the existence of the MFC run-time DLL, which is more than 1MB in size.

ATL also provides complete support for ActiveX controls. The difference is that you must write a lot of the code yourself, and to do so you need a solid understanding of COM and the ActiveX control specification. I show you how to develop such a control in Chapter 8. One of the useful things about ATL is that you can develop a full-function control that depends only on the standard C run-time DLL. This DLL is installed as part of the operating system, so your control is easier to distribute in low-bandwidth environments such as the Internet.

When you develop a COM-based component that has little or no visual aspect, ATL usually is the way to go. If you develop a Windows-based application with lots of visual functionality, you probably want to use MFC or the new Windows Template Framework (WTL) . This is just a guideline, though, and I recommend that you get some experience with both frameworks before making a final decision.

A Quick Overview of the ATL Framework

The developers of ATL succeeded at making ATL small, fast, and efficient; but in doing so, they also made it hard to understand the ATL implementation. ATL is a

C++ class library, or framework, that handles many of the routine details of COM-based development. For example, a COM component needs either a DLL or EXE housing and the component requires a class factory. The implementation of these requirements basically is the same for every component. A framework such as ATL provides this basic component support. All you have to do is use it. If you've used MFC at all, you no doubt understand this concept well.

ATL's Implementation

Because ATL is a template-based framework, include ATL's implementation as part of your implementation. In other words, to get at ATL's built-in functionality, you don't link to a series of DLLs necessarily. Instead, you include header files that compile directly into object code within your DLL or executable. In fact, ATL basically is a series of header files that contain a number of template classes. The implementation is included directly in your project. There are only a few exceptions.

Again, one of the design goals of ATL was to enable the building of small and independent components. This approach makes your executables bigger, but ATL provides several options to give you flexibility.

If you dissect a basic ATL project, you can see that you use its include files this way:

```
//
// STDAFX.H
//
#define _ATL_APARTMENT_THREADED
#include <atlbase.h>
#include <atlcom.h>
...
//
// STDAFX.CPP
//
#include "stdafx.h

// Include ATL's implementation code
#include <atlimpl.cpp>
...
//
// YourImplementation.cpp
//
#include "stdafx.h"
...
```

ATL's use of STDAFX.H and STDAFX.CPP resembles the way they are used in most Visual C++ projects. The STDAFX files include the basic requirements of the project type; you then include STDAFX.H in all your implementation files. The important point in the preceding example is that ultimately all ATL projects include

ATLBASE.H, ATLCOM.H, and ATLIMPL.CPP. By including ATLIMPL.CPP, the majority of ATL's implementation becomes an explicit part of your project and its object code becomes part of your executable.

Table 3-1 describes each of the header and implementation files included in ATL.

TABLE 3-1 ATL'S IMPLEMENTATION FILES

File	Description
ATLBASE.H	Basic include file for ATL projects.
ATLCOM.H	All ATL projects must include ATLCOM.H because it provides most of ATL's basic behavior.
ATLIMPL.CPP	The actual implementation of the classes and methods declared in ATLBASE.H and ATLCOM.H.
ATLCTL.H, ATLCTL.CPP	ATL's support for ActiveX controls. Again, both files are included in your project when you use ATL's control support.
ATLWIN.H, ATLWIN.CPP	ATL's support for windows and dialog boxes.
STATREG.H, STATREG.CPP	The implementation files for ATL's Registrar component. Depending on preprocessor symbols, the code is compiled to produce part of ATL.DLL or is included directly within your component's implementation.
ATLIFACE.IDL, ATLIFACE.H	Support files for ATL's Registrar component. The header file contains the output that results from running the IDL through the MIDL compiler, which I'll discuss in Chapter 4.

When you develop with ATL, most of its functionality is included as part of your implementation. There is no need to link to any external DLLs (other than system DLLs and possibly the C run time, which is delivered with the OS anyway). However, ATL implements some of its basic APIs in a module appropriately named ATL.DLL. The functions implemented in ATL.DLL primarily are helper functions for ATL's classes. To give you an idea of what's in ATL.DLL, here is the output of the DUMPBIN/EXPORTS command:

```
c:\winnt\system32>dumpbin /exports atl.dll
Microsoft (R) COFF Binary File Dumper Version 5.02.7132
Copyright (C) Microsoft Corp 1992-1997. All rights reserved.
```

```
Dump of file atl.dll
File Type: DLL
      Section contains the following Exports for ATL.DLL
                0 characteristics
         32E97F0B time date stamp Fri Jan 24 21:33:31 1997
             0.00 version
                1 ordinal base
               32 number of functions
               27 number of names
        ordinal hint    name
             10    0    AtlAdvise  (00002B6F)
             30    1    AtlComPtrAssign  (00002A1E)
             31    2    AtlComQIPtrAssign  (00002A47)
             26    3    AtlCreateTargetDC  (000033C5)
             29    4    AtlDevModeW2A  (00002635)
             12    5    AtlFreeMarshalStream  (00002A6E)
             27    6    AtlHiMetricToPixel  (000034E3)
             32    7    AtlInternalQueryInterface  (00002946)
             13    8    AtlMarshalPtrInProc  (00002A8A)
             15    9    AtlModuleGetClassObject  (00002EB0)
             16    A    AtlModuleInit  (00002DAC)
             17    B    AtlModuleRegisterClassObjects  (00002DFD)
             18    C    AtlModuleRegisterServer  (00002FD2)
             19    D    AtlModuleRegisterTypeLib  (000031FB)
             20    E    AtlModuleRevokeClassObjects  (00002E80)
             21    F    AtlModuleTerm  (00002F72)
             22   10    AtlModuleUnregisterServer  (0000303B)
             23   11    AtlModuleUpdateRegistryFromResourceD
(00003082)
             28   12    AtlPixelToHiMetric  (00003546)
             25   13    AtlSetErrorInfo  (00002C46)
             11   14    AtlUnadvise  (00002BDC)
             14   15    AtlUnmarshalPtr  (00002ACF)
             24   16    AtlWaitWithMessageLoop  (00002B03)
              1   17    DllCanUnloadNow  (00001378)
              2   18    DllGetClassObject  (00001387)
              3   19    DllRegisterServer  (000013A0)
              4   1A    DllUnregisterServer  (000013AF)
```

As you can see, there are a number of exported functions that appear to handle COM-like tasks for ATL. When building an ATL project, you have several options. One is to use these helper functions from ATL.DLL and distribute them as part of your software. Or you can choose to include the implementation of these helper functions directly within your module.

If you define the ATL_DLL_ symbol, your project depends on ATL.DLL. If you do not define ATL_DLL_, the ATLIMPL.CPP file includes the implementations as part of your module. I discuss this in more detail in a later section.

Component Housing Support

ATL encapsulates a component's housing support in its CComModule class. ATL hides most of the differences between the two housing types (DLL or EXE) from the developer. Also, the ATL AppWizard generates the housing code for you. Typically, you don't modify the housing support code because the default implementation provides everything your component needs.

Support for IUnknown

ATL's support for the IUnknown methods is a bit difficult to understand. However, it is encapsulated pretty well and typically you won't have to delve into the details. In this chapter, you take a look at how ATL implements QueryInterface, AddRef, and Release. The most important aspect of ATL's IUnknown implementation is your understanding of which macros to use within your implementation.

Support for Class Factories

When using ATL, you need not implement class factories for your components. ATL provides support for basic class factories in CComClassFactory, licensed class factories through CComClassFactory2, and singleton class factories through CComClassFactorySingleton. You add support for these various construction methods through the use of ATL macros.

Support for Other Aspects of COM Development

At this point, I've covered ATL's support for component housings, the IUnknown interface, and class factories—but ATL provides basic support for much more. I examine ATL's support for the other aspects of COM development throughout the book. Table 3-2 gives you a glimpse of the rest of ATL.

TABLE 3-2 ATL'S SUPPORT FOR COM

COM Functionality	ATL Support Classes
ActiveX controls	CComControl, IOleControlImpl, IOleObjectImpl, and so on to support the development of controls. IPropertyPageImpl and ISpecifyPropertyPageImpl for support of property pages

COM Functionality	ATL Support Classes
Automation	`IDispatchImpl` handles both automation and dual interfaces.
COM data types	`CComBSTR` and `CComVariant`.
Interface pointer management	`CComPtr` and `CComQIPtr`.
Error handling	`ISupportErrorInfoImpl` and `CComObject`.
Connection points	`IConnectionPointContainerImpl` and `IConnectionPointImpl`.
Asynchronous property download	`CBindStatusCallback`.
Self-registration	The ATL Registrar object (`IRegistrar`) provides self-registration support for your components.
Windows and dialog boxes	`CWindow`, `CWindowImpl`, `CDialogImpl`, and `CMessageMap`.

Using ATL's Wizards

When you're learning a large framework such as ATL, it's nice to have some base code from which to begin. This is what ATL's wizards provide.

The wizards hide many of the implementation details, and this is good when you're learning ATL. But later, when something breaks, you really need to understand what the wizards do for you. In the next few sections, I cover the details of creating ATL projects using the Visual C++ wizards. After that, I focus mostly on the ATL code.

The ATL COM AppWizard

The ATL COM AppWizard, shown in Figure 3-1, is a Visual C++ wizard that steps you through the initial creation of an ATL-based project. You use AppWizard only once per project. The purpose of AppWizard is to create the initial housing code for your components. After the project is created, you use the ATL Object wizard to add components to your project. I discuss the files created by AppWizard in the next section.

When creating a project using AppWizard, you have only a few simple options. The first is *server type*. You can select one of three options: a DLL or EXE housing for your components, or an EXE housing that executes as an NT service.

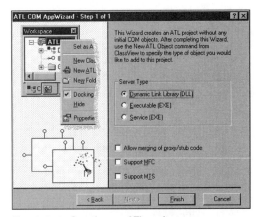

Figure 3-1: Creating an ATL project

If you choose the DLL option, you can select Allow merging of proxy/stub code and Support MFC if you wish. (I discuss proxy/stubs in Chapter 4.) This option enables your component's housing to act as the proxy/stub DLL if you provide marshaling. In other words, by checking this option and doing a bit more work, you can distribute one less DLL. If you select Support MFC, the wizard adds #includes for MFC's header files as well as additional code for MFC's CWinApp class. The Support MTS option adds the MTX.LIB to the libraries linked with your DLL or executable.

The ATL Object Wizard

The initial project created using the ATL AppWizard provides only basic housing support for your components and does not supply the files needed for building a specific component. To do that, you must use the new ATL Object wizard. You can access it through the Visual C++ Insert → Add ATL Component menu item.

Figure 3-2 shows the main Object wizard dialog box. There are three categories of objects that you can add to your project: ATL Controls, ATL Miscellaneous, and ATL Objects. The ATL Controls category provides two basic control types and a Property Page object. I discuss them in detail in Chapter 8. The ATL Miscellaneous section enables you to create a COM-based Windows dialog box.

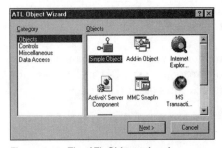

Figure 3-2: The ATL Object wizard

OBJECT WIZARD NAMES

A series of dialog boxes appears depending on the object type selected. For a simple COM object, information for two dialog boxes – Name and Attributes – must be populated. For more-complex object types, such as ActiveX controls, additional information is required. Again, I cover these objects in more detail when I show you how to build an ActiveX control with ATL in Chapter 8.

Figure 3-3 shows the Object wizard's Names dialog box. Table 3-3 lists the purpose of each option.

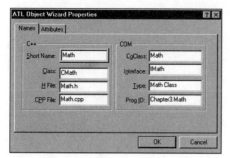

Figure 3-3: ATL Object wizard names

Table **3-3 OBJECT WIZARD NAME OPTIONS**

Field	Description
Short Name	This entry provides the basis, or prefix, for the rest of the entries on the page. It does not map directly to any particular attribute. As you change this value, the entries for the rest of the page also change.
Class	The name used for the C++ class that implements the component.
.H File and .CPP File	The component class header and implementation files.
CoClass	The name of the COM class. External clients use this name to describe the "type" of the component.
Interface	The name of the interface to create for your object. Your object initially exposes the IMath interface described in Chapter 2.
Type	The human-readable name of the component that is placed in the registry. This has no programmatic value.
ProgID	This is the programmatic identifier for the component. Clients may use this identifier to locate and instantiate a component.

OBJECT WIZARD ATTRIBUTES

The Attributes dialog box enables specification of basic COM support options for a component. Many of the details of each option are beyond the scope of this chapter, because I haven't covered concepts such as COM threading models and COM aggregation. Figure 3-4 shows the Attributes dialog box and the following sections describe each option.

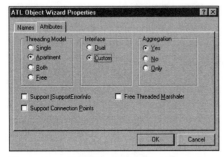

Figure 3-4: ATL Object wizard attributes

Threading Model

Several threading models are available for COM-based components. I give a quick introduction here and discuss them in more detail in Chapter 10. For these initial examples, I use the Apartment option:

◆ **Single:** Component instances can be created only in the main thread of a process.

◆ **Apartment:** Instances of the component can reside within their own apartment thread.

◆ **Free:** The component supports the free threading model. In other words, it must reside with other threads in the *multithreaded apartment (or MTA).*

◆ **Both:** Specifies that the component can support both the apartment model and the free threading model

Interface

There are two interface options: custom and dual. A *custom interface* is the standard Vtable interface discussed in Chapter 2. I haven't discussed the concept of a dual interface yet; Microsoft recommends that components support a dual interface if possible. A *dual interface* implements both a Vtable interface and the standard automation interface. In this way, the client can choose how it accesses the component's functionality. I discus this in more detail in Chapter 6.

Aggregation

Aggregation is a COM technique that enables one component to incorporate, or reuse, the functionality of another component. The internal component must support this technique explicitly by delegating its IUnknown implementation. These options enable a component to decide whether to support aggregation. The Object wizard has several support options, each of which I discuss in Chapter 5.

Support for ISupportErrorInfo

If you select this option, the Object wizard provides a default implementation for the ISupportErrorInfo interface. This arrangement provides a robust server-to-client, error-reporting mechanism. If you haven't guessed by now, I also cover this in Chapter 4. I don't want to overload you with details yet. Hang in there.

Support Connection Points

By selecting this option, you direct the wizard to provide a default implementation of COM's connection point interfaces. *Connection points* enable a client and server to communicate on a peer-to-peer basis. In other words, connection points support server callbacks or events. I discuss this in detail in Chapter 7.

Free-Threaded Marshaler

Free-threaded marshaling provides default marshaling of interface pointers among threads in a single process. Refer to Chapter 10 for more on this.

Other Object Wizard Options

Depending on the object type you insert, the Object wizard can display as many as four different tabbed dialog boxes. I've discussed the two tabbed dialogs that always display. The other two pages are used primarily for developing ActiveX controls, and I discuss them in Chapter 8.

An Example Server

To demonstrate some of the basic features of ATL, I will convert the math example from Chapter 2 to use the ATL framework. The steps for creating the math component appear at the end of this chapter. In the next few sections, I go over each line that ATL's AppWizard and Object wizard create for a basic COM server.

I decided to place the cookbook-style steps at the end of the chapter so you can focus on ATL's basic implementation. One approach is to create the example by quickly following the steps and then returning here to go through ATL's implementation. Another approach is to follow along and get a sense of what ATL is doing and then step through the example when you get to it. It's up to you.

The Structure of an ATL Project

After you run the ATL AppWizard, the initial ATL project contains files that support the component's housing. Then additional files are added for each component through the Object wizard. Table 3-4 briefly describes each file produced by AppWizard.

TABLE 3-4 ATL APPWIZARD PROJECT FILES

File	Description
ProjectName.cpp	The main project file. This file contains the support functions required by COM to provide housing for your components.
ProjectName.h	The interface declarations for the components in the housing. The MIDL compiler creates this file. The project's IDL file is compiled to produce it.
ProjectName.idl	The IDL file for your project. You add interface and method definitions here. The MIDL compiler processes this file to create a type library for the project. There is one IDL file per project, so all the components in the project share the IDL file.
ProjectName.tlb	The binary type library for the housing. Compiling the IDL file with the MIDL compiler produces this file.
ProjectName.def	Windows definition file. For DLL projects, it contains the exposed entry points. This file is not created for EXE projects.
ProjectName_i.c	A file produced by compiling the IDL file that contains definitions for all the CLSIDs and IIDs defined in the project.
ProjectName_p.c	The proxy/stub code for the project. The MIDL compiler produces this file.
ProjectNamePS.mk	The command-line make file for the project's proxy/stub DLL.
ProjectNamePS.dll	The proxy/stub DLL created by the above make file.

File	Description
DLLDATA.C	The data structure definitions for the proxy/stub DLL project.
RESOURCE.H	The resource definition file for the project.
ProjectName.rc	The resource file for the project.
STDAFX.H and STDAFX.CPP	Definitions and includes for the ATL framework.

For each component that you add through the Object wizard, you get the files listed in Table 3-5. Each component within the housing shares many of the files described in Table 3-4. I go over the files created by the Object wizard when I describe ATL's support for IUnknown, housings, class factories, and self-registration. The files provide you with basic component support; then you add your specific implementation.

TABLE 3-5 FILES CREATED BY THE OBJECT WIZARD

File	Description
ObjectName.h and ObjectName.cpp	The object's header and implementation files.
ObjectName.rgs	The object's Registrar script. This file contains the registry entries to self-register the component.

STDAFX.H and STDAFX.CPP

As I discussed earlier, every file in an ATL project includes the STDAFX.H header file, which pulls in ATL's header files. When using template-based frameworks such as ATL, you generally include all the code that your implementation needs. For example, here's a look at STDAFX.H and STDAFX.CPP. Notice the inclusion of ATLIMPL.CPP. This is where the majority of ATL's implementation is pulled into your code:

```
// stdafx.h : include file for standard system include files,
//      or project-specific include files that are used frequently
```

```
//      but are changed infrequently
#if !defined(AFX_STDAFX_H__88126992_1CC8_11D1_883A_444553540000__
INCLUDED_)
#define AFX_STDAFX_H__88126992_1CC8_11D1_883A_444553540000__INCLUDED_
#if _MSC_VER >= 1000
#pragma once
#endif // _MSC_VER >= 1000
#define STRICT
#define _WIN32_WINNT 0x0400
#define _ATL_APARTMENT_THREADED
#include <atlbase.h>

//You may derive a class from CComModule and use it
//if you want to override
//something, but do not change the name of _Module
extern CComModule _Module;

#include <atlcom.h>

//{{AFX_INSERT_LOCATION}}
// Microsoft Developer Studio will insert additional declarations
// immediately before the previous line.
#endif
// !defined(AFX_STDAFX_H__88126992_1CC8_11D1_883A_444553540000__
INCLUDED)
//

// stdafx.cpp : source file that includes just the standard includes
//
#include "stdafx.h"
#ifdef _ATL_STATIC_REGISTRY
#include <statreg.h>
#include <statreg.cpp>
#endif
#include <atlimpl.cpp>
```

I highlighted one of the comment lines to point something out. The comment warns you not to change the name of the global CComModule instance. This warning appears because many of ATL's classes have the _Module name hard-coded as part of their implementation. In other words, ATL depends heavily on the fact that there is a global class named _Module.

RESOURCE.H and ProjectName.rc

As a Windows developer, you should be familiar with the RESOURCE.H file. It primarily defines symbols for the project's resources. A basic ATL project – such as the one in this chapter – has only a few resources defined because nonvisual components like the math component don't need a lot of GUI-type resources. Following is a quick glance at the RESOURCE.H file for the ATL-based math component.

```
//{{NO_DEPENDENCIES}}
// Microsoft Developer Studio generated include file.
// Used by Chapter3_Server.rc
//
#define IDS_PROJNAME                    100
#define IDR_MATH                        101

// Next default values for new objects
//
#ifdef APSTUDIO_INVOKED
#ifndef APSTUDIO_READONLY_SYMBOLS
#define _APS_NEXT_RESOURCE_VALUE        201
#define _APS_NEXT_COMMAND_VALUE         32768
#define _APS_NEXT_CONTROL_VALUE         201
#define _APS_NEXT_SYMED_VALUE           102
#endif
#endif
```

I highlighted two lines that are specific to your project. AppWizard added the IDS_PROJNAME symbol. It identifies a string-table string that contains the name of your project. The IDR_MATH symbol identifies a binary resource that contains self-registration information for your project. This involves the ATL Registrar, which I discuss in a moment.

A basic ATL project stores four items in its projectname.rc file: version information for the housing, a binary resource containing a Registrar script, a string table with the name of the project, and a binary resource containing the type library for the component.

ProjectName.CPP, ProjectName.H, and ProjectName.DEF

These files implement the basic housing support for ATL. For DLLs, this support includes the DllMain entry point and the other exports required by COM. For executables (EXEs), it includes the WinMain function and the primary message loop for the application. I cover the details of this implementation in the housing discussion later.

ProjectName.IDL

The IDL file in an ATL project is very important. In fact, you run the IDL file through another compiler (MIDL.EXE) to create many of the files on which the projects depends. I haven't discussed what an IDL file is, but the following section provides a brief introduction. In Chapter 4, I cover IDL and the files that MIDL creates.

Interface Definition Language

Microsoft's *Interface Definition Language (IDL)* is based on the DCE RPC specification. In general, IDL describes remote procedure call interfaces; but Microsoft has extended the specification to include support for COM-based interfaces. The primary purpose of IDL — at least in the context of COM-based components — is to define a component's interfaces (its methods and parameters) in a language-independent way. The clients of the component then can use this definition. Because IDL also is used to support RPC-like capabilities, it can produce marshaling code so that a component's interfaces can function across process and network boundaries.

 Before the widespread support of IDL, Microsoft used the *Object Description Language (ODL)*. ODL was designed specifically for automation and only supports the creation of component-type libraries. Today, IDL is used instead. It is more functional than ODL and still provides support for the older ODL language.

IDL uses a C-style syntax, so defining a component's interface is similar to declaring the C++ class. You can define structure types, enumerated types, and so on using IDL. Here is the IDL file for the math component in this chapter:

```
//
// Chapter3_Server.idl : IDL source for Chapter3_Server.dll
//

// The MIDL tool processes this file to
// produce the type library (Chapter3_Server.tlb) and marshaling
code.

import "oaidl.idl";
import "ocidl.idl";
[
    object,
    uuid(8812699C-1CC8-11D1-883A-444553540000),
```

```
      helpstring("IMath Interface"),
      pointer_default(unique)
]
interface IMath : IUnknown
{
   [helpstring("method Add")]
      HRESULT Add(long lOp1, long lOp2, long* plResult);
   [helpstring("method Subtract")]
      HRESULT Subtract(long lOp1, long lOp2, long* plResult);
   [helpstring("method Multiply")]
      HRESULT Multiply(long lOp1, long lOp2, long* plResult);
   [helpstring("method Divide")]
      HRESULT Divide(long lOp1, long lOp2, long* plResult);
};


[
   object,
   uuid(6AF3DF1E-C48F-11D0-A769-D477A4000000),
   helpstring("IAdvancedMath Interface"),
   pointer_default(unique)
]
interface IAdvancedMath : IUnknown
{
   HRESULT Factorial( [in] short sFact,
                      [out, retval] long* pResult );
   HRESULT Fibonacci( [in] short sFib,
                      [out, retval] long* pResult );
};


[
   uuid(8812698E-1CC8-11D1-883A-444553540000),
   version(1.0),
   helpstring("Chapter3_Server 1.0 Type Library")
]
library CHAPTER3_SERVERLib
{
   importlib("stdole32.tlb");
   importlib("stdole2.tlb");
   [
      uuid(8812699D-1CC8-11D1-883A-444553540000),
      helpstring("Math Class")
   ]
   coclass Math
   {
      [default] interface IMath;
```

```
        interface IAdvancedMath;
    };
};
```

The first section defines the `IMath` interface. An attribute block precedes the IDL definitions. These attributes, enclosed within brackets (`[]`), provide additional information about the ensuing definition. The `IMath` interface definition begins with three attributes:

```
[
    object,
    uuid(8812699C-1CC8-11D1-883A-444553540000),
    helpstring("IMath Interface"),
    pointer_default(unique)
]
```

The object attribute specifies that you are describing a COM custom interface and not a DCE/RPC-based interface. The IDL also describes RPC interfaces. The `uuid` keyword specifies the GUID of your interface, and the `helpstring` keyword specifies some text that an object browser might display.

The `pointer_default` attribute sets the default pointer attribute for any pointers defined within the interface. Specify a default pointer attribute of `unique`. The `unique` attribute specifies that whenever a pointer is passed through an interface method, the memory associated with the pointer cannot be modified elsewhere in the application. In other words, the memory pointed to can be changed only by the method that operates on it. This is the typical case and makes marshaling more efficient. Here is the interface definition:

```
interface IMath : IUnknown
{
    [helpstring("method Add")]
        HRESULT Add( [in] long l0p1, [in] long l0p2,
                        [out, retval] long* plResult);
    [helpstring("method Subtract")]
        HRESULT Subtract( [in] long l0p1, [in] long l0p2,
                            [out, retval] long* plResult);
    [helpstring("method Multiply")]
        HRESULT Multiply( [in] long l0p1, [in] long l0p2,
                            [out, retval] long* plResult);
    [helpstring("method Divide")]
        HRESULT Divide( [in] long l0p1, [in] long l0p2,
                            [out, retval] long* plResult);
};
```

The preceding interface describes the COM-based interface in your component. This code matches almost exactly with your C++ class declaration. The major differences appear in the listing of the parameters. IDL has several keywords that can be applied to method parameters. The in and out keywords specify the direction of the parameter. By providing this information, you provide COM with information that helps to make the parameter marshaling process more efficient. The retval keyword specifies that the parameter should be treated as the return value for the method. The remaining IDL lines pertain to the housing and its contained components:

```
[
    uuid(8812698E-1CC8-11D1-883A-444553540000),
    version(1.0),
    helpstring("Chapter3_Server 1.0 Type Library")
]
library CHAPTER3_SERVERLib
{
    importlib("stdole32.tlb");
    importlib("stdole2.tlb");
    [
        uuid(8812699D-1CC8-11D1-883A-444553540000),
        helpstring("Math Class")
    ]
    coclass Math
    {
        [default] interface IMath;
        interface IAdvancedMath;
    };
};
```

The attribute block describes the type library as a whole. It has a GUID, a version, and a help string. The *help string* provides textual information for component browser applications. The library keyword specifies the name of the library and typically encloses all the definitions for the specific housing. It may have interface, module, type, and component definitions. The example server contains only one math component; it is specified using the coclass keyword. The coclass keyword specifies individual components and the interfaces that they support. The math component exposes both the IMath and the IAdvancedMath interfaces. Table 3-6 summarizes the basic IDL keywords.

TABLE 3-6 BASIC IDL KEYWORDS

Keyword	Description
object	Begins the definition for a COM-based custom interface. The object keyword is followed by several attributes that describe additional interface capabilities.
uuid	The GUID that uniquely defines the given interface, type library, or component class.
helpstring	Specifies a string that tools such as component and interface viewers display.
interface	Specifies the name of an interface. Then the name is used in the coclass section to specify the interfaces supported by a component.
coclass	Describes the interfaces supported by a given COM object. The GUID specifies the component itself.
default	Specifies the default component interface. A component object can have, at most, two default interfaces: one for the source and a second one for the sink programmable interfaces.
in/out/retval	For method calls, this keyword indicates the direction of each parameter. The retval keyword describes which parameter should be treated as the return value of the method.

Now you have an idea of how IDL describes your component and its interfaces. But the IDL file is used for much more. In fact, the IDL file provides three important things in your ATL projects. I describe them briefly next, and Figure 3-5 depicts their relationships. The important fact is that the MIDL compiler parses the IDL file to produce several files for your components.

◆ The IDL file is compiled to produce C++ header files that declare and define the interfaces, class identifiers, and interface identifiers for the project.

◆ The IDL file (or those items in the library section) is compiled into a binary representation called a type library. Component users can inspect this type library (.TLB) to determine how they should access and interact with it.

◆ The IDL file produces a series of C files and a make file to generate a proxy/stub DLL. This DLL provides marshaling support for component interfaces. I discuss this in detail in Chapter 4.

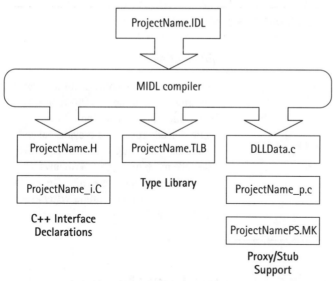

Figure 3-5: Relationship between IDL and its files

Building an ATL Project

The ATL AppWizard creates a basic ATL project that has several build options. Most of the options are the same ones you usually get when you use Visual C++, but there are a few extras related to code size and external DLL dependencies. Table 3-7 lists the various build options.

TABLE 3-7 ATL PROJECT BUILD OPTIONS

Project Option	Description
Win32 Debug	The typical debug build.
Win32 Release MinSize	Builds the module with the minimal size option. This option defines ATL_DLL_ and ATL_MIN_CRT.
Win32 Release MinDependencies	Similar to the MinSize option, but it defines the ATL_STATIC_REGISTRY symbol. By selecting this option, your module does not require distribution of the ATL Registrar, which removes any module dependencies on ATL.DLL.

Continued

TABLE 3-7 ATL PROJECT BUILD OPTIONS *(Continued)*

Project Option	Description
`Win32 Unicode Release MinSize`	Same as preceding options, but it builds the project using the `_UNICODE Win32 Unicode Release` symbol. Using a pure Unicode code build provides faster execution on `MinDependencies` native Unicode machines such as Windows NT, but it does not execute `Win32 Unicode Debug` on an ANSI operating system such as Windows 95.

ATL's Basic Housing Support: CComModule

ATL's `CComModule` class provides basic housing support for COM objects. Remember that every COM object must execute within the context of a Windows process. In the Windows environment, there are two ways to deliver object code: in a DLL or in an executable. ATL's `CComModule` class encapsulates the differences between the two housing types. You used a DLL housing in Chapter 2 and will do so again here. In Chapter 4, I cover EXE housings.

 ATL's `CComModule` class provides similar functionality to that provided by MFC's `CWinApp` class. Both classes attempt to insulate the developer from differences between the two Windows housing types. For example, `CWinApp::InitInstance` implements `WinMain` for executables and `DllMain` for DLLs.

When the ATL AppWizard generates your main project file, `CHAPTER3_SERVER.CPP`, it adds a global instance of the `CComModule` class with the name `_Module`. The `_Module` instance is a global C++ object and is created as soon as the module executes. Here is the code:

```
//
// Chapter3_Server.cpp : Implementation of DLL Exports.
//
// Note: Proxy/Stub Information
//           To build a separate proxy/stub DLL,
```

```
//              run nmake -f Chapter3_Serverps.mk in the project
directory.

#include "stdafx.h"
#include "resource.h"
#include "initguid.h"
#include "Chapter3_Server.h"
#include "Chapter3_Server_i.c"
#include "Math.h"

CComModule _Module;
```

You can ignore the proxy/stub comments, which I discuss in detail in Chapter 4. I covered most of the header files earlier in the chapter. The INITGUID.H file is included to initialize your CLSIDs and IIDs (just as described in Chapter 2). After the include files, there is a global instance of ATL's CComModule class, _Module. You can see references to that instance throughout.

Next, you encounter your first series of ATL macros.

```
BEGIN_OBJECT_MAP(ObjectMap)
    OBJECT_ENTRY(CLSID_Math, CMath)
END_OBJECT_MAP()
```

The BEGIN_OBJECT_MAP and OBJECT_ENTRY Macros

These macros set up a table of CLSIDs and their associated ATL implementation classes (in other words, components). This table of "objects" implements several aspects of an ATL component. First, ATL uses the table to update the registry with information for each component within the housing. The class's UpdateRegistry method is called. ATL automatically implements UpdateRegistry through its series of DECLARE_REGISTRY macros, which I discuss in a moment.

Second, the object map also creates instances of a component. In other words, it provides the component's class factory. Two addresses are placed in the map. The _ClassFactoryCreatorClass::CreateInstance call returns a class factory instance and _CreatorClass::CreateInstance creates an instance of the component class itself. Third, the class::GetObjectDescription method provides an implementation of the IComponentRegistrar::GetComponents method but does nothing by default. Here's a quick look at the expanded macros:

```
#define BEGIN_OBJECT_MAP(x) static _ATL_OBJMAP_ENTRY x[] = {
#define OBJECT_ENTRY(clsid, class) {
            &clsid,
            &class::UpdateRegistry,
```

```
                    &class::_ClassFactoryCreatorClass::CreateInstance,
                    &class::_CreatorClass::CreateInstance,
                    NULL, 0, &class::GetObjectDescription },
#define END_OBJECT_MAP()    {NULL, NULL, NULL, NULL}};
```

The remaining entries in your housing implementation file deal with ATL's housing support module: CComModule. By taking a look at it, you may find the housing implementation easier to understand.

CComModule

The implementation of CComModule resides in ATLBASE.H and ATLIMPL.CPP. The class has a number of methods and data members that are used throughout ATL. Table 3-8 lists the most important methods and their purposes.

TABLE 3-8 COMMONLY USED CCOMMODULE METHODS

Method	Description
Init	Initializes the CComModule instance, generally initializing internal data members and getting everything ready to go. It ultimately calls AtlModuleInit().
GetClassObject	This method is used only within DLL housings. It creates an instance of a component's class factory. In other words, it provides the implementation of your DLL housing's DllGetClassObject function.
RegisterClassObjects	This API is used to register an executable housing's class factories with the COM runtime.
RevokeClassObjects	The Revoke method deregisters the class factories when the EXE shuts down.
Lock/Unlock	You maintain a global variable in your DLL to keep track of calls to IClassFactory::LockServer. These methods provide the implementation for your ATL-based housing.
RegisterServer	Adds and removes registry entries for each component in the UnregisterServer housing

The following code implements the standard entry points for a DLL-based COM server. The DllMain entry point initializes your module on startup and shuts down properly when the DLL is unloaded. The other four entry points implement those required by a well-behaved COM DLL housing—DllCanUnloadNow checks the global lock count, DllGetClassObject returns the requested class factory, and the DllRegisterServer and DllUnregisterServer functions handle self-registration. Here is the code:

```
/////////////////////////////////////////////////////////////////////
/////////
// DLL Entry Point
extern "C"
BOOL WINAPI DllMain(HINSTANCE hInstance, DWORD dwReason, LPVOID
/*lpReserved*/)
{
    if (dwReason == DLL_PROCESS_ATTACH)
    {
        _Module.Init(ObjectMap, hInstance);
        DisableThreadLibraryCalls(hInstance);
    }
    else if (dwReason == DLL_PROCESS_DETACH)
        _Module.Term();
    return TRUE;     // ok
}


/////////////////////////////////////////////////////////////////////
/////////
// Used to determine whether the DLL can be unloaded by OLE
STDAPI DllCanUnloadNow(void)
{
    return (_Module.GetLockCount()==0) ? S_OK : S_FALSE;
}


/////////////////////////////////////////////////////////////////////
/////////
// Returns a class factory to create an object of the requested type
STDAPI DllGetClassObject(REFCLSID rclsid, REFIID riid, LPVOID* ppv)
{
    return _Module.GetClassObject(rclsid, riid, ppv);
}


/////////////////////////////////////////////////////////////////////
/////////
// DllRegisterServer - Adds entries to the system registry
STDAPI DllRegisterServer(void)
{
    // registers object, typelib, and all interfaces in typelib
```

```
    return _Module.RegisterServer(TRUE);
}


//////////////////////////////////////////////////////////////////////
//////////
// DllUnregisterServer - Removes entries from the system registry
STDAPI DllUnregisterServer(void)
{
    _Module.UnregisterServer();
    return S_OK;
}
```

As you can see, ATL's CComModule class provides basic housing functionality. With that in place, you can focus on ATL's support for components themselves.

ATL's Support for Components

The ATL AppWizard provides the basic housing support that COM components need. After you have the housing set up, use the ATL Object wizard to add basic components to your housing. All COM objects have several things in common. Each COM object must support the IUnknown interface along with other interfaces that expose its specific functionality. Each COM object also must provide a class factory so that client applications can create it. Finally, COM objects should support self-registration. ATL provides built-in support for each of these requirements. In the next few sections, I investigate this aspect of an ATL-based component.

ATL'S IUNKNOWN SUPPORT
ATL's support for COM's IUnknown methods is rather difficult to understand, so I spend quite a bit of time on it. To understand ATL's implementation of IUnknown, let's examine a number of ATL's implementation classes. The most important point to remember is that the implementation (executable code) of the three IUnknown methods isn't determined until an instance of your component class is created. ATL provides a lot of flexibility as to how an object's lifetime is managed. In most cases, the creator of the object – and not the implementer – knows how to handle an object's lifetime. I do not get into the details of this until I discuss creators and class factories, but it's important that you begin with this thought.

CCOMOBJECTROOTEX AND CCOMOBJECTROOTBASE
Each ATL class that becomes a COM object must derive from the CCom ObjectRootEx class. There is also a CComObjectRoot class, which is a typedef that I discuss next. CComObjectRootEx indirectly provides reference counting and QueryInterface support for the component. As I described earlier, the real implementation of the IUnknown methods is deferred until an instance of a component is created.

Before you can look at `CComObjectRootEx`, you must take a look at `CComObjectRootBase` from which it derives. Here is most of the declaration for `CComObjectRootBase`:

```
class CComObjectRootBase
{
public:
    CComObjectRootBase()
    {
        m_dwRef = 0L;
    }
    static HRESULT WINAPI InternalQueryInterface(void* pThis,
            const _ATL_INTMAP_ENTRY* pEntries,
            REFIID iid, void** ppvObject)
    {
        HRESULT hRes = AtlInternalQueryInterface(pThis, pEntries,
                                                     iid, ppvObject);
    }
    ULONG OuterAddRef()
    {
        return m_pOuterUnknown->AddRef();
    }
    ULONG OuterRelease()
    {
        return m_pOuterUnknown->Release();
    }
    HRESULT OuterQueryInterface(REFIID iid, void ** ppvObject)
    {
        return m_pOuterUnknown->QueryInterface(iid, ppvObject);
    }
    union
    {
        long m_dwRef;
        IUnknown* m_pOuterUnknown;
    };
};
```

`CComObjectRootBase` contains the reference count variable used to maintain your object's outstanding interface references; but it's part of a union as you can see. When a component is aggregated with another component, the lifetime of the first component is tied to that of the second so there is no need for the first (or inner) component to maintain its own reference count. Instead, it must maintain a pointer to the aggregating component's `IUnknown` implementation. Thus, only one member of the union is used per instance.

An aggregated instance also must delegate any IUnknown method calls to its outer, or aggregating, component. That's exactly what the three outer methods do here in CComObjectRootBase. CComObjectRootBase provides basic support for aggregation in components and CComObjectRootEx provides support for the non-aggregate IUnknown methods. Here's a look at its declaration:

```
template <class ThreadModel>
class CComObjectRootEx : public CComObjectRootBase
{
public:
    typedef ThreadModel _ThreadModel;
    typedef _ThreadModel::AutoCriticalSection _CritSec;
    ULONG InternalAddRef()
    {
        return _ThreadModel::Increment(&m_dwRef);
    }
    ULONG InternalRelease()
    {
        return _ThreadModel::Decrement(&m_dwRef);
    }
    void Lock() {m_critsec.Lock();}
    void Unlock() {m_critsec.Unlock();}

private:
    _CritSec m_critsec;
};
```

CComObjectRootEx provides the InternalAddRef and InternalRelease methods. These methods are used when the component is not aggregated or does not support aggregation. You have not seen the actual implementation of IUnknown::AddRef and IUnknown::Release yet, but you're getting there. Before you do, though, let's look at how the math component uses CComObjectRootEx:

```
class ATL_NO_VTABLE CMath :
    public CComObjectRootEx<CComSingleThreadModel>,
    public CComCoClass<CMath, &CLSID_Math>,
    public IMath,
    public IAdvancedMath
{
    ...
};
```

As you can see, the first class that you derive from in your CMath implementation is CComObjectRootEx. It provides basic IUnknown support. But what about that CComSingleThreadModel stuff?

The CComObjectRootEx class is template based, and the template parameter is the threading model to use for the component. (I discuss the various threading models in more detail in Chapter 10.) For now, just understand that you specify the threading models supported by your component through a parameter when building your implementation class. ATL does this so that you can change the threading models supported by your components easily.

CCOMOBJECTROOT AND THREADING

That brings me to the CComObjectRoot class, which is a simple typedef of CCom ObjectRootEx with a parameter of CComObjectThreadModel:

```
typedef CComObjectRootEx<CComObjectThreadModel> CComObjectRoot;
```

The CComObjectThreadModel parameter is defined via a preprocessor symbol. Here's how it gets set:

```
// From ATLBASE.H
#if defined(_ATL_SINGLE_THREADED)
    typedef CComSingleThreadModel CComObjectThreadModel;
    typedef CComSingleThreadModel CComGlobalsThreadModel;
#elif defined(_ATL_APARTMENT_THREADED)
    typedef CComSingleThreadModel CComObjectThreadModel;
    typedef CComMultiThreadModel CComGlobalsThreadModel;
#else
    typedef CComMultiThreadModel CComObjectThreadModel;
    typedef CComMultiThreadModel CComGlobalsThreadModel;
#endif
```

By changing a compiler directive, you can change the threading model for all the components in your project. Use CComObjectRoot instead of CComObject RootEx to declare your class this way:

```
// From MATH.H
class ATL_NO_VTABLE CMath :
    //public CComObjectRootEx<CComSingleThreadModel>,
    public CComObjectRoot,
    public CComCoClass<CMath, &CLSID_Math>,
    public IMath,
    public IAdvancedMath
```

This approach enables you to change the threading model of your component without modifying the source in any way. However, to build a truly multithreaded component you must make sure that your component is thread-safe. ATL can help, but you must do some of the work.

Where are AddRef and Release?

I've discussed how ATL implements IUnknown support, but I still haven't identified the important AddRef and Release methods. Where are they? Here's the scoop. The implementation of the reference counting methods is provided by another set of ATL classes. In other words, ATL implements reference counting in two phases. CComObjectRootEx manages reference counting through its internal and outer methods, and the CComObject series of classes handles the implementation of the exposed IUnknown methods. The problem, as you can see in the following code, is that there is no CComObject class in this implementation:

```
// From MATH.H
class ATL_NO_VTABLE CMath :
    public CComObjectRootEx<CComSingleThreadModel>,
    public CComCoClass<CMath, &CLSID_Math>,
    public IMath,
    public IAdvancedMath
{
...
};
```

The catch is that your CMath class still is not complete. You cannot instantiate CMath directly because it remains an abstract class. To instantiate your math implementation, you must derive one more template-based class. Here's a simple example of how you can instantiate an instance of the CMath class:

```
IMath* pIMath = new CComObject<CMath>
```

Figure 3-6 shows the classes necessary to implement your math component.

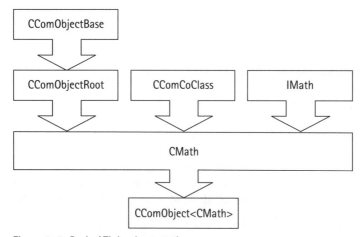

Figure 3-6: Basic ATL implementation

For a basic, non-aggregation example, CComObjectRoot gives you Internal AddRef, InternalRelease, and InternalQueryInterface; CComCoClass provides class factory support; and IMath and IAdvancedMath provide your abstract interface classes. All these combine to produce your CMath class. Then ATL goes one step further. To create instances, it uses CMath as a template parameter to CComObject, causing CComObject to derive from CMath.

CComObject

CComObject is one of a number of classes that mark the final destination in ATL's inheritance chain. Here is the majority of the implementation of CComObject:

```
// From ATLCOM.H
template <class Base>
class CComObject : public Base
{
public:
...
   STDMETHOD_(ULONG, AddRef)() {return InternalAddRef();}
   STDMETHOD_(ULONG, Release)()
   {
      ULONG l = InternalRelease();
      if (l == 0)
         delete this;
      return l;
   }
   STDMETHOD(QueryInterface)(REFIID iid, void ** ppvObject)
   {
      return _InternalQueryInterface(iid, ppvObject);
   }
};
```

Finally, you have found the declaration and implementation for the three IUnknown methods. Notice that for CComObject, these methods call directly to the internal methods (such as InternalAddRef) implemented by CComObjectRootEx and so they do not support aggregation.

There are nine CComObject-like classes that you can use to create an actual, instantiable class using ATL. Table 3-9 briefly describes each one and its specific use.

Why are there so many ways to create classes? Good question. As I've discussed, ATL focuses on creating the most efficient COM objects possible. By providing 9 different ways of implementing a component's IUnknown support, the designers of ATL give us maximum efficiency and flexibility in our implementations. It's a headache trying to figure out which one to use, but that's why we make the big money.

TABLE 3-9 CCOMOBJECT CLASSES

Class Name	Description
CComObject	Used for most typical COM components. The object does not support aggregation and handles reference counting as a typical object does. It deletes itself when the reference count reaches zero.
CComObjectNoLock	Like CComObject, except that the lifetime of the object does not affect the component housing's lock count. ATL uses this class in its implementation of a housing's class factories because their lifetimes should not affect the lifetime of the housing.
CComAggObject	Supports aggregation only. The IUnknown implementation delegates to the outer component.
CComContainedObject	Similar to an aggregate object because it delegates all calls to its outer, or parent, object. However, you can use this class when the class is contained within your implement-ation (in other words, when you aren't performing explicit aggregation).
CComPolyObject	Supports either aggregation or standard implementation. It basically is a space-saving implementation.
CComObjectStack	This implementation does not support reference counting at all. It is intended for use with COM objects created on the stack. The scope of their lifetimes is limited and well understood.
CComObjectGlobal	The lifetime of a CComObjectGlobal is equivalent to the lifetime of the component's housing. In other words, it's identical to a global C++ object. The lifetime is based on the housing's global lock count.
CComObjectCached	Once created, this object remains in a cache of objects. ATL uses this to implement a component's class factory.
CComTearOffObject	*Tear-off objects* provide a mechanism to create classes only when necessary.

The following code shows some ways that you can access the math component using C++. Remember that this code is not client code. COM clients almost always create a component through their class factories. What you're studying here is how you can implement a component that employs other COM components using ATL. COM client code uses `CoCreateInstance` and `QueryInterface`, as I discussed in Chapter 2 and will return to at the end of this chapter:

```
SomeFunction()
{
    // Create a component on the stack
    // Its lifetime is limited to this function
    CComObjectStack<CMath> tempMath;

    // Create an instance in the heap
    CComObject<CMath> *pMath;
    pMath = new CComObject<CMath>

    // Use the static CreateInstance method
    CComObject<CMath> *pMath;
    HRESULT hr = CComObject<CMath>::CreateInstance( &pMath );
}
```

 Use of `CreateInstance` is the preferred technique, especially if your implementation makes use of ATL's `FinalConstruct` idiom. I discuss this in Chapter 5.

Interfaces and Multiple Inheritance

If you look again at the class declaration for the math component, you can see that `CMath` derives from four other classes. ATL uses multiple inheritance extensively in its implementation. You get `IUnknown` support from `CComObjectRootEx`, class factory support from `CComCoClass`, and the method signatures from each of the component's unique interfaces (such as `IMath` and `IAdvancedMath`). Here's the declaration again:

```
// From MATH.H
class ATL_NO_VTABLE CMath :
    public CComObjectRootEx<CComSingleThreadModel>,
    public CComCoClass<CMath, &CLSID_Math>,
    public IMath,
    public IAdvancedMath
{
...
// IMath
public:
```

```
    STDMETHOD(Divide)(long 10p1, long 10p2, long* plResult);
    STDMETHOD(Multiply)(long 10p1, long 10p2, long* plResult);
    STDMETHOD(Subtract)(long 10p1, long 10p2, long* plResult);
    STDMETHOD(Add)(long 10p1, long 10p2, long* plResult);

// IAdvancedMath
public:
    STDMETHOD(Factorial)( short, long* );
    STDMETHOD(Fibonacci)( short, long* );
};
```

You get some functionality from the first two derivations. However, by deriving from IMath and IAdvancedMath all you get is interface inheritance. IMath and IAdvancedMath provide absolutely no functionality. Their only purpose is to provide your component with Vtables so that you can expose IMath and IAdvancedMath as COM interfaces. (I cover this in detail in Chapter 2.) The concept is still here, although it is a bit obscured in the ATL implementation of IUnknown.

ATL_NO_VTABLE

By inheriting from multiple ATL template classes, your CMath class is created. Before you go on, look at the user of ATL_NO_VTABLE. ATL_NO_VTABLE equates to __declspec(novtable). This directive tells the compiler not to produce or initialize a Vtable structure for the class, something that makes the class's construction and destruction code smaller.

But don't you need a Vtable for your class? Yes, you do – at least in your final, constructed class. But remember that your implementation class remains abstract at this point. The ATL_NO_VTABLE option enables the compiler to defer building the Vtable structure until a true instance is created, and that requires CComObject ultimately to provide its IUnknown implementation. In other words, you don't need a Vtable until you reach the end of your derivation chain so ATL_NO_VTABLE saves you some bytes as well as code.

There are a number of restrictions to remember when you use the ATL_NO_VTABLE option. In general, you should not call virtual functions or functions that result in a virtual call in the class constructor or destructor. You can remove the ATL_NO_VTABLE macro from the declaration if you're not sure whether your class follows the rules. It's just an attempt to reduce the size of the generated code.

As discussed in Chapter 2, COM interfaces are built using C++ Vtables. ATL is about building COM components, so what is this stuff about ATL_NO_VTABLE? The designers of ATL took great pains to develop a framework that does not compromise performance, and this is one example.

ATL's Class Factory Support: CComCoClass

Your CMath class also derives from CComCoClass. CComCoClass provides class factory support and basic methods to retrieve its CLSID and component-specific error information. If you develop a component that does not need a class factory because it does not support external creation, you don't need to include CComCoClass in your implementation.

As you can see from the following code, you provide the name of your implementation class as well as the actual CLSID of your component via template parameters to CComCoClass:

```
// From MATH.H
class ATL_NO_VTABLE CMath :
    public CComObjectRootEx<CComSingleThreadModel>,
    public CComCoClass<CMath, &CLSID_Math>,
    public IMath,
    public IAdvancedMath
{
...
};
```

When the template expands, you get something like the following (highlighted items are affected by your template parameters):

```
class CComCoClass
{
public:
    DECLARE_CLASSFACTORY()
    DECLARE_AGGREGATABLE( CMath )
    typedef CMath _CoClass;
    static const CLSID& WINAPI GetObjectCLSID() {return &CLSID_Math;}
    static LPCTSTR WINAPI GetObjectDescription() {return NULL;}
    static HRESULT WINAPI Error(LPCOLESTR lpszDesc,
                               const IID& iid = GUID_NULL,
                               HRESULT hRes = 0)
    {
        return AtlReportError(GetObjectCLSID(), lpszDesc, iid, hRes);
    }
...
};
```

The important thing to notice here is that CComCoClass provides your component's class factory support through the DECLARE_CLASSFACTORY macro. This macro eventually expands to provide the class with a typedef used by ATL's OBJECT_ENTRY macro. The OBJECT_ENTRY macro builds a map of creator functions for each component within a housing.

ATL's class factory support is very difficult to understand, so I quickly summarize it here and then work through each of the macros. By presenting it twice, I hope to make it a bit easier to understand.

To begin, CComCoClass contains two macros — DECLARE_CLASSFACTORY and DECLARE_AGGREGATABLE — which provide typedefs for the OBJECT_ENTRY macro:

```
#define DECLARE_CLASSFACTORY
    typedef CComCreator<CComObjectCached<CComClassFactory> > \
        _ClassFactoryCreatorClass;
#define DECLARE_AGGREGATABLE( x )
    typedef CComCreator2<CComCreator<CComObject<x> >, \
        CComCreator<CComAggObject<x> > > _CreatorClass;
```

The _ClassFactoryCreatorClass and _CreatorClass creator classes contain static CreateInstance methods through which the instances are created. The object map looks like this:

```
{
    &CLSID_CMATH,
    &CMath::UpdateRegistry,
    &CMath::_ClassFactoryCreatorClass::CreateInstance,
    &CMath::_CreatorClass::CreateInstance,
    . . .
}
```

When a client calls CoCreateInstance, COM calls DllGetClassObject. COM's call into DllGetClassObject eventually calls AtlModuleGetClassObject, which searches the object map for the CLSID_Math entry. Upon finding it, AtlModule GetClassObject calls &CMath::_ClassFactoryCreatorClass::CreateInstance and passes &CMath::_CreatorClass::CreateInstance as a parameter. This parameter is cached in the m_pfmCreateInstance member of CComClassFactory.

The &CMath::_ClassFactoryCreatorClass::CreateInstance call instantiates CComClassFactory, which (like all ATL classes) must derive from one of the CComObject classes. In this case, it's CComCachedObject because you want to cache the housing's class factory instances. The pointer to the CComClassFactory class is stored in the pCF element of the object map entry for &CLSID_CMATH.

COM (via CoCreateInstance) or the client (CoGetClassObject/Create Instance) uses CComClassFactory::CreateInstance to create component instances. This function actually calls m_pfnCreateInstance and passes pUnkOuter as a parameter. If the pUnkOuter parameter is null, which indicates the client is not aggregating, the CComCreator<CComObject<CMath>>::CreateInstance method is used. If pUnkOuter is non-null, indicating creation as an aggregate, then the CComCreator<CComAggObject<CMath>>::CreateInstance method is used instead.

Okay, now let's step through that in a bit more detail.

DECLARE_CLASSFACTORY

First, let's take a look at the `DECLARE_CLASSFACTORY` macro:

```
// From ATLCOM.H

...
#define DECLARE_CLASSFACTORY()
DECLARE_CLASSFACTORY_EX(CComClassFactory)
#define DECLARE_CLASSFACTORY_EX(cf) \
    typedef CComCreator< CComObjectCached< cf > >
                                    _ClassFactoryCreatorClass;
```

As you can tell from the above definitions, the class factory macro declares a typedef for something called `_ClassFactoryCreatorClass`. But what is going on with those nested templates? Well, let's expand it out. Here's what it eventually looks like:

```
typedef CComCreator< CComObjectCached< CComClassFactory > >
        _ClassFactoryCreatorClass
```

ATL uses something called a *creator class* that actually creates instances of your components when requested from an external client. ATL also uses the creator classes to create a component's class factory. The above typedef specifies a creator class that creates instances of the `CComObject` type specified. The creator class creates instances of a class factory using the `CComObjectCached` implementation. Instances of `CComObjectCached` are cached, so a component's class factory is created only when a client asks for it. It then hangs around until the housing is destroyed. Here's what your `CComCoClass` looks like now:

```
class CComCoClass
{
public:
    //DECLARE_CLASSFACTORY()
    typedef CComCreator< CComObjectCached< CComClassFactory > >
            _ClassFactoryCreatorClass;
    DECLARE_AGGREGATABLE( CMath )
    typedef CMath _CoClass;
    static const CLSID& WINAPI GetObjectCLSID() {return &CLSID_Math;}
    static LPCTSTR WINAPI GetObjectDescription() {return NULL;}
    static HRESULT WINAPI Error(LPCOLESTR lpszDesc,
                               const IID& iid = GUID_NULL,
                               HRESULT hRes = 0)
    {
        return AtlReportError(GetObjectCLSID(), lpszDesc, iid, hRes);
    }
...
};
```

CCOMCREATOR

What does `CComCreator` look like? Good question. Here's the code:

```
// From ATLCOM.H
template <class T1>
class CComCreator
{
public:
    static HRESULT WINAPI CreateInstance(void* pv, REFIID riid,
                                            LPVOID* ppv)
    {
        _ASSERTE(*ppv == NULL);
        HRESULT hRes = E_OUTOFMEMORY;
        T1* p = NULL;
        p = new T1( pv )
        if (p != NULL)
        {
            p->SetVoid(pv);
            p->InternalFinalConstructAddRef();
            hRes = p->FinalConstruct();
            p->InternalFinalConstructRelease();
            if (hRes == S_OK)
                hRes = p->QueryInterface(riid, ppv);
            if (hRes != S_OK)
                delete p;
        }
        return hRes;
    }
};
```

As you can see, the most important aspect of `CComCreator` is that it has a static method called `CreateInstance`. This method creates an instance of the class specified as the template parameter. It's there, in `CComCreator`, that the `new` operator is used on an ATL component. However, so far you've provided a way for ATL to create an instance of your component's class factory. How is the component actually created? Before you get to that, look at the implementation of `CComClassFactory`.

CCOMCLASSFACTORY

Most components built using ATL get their class factory through inclusion of the `CComCoClass` class. As you've seen already, the `DECLARE_CLASSFACTORY` macro handles the class factory. The macro provides a typedef used in the component's `OBJECT_ENTRY` macro entry. The typedef specifies the type of `CComObject` implementation that you want. Remember that your ATL implementation ultimately must derive from one of the `CComObject` classes.

As described already, you now have a CComCreator that "knows" how to create your class factory when necessary. In other words, when the housing is loaded, it doesn't have to instantiate class factories immediately for each component that it supports. The creation of a class factory object is deferred until a client explicitly asks for it via DllGetClassObject. This is another example of how ATL enables you to build efficient COM objects.

CComClassFactory provides the two standard class factory methods: Create Instance and LockServer. What you're interested in is that strange SetVoid function and the m_pfnCreateInstance data member. Here's a look at CComClass Factory:

```
class CComClassFactory :
   public IClassFactory,
   public CComObjectRootEx<CComGlobalsThreadModel>
{
public:
   BEGIN_COM_MAP(CComClassFactory)
      COM_INTERFACE_ENTRY(IClassFactory)
   END_COM_MAP()

   // IClassFactory
   STDMETHOD(CreateInstance)(LPUNKNOWN pUnkOuter,
                             REFIID riid, void** ppvObj);
   STDMETHOD(LockServer)(BOOL fLock);

   // helper
   void SetVoid(void* pv)
   {
      m_pfnCreateInstance = (_ATL_CREATORFUNC*)pv;
   }
   _ATL_CREATORFUNC* m_pfnCreateInstance;
};
```

As you'll see in a moment, the m_pfnCreateInstance member holds a pointer to another creator class static method that provides the component creation mechanism for the class factory. If you look back at your class's implementation of CComCoClass, you can see that you have one macro yet to expand. DECLARE_ AGGREGATABLE finally completes ATL's support for class factories – well, almost.

CCOMCREATOR2 AND DECLARE_AGGREGATABLE
Here's a look at what you have so far:

```
class CComCoClass
{
public:
```

```
    typedef CComCreator< CComObjectCached< CComClassFactory > >
            _ClassFactoryCreatorClass;
    DECLARE_AGGREGATABLE( CMath )
    typedef CMath _CoClass;
...
};
```

The default CComCoClass gives a component support for aggregation. To override this support, you can add one of several macros (for example, DECLARE_NOT_AGGREGATABLE) to your class. However, let's just plow ahead so as not to confuse the issue. The DECLARE_AGGREGATABLE macro looks like this:

```
#define DECLARE_AGGREGATABLE(x) public:\
    typedef CComCreator2< CComCreator< CComObject< x > >,\
            CComCreator< CComAggObject< x > > > _CreatorClass;
```

If you expand this template/macro in your class, you get this:

```
class CComCoClass
{
public:
    typedef CComCreator< CComObjectCached< CComClassFactory > >
            _ClassFactoryCreatorClass;
    typedef CComCreator2< CComCreator< CComObject< CMath > >,
                CComCreator< CComAggObject< CMath > > >
_CreatorClass;
typedef CMath _CoClass;
...
};
```

You now have a typedef that describes a creator class (_CreatorClass) for your component class, which appears to provide two different creators. Here's the definition for CComCreator2:

```
template <class T1, class T2>
class CComCreator2
{
public:
    static HRESULT WINAPI CreateInstance(void* pv, REFIID riid,
                                        LPVOID* ppv)
    {
        _ASSERTE(*ppv == NULL);
        HRESULT hRes = E_OUTOFMEMORY;
        if (pv == NULL)
            hRes = T1::CreateInstance(NULL, riid, ppv);
```

```
        else
            hRes = T2::CreateInstance(pv, riid, ppv);
        return hRes;
    }
};
```

CComCreator2 is a template that takes two different creator classes as parameters. The CComCreator2 class provides two ways to instantiate your CMath class. The first class (T1) uses ATL's standard, non-aggregatable CComObject implementation. The second class (T2) uses CComAggObject, which supports aggregation. The first parameter provided to CreateInstance is the outer unknown, which indicates whether the client is attempting an aggregation.

The final detail involves how the creators are accessed. I covered the OBJECT_ENTRY macros earlier in the OBJECT_ENTRY section, but they should make a bit more sense now. Here's a look at them again:

```
#define BEGIN_OBJECT_MAP(x) static _ATL_OBJMAP_ENTRY x[] = {
#define OBJECT_ENTRY(clsid, class) {
            &clsid,
            &class::UpdateRegistry,
            &class::_ClassFactoryCreatorClass::CreateInstance,
            &class::_CreatorClass::CreateInstance,
            NULL, 0, &class::GetObjectDescription },
#define END_OBJECT_MAP()   {NULL, NULL, NULL, NULL}};
```

If you look back at your housing implementation, you may notice this:

```
BEGIN_OBJECT_MAP(ObjectMap)
   OBJECT_ENTRY(CLSID_Math, CMath)
END_OBJECT_MAP()
...
BOOL WINAPI DllMain(HINSTANCE hInstance, DWORD dwReason,
                    LPVOID /*lpReserved*/)
{
...
   _Module.Init(ObjectMap, hInstance);
...
}
```

The preceding code initializes your object map with the parameters provided via the macros. Ultimately, it looks something like this:

```
static _ATL_OBJECT_ENTRY ObjectMap[] =
{
   &CLSID_Math, &CMath::UpdateRegistry,
```

```
        &CMath::_ClassFactoryCreatorClass::CreateInstance,
        &CMath::_CreatorClass::CreateInstance,
...
}
```

Now you're getting somewhere. At least you recognize the second and third parameters as the creator class typedefs. When COM asks for a specific component's class factory through `DllGetClassObject`, you can look up your class factory in the table:

```
STDAPI DllGetClassObject(REFCLSID rclsid, REFIID riid, LPVOID* ppv)
{
    // This eventually calls AtlModuleClassObject
    return _Module.GetClassObject(rclsid, riid, ppv);
}
```

Once the CLSID is found and the class factory instance is created via `_ClassFactoryCreatorClass::CreateInstance`, COM can call through `IClassFactory::CreateInstance` to create an actual component instance. Here's a condensed implementation of `CComClassFactory::CreateInstance`, which ultimately is called:

```
// From ATLIMPL.CPP
STDMETHODIMP CComClassFactory::CreateInstance(
      LPUNKNOWN pUnkOuter,
      REFIID riid, void** ppvObj)
{
    HRESULT hRes;
    hRes = m_pfnCreateInstance(pUnkOuter, riid, ppvObj);
    return hRes;
}
```

The class factory creates an instance of the math component by calling its internal `m_pfnCreateInstance` function pointer. This data member is initialized via the `SetVoid` method, which is called when the class factory initially is created. Take a look at the highlighted lines in this code:

```
ATLAPI AtlModuleGetClassObject(_ATL_MODULE* pM,
                    REFCLSID rclsid,
                    REFIID riid, LPVOID* ppv)
{
   _ATL_OBJMAP_ENTRY* pEntry = pM->m_pObjMap;
   HRESULT hRes = S_OK;
   while (pEntry->pclsid != NULL)
```

```
{
    if (InlineIsEqualGUID(rclsid, *pEntry->pclsid))
    {
        // We haven't created the class factory object yet, so do so
        if (pEntry->pCF == NULL)
        {
            // When we create the class object, pass in the address
            // of the ATL creator function for the actual component
            hRes = pEntry->pfnGetClassObject(
                    pEntry->pfnCreateInstance,
                                    IID_IUnknown,
                                    (LPVOID*)&pEntry->pCF);
        }
    }
    pEntry++;
}
    return hRes;
}
```

The m_pfnCreateInstance member is set via the pfnCreateInstance member (_CreatorClass::CreateInstance) of the ATL_OBJECT_MAP structure. Later, when COM calls IClassFactory::CreateInstance, it goes directly into the Create Instance implementation of CComCreator2.

Here's one other detail concerning ATL's class factory support. If you look closely, you notice that the creator classes are never instantiated because the CreateInstance methods are static. Again, ATL is doing whatever it can to increase performance and save space in your resulting components.

Whew. I don't know whether you followed all that. If you didn't, try going through it again later. ATL is tough stuff and may not make sense on the first pass, but hang in there. One suggestion that may help is to run the example in debug mode and set break points in the following functions of the server:

◆ DllGetClassObject: Follow the code as it traverses the object map.

◆ CComCreator::CreateInstance: Watch as the CComCreator2 address is passed via the SetVoid method.

◆ CComCreator2::CreateInstance: Watch as an instance of the math component is created via CComCreator::CreateInstance.

Self-Registration: The Registrar

All COM component housings should support *self-registration*, which is the ability of a housing to add the COM registry entries for each of its housed components automatically. In Chapter 2, I wrote registry access code to add these entries. When you create a basic ATL project with the wizards, support for self-registration is provided.

DLL housings support self-registration by exporting two standard COM functions: DllRegisterServer and DllUnregisterServer. As their names imply, these functions cause the housing either to add or remove entries in the system registry.

If you've worked with COM, OLE, or ActiveX, you probably have used the REGSVR32 utility. It takes a DLL as a parameter, as in this example:

```
c:>REGSVR32 Chapter3_Server.dll
```

The purpose of REGSVR32 is to register (or unregister via /u) components during installation on a local system. Here are the steps REGSVR32 follows to register the components in a specific housing:

1. Retrieves the name of the DLL from the command line and loads it using the Win32 API function LoadLibrary

2. Retrieves the address of the DllRegisterServer function using the Win32 API function GetProcAddress

3. Calls the entry point, which enables the DLL to add its entries to the registry

4. Calls FreeLibrary to release the DLL

In other words, you could write your own version of REGSVR32 with about 12 lines of code.

You know how self-registration works with DLLs, but what about with executables? The process differs slightly. Executables don't expose entry points, so the well-known entry point technique doesn't work. Instead, COM requires all executable housings to perform self-registration every time they execute. In that way, a user can self-register a component just by running the executable. Also, COM defines the /RegServer command-line option for those times when you want to register the components but don't want to leave the application running. The software installation process is a good example.

ATL'S REGISTRAR COMPONENT: IREGISTRAR

The *Registrar* is a simple, data-driven mechanism that updates the registry with information about a housing's components. As you probably may guess, the

Registrar is a COM object that implements the IRegistrar interface. Here's a look at IRegistrar:

```
interface IRegistrar : IUnknown
{
   HRESULT AddReplacement(
       [in] LPCOLESTR key, [in] LPCOLESTR item);
   HRESULT ClearReplacements();
   HRESULT ResourceRegisterSz(
       [in] LPCOLESTR resFileName,
       [in] LPCOLESTR szID,
       [in] LPCOLESTR szType);
   HRESULT ResourceUnregisterSz(
       [in] LPCOLESTR resFileName,
       [in] LPCOLESTR szID,
       [in] LPCOLESTR szType);
   HRESULT FileRegister([in] LPCOLESTR fileName);
   HRESULT FileUnregister([in] LPCOLESTR fileName);
   HRESULT StringRegister([in] LPCOLESTR data);
   HRESULT StringUnregister([in] LPCOLESTR data);
   HRESULT ResourceRegister(
       [in] LPCOLESTR resFileName,
       [in] UINT nID,
       [in] LPCOLESTR szType);
   HRESULT ResourceUnregister(
       [in] LPCOLESTR resFileName,
       [in] UINT nID,
       [in] LPCOLESTR szType);
};
```

As you can see, IRegistrar provides methods to update the system registry with text files, resource files, and filenames. The implementation of the Registrar component is provided in STATREG.H and STATREG.CPP and can be delivered via ATL.DLL or as part of your executable. The _ATL_STATIC_REGISTRY preprocessor symbol controls this option, as described in the "STDAFX.H and STDAFX.CPP" section earlier in this chapter. ATL uses the Registrar throughout its implementation.

DECLARE_REGISTRY_RESOURCEID
If you look closely at the math component's header file, you can see a single line that handles self-registration for your component:

```
// Math.h : Declaration of the CMath class
#include "resource.h"        // main symbols

////////////////////////
```

```
// CMath
///////////////////////
class ATL_NO_VTABLE CMath :
    public CComObjectRootEx<CComSingleThreadModel>,
    public CComCoClass<CMath, &CLSID_Math>,
    public IMath,
    public IAdvancedMath
{
...

DECLARE_REGISTRY_RESOURCEID(IDR_MATH)
...
};
```

The DECLARE_REGISTRY_RESOURCEID macro expands to a call to the Registrar. By default, the ATL Object wizard creates a ComponentName.RGS file (in this case, MATH.RGS) that contains a script for updating the registry. Here's what it looks like:

```
HKCR
{
  Chapter3.Math.1 = s 'Math Class'
  {
    CLSID = s '{8812699D-1CC8-11D1-883A-444553540000}'
  }
  Chapter3.Math = s 'Math Class'
  {
    CLSID = s '{8812699D-1CC8-11D1-883A-444553540000}'
    CurVer = s 'Chapter3.Math.1'
  }
  NoRemove CLSID
  {
    ForceRemove {8812699D-1CC8-11D1-883A-444553540000} = s 'Math
Class'
    {
      ProgID = s 'Chapter3.Math.1'
      VersionIndependentProgID = s 'Chapter3.Math'
      InprocServer32 = s '%MODULE%'
      {
        val ThreadingModel = s 'Apartment'
      }
    }
  }
}
```

The script uses a special *BNF (Backus-Nauer form)* syntax for describing each of the component's registry entries. The script is stored in the project's resource file (identified by IDR_MATH). The DECLARE_REGISTRY_RESOURCEID expands to this:

```
static HRESULT WINAPI UpdateRegistry(BOOL bRegister)
{
    return _Module.UpdateRegistryFromResource(IDR_MATH, bRegister);
}
```

This method ultimately is called by the DllRegisterServer and Dll UnregisterServer functions in CHAPTER3_SERVER.CPP. A full discussion of the ATL registry component is beyond the scope of this book. However, to modify your component's registry information, you need only edit the appropriate .RGS file and rebuild the project. It gets pulled in as a binary resource; when the component is registered, the information is updated.

ATL and Component Categories

As I discussed in Chapter 2, another important aspect of registering your components involves categorizing them using component categories. In Chapter 2, I used COM's Component Categories Manager to update the registry. ATL makes this even easier by providing a set of macros that you can use within your component implementation.

To specify that your component implements or requires a specific component category, you implement a category map using the BEGIN_CATEGORY_MAP and END_CATEGORY_MAP pair in your header file. Within this macro pair, you specify implemented categories using the IMPLEMENTED_CATEGORY macro and required categories using the REQUIRED_CATEGORY macro. The only parameter is the GUID for the category identifier. For example, the following highlighted code demonstrates adding an implemented and required category to the math component:

```
class ATL_NO_VTABLE CMath :
    public CComObjectRootEx<CComSingleThreadModel>,
    public CComCoClass<CMath, &CLSID_Math>,
    public IMath
{
...
    BEGIN_CATEGORY_MAP(CMath)
        IMPLEMENTED_CATEGORY(CATID_ATLDevGuide)
        REQUIRED_CATEGORY(CATID_SimpleFrameControl)
    END_CATEGORY_MAP()
...
};
```

Implementing the Math Component Using ATL

What follows is a step-by-step process of creating the math component using ATL's wizards. The wizards described in the preceding text produce most of the details about the case. The following step-by-step approach should make it easier to create the example quickly. You also can download the code from www.WidgetWare.com.

Create the Visual C++ Project

Start Visual C++ and create a new project, selecting ATL COM AppWizard. Give it the name Chapter3_Server. In Step 1 of 1, select Dynamic Link Library (see Figure 3-7). Select Finish and then OK to generate the project.

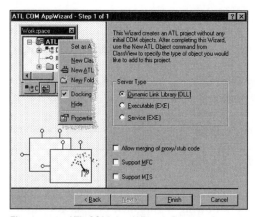

Figure 3-7: ATL COM AppWizard, Step 1 of 1

The ATL COM AppWizard

The ATL COM AppWizard is a Visual C++ wizard that steps you through the initial creation of an ATL-based project. You use AppWizard only once per project. After the project is created, you use the ATL Object wizard to add components to your project.

The ATL Object Wizard

The initial project created using the ATL AppWizard provides only basic housing support for the math component. You now need to create the component implementation files. To do that, use the new ATL Object wizard. You access it through the Visual C++ Insert → Add ATL Component menu item.

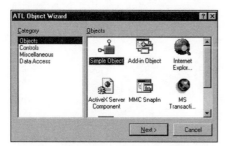

Figure 3-8: ATL Object wizard

Figure 3-8 displays the main Object wizard dialog box. For the purposes of this example, add the Simple Object type from the ATL Objects section. After clicking the Next button, you should see a dialog box like that shown in Figure 3-9.

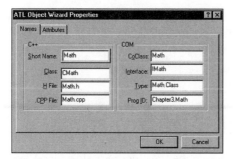

Figure 3-9: ATL Object wizard Properties dialog box, Names tab

Object Wizard Names

A series of dialog boxes is presented depending on the object type selected. For a simple COM object, information for two dialog boxes – Names and Attributes – must be populated. Figure 3-9 shows the Object wizard's Names dialog box with appropriate values for your project. You've set the Short Name to Math and changed the ProgID to `Chapter3.Math`.

Object Wizard Attributes

The Attributes dialog box enables you to specify basic COM support options for your component. Figure 3-10 reflects your selections. The only change from the defaults is that you're using a custom interface. After setting each option, click OK to create the source files for your new object.

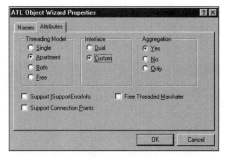

Figure 3-10: ATL Object wizard Properties dialog box, Attributes tab

The Object wizard adds these component implementation files to the project:

◆ MATH.H: CMath header file

◆ MATH.CPP: CMath implementation file

◆ MATH.RGS: Math component Registrar script file

◆ CHAPTER3_SERVER.IDL: The Object wizard also adds entries to the server's IDL file.

Implementing the IMath Interface

To add interface methods to an ATL object, access the Developer Studio's ClassView tab. In ClassView, right-click the IMath interface and select Add Method, as shown in Figure 3-11. Complete the dialog entries for the Add Method dialog box as shown in Figure 3-12, and then add the three other methods (Subtract, Multiply, and Divide) using the same technique.

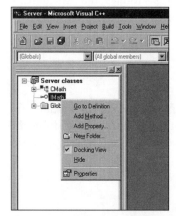

Figure 3-11: Add methods in the ClassView tab

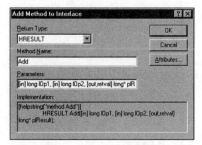

Figure 3-12: Add Method dialog box

Now it's time to write some code. Load MATH.CPP and add the following high-lighted code:

```cpp
//
// Math.cpp : Implementation of CMath
//
#include "stdafx.h"
#include "Server.h"
#include "Math.h"

/////////////////
// CMath
/////////////////

// IMath interface
STDMETHODIMP CMath::Add( long lOp1, long lOp2, long* plResult )
{
    *plResult = lOp1 + lOp2;
    return S_OK;
}
STDMETHODIMP CMath::Subtract( long lOp1, long lOp2, long* plResult )
{
    *plResult = lOp1 - lOp2;
    return S_OK;
}
STDMETHODIMP CMath::Multiply( long lOp1, long lOp2, long* plResult )
{
    *plResult = lOp1 * lOp2;
    return S_OK;
}
STDMETHODIMP CMath::Divide( long lOp1, long lOp2, long* plResult )
{
```

```
    *plResult = 10p1 / 10p2;
    return S_OK;
}
```

That's all there is to adding simple functionality. By using ATL's built-in COM functionality, you save a lot of time.

Adding IAdvancedMath and Its Methods

When you use the Object wizard to add your math component, it enables you to define only one interface (one of the deficiencies of the wizard). You must add the second interface by hand.

C++ interface declarations are built dynamically by compiling the project's IDL project with MIDL.EXE. In the earlier steps, the IDL entries for the IMath interface are added automatically. You have to do this manually for IAdvancedMath. Load CHAPTER3_SERVER.IDL and add the following code. Before you do, though, you need to use the GUIDGEN utility to generate a GUID for IAdvancedMath:

```
//
// Chapter3_Server.idl : IDL source for Chapter3_Server.dll
//
...
import "oaidl.idl";
import "ocidl.idl";
    [
        object,
        uuid(8812699C-1CC8-11D1-883A-444553540000),
        helpstring("IMath Interface"),
        pointer_default(unique)
    ]
    interface IMath : IUnknown
    {
        // This was added automatically by the IDE
        HRESULT Add( [in] long, [in] long,
                    [out, retval] long* plResult );
        HRESULT Subtract( [in] long, [in] long,
                        [out, retval] long* plResult );
        HRESULT Multiply( [in] long, [in] long,
                        [out, retval] long* plResult );
        HRESULT Divide( [in] long, [in] long,
                        [out, retval] long* plResult );
    };
```

```
   [
     object,
     // We have to create this new GUID
     uuid(6AF3DF1E-C48F-11D0-A769-D477A4000000),
     helpstring("IAdvancedMath Interface"),
     pointer_default(unique)
   ]
   interface IAdvancedMath : IUnknown
   {
     HRESULT Factorial( [in] short sFact,
                        [out, retval] long* pResult );
     HRESULT Fibonacci( [in] short sFib, [out, retval] long* pResult
);
   };


[
   uuid(8812698E-1CC8-11D1-883A-444553540000),
   version(1.0),
   helpstring("Chapter3_Server 1.0 Type Library")
]
library SERVERLib
{
     ...
     coclass Math
     {
         [default] interface IMath;
         // Add the interface to the component's description
         interface IAdvancedMath;
     };
};
```

Updating MATH.H

Once you add the interface declaration to the IDL file, you declare and implement
the interface in MATH.H and MATH.CPP. First, MATH.H:

```
// Math.h : Declaration of the CMath class
#ifndef __MATH_H_
#define __MATH_H_
#include "resource.h"        // main symbols
/////////////////////
// CMath
/////////////////////
class ATL_NO_VTABLE CMath :
   public CComObjectRootEx<CComSingleThreadModel>,
```

```
    public CComCoClass<CMath, &CLSID_Math>,
    public IMath,
    public IAdvancedMath
{
...
BEGIN_COM_MAP(CMath)
    COM_INTERFACE_ENTRY(IMath)
    COM_INTERFACE_ENTRY(IAdvancedMath)
END_COM_MAP()
// IMath
public:
    STDMETHOD(Divide)(long lOp1, long lOp2, long* plResult);
    STDMETHOD(Multiply)(long lOp1, long lOp2, long* plResult);
    STDMETHOD(Subtract)(long lOp1, long lOp2, long* plResult);
    STDMETHOD(Add)(long lOp1, long lOp2, long* plResult);

// IAdvancedMath
public:
    STDMETHOD(Factorial)( short, long* );
    STDMETHOD(Fibonacci)( short, long* );
};
#endif //__MATH_H_
```

Updating MATH.CPP

Next, update MATH.CPP. This code is nearly identical to the code from the Chapter 2 example. It's the implementation of your component's interface:

```
//
// Math.cpp : Implementation of CMath
//
#include "stdafx.h"
#include "Server.h"
#include "Math.h"

/////////////////
// CMath
/////////////////

// IMath interface
STDMETHODIMP CMath::Add( long lOp1, long lOp2, long* plResult )
{
    *plResult = lOp1 + lOp2;
    return S_OK;
```

```
}
...
// IAdvancedMath interface
long calcFactorial( short n )
{
   if ( n > 1 )
      return n * calcFactorial( n - 1 );
   else
      return 1;
}

STDMETHODIMP CMath::Factorial( short sOp, long* pResult )
{
   *pResult = calcFactorial( sOp );
   return S_OK;
}

long calcFibonacci( short n )
{
   if ( n <= 1 )
      return 1;
   return calcFibonacci( n - 1 ) + calcFibonacci( n - 2 );
}

STDMETHODIMP CMath::Fibonacci( short sOp, long* pResult )
{
   *pResult = calcFibonacci( sOp );
   return S_OK;
}
```

Building the Project

That's it — using ATL saves quite a bit of coding and you don't have to worry about implementing the IUnknown methods or your component's class factory. ATL also provides self-registration code for the server. Now, let's build the project. Before you move on to developing a client application, you quickly should test your new component using OLEVIEW. This is shown in Figure 3-13.

Your component shows up under All Objects with the name Math Class instead of Chapter3.Math. This is because of the way the ATL Object wizard creates the RGS file. Next, take a look at the RGS file.

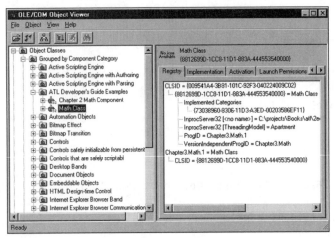

Figure 3-13: The ATL math component in OLEVIEW

Here is the code:

```
HKCR
{
  Chapter3.Math.1 = s 'Math Class'
  {
    CLSID = s '{8812699D-1CC8-11D1-883A-444553540000}'
  }
  Chapter3.Math = s 'Math Class'
  {
    CLSID = s '{8812699D-1CC8-11D1-883A-444553540000}'
    CurVer = s 'Chapter3.Math.1'
  }
  NoRemove CLSID
  {
    ForceRemove {8812699D-1CC8-11D1-883A-444553540000} = s 'Math
Class'
    {
      ProgID = s 'Chapter3.Math.1'
      VersionIndependentProgID = s 'Chapter3.Math'
      InprocServer32 = s '%MODULE%'
      {
        val ThreadingModel = s 'Apartment'
      }
    }
  }
}
```

In Figure 3-13, also notice that your component is shown under the ATL Developer's Guide Examples component category. To obtain this behavior, you need to add a component category map to your component's header file and include the ATLDEVGUIDE.H file that defines your category ID. Here's the code:

```
// Math.h : Declaration of the CMath

#ifndef __MATH_H_
#define __MATH_H_

#include "resource.h"        // main symbols
#include "atldevguide.h"

class ATL_NO_VTABLE CMath :
    public CComObjectRootEx<CComSingleThreadModel>,
    public CComCoClass<CMath, &CLSID_Math>,
    public IMath,
    public IAdvancedMath
{
...

    BEGIN_CATEGORY_MAP(CMath)
        IMPLEMENTED_CATEGORY(CATID_ATLDevGuide)
        REQUIRED_CATEGORY(CATID_SimpleFrameControl)
    END_CATEGORY_MAP()
...
};
```

Build Another COM Client

Your client application is similar to the one you developed in Chapter 2. The quickest way to build this project is to copy the project from your Chapter 2 directory and make the modifications highlighted next in CLIENT.CPP. Instead of using CoGetClassObject, you now use CoCreateInstance — the normal approach to instantiating COM objects. Here's the complete code for Chapter3_Client. I highlighted those lines that I need to discuss:

```
//
// Chapter3_Client.cpp
//
#include <windows.h>
#include <tchar.h>
#include <iostream.h>
#include <initguid.h>

#include "..\Chapter3_Server\Chapter3_Server_i.c"
```

```cpp
#include "..\Chapter3_Server\Chapter3_Server.h"

int main( int argc, char *argv[] )
{
    cout << "Initializing COM" << endl;
    if ( FAILED( CoInitialize( NULL )))
    {
        cout << "Unable to initialize COM" << endl;
        return -1;
    }

    // Use CoCreateInstance
    IMath* pMath;
    HRESULT hr = CoCreateInstance( CLSID_Math,
                                   NULL,
                                   CLSCTX_INPROC,
                                   IID_IMath,
                                   (void**) &pMath );
    if ( FAILED( hr ))
    {
        cout.setf( ios::hex, ios::basefield );
        cout << "Failed to create server instance. HR = " << hr <<
                                                              endl;
        return -1;
    }
    cout << "Instance created" << endl;

    long result;
    pMath->Multiply( 100, 8, &result );
    cout << "100 * 8 is " << result << endl;
    pMath->Subtract( 1000, 333, &result );
    cout << "1000 - 333 is " << result << endl;

    // Try IAdvancedMath, QI through IMath
    IAdvancedMath* pAdvMath = NULL;
    hr = pMath->QueryInterface( IID_IAdvancedMath,
                                (LPVOID*)&pAdvMath );
    if ( FAILED( hr ))
    {
        cout << "QueryInterface() for IAdvancedMath failed" << endl;
        pMath->Release();
        CoUninitialize();
        return -1;
    }
```

```
pAdvMath->Factorial( 10, &result );
cout << "10! is " << result << endl;
pAdvMath->Fibonacci( 10, &result );
cout << "The Fibonacci of 10 is " << result << endl;

cout << "Releasing IMath interface" << endl;
pMath->Release();

cout << "Releasing IAdvancedMath interface" << endl;
pAdvMath->Release();

cout << "Shutting down COM" << endl;
CoUninitialize();

return 0;
}
```

You have to make only a few adjustments to your client applications. First, change how you reference the server's interface declarations. Because MIDL now generates them automatically from the IDL file, include them instead. CHAPTER3_ SERVER.H contains the IMath and IAdvancedMath interface declarations and CHAPTER3_SERVER_I.C contains the definitions of the component's CLSIDs and IIDs.

The other difference is that you now use CoCreateInstance instead of CoGetClassObject. CoCreateInstance handles the details of getting the class factory and calling IClassFactory::CreateInstance. These details always remain the same, so let COM handle them.

Test the Server

After you make the preceding change, build the client project and run it in debug. It should behave just as it did in Chapter 2. The best way to learn COM and ATL is to step through this code in debug. When you get to an interface call, step into the call and begin debugging the server code.

Summary

That covers your introduction to ATL. You reimplemented the math component using ATL; I'm sure you can see that it's quite a bit easier than doing it with C++. More specifically, you:

♦ Learned that the ATL framework provides implementations for much of the low-level work that we did ourselves in Chapter 2.* Now understand the basics of using ATL's AppWizard and Object Wizard.

◆ Learned what files are created for you and what files you must modify to add functionality to your COM components.

◆ Learned that the source code for the ATL framework is included with your own code.

◆ Now understand the basic macros used by ATL and what they do. In Chapter 4, you delve into the requirements for housing the components in executables instead of in DLLs. You take a look at marshaling and study the files produced by the MIDL compiler. Let's get started.

Chapter 4

Interfaces, IDL, and Marshaling

IN THIS CHAPTER

- ◆ The various COM interface types
- ◆ The marshaling process
- ◆ COM's proxy/stub architecture
- ◆ The Interface Definition Language (IDL)
- ◆ COM data types and memory management
- ◆ Error handling in COM

NOW YOU SHOULD have an understanding of what COM is about, as well as an idea of how ATL facilitates the creation of COM-based components. In this chapter, you delve a bit deeper into the various interface mechanisms provided by COM. In particular, I cover the Interface Definition Language (IDL) and marshaling, as well as details such as COM error handling, COM memory management, and basic COM data types. The following sections provide a brief summary of each interface type.

A Brief Summary of COM Interface Types

In Chapter 2, I described COM interfaces by using the C++ Vtable structure as their implementation mechanism. Interfaces that use the Vtable structure exclusively are known as Vtable, or custom, interfaces. COM also supports two other interface types: *dispinterfaces* (based on the standard IDispatch) and *dual interfaces.*

Vtable Interfaces

You're familiar with the implementation of a Vtable interface. A COM component exposes its functionality through this Vtable interface. One of the drawbacks of a Vtable-style interface is that it requires some form of compile-time binding with the client (basically, the exact layout of the Vtable). In other words, the client must

147

have compile-time knowledge of the interface methods and parameters. However, this static knowledge does not include the actual implementation of the methods in the component.

This is where COM's polymorphic behavior enters. An interface's signature is defined at compile time, but not the actual implementation of the interface methods. This enables you to "plug in" component functionality at run time.

IDispatch Interfaces: Dispinterfaces

What makes a dispinterface different from a Vtable interface is that its clients do not require any compile-time binding information (except to the IDispatch itself, which is well known). A client application can determine, at run time, the method names and parameters. This arrangement removes any compile-time requirement on the client application. It sounds great, but the drawback is that dispinterfaces are much slower because they require an extra level of indirection in their implementation. I discuss this interface in detail in Chapter 6.

Dual Interfaces

Once you understand the concept of a Vtable and a dispinterface, a dual interface is easy. A *dual interface* is a combination of a regular COM Vtable interface and a dispinterface. This combination gives the client additional flexibility. A client of a component that supports a dual interface can choose the more efficient Vtable interface and bind to it at compile time. A client also can choose to bind late (at run time), which is less efficient but offers additional capabilities. I discuss implementing and accessing a dual interface in detail in Chapter 6.

Describing a Component and Its Interfaces

Client applications that need to access a component's interface require a technique to obtain information about the interfaces. Interfaces must be described for several reasons. First, potential clients need to understand both the Vtable layout and the number and type of parameters in each method. Without this information, you have to distribute language-dependent files (such as C++ header files) along with your component. Second, an interface description is useful for generating language-specific bindings – something that is handy when you develop components in a particular language such as C++. Third, as I discussed in Chapter 2, COM-based components support the concept of location transparency. The client's capability to access a component's functionality across process and machine boundaries is important. However, to support this capability, COM requires marshaling support for its interfaces. If you describe an interface in a canonical way, tools can produce marshaling support code automatically.

Type Information

Before a client application can access the services provided by a Vtable-based COM component, the client must know the structure of the component's interfaces. It must know information such as which interfaces are supported, which parameters each method takes, and so on. COM provides a way for components to describe their functionality through a binary, language-independent file called a *type library*.

As I discussed in Chapter 3, a component describes its interfaces with IDL. When you use ATL, each component housing has an associated IDL file that contains type information for components within the housing. This file is compiled into a type library using Microsoft's IDL compiler (MIDL.EXE). After compiling the type information, you distribute it along with the component within the housing itself or as a separate .TLB file. The HKCR\TypeLib registry entry provides a way for client applications and object browsers to locate a component's type information. The type library provides all the needed information so that client applications can support compile-time type checking and early binding to a component's methods.

LANGUAGE BINDINGS

IDL also generates language-specific files for the described component. The MIDL compiler generates bindings (as .H and .C files) only for the C/C++ language. All other languages use the type library to generate compile-time bindings. Both Visual Basic and Visual J++ create wrapper classes for components by reading a component's type library and generating internal support code.

PROXY/STUB GENERATION

Another important aspect of IDL is its capability of producing proxy/stub DLLs for your component's interfaces. By describing your interfaces, methods, and parameters with IDL and compiling it with MIDL, you get code and a make file for a proxy/stub DLL. The proxy/stub DLL implements standard marshaling for each of your component interfaces.

Marshaling

Marshaling is the process of transferring function arguments and return values across process and machine boundaries. Intrinsic types, such as shorts and longs, are easy to marshal; most others, such as pointers to structures, are a bit more difficult. You can't just make a copy of a pointer because its value (an address) has no meaning in the context of another process, especially if that process is on another machine.

I've mentioned that COM objects are housed in either a Windows executable or a Windows DLL. When the component housing is a DLL, it is called an in-process server to denote that the server component executes within the context of the client's address space (executable). This method is the most efficient way to interact with a COM-based component because marshaling usually is not necessary. However, as you'll see in Chapter 10, COM uses marshaling to synchronize access to components in multithreaded applications. So, in some cases you may need marshaling support even if your component supports only in-process execution.

COM's implementation of marshaling uses a proxy and a stub. When marshaling is required, COM creates a proxy object in the client's process space and a stub in the component's process space. The client application then interacts with the proxy as if it has a direct connection to the component. The component also interacts with the stub as if it is connected directly to the client. This important COM feature is what enables location transparency. The complexity of marshaling, which may require moving interface pointers from one machine to another, is hidden from the developer. Figure 4-1 shows the relationship of clients, proxies, servers, and stubs.

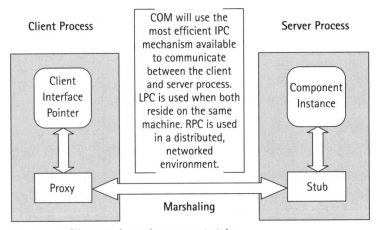

Figure 4-1: Client proxies and component stubs

Marshaling is required in the following situations:

◆ When you access a component in a different process on the same machine

◆ When you access a component on a different machine (DCOM)

◆ When you pass interface pointers between COM apartments in the same process

COM handles the majority of these cases. By automatically managing the marshaling process among clients and components, COM makes module interoperability quite a bit easier.

Distributed COM

Distributed COM is COM's ability to distribute components and access them from different machines in a network. This means that you can deploy a COM-based component on a machine in New York and access its services on a client machine in Kansas City. The benefit is that the client software is oblivious to the location of the server component. It can reside locally on the client machine, on a different machine in Kansas City, or on a machine in New York.

The COM-client software doesn't care and doesn't need to know in what address space the server executes. All this happens through the magic of marshaling. However, DCOM raises several additional issues – primarily security – which I do not discuss in this book. DCOM mostly involves getting the security right and managing component lifetimes in the more hostile, unstable network environment. (For more details, see *Professional DCOM Programming* (Wrox Press, 1997) by Richard Grimes.)

Standard Marshaling

When you describe your component's interfaces via IDL, the MIDL compiler generates a series of files (shown in Table 4-1) that produces a standard proxy/stub DLL. By building and registering the proxy/stub DLL, you provide standard marshaling for your components. For custom Vtable interfaces that you define, you must distribute and register the proxy/stub DLL with your components. Also, the proxy/stub must be registered on each client machine. Standard COM interfaces provided by Microsoft (such as `IClassFactory`) also have proxy/stub DLLs, but they are shipped as part of the operating system.

TABLE 4-1 MIDL-GENERATED PROXY/STUB FILES

File	Description
`ProjectNamePS.mk`	The make file that generates the proxy/stub DLL named `ProjectNamePS.DLL`
`ProjectName.h`	A header file with the C- and C++-compatible interface declarations
`ProjectName_p.c`	The code that implements the proxy/stub
`ProjectName_i.c`	A C file that contains the interface GUIDs
`DLLDATA.C`	A C file that implements a DLL for the proxy/stub code

Type Library (Universal) Marshaling

If you don't like the idea of shipping a proxy/stub DLL for each of your components, you have another option. Type library marshaling uses the standard automation marshaler that comes with the operating system. The one caveat with type library marshaling is that you can use only automation-compatible types in your interface methods, which I cover in Chapter 6.

To enable type library marshaling for your components, make sure that you use only automation types and add the `oleautomation` attribute to your interface declaration in your IDL file. Here's an example for the math component. The `IMath` interface uses automation-compatible types, so you can use type library marshaling:

```
[
    object,
    uuid(8C30BC10-B8F2-11D0-A756-B04A12000000),
    oleautomation,
    helpstring("IMath Interface"),
    pointer_default(unique)
]
interface IMath : IUnknown
{
    HRESULT Add( [in] long, [in] long, [out, retval] long* pResult );
    HRESULT Subtract( [in] long, [in] long,
                    [out, retval] long* pResult );
    HRESULT Multiply( [in] long, [in] long,
                    [out, retval] long* pResult );
    HRESULT Divide( [in] long, [in] long,
                    [out, retval] long* pResult );
};
```

Another required step for type library marshaling is that you register your component's type library via COM's `RegisterTypeLibrary` function. ATL automatically registers your type library as part of its normal registration process, so only the changes to your interface declarations are required when you use ATL. Figure 4-2 shows the registry entries when you use type library marshaling. Notice that the proxy/stub entry is `OLEAUT32.DLL`, which is the proxy/stub DLL provided by the OS.

Custom Marshaling

If standard marshaling and type library marshaling do not meet your needs, you can perform your own custom marshaling. Custom marshaling requires that your component implement the `IMarshal` interface. When a client creates a component, COM queries for the `IMarshal` interface. Standard and type library marshaling implement the `IMarshal` interface for the component, but the `IMarshal` interface returned is implemented directly within the component in custom marshaling.

One of the benefits of custom marshaling is that you can use any mechanism for interprocess communication. For example, standard marshaling uses Microsoft's RPC implementation for cross-machine marshaling in a DCOM scenario. By implementing your own `IMarshal` interface, you can decide to use TCP/IP packets to marshal interface parameters from machine to machine.

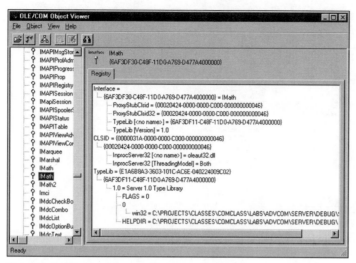

Figure 4-2: IMath with type library marshaling

A component developer typically chooses to implement custom marshaling either because COM does not support the desired behavior or because the developer has intimate knowledge of the client/component interaction and wants to use this knowledge to increase performance.

Building the Proxy/Stub DLL

To build and register the proxy/stub DLL produced by the MIDL compiler, you must work from the command line. First, locate the ProjectNamePS.mk make file and use NMAKE to create the DLL. It looks something like this:

```
c:\MyProject\NMAKE -f Chapter4_ServerPS.mk
```

Once the DLL is created, add it to the registry using REGSVR32.

```
c:\MyProject\REGSVR32 Chapter4_ServerPS.DLL
```

COM locates the proxy/stub DLL for a component by looking it up in the registry. Whenever a client application queries for an interface (usually through CoCreateInstance or QueryInterface), COM determines whether a proxy is required; if it is, COM looks up the location of the DLL via the registry. The HKCR\Interfaces key lists the proxy/stub DLLs for all interfaces on the system that support it. For example, Figure 4-3 shows the entry for your math component.

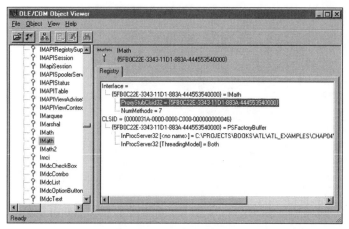

Figure 4-3: The proxy/stub registry entry

When you load a component with the OLEVIEW utility, OLEVIEW determines which interfaces the component supports by calling QueryInterface with every potential interface under the HKCR\Interfaces registry key. (Yes, that's several hundred QIs, but remember that a component is defined by the interfaces it supports and this is one way to check.) If your component does not show that it supports a certain implemented interface, add the IID under the HKCR\Interfaces key to make it appear.

The Interface Definition Language

I discussed IDL briefly in Chapter 3. In this chapter, I cover it in a bit more detail. In particular, I discuss how IDL produces type information, language bindings, and proxy/stub code for components.

Basic Syntax and Layout

The syntax of IDL is similar to standard C++ syntax. You can define structures, enums, and so on. One primary difference is that you declare interfaces instead of classes. In fact, there is no executable code within the IDL file. As its name implies, IDL describes an interface and its related details. The implementation of the resulting descriptions is performed later using a specific language.

Attributes can precede keywords in IDL. These attributes, contained within a bracket pair, modify the keyword. For example, the uuid, helpstring, and pointer_default attributes modify the following interface:

```
[
    uuid(5FB0C22E-3343-11D1-883A-444553540000),
    helpstring("IMath Interface"),
```

```
        pointer_default(unique)
]
interface IMath : IUnknown
{
...
};
```

If the IDL file contains the library keyword, the MIDL compiler generates a type library. As you can see in the following code, each IDL keyword is modified by its preceding attributes. The type library has a GUID, a version, and a help string:

```
[
    uuid(5FB0C221-3343-11D1-883A-444553540000),
    version(1.0),
    helpstring("Chapter4_Server 1.0 Type Library")
]
library CHAPTER4_SERVERLib
{
    importlib("stdole32.tlb");
    importlib("stdole2.tlb");
    [
        uuid(5FB0C22F-3343-11D1-883A-444553540000),
        helpstring("Math Class")
    ]
    coclass Math
    {
        [default] interface IMath;
        interface IMath2;
        interface IAdvancedMath;
        interface IComponentInfo;
    };
};
```

Items declared globally outside the library block generate C/C++ code when passed through the MIDL compiler.

Declaring Interfaces: Methods and Properties

Declaring interfaces in IDL follows the basic IDL syntax. You specify any special interface attributes prior to the interface keyword and then declare the methods that the interface supports. For example, here's the interface declaration for the IMath interface:

```
[
    object,
```

```
    uuid(5FB0C22E-3343-11D1-883A-444553540000),
    helpstring("IMath Interface"),
    pointer_default(unique)
]
interface IMath : IUnknown
{
  [helpstring("method Add")]
   HRESULT Add([in] long l0p1,[in] long l0p2,
               [out,retval] long* plResult);
  [helpstring("method Subtract")]
   HRESULT Subtract([in] long l0p1,[in] long l0p2,
                    [out,retval] long* plResult);

   ...
};
```

I described this interface in Chapter 3. COM also supports the concept of a property — a characteristic of the component that a data member usually handles internally. The data members of a class provide its state, and its methods operate on that state. COM components can expose their data members through standard accessor methods, but COM provides properties so that development tools can present them as explicit data members of the component. For example, if you add a VersionNumber property to your math component, you describe it in IDL this way:

```
interface IMath2 : IUnknown
{

...

   [propget, helpstring("property VersionNumber")]
      HRESULT VersionNumber([out, retval] long *pVal);
   [propput, helpstring("property VersionNumber")]
      HRESULT VersionNumber([in] long newVal);
};
```

If you specify the propget and propput attributes for your accessor methods, client applications such as Visual Basic can provide a special syntax that enables the user to treat VersionNumber as a directly accessible data member of the component. The Visual Basic syntax looks like this:

```
Dim objMath as New Math
objMath.VersionNumber = 100
' or
txtVersion.Text = objMath.VersionNumber
```

The primary difference from a user's perspective lies in using the assignment operator instead of the method call syntax. Properties are used heavily in automation, which I discuss in Chapter 6.

The native COM support in Visual C++ 6 also provides this syntax as part of its #import keyword implementation. (See the Appendix for more details.)

IDL Data Types

IDL supports a number of built-in data types, including the typical C++ data types. Table 4-2 lists the base types supported by IDL. When designing interfaces for your components, you should use these base types or structures based on these types. You also can use any of the automation-compatible types listed in Table 4-3. By limiting your interface parameters to automation types, you can use the built-in automation marshaler that I described earlier in this chapter.

TABLE 4-2 IDL BASE TYPES

Base Type	Description
boolean	8-bit data item
byte	8-bit data item
char	8-bit unsigned data item
double	64-bit floating-point number
float	32-bit floating-point number
handle_t	Primitive handle type
hypersigned	64-bit signed integer
int	32-bit signed integer
long	32-bit signed integer
short	16-bit signed integer
small	8-bit signed integer
void*	32-bit context handle pointer type
wchar_t	16-bit unsigned data item

TABLE **4-3 AUTOMATION TYPES**

Base Type	Description
boolean	Uses the VARIANT_BOOL type
unsigned char	8-bit unsigned data item
Double	64-bit IEEE floating-point number
Float	32-bit IEEE floating-point number
Int	Integer whose size is system-dependent
Long	32-bit signed integer
Short	16-bit signed integer
BSTR	Length-prefixed string
CY	8-byte fixed-point number
DATE	64-bit floating-point fractional number of days since December 31, 1899
SCODE	Built-in error type that corresponds to HRESULT
Enum	Signed integer, whose size is system-dependent
IDispatch *	Pointer to IDispatch interface (VT_DISPATCH)
IUnknown *	Pointer to an IUnknown interface

Arrays

Using IDL, you can declare arrays of the basic types. It is easy to do because the declaration is similar to a declaration in C++. Here's an example of a method that takes an array of integers:

```
HRESULT Sum( [in] short sArray[5], [out, retval] long* plResult );
```

In this example, the component knows the size of the array in advance. More typically, it is useful to sum a user-defined series of numbers. You can use the IDL size_is attribute to pass an arbitrary size to the server — something like this:

```
HRESULT Sum( [in] short sArraySize,
             [in, size_is( sArraySize )] short sArray[],
             [out, retval] long* plResult );
```

The server code is easy to implement:

```
STDMETHODIMP CMath::Sum( short sArraySize,
                         short sArray[],
                         long* plResult )
{
   *plResult = 0;
   while( sArraySize )
   {
      *plResult += sArray[--sArraySize];
   }
   return S_OK;
}
```

You can use the method from the client just as easily:

```
short sArray[3] = { 3,4,5 };
long lResult = 0;
pMath2->Sum( 3, sArray, &lResult );
```

Strings

You use strings constantly when developing software. The IDL string attribute is a shorthand technique for describing a one-dimensional array. Following is a simple structure declaration that includes the string attribute:

```
typedef struct COMPONENT_INFO
{
   [string] char*    pstrAuthor;
   ...
} COMPONENT_INFO;
```

Structures

If COM interfaces enabled you to pass only native types back and forth, it would be difficult to build large, efficient components. Because IDL automatically generates proxy/stub code for your methods, you can build complex structures while the MIDL compiler handles the details of marshaling the structures across processes and machines. For example, here's a simple structure that you can use in your math component:

```
typedef struct COMPONENT_INFO
{
   [string] char*    pstrAuthor;
   short             sMajor;
   short             sMinor;
```

```
    BSTR                bstrName;
} COMPONENT_INFO;
```

You also can add a new interface called IComponentInfo that returns details of a component to its user. Here's the declaration:

```
interface IComponentInfo : IUnknown
{
    [helpstring("method get_Info")]
        HRESULT get_Info( [out] COMPONENT_INFO** pInfo );
    [helpstring("method get_Name")]
        HRESULT get_Name( [out] BSTR* bstrName );
};
```

Wouldn't it be nice if every component implemented this interface? You would have a standard way to query for version information directly from the component. The About dialog box for each application would be easy to write and would display information about each component within the application. This is a simple example of an interface that uses structures, but it also demonstrates the power of COM as a component architecture.

The get_Info method takes a COMPONENT_INFO structure pointer through which the component's information is returned. We've defined the get_Info method to take a pointer to a pointer because the component allocates the structure and returns it to the client. I discuss this process later when I describe how COM components manage memory.

Enums

IDL also supports enumerated types in a language-independent way. By describing your enumerated types in IDL, you can use them within your C++ projects as well as in Visual Basic, Java, and any language that can read a type library. Following is an example that I use in the math component. You add a new method called Compute that takes as a parameter the type of computation to perform. The type is specified as one of the mathOPERATION constants.

```
typedef
[
    uuid(984D09A4-3379-11d1-883A-444553540000),
    helpstring("Math Operation Type"),
]
enum mathOPERATION
{
    [helpstring("Add")]      mathAdd      = 0x0001,
    [helpstring("Subtract")] mathSubtract = 0x0002,
    [helpstring("Multiply")] mathMultiply = 0x0003,
```

```
    [helpstring("Divide")]    mathDivide   = 0x0004
} mathOPERATION;
```

Then you can use this new type in the declaration of the Compute method:

```
[helpstring("method Compute")]
HRESULT Compute( [in] mathOPERATION enumOp,
                 [in] long lOp1,
                 [in] long lOp2,
                 [out,retval] long* plResult );
```

After you run the preceding code through the MIDL compiler, it produces a C construct as part of your Chapter4_Server header file:

```
// From Chapter4_Server.h
typedef enum mathOPERATION
{
    mathAdd      = 0x1,
    mathSubtract    = 0x2,
    mathMultiply    = 0x3,
    mathDivide     = 0x4
} mathOPERATION;
```

You can use this type in the implementation of your component's method:

```
STDMETHODIMP CMath::Compute( mathOPERATION enumOp,
                             long lOp1,
                             long lOp2,
                             long * plResult)
{
    switch( enumOp )
    {
    case mathAdd:
        return Add( lOp1, lOp2, plResult );
    case mathSubtract:
        return Subtract( lOp1, lOp2, plResult );
    case mathMultiply:
        return Multiply(  lOp1, lOp2, plResult );
    case mathDivide:
        return Divide( lOp1, lOp2, plResult );
    }
    return S_OK;
}
```

The type library that MIDL produces for your component also contains this definition, so non-C++ tools also can use the enumeration. Figure 4-4 shows the Object Browser in Visual Basic with your `mathOPERATION` type highlighted. The Visual Basic example at the end of the chapter demonstrates the use of this type.

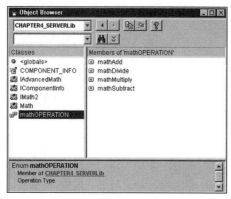

Figure 4-4: The enumerated type in Visual Basic's Object Browser

ATL and COM Data Types

When building COM components, you typically deal with several COM-based data types. In the next few sections, you take a look at these basic data types and discover how ATL provides wrapper classes for them. We begin with COM interface pointers and ATL's smart pointers and finish with the basic COM string type: the binary string, or BSTR.

Interface Pointers

The only way to access functionality in a COM component is through its interface. One of the most primitive types in COM is a `Vtable` interface. You've dealt with Vtables quite a bit so far, and you understand that interface pointers really are pointers to a C++ abstract class `Vtable`.

Sometimes it is necessary to return interface pointers as part of your method or property implementations. The IDL syntax is straightforward. For example, let's add a new property to the `IMath2` interface. The new `AdvancedMath` property returns a pointer to the `IAdvancedMath` interface within the math component:

```
// IDL entry
[propget, helpstring("property AdvancedMath")]
    HRESULT AdvancedMath([out, retval] IAdvancedMath **ppVal);


// Implementation
```

```
STDMETHODIMP CMath::get_AdvancedMath(IAdvancedMath** ppVal)
{
    GetUnknown()->QueryInterface( IID_IAdvancedMath,
                                  (void**) ppVal );
    return S_OK;
}
```

The implementation uses ATL's GetUnknown function to get an IUnknown pointer through which you query for the IAdvancedMath interface. QueryInterface automatically increments the reference counter for the component, so you don't have to call IUnknown::AddRef explicitly. The client application is responsible for releasing the interface pointer.

C++ Smart Pointers

Smart pointers are C++ classes that hide many of the details of memory management when working with pointers. The smart pointer idiom also can be used with COM interface pointers. As I discussed in Chapter 2, you must treat interface pointers like a system resource. When the interface is retrieved, copied, or passed to another logical user, its reference count must be incremented. When you're finished using an interface pointer, you must release it. In this way, a component instance manages its own lifetime.

Smart pointers encapsulate the QueryInterface()/Release() and CoCreate Instance()/Release() pairs so that the user of the class doesn't have to worry about explicitly releasing COM pointers. Because the pointer operator is modified, access to the interface's methods proceeds as usual. ATL provides two smart pointer classes: CComPTR and CComQIPtr. Both classes are templatized to take an interface pointer type. CComQIPtr also takes an IID to perform an implicit QueryInterface. I discuss these two classes in the next few sections.

Visual C++ also provides a set of smart pointers for managing COM interfaces; in fact it provides more functionality than that of ATL. However, the ATL classes preceded Visual C++ 6.0 and they provide a compiler-independent smart pointer implementation.

CComPtr

ATL's CComPtr template class provides basic smart pointer functionality. You can use the class as a COM interface pointer, with the added benefit that when it goes out of scope the class calls Release() automatically. Here's how you can use the CComPtr class:

```
CComPtr< IMath > ptrMath;
HRESULT hr;
// This time use CoCreateInstance
hr = CoCreateInstance( CLSID_Math,
                       NULL,
```

```
                        CLSCTX_LOCAL_SERVER,
                        IID_IMath,
                        (void**) &ptrMath );

    ...
    // Access the IMath interface
    long lResult;
    ptrMath->Add( 134, 353, &lResult );
    cout << "134 + 353 = " << lResult << endl;
    ...
    }
```

In the preceding example, you don't have to call Release. However, you can release explicitly by calling CComPtr::Release or by using the assignment operator:

```
ptrMath.Release();
// or
ptrMath = 0;
```

Smart pointers are useful, but they don't make it much easier to work with COM interfaces. Because CComPtr directly exposes a Release method, you accidentally can release an interface twice – explicitly (as you're used to) and again when the instance goes out of scope. Because of the reference counting scheme used by COM (discussed in Chapter 2), calling release more times than necessary will result in an eventual access violation.

CComQIPtr

When you work with COM (especially when you're a client), you often call QueryInterface on one interface pointer to get another one. You've done this in your client examples and will do it again in the examples at the end of the chapter. ATL provides another smart pointer class that performs a QueryInterface automatically when it's instantiated. CComQIPtr takes an additional parameter – the IID of the requested interface. Here's how you can use it:

```
// Access IAdvancedMath
CComQIPtr<IAdvancedMath,
        &IID_IAdvancedMath> ptrAdvancedMath( ptrMath );
if ( ptrAdvancedMath )
{
    ptrAdvancedMath->Factorial( 12, &lResult );
    cout << "12! = " << lResult << endl;
    ptrAdvancedMath->Fibonacci( 12, &lResult );
    cout << "The Fibonacci of 12 = " << lResult << endl;
}
```

Visual C++ 6.0 provides a native implementation of smart pointers for COM interfaces. The _com_ptr_ class provides this implementation and is part of Visual C++'s native COM support. See the Appendix for more coverage of this concept.

BSTRs

COM uses a special string data type called a *binary* or *basic string*, or *BSTR*. A BSTR is declared as an OLECHAR*, which indicates that it's a Unicode string. However, COM provides a number of Win32 functions that act directly on the BSTR type. In other words, if you use these special functions, a standard Unicode or ANSI string can become a BSTR. The primary API, SysAllocString, creates and stores a DWORD value at the front of a Unicode string that describes its length. This is handy because it enables the use of embedded nulls within the string. Also, by providing the string's length, you can perform marshaling more efficiently because there is no need to scan the string to determine its length.

BSTRs are Visual Basic strings and are described as automation-compatible types. Because the operating system provides APIs to manage them and because default marshaling code also is provided, the BSTR type is the de facto COM string and is used extensively outside of its humble automation roots. Figure 4-5 depicts the structure of a BSTR. The DWORD count is the actual number of bytes, which is twice the number of Unicode characters.

BSTR – OLECHAR*

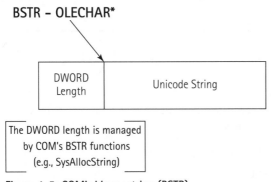

Figure 4-5: COM's binary string (BSTR)

Conversion of BSTRs into ANSI strings is easy because BSTRs are represented as OLECHAR pointers. To convert a BSTR to ANSI, you can use the standard

Unicode-to-ANSI macros described in Chapter 2. Here's a quick excerpt from the chapter example:

```
BSTR bstrDescription = 0;
BSTR bstrSource = 0;
pEI->GetDescription( &bstrDescription );
pEI->GetSource( &bstrSource );

USES_CONVERSION;
cout << OLE2T( bstrDescription ) << endl;
cout << OLE2T( bstrSource ) << endl;

::SysFreeString( bstrDescription );
::SysFreeString( bstrSource );
```

This example shows how you declare a BSTR and pass it to a COM method, which allocates and returns the BSTR. You then convert it to ANSI for display and deallocate the memory using the SysFreeString function. This is an example of COM's memory management rules, which I discuss shortly.

CComBSTR

ATL's CComBSTR class acts as a wrapper around COM's BSTR data type. By using CComBSTR, you can avoid looking up the BSTR APIs. However, CComBSTR is a thin wrapper around BSTR; many developers forgo it and instead use the BSTR type. I take the latter approach in this chapter, but use CComBSTR extensively in later chapters. Table 4-4 lists some of CComBSTR's methods.

Table 4-4 CCOMBSTR METHODS

Member	Description
CComBSTR(...)	The class has several constructors for each of the ANSI, Unicode, and BSTR string types.
Append	Appends an ANSI string to the BSTR
AppendBSTR	Appends a BSTR
Copy	Returns a copy of the BSTR
Length	Returns the length, in characters, of the string

The CComBSTR class has a few useful operators. Two conspicuously missing ones are the comparison and char* operators. If you want to compare two CComBSTR strings, you can use the following code or use the `CComVariant` class, which I describe in Chapter 6:

```
// BSTR comparison...
CComBSTR bstrA( "COM" );
CComBSTR bstrB( "COM" );
if ( ::SysStringByteLen( bstrA ) == ::SysStringByteLen( bstrB ) &&
     ::memcmp( bstrA, bstrB, ::SysStringByteLen( bstrA )) == 0 )
{
    cout << "bstrA == bstrB" << endl;
}
```

 Visual C++ also provides a native implementation of the BSTR type via the `_bstr_t_` class. See the Appendix for more details.

COM Memory Management

In a distributed environment in which clients and servers execute in different processes or on different machines, memory management is an important issue. In many cases, a component may have to allocate memory and return it to a client application without the component knowing when the client is finished using the allocated memory. COM handles this situation by providing a few special APIs, along with rules for how you should use them.

CoTaskMemAlloc and CoTaskMemFree

These are helper functions for COM's `IMalloc` interface. `IMalloc` provides an abstraction of the familiar C run-time memory functions: `malloc` and `free`. You typically do not use the interface directly, though, because `CoTaskMemAlloc` and `CoTaskMemFree` act as wrapper functions.

You use `CoTaskMemAlloc` and `CoTaskMemFree` just as you do the C run-time equivalents. Here's an example:

```
COMPONENT_INFO* pInfo = (COMPONENT_INFO *)
       CoTaskMemAlloc( sizeof( COMPONENT_INFO ));
ZeroMemory( pInfo, sizeof( COMPONENT_INFO ));
// Do something with the structure
...
// Now free it
CoTaskMemFree( pInfo );
```

The preceding example is easy to understand. However, things get complicated when you need to allocate and deallocate memory across processes – something that occurs all the time in COM. One other requirement states that the client and server applications are oblivious to each other's location. Again, because of COM's support for location transparency, the cooperating entities need hard and fast rules to follow. COM provides this through the IDL description of an interface's methods.

IDL and Memory Management

To determine responsibility for allocating and deallocating memory, you must look at the declaration of the method in IDL. The entity responsible for allocating and freeing parameters of an interface method is specified via IDL's `in` and `out` parameter attributes. The following rules apply:

- For `in`-only parameters, the client (caller) is responsible for allocating and freeing the memory.

- For `out`-only parameters, the server (callee) is responsible for allocating the memory and the client (caller) is responsible for freeing the memory.

- For `in/out` parameters, the client (caller) allocates the memory and is responsible for freeing the memory. However, the component (callee) has the option of reallocating memory if needed.

You also may have to use COM's memory management functions when using certain COM APIs – particularly those functions that take a pointer to a pointer, such as COM's `ProgIDFromCLSID` function. Help for `ProgIDFromCLSID` indicates that the second parameter is an `out` parameter. Thus, you need to free the memory:

```
// Look up the ProgID
WCHAR* pProgID = 0;
ProgIDFromCLSID( guids[0], &pProgID );

// Add it to the listbox
USES_CONVERSION;
m_ControlList.AddString( W2A( pProgID ));

// Free the memory
CoTaskMemFree( pProgID );
```

COM Error Handling

All COM interface methods must return either `void` or an `HRESULT`; `void` returns won't work until COM supports asynchronous calls in Windows 2000. For now, the primary mechanism of reporting errors from a component to its client is through the HRESULT return code. Recently, though, COM has added a rich error-handling model that enables a component to report detailed information. In this section, I describe three new interfaces and three new API functions and discuss how clients and server applications use these facilities. I also reveal how ATL makes error handling a bit easier to implement.

ISupportErrorInfo

If a component wants to support COM error handling, its first step is to provide an implementation of the ISupportErrorInfo interface. ISupportErrorInfo has only one method: InterfaceSupportsErrorInfo. The component specifies, via its implementation of InterfaceSupportsErrorInfo, which of its interfaces can return rich error information. The method itself is easy to implement, especially when you use ATL.

CreateErrorInfo and ICreateErrorInfo

Once a component indicates that it can return error information, it creates it by using the CreateErrorInfo function. This function returns an interface pointer to the created error object. Interaction with the error object proceeds through ICreateErrorInfo. ICreateErrorInfo contains a number of methods, all of which enable the setting of various attributes within the error object. Examples include SetGUID, SetSource (which is the ProgID), SetDescription, and so on. The following example, which I adapted from ATL's implementation, demonstrates how to create and initialize an error object within a component:

```
ICreateErrorInfo* pICEI;
if ( SUCCEEDED( CreateErrorInfo( &pICEI )))
{
    // Set the GUID
    pICEI->SetGUID( iid );

    // Set the ProgID
    LPOLESTR lpsz;
    ProgIDFromCLSID( clsid, &lpsz );
    if (lpsz != NULL)
    {
        pICEI->SetSource( lpsz );
        CoTaskMemFree( lpsz );
    }

    // Set any help information
    if (dwHelpID != 0 && lpszHelpFile != NULL)
    {
        pICEI->SetHelpContext( dwHelpID );
```

```
        pICEI->SetHelpFile( const_cast<LPOLESTR>( lpszHelpFile ));
    }

    // Set the actual description of the problem
    pICEI->SetDescription((LPOLESTR)lpszDesc);

    // Associate the error with the current execution context
    IErrorInfo* pErrorInfo;
    if ( SUCCEEDED(pICEI->QueryInterface( IID_IErrorInfo,
                                        (void**) &pErrorInfo )))

        SetErrorInfo(0, pErrorInfo);

    // Release the interfaces
    pICIE->Release();
    pErrorInfo->Release();
}
```

SetErrorInfo and IErrorInfo

An error object is created using `CreateErrorInfo` and the `ICreateErrorInfo` interface. After everything is set up, the error object must be associated with the current thread of execution through the `IErrorInfo` interface and the `SetError Info` function. The last few lines of the preceding code demonstrate this technique.

The `IErrorInfo` interface provides a corresponding `Get` method for each `Set` method in `ICreateErrorInfo`. In other words, the client application ultimately uses `IErrorInfo` to retrieve the error information.

 Visual C++ 6.0 provides several native COM exception-handling classes. These classes encapsulate the details of working with the low-level aspects of COM error handling. See the Appendix for more details.

Clients and GetErrorInfo

Now you know how to implement error handling within the component itself. Next, I discuss how a client application retrieves the information. Initially, the client is notified when an error occurs via an unsuccessful `HRESULT` return like this:

```
long lResult;
IMath* pMath;
...
```

```
if ( FAILED( pMath->Divide( 0, 0, &lResult ))
{
    HandleError( pMath, IID_IMath );
}
```

Once an error is indicated, as in the preceding example, the client determines whether the component supports rich error information; the client queries for ISupportErrorInfo. If the QI succeeds, the client can continue retrieving the IErrorInfo interface. Following is the complete code for determining whether a component supports error info and, when it does, getting the COM error object and displaying the information:

```
void HandleError( IUnknown* pUnk, REFIID riid )
{
    HRESULT hr;
    // See if the object supports rich error info
    ISupportErrorInfo* pSEI = 0;
    hr = pUnk->QueryInterface( IID_ISupportErrorInfo,
                              (void**) &pSEI );
    if (SUCCEEDED( hr ))
    {
        hr = pSEI->InterfaceSupportsErrorInfo( riid );
        if ( SUCCEEDED( hr ))
        {
            // Get the error info
            IErrorInfo* pEI;
            if ( SUCCEEDED( GetErrorInfo( 0, &pEI )))
            {
                USES_CONVERSION;
                BSTR bstrDescription = 0;
                BSTR bstrSource = 0;
                pEI->GetDescription( &bstrDescription );
                pEI->GetSource( &bstrSource );
                cout << OLE2T( bstrDescription ) << endl;
                cout << OLE2T( bstrSource ) << endl;
                ::SysFreeString( bstrDescription );
                ::SysFreeString( bstrSource );
                pEI->Release();
            }
        }
        pSEI->Release();
    }
}
```

Whew! That's a lot of work just to get the error information, but that's what you have to do. Once you determine that the component supports error information on the specified interface, call the `GetErrorInfo` API to return the `IErrorInfo` interface. Through `IErrorInfo`, you can retrieve and display the information passed by the server.

ATL's Support for Error Handling

When you initially create a component object using the ATL Object wizard, the first tabbed dialog box gives you an option called Support `ISupportErrorInfo`. By checking this option, you add an implementation of the `ISupportErrorInfo` interface to your component. The following code highlights the code added by the Object wizard:

```
// Math.h
...
class ATL_NO_VTABLE CMath :
    public CComObjectRootEx<CComSingleThreadModel>,
    public CComCoClass<CMath, &CLSID_Math>,
    public ISupportErrorInfo,
    public IMath
{
...
BEGIN_COM_MAP(CMath)
    COM_INTERFACE_ENTRY(IMath)
    COM_INTERFACE_ENTRY(ISupportErrorInfo)
END_COM_MAP()

public:
// ISupportsErrorInfo
    STDMETHOD(InterfaceSupportsErrorInfo)(REFIID riid);

// IMath
    STDMETHOD(Add)( long, long, long* );
    ...
};

// Math.cpp
...
STDMETHODIMP CMath::InterfaceSupportsErrorInfo(REFIID riid)
{
    static const IID* arr[] =
    {
        &IID_IMath
```

```
};
for (int i=0;i<sizeof(arr)/sizeof(arr[0]);i++)
{
   if (InlineIsEqualGUID(*arr[i],riid))
      return S_OK;
}
return S_FALSE;
}
```

As you can see, it adds the new interface to your inheritance chain, adds your interface map, and then adds the declaration and definition for the Interface SupportsErrorInfo method. The method itself searches through a static table to determine whether the specified IID supports rich error handling. For the math component, you add error handling to the IMath interface. Specifically, you ensure that the client doesn't try to divide by zero.

CComCoClass::Error

Because ATL is mostly about creating components, it provides methods that encapsulate the creation of error information within components. Meanwhile, it doesn't do anything for the client side. The CComCoClass::Error method is overloaded to take every parameter specified via ICreateErrorInfo. Here are a few of the overloaded Error methods:

```
static HRESULT WINAPI Error( LPCOLESTR lpszDesc,
   const IID& iid = GUID_NULL, HRESULT hRes = 0 )
{
   return AtlReportError( GetObjectCLSID(), lpszDesc, iid, hRes );
}
static HRESULT WINAPI Error( LPCOLESTR lpszDesc, DWORD dwHelpID,
   LPCOLESTR lpszHelpFile, const IID& iid = GUID_NULL, HRESULT hRes
= 0)
{
   return AtlReportError( GetObjectCLSID(), lpszDesc, dwHelpID,
                         lpszHelpFile,iid, hRes );
}
static HRESULT WINAPI Error( UINT nID, const IID& iid = GUID_NULL,
   HRESULT hRes = 0, HINSTANCE hInst = _Module.GetResourceInstance())
{
   return AtlReportError(GetObjectCLSID(), nID, iid, hRes, hInst);
}
static HRESULT WINAPI Error( UINT nID, DWORD dwHelpID,
   LPCOLESTR lpszHelpFile, const IID& iid = GUID_NULL,
   HRESULT hRes = 0, HINSTANCE hInst = _Module.GetResourceInstance())
{
```

```
        return AtlReportError( GetObjectCLSID(), nID, dwHelpID,
                               lpszHelpFile, iid, hRes, hInst );
}
```

Each method ultimately calls an overloaded `AtlReportError`. Take a look at `ATLIMPL.CPP`. You can see that this method in turn calls `AtlSetErrorInfo`, which basically reflects the earlier server-side implementation. Following is an example of using `CComCoClass::Error`.

```
STDMETHODIMP CMath::Divide( long lOp1, long lOp2, long* pResult )
{
    // Handle divide-by-zero error
    if ( lOp2 == 0 )
    {
        return Error( "Divide by zero attempted." );
    }
    *pResult = lOp1 / lOp2;
    return S_OK;
}
```

ISupportErrorInfoImpl

ATL also provides an implementation class for adding `ISupportErrorInfo` functionality. However, it is limited in that it enables you to support error handling for only one interface. You specify the IID of the interface as a template parameter.

Creating the Math Component in an EXE Housing

What follows is a step-by-step process of creating the math component using ATL's wizards. The example that I develop is called `Chapter4_Server`. What follows, though, mostly describes how you modify the math component to reside within an executable housing instead of a DLL. You also add rich error handling and implement an `IMath2` interface as well as a new `IComponentInfo` interface.

Step 1: Create the Visual C++ Project

Start Visual C++ and create a new project, selecting ATL COM AppWizard. Give it the name `Chapter4_Server`. In Step 1 of 1, select Executable (EXE). Click Finish to generate the project.

Step 2: Use the ATL Object Wizard

Next, using the ATL Object wizard, insert an object of type `Simple Object`. After clicking the Next button, populate the Names dialog box as follows:

◆ `Short Name:Math.` Take the defaults provided for `Class`, `.H file`, and `.CPPfile`.

◆ `CoClass:Math`

◆ `Interface:IMath`

◆ `Type:Math Class`

◆ `ProgID:Chapter4.Math`

Move to the Attributes dialog box and populate it with the following:

◆ `Threading Model:Apartment`

◆ `Interface:Custom`

◆ `Aggregation:Yes`

◆ `Support ISupportErrorInfo:Yes`

◆ `Support Connection Points:No`

◆ `Free Threaded Marshaler:No`

Step 3: Add the IMath and IAdvancedMath

At this point, you should follow the steps in Chapter 3 that describe how to implement the `IMath` and `IAdvancedMath` interfaces. I've covered this process already, so I do not discuss it here. Instead, I focus on adding support for rich error handling and implementing two additional interfaces in your math component.

Step 4: Handle the Divide-By-Zero Problem

Because you checked the `Support ISupportErrorInfo` option when creating this project, ATL adds the support for `ISupportErrorInfo`. To throw back an error in your `Divide` method, you need only use the `CComCoClass::Error` method. (I described this in detail earlier in this chapter):

```
STDMETHODIMP CMath::Divide( long lOp1, long lOp2, long* pResult )
{
   // Handle divide-by-zero error
   if ( lOp2 == 0 )
   {
      return Error( "Divide by zero attempted." );
```

```
    }
    *pResult = 10p1 / 10p2;
    return S_OK;
}
```

Step 5: Add the IMath2 Interface

To demonstrate the required process to "version" an interface within a component, add three new methods to the IMath interface. Remember, though, that COM interfaces should not change once you deploy them. Follow this rule by adding a new interface, IMath2, to your component. Existing clients can continue to use IMath, but new clients can opt to use the feature-rich IMath2 interface instead. The following code updates the IDL, MATH.H, and MATH.CPP files:

```
// Chapter4_Server.idl
...
typedef
[
    uuid(984D09A4-3379-11d1-883A-444553540000),
    helpstring("Operation Type"),
]
enum mathOPERATION
{
    [helpstring("Add")]        mathAdd      = 0x0001,
    [helpstring("Subtract")]   mathSubtract = 0x0002,
    [helpstring("Multiply")]   mathMultiply = 0x0003,
    [helpstring("Divide")]     mathDivide   = 0x0004
} mathOPERATION;


[
    uuid(984D09A2-3379-11d1-883A-444553540000),
    helpstring("IMath2 Interface"),
    pointer_default(unique)
]
interface IMath2 : IUnknown
    {
        [helpstring("method Add")]
          HRESULT Add([in] long 10p1,[in] long 10p2,
                      [out,retval] long* plResult);
        [helpstring("method Subtract")]
          HRESULT Subtract([in] long 10p1,[in] long 10p2,
                           [out,retval] long* plResult);
        [helpstring("method Multiply")]
          HRESULT Multiply([in] long 10p1,[in] long 10p2,
                           [out,retval] long* plResult);
```

```
       [helpstring("method Divide")]
         HRESULT Divide([in] long lOp1,[in] long lOp2,
                     [out,retval] long* plResult);
       [helpstring("method Sum" )]
         HRESULT Sum( [in] short sArraySize,
                     [in, size_is( sArraySize )] short sArray[],
                     [out, retval] long* lResult );
       [helpstring("method Compute")]
                   HRESULT Compute( [in] mathOPERATION enumOp,
                     [in] long lOp1,
                     [in] long lOp2,
                     [out,retval] long* plResult);
       [propget, helpstring("property AdvancedMath")]
         HRESULT AdvancedMath([out, retval] IAdvancedMath **ppVal);
     };

coclass Math
{
   [default] interface IMath;
   interface IAdvancedMath;
   interface IMath2;
};

// Math.h
...
class ATL_NO_VTABLE CMath :
   ...
   public ISupportErrorInfo,
   public IMath,
   public IAdvancedMath,
   public IMath2
{
...
BEGIN_COM_MAP(CMath)
   COM_INTERFACE_ENTRY(IMath)
   COM_INTERFACE_ENTRY(IAdvancedMath)
   COM_INTERFACE_ENTRY(IMath2)
   COM_INTERFACE_ENTRY(ISupportErrorInfo)
END_COM_MAP()
...
// IMath2
public:
   STDMETHOD(Sum)( short sArraySize,
                   short sArray[],
                   long* plResult );
   STDMETHOD(Compute)( mathOPERATION enumOp,
```

```
                               long l0p1,
                               long l0p2,
                               long* plResult );
      STDMETHOD(get_AdvancedMath)(IAdvancedMath** ppVal);
...
};

// From Math.cpp

...
// New IMath2 methods
STDMETHODIMP CMath::Sum( short sArraySize,
                 short sArray[],
                 long* plResult )
{
   *plResult = 0;
   while( sArraySize )
   {
      *plResult += sArray[--sArraySize];
   }
   return S_OK;
}


STDMETHODIMP CMath::Compute( mathOPERATION enumOp,
                             long l0p1,
                             long l0p2,
                             long * plResult)
{
   switch( enumOp )
   {
   case mathAdd:
      return Add( l0p1, l0p2, plResult );
   case mathSubtract:
      return Subtract( l0p1, l0p2, plResult );
   case mathMultiply:
      return Multiply(  l0p1, l0p2, plResult );
   case mathDivide:
      return Divide( l0p1, l0p2, plResult );
   }
   return S_OK;
}

STDMETHODIMP CMath::get_AdvancedMath(IAdvancedMath** ppVal)
{
   GetUnknown()->QueryInterface( IID_IAdvancedMath, (void**) ppVal);
   return S_OK;
}
```

Step 6: Add the IComponentInfo Interface

To demonstrate marshaling structures from component to client, you add another interface to the example. The math component implements IComponentInfo so that it can pass back details concerning its author, name, and version number. Here are the major details from the IDL and .CPP files; you can fill in the rest:

```
// From Chapter4_Server.idl
...
typedef struct COMPONENT_INFO
{
   [string] char*  pstrAuthor;
   short   sMajor;
   short   sMinor;
   BSTR    bstrName;
} COMPONENT_INFO;
[
   uuid(1E405AA0-3396-11d1-883A-444553540000),
   helpstring("IComponentInfo Interface"),
   pointer_default(unique)
]
interface IComponentInfo : IUnknown
{
   [helpstring("method get_Info")]
      HRESULT get_Info( [out] COMPONENT_INFO** pInfo );
   [helpstring("method get_Name")]
      HRESULT get_Name( [out] BSTR* bstrName );
};


// From Math.cpp
...
STDMETHODIMP CMath::get_Info( COMPONENT_INFO** ppInfo )
{
   *ppInfo = (COMPONENT_INFO *)
           CoTaskMemAlloc( sizeof( COMPONENT_INFO ));
   ZeroMemory( *ppInfo, sizeof( COMPONENT_INFO ));

   // Make these globals or defines
   (*ppInfo)->sMajor = 1;
   (*ppInfo)->sMinor = 0;
   char szBuffer[128];
   if ( LoadString( _Module.GetResourceInstance(),
              IDS_AUTHOR,
              szBuffer,
              sizeof( szBuffer ) ))
   {
```

```
            (*ppInfo)->pstrAuthor = (unsigned char*)
                    CoTaskMemAlloc( lstrlen( szBuffer ) + 1 );
        memcpy( (*ppInfo)->pstrAuthor,
                szBuffer,
                lstrlen( szBuffer ) + 1 );
    }
    if ( LoadString( _Module.GetResourceInstance(),
                IDS_NAME,
                szBuffer,
                sizeof( szBuffer ) ))
    {
        USES_CONVERSION;
        (*ppInfo)->bstrName = SysAllocString( A2W( szBuffer ));
    }
    return S_OK;
}

STDMETHODIMP CMath::get_Name( BSTR* pbstrName )
{
    char szBuffer[128];
    if ( LoadString( _Module.GetResourceInstance(),
                IDS_NAME,
                szBuffer,
                sizeof( szBuffer ) ))
    {
        USES_CONVERSION;
        *pbstrName = SysAllocString( A2W( szBuffer ));
    }
    return S_OK;
}
```

Step 7: Build the Project

After adding the code described earlier (or downloading the example source from www.WidgetWare.com), build the project. As part of the build process, a custom build step executes the server that adds its entries to the registry.

Step 8: Build and Register the Proxy/Stub DLL

When building an ATL project, the MIDL compiler produces a number of supporting files. You're interested in those files used to build a proxy/stub DLL for your component. Because the example in this chapter is implemented via an EXE housing, you must provide a proxy/stub DLL for both client and component. MIDL generates the code; you compile, link, and register it. Here's all it takes:

```
nmake -f serverps.mk
```

After the make finishes, register the DLL using `REGSVR32.EXE`.

```
REGSVR32 serverps.dll
```

This creates the necessary entries in the registry. Figure 4-6 shows the `IMath` interface and your new proxy/stub DLL. Look under the Interfaces section of `OLEVIEW`.

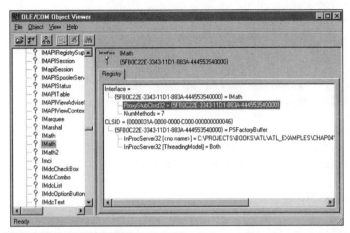

Figure 4-6: Proxy/stub DLL registered

Building the COM Client

This client application is similar to the one you developed in Chapter 3. The primary differences are that you now use `CoCreateInstance` instead of `CoGetClass Object`; implement error handling to catch the divide-by-zero error; and demonstrate the use of enumerators, properties, structures, and memory management. I highlighted the new code and commented it liberally:

```
//
// Chapter4_Client.cpp
//
#include <windows.h>
#include <tchar.h>
#include <iostream.h>

// Include this for Unicode conversion macros
#include <atlbase.h>

// GUIDs, enumerates types, interface declarations, etc.
```

```
// Remember, these files are generated by the MIDL compiler
#include "..\Chapter4_Server\Chapter4_Server_i.c"
#include "..\Chapter4_Server\Chapter4_Server.h"

void HandleError( IUnknown* pUnk, REFIID riid )
{
    HRESULT hr;
    // See if the object supports rich error info
    ISupportErrorInfo* pSEI = 0;
    hr = pUnk->QueryInterface( IID_ISupportErrorInfo,
                               (void**) &pSEI );
    if (SUCCEEDED( hr ))
    {
        hr = pSEI->InterfaceSupportsErrorInfo( riid );
        if ( SUCCEEDED( hr ))
        {
            // Get the error info
            IErrorInfo* pEI;
            if ( SUCCEEDED( GetErrorInfo( 0, &pEI )))
            {
                USES_CONVERSION;
                BSTR bstrDescription = 0;
                BSTR bstrSource = 0;
                pEI->GetDescription( &bstrDescription );
                pEI->GetSource( &bstrSource );
                cout << OLE2T( bstrDescription ) << endl;
                cout << OLE2T( bstrSource ) << endl;
                ::SysFreeString( bstrDescription );
                ::SysFreeString( bstrSource );
                pEI->Release();
            }
        }
        pSEI->Release();
    }
}

int main( int argc, char *argv[] )
{
    cout << "Initializing COM" << endl;
    if ( FAILED( CoInitialize( NULL )))
    {
        cout << "Unable to initialize COM" << endl;
        return -1;
    }
```

```
IMath* pMath;
HRESULT hr;
// This time use CoCreateInstance
hr = CoCreateInstance( CLSID_Math,
                       NULL,
                       CLSCTX_LOCAL_SERVER,
                       IID_IMath,
                       (void**) &pMath );
if ( FAILED( hr ))
{
   cout.setf( ios::hex, ios::basefield );
   cout << "Failed to create server instance. HR = " << hr <<
                                                     endl;
   CoUninitialize();
   return -1;
}
// Access the IMath interface
long lResult;
pMath->Add( 134, 353, &lResult );
cout << "134 + 353 = " << lResult << endl;

// Try to divide by zero
hr = pMath->Divide( 0, 0, &lResult );
if ( FAILED( hr ))
{
   // Use our new HandleError function to
   // display any rich error information
   HandleError( pMath, IID_IMath );
}

// Access IMath2
IMath2* pMath2;
hr = pMath->QueryInterface( IID_IMath2,
                            (void**) &pMath2 );
if ( SUCCEEDED( hr ))
{
   // Here's our new Compute method that
   // uses the mathOPERATOR enumerated type
   pMath2->Compute( mathAdd,
                    100,
                    200,
                    &lResult );
   cout << "100 + 200 = " << lResult << endl;
   // Our example of using arrays in an interface method
   short sArray[3] = { 3,4,5 };
```

```
        pMath2->Sum( 3,
                     sArray,
                     &lResult );
      cout << "3 + 4 + 5 = " << lResult << endl;
}


// Access IAdvancedMath
IAdvancedMath* pAdvancedMath = 0;
hr = pMath->QueryInterface( IID_IAdvancedMath,
                            (void**) &pAdvancedMath );
if ( SUCCEEDED( hr ))
{
   pAdvancedMath->Factorial( 12, &lResult );
   cout << "12! = " << lResult << endl;
   pAdvancedMath->Fibonacci( 12, &lResult );
   cout << "The Fibonacci of 12 = " << lResult << endl;
}


// Access IComponentInfo
IComponentInfo* pCompInfo;
hr = pMath->QueryInterface( IID_IComponentInfo,
                            (void**) &pCompInfo );
if ( SUCCEEDED( hr ))
{
   // Pass in a pointer. The component
   // will allocate and return the structure
   COMPONENT_INFO* pInfo = 0;
   pCompInfo->get_Info( &pInfo );

   // Display the contents of the structure
   cout << "Component author is " << pInfo->pstrAuthor << endl;
   cout << "Component version is " << pInfo->sMajor << "."
        << pInfo->sMinor << endl;

   USES_CONVERSION;
   cout << "Component name is " << OLE2T( pInfo->bstrName )
                                << endl;

   // Free any memory allocated by the component
   if ( pInfo->pstrAuthor )
      CoTaskMemFree( pInfo->pstrAuthor );
   if ( pInfo->bstrName )
      SysFreeString( pInfo->bstrName );
   if ( pInfo )
```

```
        CoTaskMemFree( pInfo );
    }

    // Release all of our interfaces
    if ( pMath )
        pMath->Release();
    if ( pMath2 )
        pMath2->Release();
    if ( pAdvancedMath )
        pAdvancedMath->Release();
    if ( pCompInfo )
        pCompInfo->Release();

    CoUninitialize();

    return 0;
}
```

The examples in this chapter include a project called Chapter4_ATLClient that implements the preceding code using ATL's CComPtr and CComQIPtr classes. The code in the Appendix also implements the preceding code, but it uses the Visual C++ native COM support. See Chapter4_NativeClient for details.

After typing in the preceding code (or downloading it as described in the Introduction), build the client project and run it in debug. It should behave just as it did in the Chapter 3 example. This time, however, the component resides in an executable and all the interface calls are marshaled by the proxy/stub DLL that you developed.

Building a Visual Basic Client

To demonstrate COM's language independence, let's write a simple Visual Basic application that uses the Chapter 4 math component. Start Visual Basic, choose Standard EXE, and follow the steps listed next. (The project also is part of the example download. You can access it in the Chapter4_VBClient directory.)

Step 1: Build the Form

Place three text boxes and eight command buttons on the form in an arrangement like that shown in Figure 4-7.

Be sure to use good Hungarian notation when naming the controls. Give the text boxes the names txtOp1, txtOp2, and txtResult. Name the command buttons in a similar fashion: cmdAdd, cmdSubtract, cmdMultiply, cmdDivide, and so on.

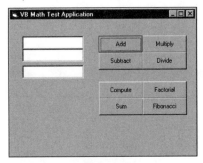

Figure 4–7: Visual Basic form

Step 2: Insert a Reference for the Math Component

From the Project → References menu, locate your math component's entry under Server 1.0 Type Library. Check the entry and add the reference to your Visual Basic project. Figure 4-8 shows the insertion of the component reference.

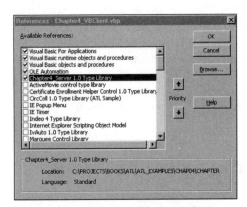

Figure 4–8: Adding the component reference

Visual Basic reads the type library for the math component and sets up a new Visual Basic type that you can use. You can check this out using Visual Basic's Object Browser. Select View → Object Browser or press F2. Figure 4-9 shows your math component in the Object Browser.

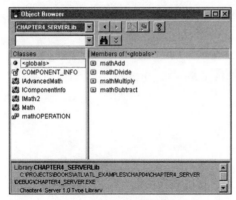

Figure 4-9: Visual Basic's Object Browser

Step 3: Add the Code

You now can use the math component and its IMath, IMath2, and IAdvancedMath interfaces from Visual Basic. Add the following code:

```
' this code goes in the "General" section
' We have to include the library name because
' "Math" is a reserved word in Visual Basic
Dim iMath As New CHAPTER4_SERVERLib.Math
Dim iAdvMath As CHAPTER4_SERVERLib.IAdvancedMath
Dim IMath2 As CHAPTER4_SERVERLib.IMath2

Private Sub cmdAdd_Click()
    txtResult = iMath.Add(txtOp1, txtOp2)
End Sub

Private Sub cmdDivide_Click()
    txtResult = iMath.Divide(txtOp1, txtOp2)
End Sub

Private Sub cmdMultiply_Click()
    txtResult = iMath.Multiply(txtOp1, txtOp2)
End Sub

Private Sub cmdSubtract_Click()
    txtResult = iMath.Subtract(txtOp1, txtOp2)
End Sub
```

Once you get the code working, add code for the cmdFactorial and cmdFibonacci buttons:

```
Private Sub cmdFactorial_Click()
    ' VB's Set command actually does a QueryInterface
    Set iAdvMath = iMath
    txtResult = iAdvMath.Factorial(txtOp1)
End Sub

Private Sub cmdFibonacci_Click()
    Set iAdvMath = iMath
    txtResult = iAdvMath.Fibonacci(txtOp1)
End Sub
```

Pretty cool. The Visual Basic Set keyword performs a QueryInterface. Let's use it again to access the IMath2 interface:

```
Private Sub cmdCompute_Click()
    Set IMath2 = iMath
    ' Here's an example of using our enumerated type
    txtResult = IMath2.Compute(mathAdd, txtOp1, txtOp2)
End Sub
Private Sub cmdSum_Click()
    Set IMath2 = iMath
    Dim sArray(3) As Integer
    sArray(1) = 3
    sArray(2) = 4
    sArray(3) = 5
    txtResult = IMath2.Sum(3, sArray(1))
End Sub
```

The application's behavior should closely resemble that of the C++ client example. When you attempt to divide by zero, the message is passed to the Visual Basic run time and is displayed as part of Visual Basic's exception mechanism. Figure 4-10 shows the error dialog box.

Figure 4-10: Divide by zero in Visual Basic

Summary

In this chapter, you learned the basics of interface design, memory management, and error handling when working with COM and ATL. In particular, you learned:

◆ How COM supports location transparency, which hides the details of cross-process and cross-machine communication.

◆ That there are several different COM interface types and determining which type to use has important implications for your COM-based projects.

◆ The Interface Definition Language (IDL) is an important tool for the COM developer.

◆ COM has built-in support for rich error handling that works across process as well as across machine boundaries.

◆ There are several standard data types used by COM and understanding these types is important during interface design.

In Chapter 5, I describe COM's binary reuse mechanisms – containment and aggregation – in the context of ATL.

Chapter 5

Containment and Aggregation

IN THIS CHAPTER

◆ COM and binary reuse

◆ COM containment and aggregation

◆ Creating aggregate components

◆ ATL's support for containment and aggregation

ONE IMPORTANT FEATURE of COM is its support for software module reuse at a binary level. In this chapter, you take a look at COM's binary reuse techniques: containment and aggregation. After a quick introduction to the two techniques, you examine how ATL provides support for developing components that support and use containment and aggregation.

Binary Reuse

Binary reuse enables a developer to create a software component for use across languages, tools, and platforms by distributing only a binary component (such as a DLL). This approach is a boon for software developers because they can choose the best language and tool to develop and deliver their components without worrying (as much) about which language or tool the user of the component employs.

One important aspect of binary reuse is that it gives COM language independence. (I discuss this in detail in Chapter 4.) Another aspect of binary reuse is that developers can incorporate existing COM components directly within their own component implementations.

For example, say you build a comprehensive text editor component that provides spell checking and a thesaurus. You know that a third party developed a full-featured spell-checking component. You also know that the spell-checking component exposes its functionality via a set of COM interfaces. By using either containment or aggregation, you can expose the spell-checking component's interfaces from within your component as if your component implemented them directly. You must follow licensing requirements for the third-party component, but the potential is there.

Binary reuse isn't always as easy as it sounds. You must overcome several difficulties when implementing binary reuse. COM provides good support for it, but several limitations do exist.

The first limitation is that you don't understand the internal implementation of the third-party component necessarily, and the public methods may have interdependencies that aren't documented (even if you have access to documentation). In other words, a method may change the internal state of a component, so you cannot replace the method directly. Also, if a component exposes a number of interfaces, you can't replace one interface with a new one because the internal state of a component is not exposed.

The second limitation involves the issue of type information. Should a component that exposes another component's functionality describe this functionality as part of its description (that is, in its own type library)? In most cases the answer is yes, but this adds a bit more complexity to your component's implementation.

COM Containment

COM *containment* (also called *delegation*) is nearly identical to the C++ technique of *class composition*. You may not recognize the name for this C++ technique (also called *embedding*), but you probably use it all the time when creating C++ classes. You typically use class composition when the relationship within a set of classes follows the "has a" relationship. (For example, a car "has an" engine.) A C++ implementation looks something like this:

```
class Engine
{
public:
   void Start();
   void Stop();
};

class Car
{
public:
   // Use the embedded Engine implementation
   Go() { m_Engine.Start(); }

   // Expose Engine functionality directly
   Start() { m_Engine.Start(); }

private:
   Engine m_Engine;
};
```

The preceding example is rather abstract, but you get the idea. You contain an instance of the Engine class and use it internally as part of the Car implementation. The example also demonstrates what is required to expose some of the Engine class functionality directly through the Car class. To demonstrate real class composition, let's return to the simple math example:

```
class CSimpleMath
{
public:
    long Add( long lOp1, long lOp2 )
        { return lOp1 + lOp2 };
    long Subtract( long lOp1, long lOp2 )
        { return lOp1 - lOp2 };
    long Multiply( long lOp1, long lOp2 )
        { return lOp1 * lOp2 };
    long Divide( long lOp1, long lOp2 )
        { return lOp1 / lOp2 };
};


class CMath
{
public:
    long Factorial( short sOp ) { ... };
    long Fibonacci( short sOp ) { ... };

private:
    CSimpleMath m_SimpleMath;
}
```

The CSimpleMath class contains the functionality of the earlier IMath interface. When implementing the CMath class, use the functionality of CSimpleMath. To demonstrate containment, you embed an instance of CSimpleMath and reexpose its methods via CMath's public interface. You also can use the instance as part of your Factorial and Fibonacci implementation. It looks something like this:

```
class CMath
{
private:
    long CalcFactorial( short n )
    {
        // Use our embedded class in our implementation
        if ( n > 1 )
            return m_SimpleMath.Multiply( n, calcFactorial( n - 1 ));
        else
            return 1;
```

```
   }

public:
   long Factorial( short sOp )
   {
      CalcFactorial( sOp );
   };
   long Fibonacci( short sOp )
   {
      ...
   };

   // We explicitly expose the SimpleMath methods
   long Add( long lOp1, long lOp2 )
   {
      return m_SimpleMath.Add( lOp1, lOp2 );
   }
   long Subtract( long lOp1, long lOp2 )
   {
      return m_SimpleMath.Subtract( lOp1, lOp2 );
   }
   long Multiply( long lOp1, long lOp2 )
   {
      return m_SimpleMath.Multiply( lOp1, lOp2 );
   }
   long Divide( long lOp1, long lOp2 )
   {
      return m_SimpleMath.Divide( lOp1, lOp2 );
   }

private:
   CSimpleMath m_SimpleMath;
}
```

This example doesn't make much sense as a C++ implementation, but it describes COM containment accurately. Both composition and containment achieve reuse by using the services of a C++ class or COM component internally. The interface of the contained component is exposed only indirectly (if at all) via methods provided by the containing (or outer) component. The outer COM object employs the internal (or inner) COM component's interfaces in the implementation of its interfaces. If it chooses, the outer component can expose the inner component's interfaces.

In COM containment, just as in C++ composition, the outer component completely controls the lifetime of the inner object. An important aspect of containment is that a COM component supports containment by default. It does not have to do anything to support its use as an inner or contained object.

When you use containment with COM, the two (or more) components need not follow the "has a" relationship. Instead, the important aspect is that you gain binary reuse of another component. Another way of looking at it is that the outer component acts as a client of the inner component.

A third party may have developed the component that you "contain". It doesn't matter who implemented the component or in what language the component was implemented because you're reusing it via COM's binary support for component interfaces and uniform instantiation. However, because you are reusing the component through its client interfaces, you do not have any special knowledge of its implementation; sometimes this makes full reuse very difficult to achieve.

To demonstrate containment, the example at the end of this chapter implements the math component; this time it does so in a two-step process with two distinct components. To give you a preview of how containment is implemented, here's the most important step – the creation of the inner component and the implementation of the outer component's IMath interface:

```
// Instantiate the contained component
HRESULT FinalConstruct()
{
    HRESULT hr = CoCreateInstance( CLSID_SimpleMath,
                                   0,
                                   CLSCTX_INPROC_SERVER,
                                   IID_IMath,
                                   (void**) &m_pSimpleMath );
    return hr;
}


// Utilize the inner component's interface in our implementation
STDMETHODIMP CAdvancedMath::Add(long lOp1, long lOp2, long * plResult)
{
    return m_pSimpleMath->Add( lOp1, lOp2, plResult );
}
STDMETHODIMP CAdvancedMath::Subtract(long lOp1, long lOp2,
                                        long * plResult)
{
    return m_pSimpleMath->Subtract( lOp1, lOp2, plResult );
}
STDMETHODIMP CAdvancedMath::Multiply(long lOp1, long lOp2,
                                        long * plResult)
{
    return m_pSimpleMath->Multiply( lOp1, lOp2, plResult );
}
STDMETHODIMP CAdvancedMath::Divide(long lOp1, long lOp2,
                                      long * plResult)
```

```
{
    return m_pSimpleMath->Divide( 1Op1, 1Op2, plResult );
}
```

COM Aggregation

Aggregation is similar to component containment except that the inner component's interfaces are exposed directly. The aggregate object doesn't need or use the functionality of the contained object internally; instead it exposes the inner object's interfaces directly as if they were its own.

The IUnknown interface of the outer object provides access to some or all of the interfaces of the inner component. This little detail makes implementing aggregation a bit more complicated. The management of the lifetimes of the outer and inner objects must be coordinated through the outer component's IUnknown implementation. In other words, if a client calls AddRef through an interface on the inner component, it must increment the outer component's reference count. This is because the outer object manages the lifetime of the aggregate object, so clients of the aggregate never access the IUnknown of the inner component.

Successful lifetime management of the aggregate requires that the inner component provide support for the *controlling unknown*, which is the outer component's IUnknown implementation. When the inner component is created as part of an aggregate, it is passed a pointer to the outer object's IUnknown implementation. The inner component then delegates its IUnknown implementation to that of the outer component. This arrangement provides a consistent approach to the management of the aggregate object's lifetime.

Another requirement dictates that a QueryInterface on any interface of the aggregate must behave exactly the same way. Again, the inner component should delegate any QueryInterface calls to the outer component. The outer component then can determine whether the QI is for an interface it has implemented; if not, the outer component can pass the QI call back to the inner component.

COM components support their containment by default. They don't have to do anything special to handle their containment. However, a component must provide explicit support to act as an inner component in aggregation. To support its aggregation, a component must provide two different implementations of its IUnknown interface: one that behaves conventionally and one that delegates all IUnknown calls to an outer, aggregating component. This second IUnknown implementation is called the *delegating unknown*.

Supporting Aggregation

Developing a component that supports aggregation is easy when you use a COM-capable framework such as MFC and ATL. In fact, with ATL, it's just a checkbox in the Object wizard dialog box so I don't go into detail on implementing an aggregatable object. However, I suggest you review the following rules for developing a component that supports aggregation:

- The component's implementation of the IUnknown interface methods must not delegate to the outer component's IUnknown implementation.

- QueryInterface, AddRef, and Release for all other interfaces must delegate their implementations to that of the outer object. This implementation uses the pUnkOuter parameter passed to the inner component during its creation via CoCreateInstance (and other) functions. The component should store this pointer and use it when delegating.

- The component must not call AddRef through the outer component's IUnknown pointer.

- When the component is created as an aggregate (indicated by the pUnkOuter parameter in IClassFactory::CreateInstance), it must fail if an interface other than IUnknown is requested. The component must return the IUnknown implementation described in the first rule of this bulleted list.

ATL's aggregate implementation follows all of the preceding rules. By adding a simple macro to your component's implementation, you get support for aggregation.

Creating Aggregate Components

Most frameworks make it easy to develop aggregatable components. However, most of them lack support for creating aggregates. ATL, though, provides good support (although not through the wizards), which I cover in a moment. Before I do, I cover the rules for creating aggregate objects. The following rules apply to those components that expose some of their functionality by aggregating another component:

- The outer, aggregating component completely manages the inner component's lifetime. When creating the inner component (usually via CoCreateInstance), you must ask for the inner component's IUnknown explicitly. CoCreateInstance must return an IUnknown pointer.

- The outer component must protect its implementation of IUnknown::Release from reentrancy with an artificial reference count around its destruction code.

- The outer object must call its controlling IUnknown's Release if it queries for a pointer to any of the inner object's interfaces. To free this pointer, the outer object calls its controlling IUnknown's AddRef, followed by Release on the inner object's pointer.

◆ The outer component should not delegate a QueryInterface blindly to the inner component if it does not recognize the interface. However, the outer component can do this if it is part of the design. This distinction marks the difference between selective and blind aggregation.

Selective Aggregation

Microsoft recommends that you use selective aggregation when aggregating; it is a good programming practice. With *selective aggregation*, you expose only those interfaces on the inner component that you want. For example, here's how the outer component's QueryInterface is implemented for selective aggregation:

```
// Demonstrates selective aggregation
HRESULT COuterComponent::QueryInterface( REFIID riid, void** ppv )
{
    // Do we implement the interface?
    if ( IID_IAdvancedMath == riid || IID_IUnknown == riid )
    {
        *ppv = this;
        ...
        return S_OK;
    }
    // Determine if it's one of the interfaces in our aggregate
    //
    else ( IID_IMath == riid )
    {
        // Get it from the inner component
        return pInnerUnk->QueryInterface( riid, ppv );
    }

    // The client asked for an interface we don't support
    return E_NOINTERFACE;
}
```

Blind Aggregation

Blind aggregation is not recommended, but it is up to the implementer to decide whether to use it. *Blind aggregation* means that the outer component blindly passes all QueryInterface calls to the inner component if it does not recognize the requested interface. Here's an example of a blind aggregation QueryInterface:

```
// Demonstrates blind aggregation
HRESULT COuterComponent::QueryInterface( REFIID riid, void** ppv )
{
    // Do we implement the interface?
```

```
    if ( IID_IAdvancedMath == riid || IID_IUnknown == riid )
    {
        *ppv = this;
        ...
        return S_OK;
    }

    // Blindly ask the inner component if it
    // supports the requested interface
    return pInnerUnk->QueryInterface( riid, ppv );
}
```

That finishes our discussion of the basic concepts of containment and aggregation. In the next few sections, I discuss containment and aggregation in the context of ATL. The code demonstrated derives from the chapter examples. First, I show you how to develop a simple math component that implements only the IMath interface. Then, using this as an inner component, I show you how to implement an AdvancedMath component with both containment and aggregation. The AdvancedMath component contains an IMath interface (from the inner component) and an IAdvancedMath interface (from the outer component).

ATL's Support for Containment

As I described earlier, a component doesn't have to do anything special to support its containment by another component. All of those components that you develop using ATL can be contained; you cannot do anything to disable this support. ATL provides additional help when building a component that uses containment to expose the functionality of another component. I cover this concept next.

The first step in containing another component is to create it. ATL provides two methods — FinalConstruct and FinalRelease — as part of the CComObjectRootEx class, which is the perfect place to perform this creation. Because the outer object's functionality depends on the capabilities of the inner component, you must create the inner component as soon as possible. The outer component, however, can't perform this creation in its constructor because constructors don't have return values.

When a client attempts to instantiate a component (such as CoCreateInstance), an HRESULT is returned to indicate the success or failure of the creation. When a component implements containment, some mechanism must be provided to communicate whether a failure occurs during creation of the inner component. ATL provides a hook in the creation process so that a component can indicate success or failure to the client.

FinalConstruct and FinalRelease

The creation of a component in ATL proceeds via a two-step process. When a component is created through ATL's creator class static method, the class is instantiated. After instantiation and before returning to the client, ATL calls the component's FinalConstruct method, thereby giving the implementation a chance to perform any last-second initialization. Here's the code from CComCreator::CreateInstance in Chapter 3:

```
// From ATLCOM.H
template <class T1>
class CComCreator
{
public:
    static HRESULT WINAPI CreateInstance(void* pv,
                                         REFIID riid, LPVOID* ppv)
    {
        _ASSERTE(*ppv == NULL);
        HRESULT hRes = E_OUTOFMEMORY;
        T1* p = NULL;
        p = new T1( pv )
        if (p != NULL)
        {
            ...
            hRes = p->FinalConstruct();
            ...
            if (hRes == S_OK)
                hRes = p->QueryInterface(riid, ppv);
            if (hRes != S_OK)
                delete p;
        }
        return hRes;
    }
};
```

The FinalConstruct method is the perfect place for you to create an inner component. The default implementation, which you can determine by looking at the source for ATL, does nothing, so a simple override works:

```
HRESULT FinalConstruct()
{
    HRESULT hr = CoCreateInstance( CLSID_SimpleMath,
                                   0,
                                   CLSCTX_INPROC_SERVER,
                                   IID_IMath,
```

```
                                   (void**) &m_pSimpleMath );
    return hr;
}
```

If creation of the inner component fails, you can return the error. This also fails the creation of the outer component. The error propagates all the way back to the client application through its call to IClassFactory::CreateInstance (usually via CoCreateInstance).

ATL also provides a FinalRelease method, whereby you can destroy the contained instance. You only need to call this method if the creation succeeds. Here's a basic implementation of FinalRelease:

```
void FinalRelease()
{
    if ( m_pSimpleMath )
        m_pSimpleMath->Release();
}
```

You manage the lifetime of your inner component by maintaining a pointer to its IMath interface. You also need this interface as part of your implementation because containment requires that you reimplement each of the IMath methods by calling through the inner component's IMath. It looks something like this:

```
// Implementation needed with containment
// However, we just pass the call on to the contained component
STDMETHODIMP CAdvancedMath::Add(long l0p1, long l0p2,
                                long * plResult)
{
    return m_pSimpleMath->Add( l0p1, l0p2, plResult );
}


STDMETHODIMP CAdvancedMath::Subtract(long l0p1,
                                     long l0p2, long * plResult)
{
    return m_pSimpleMath->Subtract( l0p1, l0p2, plResult );
}


STDMETHODIMP CAdvancedMath::Multiply(long l0p1,
                                     long l0p2, long * plResult)
{
    return m_pSimpleMath->Multiply( l0p1, l0p2, plResult );
}


STDMETHODIMP CAdvancedMath::Divide(long l0p1,
                                   long l0p2, long * plResult)
```

```
{
    return m_pSimpleMath->Divide( lOp1, lOp2, plResult );
}
```

As you can see, implementing containment using ATL is relatively straightforward.

ATL's Support for Aggregation

ATL supports the creation of components that allow aggregation as well as for building components that aggregate with other components. As described in Chapter 3, a basic ATL component supports acting as an aggregate through the default implementation of CComCoClass. When you use ATL, building a component that aggregates another one resembles building the containment example. There are, however, a few additional details. I cover both aspects of aggregation in the next few sections.

Implementing Aggregatable Components

When initially creating a component using the ATL Object wizard, you are presented with three aggregation options in the Attributes dialog box:

◆ Yes – Support being aggregated. This is the default provided by the CComCoClass implementation.

◆ No – Disallow the component from being aggregated. The wizard adds the DECLARE_NOT_AGGREGATABLE macro to your class declaration.

◆ Only – Allow the component's instantiation only as an aggregate. The DECLARE_ONLY_AGGREGATABLE macro is added to your class declaration.

DECLARE_AGGREGATABLE

The DECLARE_AGGREGATABLE macro is the default when you create an ATL component. CComCoClass adds the macro as part of its implementation:

```
#define DECLARE_AGGREGATABLE(x) public: \
    typedef CComCreator2< CComCreator< CComObject< x > >, \
        CComCreator< CComAggObject< x > > > _CreatorClass;
template <class T, const CLSID* pclsid> class CComCoClass
{
public:
    DECLARE_AGGREGATABLE(T)
...
};
```

The creator class implementation provides a static CreateInstance method for both non-aggregate and aggregate creations. If the pUnkOuter parameter contains a value, the client is attempting aggregation. If it is NULL, then normal, non-aggregate creation is occurring. Again, the creator handles this:

```
template <class T1, class T2>
class CComCreator2
{
public:
    static HRESULT WINAPI CreateInstance(void* pv,
                                         REFIID riid, LPVOID* ppv)
    {
        _ASSERTE(*ppv == NULL);
        HRESULT hRes = E_OUTOFMEMORY;
        if (pv == NULL)
            hRes = T1::CreateInstance(NULL, riid, ppv);
        else
            hRes = T2::CreateInstance(pv, riid, ppv);
        return hRes;
    }
};
```

DECLARE_NOT_AGGREGATABLE

By default, ATL's CComCoClass implementation provides support for aggregation. To disable aggregation in a basic ATL component class, add the DECLARE_NOT_AGGREGATABLE macro to your implementation header file or select No in the Aggregate option of the Attributes tab when you initially create the component:

```
class ATL_NO_VTABLE CMath :
    public CComObjectRootEx<CComSingleThreadModel>,
    public CComCoClass<CSimpleMath, &CLSID_SimpleMath>,
    public IMath,
{
    DECLARE_NOT_AGGREGATABLE( CMath );
...
};
```

The macro works by using ATL's CComFailCreator class.

```
#define DECLARE_NOT_AGGREGATABLE(x) public:\
    typedef CComCreator2< CComCreator< CComObject< x > >, \
    CComFailCreator<CLASS_E_NOAGGREGATION> > _CreatorClass;
```

If the client attempts to aggregate with the component by passing a valid pUnkOuter parameter to CoCreateInstance, ATL's implementation returns the CLASS_E_NOAGGREGATION error. It does so through its CComFailCreator implementation. Here it is:

```
template <HRESULT hr>
class CComFailCreator
{
public:
    static HRESULT WINAPI CreateInstance(void*, REFIID, LPVOID*)
    {
        return hr;
    }
};
```

There's nothing difficult to understand here. The CComFailCreator::CreateInstance implementation just returns the HRESULT provided. No attempt is made to instantiate a component.

DECLARE_ONLY_AGGREGATABLE

This aggregation option implements your component so that it only supports being aggregated. Again, the CComFailCreator class is used – this time when the client does not specify a value for the pUnkOuter parameter:

```
#define DECLARE_ONLY_AGGREGATABLE(x) public:\
    typedef CComCreator2< CComFailCreator<E_FAIL>,
    CComCreator< CComAggObject< x > > > _CreatorClass;
```

DECLARE_POLY_AGGREGATABLE

You can use the DECLARE_POLY_AGGREGATABLE macro for your component instead of the default DECLARE_AGGREGATABLE if you want to save space in your implementation. If you use the POLY macro, ATL employs CComPolyObject for your component's IUnknown implementation. The default implementation uses both a CComObject and a CComAggObject implementation to support the non-aggregating and aggregating cases. By using the POLY macro, you instead use CComPolyObject. This class supports both cases in a single implementation. You may find this approach beneficial if your component has several interfaces in its implementation:

```
#define DECLARE_POLY_AGGREGATABLE(x) public:\
        typedef CComCreator< CComPolyObject< x > > _CreatorClass;
```

Implementing Aggregation

The previous discussion focused on ATL's support for building components that support their own aggregation. This section covers the requirements to implement a component that aggregates another component. Aggregating another component is very similar to containment. First, you must create the inner component in your FinalConstruct method. This time, however, ask explicitly for the inner component's IUnknown interface. This is a requirement for aggregation.

```
HRESULT FinalConstruct()
{
    HRESULT hr = CoCreateInstance( CLSID_SimpleMath,
                        GetControllingUnknown(),
                        CLSCTX_INPROC_SERVER,
                        IID_IUnknown,
                        (void**) &m_pSimpleUnknown );
    return hr;
}
```

After you create the component and obtain its IUnknown implementation, you must decide which interfaces you want to expose directly. With aggregation, you don't have to reimplement any interface methods. Instead you expose them directly using a number of ATL macros. You must choose to expose the inner component's interfaces selectively or blindly.

 Another requirement when you aggregate a component is that the component must be in-process. Aggregation currently is not supported across processes, so don't try it with local or remote servers.

COM_INTERFACE_ENTRY_AGGREGATE

For each interface in the aggregated object that you want to expose, you must add a COM_INTERFACE_ENTRY_AGGREGATE macro (or one of its counterparts) to your component's interface map. In the math example, you expose the IMath interface this way:

```
class ATL_NO_VTABLE CAdvancedMath :
    public CComObjectRootEx<CComSingleThreadModel>,
    public CComCoClass<CAdvancedMath, &CLSID_AdvancedMath>,
    public IAdvancedMath
{
...
BEGIN_COM_MAP(CAdvancedMath)
```

```
    COM_INTERFACE_ENTRY(IAdvancedMath)
    COM_INTERFACE_ENTRY_AGGREGATE( IID_IMath, m_pSimpleUnknown )
END_COM_MAP()
...
};
```

Here you selectively expose the IMath interface. The ATL implementation queries for the specified interface (IID_IMath) by delegating to the IUnknown provided as the second parameter.

COM_INTERFACE_ENTRY_AGGREGATE_BLIND

To blindly expose all interfaces of the aggregated component, you can use ATL's AGGREGATE_BLIND macro. The only parameter required is the IUnknown* pointer for the inner component. If an interface is not found in the outer component's map, the result of a QueryInterface on the inner component's unknown is returned. Remember, though, that I do not recommend blind aggregation unless you really understand the consequences. Here's how you implement blind aggregation for the math component example:

```
class ATL_NO_VTABLE CAdvancedMath :
    public CComObjectRootEx<CComSingleThreadModel>,
    public CComCoClass<CAdvancedMath, &CLSID_AdvancedMath>,
    public IAdvancedMath
{
...
BEGIN_COM_MAP(CAdvancedMath)
    COM_INTERFACE_ENTRY(IAdvancedMath)
    // Blindly expose all interfaces of the inner
    COM_INTERFACE_ENTRY_AGGREGATE_BLIND( m_pSimpleUnknown )
END_COM_MAP()
...
};
```

COM_INTERFACE_ENTRY_AUTOAGGREGATE and COM_INTERFACE_ENTRY_AUTOAGGREGATE_BLIND

The AUTOAGGREGATE macros basically are the same as the previous AGGREGATE macros, except that the named component is instantiated automatically. By using the AUTOAGGREGATE macro, you skip the step of explicitly creating the component in the FinalConstruct method. Using AUTOAGGREGATE, your code looks like this:

```
class ATL_NO_VTABLE CAdvancedMath :
    public CComObjectRootEx<CComSingleThreadModel>,
    public CComCoClass<CAdvancedMath, &CLSID_AdvancedMath>,
```

```
        public IAdvancedMath
{
...
BEGIN_COM_MAP(CAdvancedMath)
    COM_INTERFACE_ENTRY(IAdvancedMath)
    COM_INTERFACE_ENTRY_AUTOAGGREGATE( IID_IMath,
                                       m_pSimpleUnknown,
                                       CLSID_SimpleMath )
END_COM_MAP()
...
};
```

DECLARE_GET_CONTROLLING_UNKNOWN

When you create the inner component of an aggregate, the outer component must pass its IUnknown implementation. ATL provides the DECLARE_GET_ CONTROLLING_UNKNOWN macro for just this purpose.

```
#define DECLARE_GET_CONTROLLING_UNKNOWN() public:\
    virtual IUnknown* GetControllingUnknown() {return
GetUnknown();}
```

You add the macro to your component's header file in order to use the GetControllingUnknown method when calling CoCreateInstance. It looks something like this:

```
DECLARE_GET_CONTROLLING_UNKNOWN()
HRESULT FinalConstruct()
{
    HRESULT hr = CoCreateInstance( CLSID_SimpleMath,
                        GetControllingUnknown(),
                        CLSCTX_INPROC_SERVER,
                        IID_IUnknown,
                        (void**) &m_pSimpleUnknown );
    return hr;
}
```

Creating the Simple Math Component

To demonstrate the two binary reuse mechanisms available in COM, I built the previous math component using two COM components. First, I built a component that implements only the IMath interface. Then I built a component that implements IAdvancedMath and exposes IMath through aggregation. After that, I built the math component using containment to expose the inner component's IMath interface.

Step 1: Create the Simple Math Component that Implements IMath

Start Visual C++ and create a new project, selecting ATL COM AppWizard. Give it the name Chapter5_Simple. In Step 1 of 1, select a type of DLL. Select Finish to generate the project. Using the ATL Object wizard, insert a simple component with the following options:

◆ Use a Short Name of SimpleMath.

◆ Make sure the interface name is IMath.

◆ Change the ProgID to Chapter5.SimpleMath.

◆ On the Attributes tab, select the Custom interface. Use the defaults on the rest of the attributes.

Step 2: Implement the IMath Interface

Use the Add Method option by right-clicking the ClassView tab and adding the methods from your previous IMath interface. Here is the implementation:

```
// SimpleMath.h : Declaration of the CMath

#ifndef __SIMPLEMATH_H_
#define __SIMPLEMATH_H_
#include "resource.h"        // main symbols

/////////////////////////////
// CSimpleMath
/////////////////////////////
class ATL_NO_VTABLE CSimpleMath :
    public CComObjectRootEx<CComSingleThreadModel>,
    public CComCoClass<CSimpleMath, &CLSID_SimpleMath>,
    public IMath,
{
...
// IMath
public:
    STDMETHOD(Add)( long lOp1, long lOp2, long* plResult );
    STDMETHOD(Subtract)( long lOp1, long lOp2, long* plResult );
    STDMETHOD(Multiply)( long lOp1, long lOp2, long* plResult );
    STDMETHOD(Divide)( long lOp1, long lOp2, long* plResult );
};
//
// SimpleMath.cpp : Implementation of CSimpleMath
//
```

```
...
// IMath interface
STDMETHODIMP CSimpleMath::Add( long l0p1, long l0p2,
                                long* plResult )
{
   *plResult = l0p1 + l0p2;
   return S_OK;
}
STDMETHODIMP CSimpleMath::Subtract( long l0p1, long l0p2,
                                     long* plResult )
{
   *plResult = l0p1 - l0p2;
   return S_OK;
}
STDMETHODIMP CSimpleMath::Multiply( long l0p1, long l0p2,
                                     long* plResult )
{
   *plResult = l0p1 * l0p2;
   return S_OK;
}
STDMETHODIMP CSimpleMath::Divide( long l0p1, long l0p2,
                                   long* plResult )
{
   *plResult = l0p1 / l0p2;
   return S_OK;
}
```

Step 3: Build the Project (Simple)

That's it. Now build the project. This simple COM component implements only the IMath interface. Next, you aggregate with this object to create a more advanced math component.

Implementing the Math Component with Aggregation

Start Visual C++ and create a new project, selecting ATL COM AppWizard. Give it the name Chapter5_Aggregate. In Step 1 of 1, select a type of DLL. Select Finish to generate the project. Using the ATL Object wizard, insert a simple component with the following options:

- ◆ Use a Short Name of AdvancedMath.

- ◆ Make sure the interface name is IAdvancedMath.

◆ Change the ProgID to `Chapter5.Aggregate`.

◆ On the Attributes tab, make sure the interface type is `Custom`. You can take the defaults on the rest of the attributes.

◆ Add the `IAdvancedMath` declarations and definitions to the `AdvancedMath` component, as in the previous examples.

Step 1: Implement the IAdvancedMath Interface

The implementation of the `IAdvancedMath` interface is the same as before. You can use your favorite technique to add the declarations to the `.IDL` and `.H` files. Here's the implementation:

```
// IAdvancedMath interface
long calcFactorial( short n )
{
    if ( n > 1 )
        return n * calcFactorial( n - 1 );
    else
        return 1;
}
STDMETHODIMP CAdvancedMath::Factorial( short sOp, long* plResult )
{
    *plResult = calcFactorial( sOp );
    return S_OK;
}
long calcFibonacci( short n )
{
    if ( n <= 1 )
        return 1;
    return calcFibonacci( n - 1 ) + calcFibonacci( n - 2 );
}
STDMETHODIMP CAdvancedMath::Fibonacci( short sOp, long* plResult )
{
    *plResult = calcFibonacci( sOp );
    return S_OK;
}
```

Step 2: Aggregate with the Simple Math Component

All the prior work was familiar ground. Now let's enhance the advanced math component to aggregate with the simple math component. This enables `AdvancedMath` to expose the `IMath` interface directly, along with its own `IAdvancedMath` interface. Take the following steps to implement the aggregation.

Step 3: Include the Definitions for the Aggregate's CLSID and IID

To begin, you need the class ID and interface ID of the aggregate component:

```
//
// AdvancedMath.h : Declaration of the CAdvancedMath
//
...
// Include the CLSID and IID of the inner component
#include "..\Chapter5_Simple_i.c"
/////////////////////////////////////////////////////////////////////
/////////
// CAdvancedMath
class ATL_NO_VTABLE CAdvancedMath :
    public CComObjectRootEx<CComSingleThreadModel>,
...
```

Step 4: Add an IUnknown Pointer to Your Class

An important step in aggregation involves managing the lifetime of the aggregated (or inner) component. The best way to accomplish this is to maintain an interface pointer throughout the lifetime of the aggregating object, so add a member variable to hold the IUnknown* for the aggregate. You also need to maintain this IUnknown interface pointer so that you can delegate QueryInterface calls for the inner interfaces:

```
class ATL_NO_VTABLE CAdvancedMath :
    public CComObjectRootEx<CComSingleThreadModel>,
    public CComCoClass<CAdvancedMath, &CLSID_AdvancedMath>,
    public IAdvancedMath
{
public:
   CAdvancedMath() : m_pSimpleUnknown( 0 )
   {
   }
private:
   IUnknown* m_pSimpleUnknown;
};
```

Step 5: Override FinalConstruct

Now that you have the IUnknown pointer, you need to create an instance of the simple component as soon as the advanced component is created. ATL provides an overridable member called FinalConstruct that provides the perfect place to create

the instance. `FinalConstruct` is called right after a client calls `IClassFactory:`
`:CreateInstance`; it enables you to return an `HRESULT` to indicate any problems.
Here's the code:

```
class ATL_NO_VTABLE CAdvancedMath :
    public CComObjectRootEx<CComSingleThreadModel>,
    public CComCoClass<CAdvancedMath, &CLSID_AdvancedMath>,
    public IAdvancedMath
{
public:
   CAdvancedMath() : m_pSimpleUnknown( 0 )
   {
   }
   DECLARE_GET_CONTROLLING_UNKNOWN()
   HRESULT FinalConstruct()
   {
      HRESULT hr = CoCreateInstance( CLSID_SimpleMath,
                         GetControllingUnknown(),
                         CLSCTX_INPROC_SERVER,
                         IID_IUnknown,
                         (void**) &m_pSimpleUnknown );

      return hr;
   }
```

Step 6: Add the Aggregated Component's Interface to the Interface Map

When a client uses `QueryInterface` to query for either `IMath` or `IAdvancedMath`,
the query occurs through your advanced component's `QI` implementation. You
need to add the aggregate's interface to ATL's interface map. ATL provides a special
macro just for this purpose: `COM_INTERFACE_ENTRY_AGGREGATE`. The macro takes
two parameters:

```
class ATL_NO_VTABLE CAdvancedMath :
    public CComObjectRootEx<CComSingleThreadModel>,
    public CComCoClass<CAdvancedMath, &CLSID_AdvancedMath>,
    public IAdvancedMath
{
...
BEGIN_COM_MAP(CAdvancedMath)
   COM_INTERFACE_ENTRY(IAdvancedMath)
   COM_INTERFACE_ENTRY_AGGREGATE( IID_IMath, m_pSimpleUnknown )
END_COM_MAP()
```

Step 7: Release the Aggregated Component

When your component is destroyed, you also must destroy the aggregated component. The best place to do this in ATL is in the `FinalRelease` call. When you release the inner component's `IUnknown`, its reference count goes to zero.

```
class ATL_NO_VTABLE CAdvancedMath :
    public CComObjectRootEx<CComSingleThreadModel>,
    public CComCoClass<CAdvancedMath, &CLSID_AdvancedMath>,
    public IAdvancedMath
{
...
   void FinalRelease()
   {
      if ( m_pSimpleUnknown )
         m_pSimpleUnknown->Release();
   }
...
}
```

Step 8: Test the Aggregation-Based Component

Now, modify either the Chapter 3 or the Chapter 4 client to test the `AdvancedMath` component. If you need help, the downloadable examples contain a `Chapter5_Client` project that provides everything you need.

Implementing the Advanced Math Component with Containment

Once you implement aggregation, containment is a little easier. The following steps modify your project to use containment instead of aggregation. The important point is that you still create the inner component when your advanced math component is created. However, you do not pass the `IUnknown*` to `CoCreateInstance`. You pass null instead, and ask for the `IMath` interface. Then you maintain this pointer and use it to provide the `IMath` implementation.

Because the outer component exposes `IMath` directly, you must include the declaration for `IMath` and add `IMath` in the `coclass` entry to the IDL file. This example raises the issue of how to manage type information when using containment. Again, you must expose each parameter type and interface description for interfaces that you reuse from the contained component:

```
// Math.h : Declaration of the CAdvancedMath
#include "resource.h"       // main symbols
```

```cpp
// This is needed for containment
// for the declaration of IMath
#include "..\Simple.h"
//////////////////////////////////////////////////////////////////
////
// CAdvancedMath
class ATL_NO_VTABLE CAdvancedMath :
    public CComObjectRootEx<CComSingleThreadModel>,
    public CComCoClass<CAdvancedMath, &CLSID_AdvancedMath>,
    public IAdvancedMath,
    // We have to include this for our implementation
    public IMath
{
public:
    CAdvancedMath() : m_pSimpleMath( 0 )
    {
    }

    // Don't need this anymore
    //DECLARE_GET_CONTROLLING_UNKNOWN()
    HRESULT FinalConstruct()
    {
        HRESULT hr = CoCreateInstance( CLSID_SimpleMath,
                                // GetControllingUnknown(),
                                0,
                                CLSCTX_INPROC_SERVER,
                                IID_IMath,
                                //(void**) &m_pSimpleUnknown );
                                (void**) &m_pSimpleMath );
        return hr;
    }
    void FinalRelease()
    {
        if ( m_pSimpleMath )
            m_pSimpleMath->Release();
    }

    DECLARE_REGISTRY_RESOURCEID(IDR_ADVANCEDMATH)
    BEGIN_COM_MAP(CAdvancedMath)
        COM_INTERFACE_ENTRY(IAdvancedMath)
        // COM_INTERFACE_ENTRY_AGGREGATE( IID_IMath, m_pSimpleUnknown )
        COM_INTERFACE_ENTRY(IMath)
    END_COM_MAP()

private:
    //IUnknown* m_pSimpleUnknown;
```

```
    IMath* m_pSimpleMath;

// IMath - We now must explicitly implement these methods
// If you use ClassView/Add Method.. these will already be here
public:
    STDMETHOD(Divide)(long l0p1, long l0p2, long* plResult);
    STDMETHOD(Multiply)(long l0p1, long l0p2, long* plResult);
    STDMETHOD(Subtract)(long l0p1, long l0p2, long* plResult);
    STDMETHOD(Add)(long l0p1, long l0p2, long* plResult);


// IAdvancedMath
public:
    STDMETHOD(Fibonacci)(short s0p, long* plResult);
    STDMETHOD(Factorial)(short s0p, long* plResult);
};
```

Step 1: Add the Implementation for IMath

This IMath implementation is just a pass-through via the m_pSimpleMath interface pointer. However, as described earlier, you need the declaration for IMath in your IDL file as well as the header file of your implementation. It's easiest to add the methods using ClassView → Add Method.

```
// Implementation needed with containment
// However, we just pass the call on to the contained component
STDMETHODIMP CAdvancedMath::Add(long l0p1, long l0p2,
                                long * plResult)
{
    return m_pSimpleMath->Add( l0p1, l0p2, plResult );
}
STDMETHODIMP CAdvancedMath::Subtract(long l0p1, long l0p2,
                                     long * plResult)
{
    return m_pSimpleMath->Subtract( l0p1, l0p2, plResult );
}
STDMETHODIMP CAdvancedMath::Multiply(long l0p1, long l0p2,
                                     long * plResult)
{
    return m_pSimpleMath->Multiply( l0p1, l0p2, plResult );
}
STDMETHODIMP CAdvancedMath::Divide(long l0p1, long l0p2,
                                   long * plResult)
{
    return m_pSimpleMath->Divide( l0p1, l0p2, plResult );
}
```

Step 2: Test the Containment-Based Component

The client application that you developed earlier to test the aggregation-based component should work just fine — even without a recompile — with your new containment-based `AdvancedMath` component. For a comparison of the two reuse techniques, the examples include two projects: `Chapter5_Aggregate` and `Chapter5_Contain`.

Summary

In this chapter, you learned the basics of COM's reuse mechanisms. In particular, you learned:

♦ COM uses binary reuse techniques that enable language-independent reuse of your components.

♦ The two primary COM techniques are called containment (also delegation) and aggregation.

♦ ATL provides lots of support for using both of these techniques in the components that you build.

In Chapter 6, I cover an important aspect of COM: automation. Automation provides certain dynamic calling techniques that Vtable interfaces do not provide. `IDispatch`, automation's primary interface, gives the implementer and user the ability to perform late binding of component functionality. Additionally, automation is important because it is the only mechanism for exposing functionality in components that must work in Microsoft's scripting environments (such as Internet Explorer).

Chapter 6

Automation

IN THIS CHAPTER

+ Late function binding techniques in COM

+ The IDispatch interface

+ Dual interfaces

+ The BSTR, Variant, and other automation data types

+ ATL's support for building automation -capable components

+ Automation versioning techniques

AUTOMATION IS THE COM-based technology that almost all Windows developers are familiar with — at least from a user's perspective. Visual Basic uses automation extensively; ActiveX controls expose their functionality through automation. It's hard to be a Windows developer today without encountering these forms of automation.

Early in the history of COM and OLE, automation was the preferred technique for building components primarily because it is well supported within MFC. Custom Vtable interfaces (see Chapter 2) aren't supported very well within MFC, especially via its wizards. For example, MFC (version 4.21) still uses the older, automation-specific ODL technique of describing a component. You must use ATL to get built-in support for the more useful IDL.

Automation remains an important technology, but newer tools such as ATL take precedence. Many developers use COM as an architecture with which to build their applications; the most efficient and robust technique for this purpose is to use custom Vtable interfaces and IDL. However, automation is required and useful in many cases (for example, ActiveX controls), so I cover it in this chapter. Also, when developing an ATL-based component, you can use either a custom or a dual interface; the latter depends heavily on automation.

Nearly every Windows development environment supports automation. By building a component that supports automation, you ensure that the component works in every major development tool. For some developers, this requirement is important; for others, it's not important at all. It all depends on your target market (in-house application architectures, shrink-wrap component markets, and so on).

Another important aspect of automation is that it enables you to expose the functionality of a whole application. In other words, the application itself becomes a reusable component. If you need the services of a good word processor in your application, you can purchase a word processor that exposes its capabilities via automation and use it within your application. Microsoft Word, Microsoft Project, and Internet Explorer provide access to nearly all their capabilities through automation and you can use them as components of other applications.

Late Binding

Late binding is what sets automation apart from the other COM technologies that I've discussed. Vtable interfaces require that the client bind to the Vtable structure at compile time; the client needs a header file or some other way of discovering how to build its call stack. Also, because COM interfaces are typed rigidly, parameter type checking is performed at compile time. Vtable interfaces provide certain types of dynamic behavior (such as dynamic instantiation of different implementations of an interface definition), but they still require some compile-time knowledge.

Automation provides true late binding by adding a level of indirection to interface method invocations. The client still binds to a Vtable interface at compile time, but it binds to the standard IDispatch interface. The IDispatch implementation then provides run-time determination and invocation of a component's methods. Automation provides this late-binding mechanism not only within a single language but also across languages.

Late binding isn't the best technique to use when you develop robust applications because type checking isn't performed until run time, and that makes effective testing difficult. However, certain Microsoft tools and technologies (such as Visual Basic for Applications, Internet Explorer's VBScript, and Internet Information Server's Active Server Pages) require late-binding behavior because of their interpreted nature. In these cases, component developers must expose functionality through automation so that they can use the components.

The Dispinterface

Automation is based on COM's IDispatch interface. IDispatch provides a series of methods that enable a client application to access functionality dynamically within an automation-based server. This dynamic invocation differs from the COM custom interface technique used in your custom interface-based math component. When using a custom interface, the client application requires some compile-time knowledge of the component's interface – either through a type library or by including the component's interface declaration at compile time (for example, IMATH.H). This approach implements early binding of the component's interface.

A component that implements its methods using IDispatch instead of a custom interface provides a number of additional capabilities. The interaction between the client and server applications must employ late binding of the component's interface methods. This arrangement makes it easy for a server component to change its interface (even at run time!) without requiring client applications to be recompiled or relinked. If the interface methods are changed, these changes should be communicated to the client application so that it can take advantage of the new features.

Another significant feature you gain by using IDispatch is *universal* (or *type library*) *marshaling*. The default COM implementation provided by Windows contains a number of data types that components implementing the IDispatch interface can use. Intrinsic support for these data types makes it easy to build components that work across local and remote processes without the requirement to build and ship a proxy/stub DLL.

Most COM interfaces resemble the IMath example. They provide a structure that requires a rigid implementation of an abstract class. COM defines the abstract class (interface), but the application developer must provide a unique implementation of that abstract class. IDispatch is a little different because it adds a level of indirection to the Vtable-style interfaces. One term for this new interface type is *dispinterface*, for *dispatch interface*. That term succinctly describes how IDispatch differs from the standard Vtable implementation. The client does not access a component's functionality through the Vtable pointer as you did with IMath; instead, the client first must "look up" the function, provide an internal identifier for the desired function, and finally invoke or "dispatch" the function. Figure 6-1 illustrates this process.

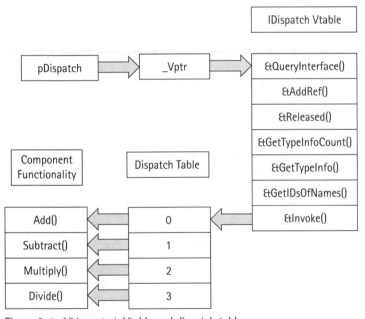

Figure 6-1: IDispatch Vtable and dispatch table

The dispatch table in Figure 6-1 is an abstract construct. In code, it's just a set of integers that uniquely identify each exposed method or property within a component.

As you can see from the illustration, the IDispatch interface is more complicated than the usual Vtable interaction. The client still gets a Vtable pointer, but now the Vtable doesn't have direct access to the `IMath` methods. Instead, the call first must go through `IDispatch::Invoke`, which contains a parameter that maps the method call to a specific entry in the dispatch map. This additional level of indirection provides for late binding to a component's methods. Table 6-1 describes the four methods of the `IDispatch` interface.

TABLE 6-1 IDISPATCH METHODS

Method	Description
Invoke	Invoke provides most of the functionality of the IDispatch interface. It takes eight parameters, the most important of which is the DISPID. The DISPID is mapped to a specific offset within the dispatch table; it determines which component method is invoked.
GetIDsOfNames	GetIDsOfNames provides a facility for the client to map the textual automation server property or method name, such as Add, to its numeric DISPID. Then you can use the DISPID with the Invoke function to access the method in the component.
GetTypeInfo	A client that provides dynamic lookup and calling of automation methods typically does not have all the type information necessary to populate the Invoke DISPPARAMS structure. An automation client can call GetTypeInfoCount to determine whether the component can provide type information through this method.
GetTypeInfoCount	The client uses GetTypeInfoCount to determine whether the component object implements the GetTypeInfo method. Setting the passed-in parameter to 1 indicates that type information is available; zero indicates that no type information is available.

To give you a brief example of how a dispinterface works, let's examine some common Visual Basic code that demonstrates late-binding functionality:

```
Dim objMath as Object
Dim nResult as Integer
Set objMath = CreateObject( "Chapter6.Math" )
nResult = objMath.Add( 100, 55 )
Set objMath = Nothing
```

The `Object` type in Visual Basic holds an `IDispatch` pointer, and the `CreateObject` procedure creates an instance of the component specified by the ProgID. Visual Basic goes through these steps in C++ code to perform the preceding functions:

```
// Create an instance of the math component
// and QI for IDispatch
CLSIDFromProgID( "Chapter6.Math", &clsid );
IDispatch pDispatch = 0;
CoCreateInstance( clsid,
                     ...
                  IID_IDispatch,
                  (void**) &pDispatch );

// Get the DISPID for Add
DISPID dispid;
pDispatch->GetIDsOfNames( "Add", &dispid );

// Build the parameters based on the context of the call
// and then invoke the method
pDispatch->Invoke( dispid, parameters, &result, ... );

// Release the pointer
pDispatch->Release();
```

The most important aspect of late binding is that the client gets the name of a method and the parameters that should be passed from the call itself. The preceding example does not use any compile-time bindings other than that for the standard `IDispatch` interface. Visual Basic gets the `DISPID` for the `Add` method at run time and determines which parameters to pass to the `Invoke` method from the call itself. Suppose you write it this way:

```
Dim objMath as Object
Dim nResult as Integer
Set objMath = CreateObject( "Chapter6.Math" )
nResult = objMath.Add( 100, 55, 77, 99 )
Set objMath = Nothing
```

In this case, you get an "Invalid number of parameters" error at run time instead of at compile time because the `Add` method does not accept four parameters. Dispinterface provides this true late binding of functionality compared with a straight COM Vtable interface.

The Dual Interface

You now have all the pieces you need to understand the concept of a dual interface. *Dual interfaces,* implemented by a server component, provide the client application two different ways to access its functionality. A dual interface combines a custom interface (such as IMath) with the standard IDispatch interface. This arrangement enables the client to choose the interface (and thus the binding technique) it wants to use.

Figure 6-2 depicts your math component with a dual interface. It is a combination of your custom interface (IMath) and the IDispatch that you'll implement using ATL. The math methods are exposed directly through your Vtable and indirectly through IDispatch.

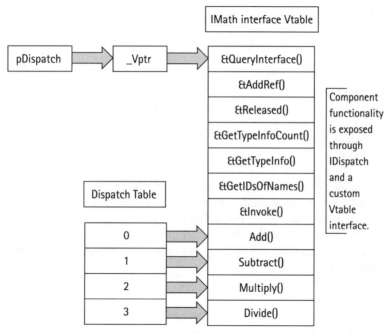

Figure 6-2: Math **class with a dual interface**

Why should you expose two interfaces that provide basically the same functionality? The primary reason is performance. If the server has an in-process (DLL) implementation, it does not require marshaling. The client can bind directly to the custom interface methods and make very efficient calls. The performance of this method identically matches that of direct C or C++ function bindings.

However, if the client requires late-binding functionality, it can use the IDispatch implementation. This technique is slower because more of the work is performed at run time instead of compile time, but in many instances late binding is necessary. You take another look at various client binding techniques later in this chapter.

Automation Data Types

Automation provides standard marshaling of parameters and return values across process and apartment boundaries using the universal marshaler (OLEAUT32.DLL). This approach makes it a bit easier to implement your components within a local or remote server because you don't have to ship a proxy/stub DLL along with your component. To provide universal marshaling for automation, however, COM defines and limits the data types that you can use. I introduced these types in Chapter 4; this chapter covers the major ones in more detail. To begin, Table 6-2 describes each of the automation data types.

TABLE 6-2 AUTOMATION DATA TYPES

Data Type	Description
BSTR	A binary string that stores the length of the string in the first four bytes of the structure and the actual string directly after. The string data is Unicode.
short, long, float, double	Intrinsic types.
Byte	An unsigned character.
BOOL	A Boolean value.
CURRENCY	A currency value stored in an eight-byte integer. Used for fixed-point representation of a number. The integer represents the value multiplied by 10,000.
DATE	A date stored in a double, in which January 1, 1900, is 2.0, January 2 is 3.0, and so on. COM provides functions to help in the manipulation of the date type.
IUnknown*	A pointer to an IUnknown interface.
IDispatch*	A pointer to an IDispatch interface.
SafeArray	An array of one of the preceding data types, including an array of VARIANTs.
VARIANT	A structure containing any one of the preceding types, including a pointer to a SafeArray.

When designing a component that exposes its functionality through a dispinterface or dual interface, you can use only the data types described in Table 6-2. Many of the types are basic, and you probably use them all the time. The VARIANT data type is special, and used frequently in automation, so let's take a look at it.

The VARIANT Data Type

The VARIANT data type provides an effective mechanism to pass around arbitrary automation data because the variant contains both the data type and its value. Also, because a variant can contain any of a number of different data types, it provides a rudimentary overloading mechanism (which I discuss in a moment). In the following condensed version of the VARIANT structure, the comments indicate the symbol used for the VARTYPE value. A value of VT_EMPTY indicates that the variant does not contain a type or value:

```
struct tagVARIANT
{
    VARTYPE vt;
    union
    {
        LONG lVal;          // VT_I4
        SHORT iVal;         // VT_I2
        FLOAT fltVal;       // VT_R4
        DOUBLE dblVal;      // VT_R8
        VARIANT_BOOL boolVal;   // VT_BOOL
        SCODE scode;        // VT_ERROR
        CY cyVal;           // VT_CY
        DATE date;          // VT_DATE
        BSTR bstrVal;       // VT_BSTR
        IUnknown *punkVal;      // VT_UNKNOWN
        IDispatch *pdispVal;    // VT_DISPATCH
        SAFEARRAY *parray;      // VT_ARRAY
        SHORT *piVal;       // VT_I2 | VT_BYREF
        LONG *plVal;        // VT_I4 | VT_BYREF
        FLOAT *pfltVal;     // VT_R4 | VT_BYREF
        DOUBLE *pdblVal;    // VT_R8 | VT_BYREF
        BSTR *pbstrVal;     // VT_BSTR | BT_BYREF
        SAFEARRAY **pparray;    // VT_ARRAY | VT_BYREF
        VARIANT *pvarVal;       // VT_VARIANT | VT_BYREF
    }
};

typedef tagVARIANT VARIANT;
```

A VARIANT is just a big union of different types and an identifier indicating which type value resides within the union. The vt member indicates the data type, and that enables the receiver to extract the data from the appropriate union element. Here's a simple example of initializing a variant to contain a long with a value of 1,045:

```
// Declare and initialize the variant
VARIANT varResult;
VariantInit( &varResult );
// Set the type to long (I4)
varResult.vt = VT_I4;
// Set its value to 1045
varResult.lVal = 1045;
```

You now can pass this variant through a COM interface method; the data is marshaled automatically. There are several COM APIs and macros that make working with variants easier. Table 6-3 shows some of the common variant APIs.

TABLE 6-3 VARIANT-BASED APIS

Function	Purpose
VariantInit	Initializes a variant to VT_EMPTY.
VariantClear	Initializes a variant by first freeing any memory used within the variant. This is useful for client-side applications in which you need to clear a variant passed from a server.
VariantChangeType	Coerces a variant from one type to another. For example, this method changes a long (VT_I4) to a BOOL and an IDispatch pointer to a BSTR.
VariantCopy	Makes a copy of a variant and frees any existing memory in the destination before making the copy.

You can use variants to overload automation methods. In the following example, you rewrite the IMath methods to use variants, giving the client additional flexibility. For example, the client now can pass strings containing the numeric operands instead of passing only longs:

```
STDMETHODIMP CMath::Add(VARIANT varOp1, VARIANT varOp2,
                        VARIANT *pvarResult)
{
    HRESULT hr;
```

```
// Coerce the first variant into the desired type
// In this case we would like a long
hr = VariantChangeType( &varOp1,
                        &varOp1,
                        0,
                        VT_I4 );

// If we can't get a long return invalid argument
if ( FAILED( hr ))
    return( DISP_E_TYPEMISMATCH );

// Coerce the second variant into the desired type
// In this case we would like a long
hr = VariantChangeType( &varOp2,
                        &varOp2,
                        0,
                        VT_I4 );
// If we can't get a long return invalid argument
if ( FAILED( hr ))
    return( DISP_E_TYPEMISMATCH );

// Initialize the return value
// If there isn't one, then just return
if ( pvarResult )
{
    VariantInit( pvarResult );
    pvarResult->vt = VT_I4;
    pvarResult->lVal = varOp1.lVal + varOp2.lVal;
}
return S_OK;
}
```

The Add method takes two variant parameters and returns a variant. By accepting a variant parameter, you enable a client to pass any automation type (for example, a BSTR instead of a long, a short, or a BOOL). You then use COM's variant coercion function, VariantChangeType, to ensure that you have a long before you do your calculations.

If the coercion fails, you return a type mismatch error. However, Variant ChangeType can coerce almost anything. It handles string-to-numeric, numeric-to-string, by-reference to value, value to by-reference, and a few other conversions automatically. In the preceding example, Visual Basic code such as this actually works:

```
Dim result as Long
result = objMath.Add( "123", "345" )
```

This works because `VariantChangeType` can convert the BSTRs to longs. However, this behavior may not reflect what you want. In other words, the component code can behave differently depending on the passed-in data types. If the client passes two strings, instead of coercing them to longs and performing addition, you can create a new string by concatenating the string parameters. Here's an example:

```
// If we have two strings, append them
if ( varOp1.vt == VT_BSTR &&
     varOp2.vt == VT_BSTR )
{
   VariantInit( pvarResult );
   CComBSTR bstr( varOp1.bstrVal );
   bstr.AppendBSTR( varOp2.bstrVal );

   // Return the concatenated string
   pvarResult->vt = VT_BSTR;
   pvarResult->bstrVal = bstr.Copy();
   return S_OK;
}
```

The method provides different functionality based on the parameters; because you also return your result via a variant, you can pass back either a long or a BSTR depending on your overloaded behavior.

The SafeArray Data Type

The `SafeArray` data type and its associated APIs provide a mechanism to move arrays of automation-compatible types between local and remote processes. The `SafeArray` began as a Visual Basic type but is now part of COM because it is an automation type. Here's a look:

```
typedef struct   tagSAFEARRAY
{
   USHORT cDims;
   USHORT fFeatures;
   ULONG cbElements;
   ULONG cLocks;
   PVOID pvData;
   SAFEARRAYBOUND rgsabound[ 1 ];
} SAFEARRAY;

typedef struct   tagSAFEARRAYBOUND
{
   ULONG cElements;
```

```
    LONG lLbound;
} SAFEARRAYBOUND;
```

A safe array can have multiple dimensions; it uses a reference counter to help with cross-process memory management. When working with safe arrays, you shouldn't access the data members directly. Instead, use a series of APIs provided by COM. Table 6-4 describes the basic safe array APIs.

TABLE 6-4 SAFE ARRAY APIS

Function	Purpose
SafeArrayCreate	Creates a safe array
SafeArrayDestroy	Destroys a safe array
SafeArrayGetElement	Gets a specified element from an array
SafeArrayPutElement	Puts an element into the array
SafeArrayGetLBound	Gets the lower bound
SafeArrayGetUBound	Gets the upper bound

The lower- and upper-bound APIs are required because safe arrays do not begin at zero or 1 necessarily. Instead, the developer arbitrarily can supply the bounds. For example, a Visual Basic developer can create an array such as this:

```
Private Sub cmdSum_Click()
    'Build a safe array of longs
    Dim longArray(-4 To 4) As Long
    For i = -4 To 4
        longArray(i) = i
    Next
    txtResult = objMath2.Sum(longArray)
End Sub
```

The corresponding component code looks like this:

```
STDMETHODIMP CMath::Sum(VARIANT varOp1, long * plResult)
{
    // Make sure we have an array of longs
    if (! (varOp1.vt & VT_I4 ))
        return DISP_E_TYPEMISMATCH;
```

```
if (! (varOp1.vt & VT_ARRAY ))
   return DISP_E_TYPEMISMATCH;

// The parameter may be a reference
SAFEARRAY* psa;
if ( varOp1.vt & VT_BYREF )
   psa = *(varOp1.pparray);
else
   psa = varOp1.parray;

// Get the lower and upper bounds
long lLBound, lUBound;
SafeArrayGetLBound( psa,
                    1, &lLBound );
SafeArrayGetUBound( psa,
                    1, &lUBound );

// Sum the elements of the array
long lSum = 0;
for( long i = lLBound; i <= lUBound; i++ )
{
   long lValue;
   SafeArrayGetElement( psa,
                        &i, &lValue );
   lSum += lValue;
}
*plResult = lSum;
return S_OK;
}
```

In the preceding example, you accept the safe array through a variant. Visual Basic likes to work with variants. Next, you check the variant type to make sure that it is an array of longs. You then check to see whether the safe array is passed by reference. If it is, you must extract the pointer from a different member of the union.

Another important point is that you don't access the safe array structure directly. Instead, you use the safe array API functions to get the lower and upper bounds of the array and use these values to iterate over the elements and return the sum.

Passing a safe array in C++ resembles what you do in Visual Basic, but you must use the APIs directly. Here's an example of passing a safe array to the Sum method:

```
// Try calling our Sum method
// We first have to build a safe array
// It's an array of 10 longs with
// the values 0,1,2,3,4...
```

```
SAFEARRAY        *psaArray = 0;
SAFEARRAYBOUND  rgsabound[1];
rgsabound[0].lLbound = 0;
rgsabound[0].cElements = 10;
psaArray = SafeArrayCreate( VT_I4,
                            1, rgsabound );

// Fill the array with values
for( int i = 0; i < 10; i++ )
{
    SafeArrayPutElement( psaArray,
                         (long *) &i, &i );
}
VARIANT varArray;
VariantInit( &varArray );
V_VT( &varArray ) = VT_ARRAY | VT_I4;
V_ARRAY( &varArray) = psaArray;

// Call the method
long lResult;
pMath2->Sum( varArray, &lResult );
```

You fill out the SAFEARRAY and SAFEARRAYBOUND structures and create the array by calling SafeArrayCreate. Next, you pack the array in a variant and pass it to the appropriate method. The V_VT and V_ARRAY macros, defined in OLEAUTO.H, provide a shorthand technique for setting the appropriate fields of the variant. Specifically, the two macros expand to this:

```
// V_VT( &varArray ) = VT_ARRAY | VT_I4;
(&varArray)->vt = VT_ARRAY | VT_I4;
// V_ARRAY( &varArray) = psaArray;
(&varArray)->pArray = psaArray;
```

Implementing a Dispinterface

Before I examine how ATL provides support for building automation components, let's look at how you do it in C++. In this section, I cover the server-side implementation of both a dispinterface and a dual interface, and then I examine how a client can access this functionality.

Implementing IDispatch

A component that exposes its functionality through IDispatch is considered an *automation component*. Microsoft recommends that components expose their functionality through a dual interface, which combines both the standard IDispatch and custom Vtable interfaces into one Vtable. A component that implements only IDispatch provides a dispinterface; that's what I describe here.

IDL provides a special interface type for IDispatch-based interfaces. The dispinterface keyword identifies an interface that implements only the four IDispatch methods. The description of a dispinterface differs from that of a straight Vtable interface because a dispinterface must provide the *dispatch identifier (DISPID)* for each method. For example, here's how you can declare a dispinterface that implements your IMath functionality:

```
[
    uuid( B8721602-4A3D-11d1-883A-444553540000),
    helpstring("DMath dispinterface")
]
dispinterface DMath
{
    properties:
    methods:
        [id(1)] long Add( long lOp1, long lOp2 );
        [id(2)] long Subtract( long lOp1, long lOp2 );
        [id(3)] long Multiply( long lOp1, long lOp2 );
        [id(4)] long Divide( long lOp1, long lOp2 );
}
...
coclass Math
{
    [default] dispinterface DMath;
}
```

Conventionally, you prefix dispinterfaces with a "D" instead of an "I". As you can see, the declaration is very similar to those of the earlier IMath interfaces. Notice, though, that dispinterface methods don't return HRESULTs like Vtable interfaces do. The dispinterface keyword comes from Microsoft's earlier Object Description Language (ODL) implementation, which did not have the retval attribute so return values were handled this way. Alternatively, you can describe the same preceding interface using IDL:

```
[
    object,
    uuid(D6F16BC1-4B83-11d1-883A-444553540000),
    helpstring("IMath Dispinterface")
]
interface IMath : IDispatch
{
    [id(1)] HRESULT Add( [in] long lOp1,
```

```
                              [in] long lOp2,
                              [out,retval] long* plResult );
     [id(2)] HRESULT Subtract( [in] long lOp1,
                               [in] long lOp2,
                               [out,retval] long* plResult);
     [id(3)] HRESULT Multiply( [in] long lOp1,
                               [in] long lOp2,
                               [out,retval] long* plResult );
     [id(4)] HRESULT Divide( [in] long lOp1,
                             [in]long lOp2,
                             [out,retval] long* plResult );
}
...
coclass Math
{
   [default] interface IMath;
}
```

This represents the preferred technique because IDL syntax has replaced ODL and, as described in Chapter 4, IDL provides several additional capabilities. You implement the dispinterface (IDispatch) just as you do any COM Vtable interface. Here's an excerpt from MATH.H in the Chapter6_NativeServer example:

```
class CMath : public IDispatch
{
...
public:
   // IUnknown
   STDMETHOD(QueryInterface)( REFIID, void** );
   STDMETHOD_(ULONG, AddRef());
   STDMETHOD_(ULONG, Release());

   // IDispatch
   STDMETHOD(GetTypeInfoCount)( UINT* pctinfo );
   STDMETHOD(GetTypeInfo)( UINT itinfo,
                           LCID lcid,
                           ITypeInfo** pptinfo );
   STDMETHOD(GetIDsOfNames)( REFIID riid,
                             OLECHAR** rgszNames,
                             UINT cNames,
                             LCID lcid,
                             DISPID* rgdispid );
   STDMETHOD(Invoke)( DISPID dispid,
                      REFIID riid,
                      LCID lcid,
```

```
                              WORD wFlags,
                              DISPPARAMS FAR* pDispParams,
                              VARIANT FAR* pvarResult,
                              EXCEPINFO FAR* pExcepInfo,
                              unsigned int FAR* puArgErr );
};
```

To implement a dispinterface, you typically need to implement only the GetIDsOfNames and Invoke methods. GetTypeInfoCount and GetTypeInfo enable a client to obtain type information. Most clients, though, get type information through a component's binary type library, so there isn't much need to implement these two methods. Getting a component's type information from its type library is more efficient anyway because the client doesn't have to instantiate the component. So, for your native automation implementation, implement GetIDsOfNames and Invoke. Here's a look at GetIDsOfNames for the math component:

```
// Method tokens (DISPIDs)
const DISPID_ADD = 1;
const DISPID_SUBTRACT = 2;
const DISPID_MULTIPLY = 3;
const DISPID_DIVIDE = 4;
...
STDMETHODIMP CMath::GetIDsOfNames( REFIID riid,
                           OLECHAR** rgszNames, UINT cNames,
                           LCID lcid, DISPID* rgdispid )
{
   // We only support one name at a time
   if ( cNames > 1 )
      return( E_INVALIDARG );

   // Convert the name to ANSI
   USES_CONVERSION;
   char* szAnsi = OLE2T( rgszNames[0] );
   if ( strncmp( "Add", szAnsi, 3 ) == 0 )
      rgdispid[0] = DISPID_ADD;
   else if ( strncmp( "Subtract", szAnsi, 8 ) == 0 )
      rgdispid[0] = DISPID_SUBTRACT;
   ...
   else
      return( DISPID_UNKNOWN );
   return S_OK;
}
```

With automation, the client application doesn't have any knowledge necessarily of a component's method signatures and DISPIDs at compile time. GetIDsOfNames provides the client with a way to specify a method name at run time and have the component pass back a token identifying the code associated with the method name.

The client calls this function to get the specific DISPID for a method within the math component. Map the member name to its DISPID. The `rgszNames` parameter is an array of member names provided by the client. The array consists of a method or property name in the first element, followed (optionally) by named parameter elements.

All COM method calls use native Unicode, so convert the Unicode string to ANSI. Then do a simple string compare; if you get a match, you return the respective DISPID. If you don't get a match, you return the required `DISPID_UNKNOWN` error. After the client obtains a DISPID, it invokes the associated code by calling `IDispatch::Invoke`, passing the DISPID and any parameters needed for the method. Listing 6-1 shows the implementation.

Listing 6-1: Implementation of the Invoke method

```
STDMETHODIMP Math::Invoke( DISPID dispid,
                           REFIID riid,
                           LCID lcid,
                           WORD wFlags,
                           DISPPARAMS FAR* pDispParams,
                           VARIANT FAR* pvarResult,
                           EXCEPINFO FAR* pExcepInfo,
                           unsigned int FAR* puArgErr )
{
   // All of our methods take two parameters
   if ( !pDispParams ||
        pDispParams->cArgs != 2 )
     return( DISP_E_BADPARAMCOUNT );

   // We don't support named arguments
   if ( pDispParams->cNamedArgs > 0 )
     return( DISP_E_NONAMEDARGS );

   // Break out the parameters and coerce them
   // to the proper type
   HRESULT hr;
   VARIANT varOp1;
   VARIANT varOp2;

   // Coerce the variant into the desired type
   // In this case we would like a long
   VariantInit( &varOp1 );
   hr = VariantChangeType(  &varOp1,
                           &(pDispParams->rgvarg[1]),
                           0,
```

```
                      VT_I4 );

// If we can't get a long, return invalid argument
if ( FAILED( hr ))
   return( DISP_E_TYPEMISMATCH );

// Coerce the variant into the desired type
// In this case we would like a long
VariantInit( &varOp2 );
hr = VariantChangeType( &varOp2,
                  &(pDispParams->rgvarg[0]),
                  0,
                  VT_I4 );
// If we can't get a long, return 'invalid argument' error
if ( FAILED( hr ))
   return( DISP_E_TYPEMISMATCH );

// Initialize the return value
// If there isn't one, then just return
if ( pvarResult )
{
   VariantInit( pvarResult );
   pvarResult->vt = VT_I4;
}
else
   return S_OK;

// Now, perform the appropriate calculation
switch( dispid )
{
   case DISPID_ADD:
      pvarResult->lVal = varOp1.lVal + varOp2.lVal;
      return S_OK;
   case DISPID_SUBTRACT:
      pvarResult->lVal = varOp1.lVal - varOp2.lVal;
      return S_OK;
   case DISPID_MULTIPLY:
      pvarResult->lVal = varOp1.lVal * varOp2.lVal;
      return S_OK;
   case DISPID_DIVIDE:
      pvarResult->lVal = varOp1.lVal / varOp2.lVal;
      return S_OK;
   default:
      return( DISP_E_MEMBERNOTFOUND );
}
}
```

There's quite a bit going on here, but I discussed the use of Variants as parameters earlier in this chapter, so this code should look familiar. The client must fill the DISPPARAMS structure with any method parameters (stored in variants) and must supply the pvarResult parameter if a return value is expected. Check these to ensure that they match your implementation, coerce the variants into longs, and finally perform the math computation. Then, package the result in the provided variant and pass it back to the client.

As you can see, the server-side support code for automation is considerable. This is because you are handling things that the compiler normally manages. The added complexity of breaking out a parameter structure is part of providing the flexibility of run-time binding.

The IDispatch API Functions

To make it easier to implement a dispinterface, Microsoft provides a set of APIs that handle some of the work. These APIs generate an IDispatch interface implementation automatically, based upon the component's type library. The type library contains nearly all the information needed to implement an IDispatch interface. It contains the type information for GetTypeInfoCount and GetTypeInfo, contains the DISPIDs for GetIDsFromNames, and knows the structure of the parameters for each method call. Table 6-5 shows the primary API functions.

TABLE 6-5 DISPATCH API FUNCTIONS

Function	Description
CreateStdDispatch	Creates an IDispatch interface based on the provided type information
CreateDispTypeInfo	Creates type information for use when implementing a simple IDispatch interface
LoadTypeLib	Loads a type library and returns its description through an ITypeInfo interface
DispGetIDsOfNames	Uses type information to convert a set of names into its respective DISPIDs
DispInvoke	Automatically calls a method on an interface based on the type information for that interface

Implementing a Dual Interface

I've covered how to implement Vtable interfaces in most of the previous chapters, and from the preceding discussion you now understand what is required to implement a dispinterface. Implementing a dual interface is a combination of both techniques. A dual interface implements the IDispatch methods as well as any methods provided by your component's custom interface. One key aspect is that the functionality exposed through both techniques must be the same. In other words, you don't want to expose methods through your Vtable that aren't available through your dispinterface. Here's how you describe the IMath interface as a dual interface:

```
[
   object,
   uuid(D6F16BC1-4B83-11d1-883A-444553540000),
   dual,
   helpstring("IMath Dual Interface")
]
interface IMath : IDispatch
{
   [id(1)] HRESULT Add( [in] long lOp1,
                        [in] long lOp2,
                        [out,retval] long* plResult );

   ...
}
```

The only difference here is the addition of the dual keyword. The dual keyword requires the implementation of the described methods as part of the Vtable interface, which differs from the dispinterface case. The preceding declaration requires you to implement both IDispatch and the IMath interface methods. Here's a look at the header file from the Chapter6_DualServer example:

```
class CMath : public IMath
{
public:
   // IUnknown
   STDMETHOD(QueryInterface)( REFIID, void** );
   STDMETHOD_(ULONG, AddRef());
   STDMETHOD_(ULONG, Release());
```

```
// IDispatch
STDMETHOD(GetTypeInfoCount)( UINT* pctinfo );
STDMETHOD(GetTypeInfo)( UINT itinfo,
                        LCID lcid,
                        ITypeInfo** pptinfo );
STDMETHOD(GetIDsOfNames)( REFIID riid,
                          OLECHAR** rgszNames,
                          UINT cNames,
                          LCID lcid,
                          DISPID* rgdispid );
STDMETHOD(Invoke)( DISPID dispid,
                   REFIID riid,
                   LCID lcid,
                   WORD wFlags,
                   DISPPARAMS FAR* pDispParams,
                   VARIANT FAR* pvarResult,
                   EXCEPINFO FAR* pExcepInfo,
                   unsigned int FAR* puArgErr );

// IMath
STDMETHOD(Add)( long, long, long* );
STDMETHOD(Subtract)( long, long, long* );
STDMETHOD(Multiply)( long, long, long* );
STDMETHOD(Divide)( long, long, long* );
};
```

This chapter uses code from three different examples. `Chapter6_NativeServer` demonstrates implementing a dispinterface in straight C++, `Chapter6_DualServer` demonstrates implementing a dual interface in straight C++, and `Chapter6_Server`, which uses ATL, appears at the end of the chapter. Only the `Chapter6_Server` example uses ATL. All of these examples are included in the downloadable package at `www.widgetware.com`.

The implementation of the preceding code reiterates what I've already covered. However, the `CMath` class has only one Vtable with 11 functions. It's a dual interface with both `IDispatch` and `IMath` implementations in the same interface (`IMath`).

The client now has the flexibility of querying for the dispinterface (`IDispatch`) or the Vtable (`IMath`) interface to access your functionality. The implementation of `QueryInterface` is interesting:

```
STDMETHODIMP CMath::QueryInterface( REFIID riid, void** ppv )
{
    *ppv = NULL;
    if ( riid == IID_IUnknown  ||
         riid == IID_IDispatch ||
```

```
        riid == IID_IMath )
      *ppv = this;

  if ( *ppv )
  {
     ((IUnknown*)*ppv)->AddRef();
     return( S_OK );
  }
  return E_NOINTERFACE;
}
```

The one Vtable handles a request for any of your component's three implemented interfaces. This works because they are all lined up in the same Vtable. (This becomes clear when I cover the client side in the next section.) The complete source for this example appears in the `Chapter6_DualServer` project. It demonstrates implementing a dual interface using straight C++.

Accessing an IDispatch–Based Interface

A client of either a dispinterface or a dual interface has several options concerning how it binds to an automation component's functionality. If the component implements only a dispinterface and does not provide a type library, late binding is the only option. If the component implements a dispinterface and provides a type library, a component can choose late binding or something called *ID binding*. If the component implements a dual interface and provides a type library (basically a requirement with a dual), the client can choose between late binding, ID binding, and early binding. Each option has its strengths and weaknesses.

Late Binding (Dynamic Binding)

Late binding is one of the more powerful features of automation. It enables a client application to determine a component's functionality at run time. The method names and parameter types are not checked during the client development process. Instead, the functionality is queried for and called at run time. In other words, the client application queries for the DISPID of the method and then populates the `DISPPARAMS` structure and calls `Invoke` through the `IDispatch` interface. This is the most expensive technique and it provides no compile-time type checking. The server performs all type checking at run time as the method is called. If an incorrect type is passed, a run-time error results.

Because of the run-time aspect of this technique, it also is the slowest technique. However, it is the most flexible. If the server interface changes, the client does not have to be recompiled to take advantage of these changes. The following code demonstrates the use of late binding in Visual Basic:

```
Dim objMath as Object
Dim nResult as Integer
Set objMath = CreateObject( "Chapter6.Math" )
nResult = objMath.Add( 100, 55 )
Set objMath = Nothing
```

I discussed this earlier in the chapter. Following is complete C++ code that performs exactly as the preceding Visual Basic code:

```
IDispatch* pDispatch;
HRESULT hr = CoCreateInstance( CLSID_Math,
                               NULL,
                               CLSCTX_SERVER,
                               IID_IDispatch,
                               (void**) &pDispatch );
if ( FAILED( hr ))
{ ... }


// Get the DISPID
LPOLESTR lpOleStr = L"Add";
DISPID dispid;
hr = pDispatch->GetIDsOfNames( IID_NULL,
                               &lpOleStr,
                               1,
                               LOCALE_SYSTEM_DEFAULT,
                               &dispid );
if (FAILED( hr ))
{ ... }

// Call the Add method after setting up the parameters
DISPPARAMS dispparms;
memset( &dispparms, 0, sizeof( DISPPARAMS ));
dispparms.cArgs = 2;

// allocate memory for parameters
VARIANTARG* pArg = new VARIANTARG[dispparms.cArgs];
dispparms.rgvarg = pArg;
memset(pArg, 0, sizeof(VARIANT) * dispparms.cArgs);

// The parameters are entered right to left
dispparms.rgvarg[0].vt = VT_I4;
dispparms.rgvarg[0].lVal = 55;
```

```
dispparms.rgvarg[1].vt = VT_I4;
dispparms.rgvarg[1].lVal = 100;

// This method returns a value so we need a VARIANT to store it in
VARIANTARG vaResult;
VariantInit( &vaResult );
hr = pDispatch->Invoke( dispid,
                        IID_NULL,
                        LOCALE_SYSTEM_DEFAULT,
                        DISPATCH_METHOD,
                        &dispparms,
                        &vaResult,
                        0, NULL );
pDispatch->Release();
```

That's a lot of code to add two numbers, but there are no header files involved in the preceding implementation except for those that are part of the development environment (such as WINDOWS.H).

To understand all of what's going on, I need to discuss the automation DISPPARAMS structure. DISPPARAMS passes parameters to the method call. Here's its declaration:

```
typedef struct tagDISPPARAMS
{
    // An array of variants containing the arguments
    VARIANTARG *rgvarg;
    // An array of DISPIDs for named arguments
    DISPID  *rgdispidNamedArgs;
    // The number of arguments in the rgvarg array
    UINT cArgs;
    // The number of DISPIDs in the rgdispidNamedArgs array
    UINT cNamedArgs;
} DISPPARAMS;
```

In the preceding code, you first allocate space for two variants; you then set the cArgs count to 2 and fill the variant parameters. An important point is that the array holds the parameters in right-to-left order.

ID Binding (Early Binding)

In the previous example, the client must call IDispatch::GetIDsOfNames before invoking the component's Add method. No type checking is performed because the client has not used the component's type information. A second binding technique, called ID binding, provides increased performance and the benefit of compile-time type checking.

The Visual Basic References option adds a type library to your project. You then can treat the imported type as a native Visual Basic type. As your project is compiled, Visual Basic checks the syntax and parameter types against your component's type information. Also, Visual Basic caches the DISPIDs for each method and property. This removes the run-time requirement to query for each member DISPID. One of the drawbacks of this approach is that a recompile is necessary if the interface to a component changes. This code demonstrates ID binding:

```
Dim objMath as New Chapter6_Server.Math
Dim nResult as Integer
nResult = objMath.Add( 100, 55 )
```

In this case, the component implements only a dispinterface. However, because it provides a type library, Visual Basic can load the DISPIDs and cache them as part of the build process. Visual Basic also can ensure that you provide the correct number and types of parameters when calling the component's methods.

To demonstrate the C++ code that implements ID binding, you need to look at how MFC supports IDispatch. When you use ClassWizard's Add Class. . .→From TypeLib option, it produces a wrapper class for an automation component. This wrapper class provides ID binding because it hard-codes the DISPID in the source. Compile-time type checking is supported because the methods of the wrapper class mirror those described in the type library. Only the Invoke method is needed to access a component's functionality. Here's a peek at an MFC wrapper class method for the math component:

```
//
// IMath wrapper class
//
class IOMath : public COleDispatchDriver
{
public:
    IOMath() {}
    IOMath( IDispatch* pDisp );
public:
    long Add( long l0p1, l0p2 );
    long Subtract( long l0p1, l0p2 );
    long Multiply( long l0p1, l0p2 );
    long Divide( long l0p1, l0p2 );
};
...
long IOMath::Add( long l0p1, l0p2 )
{
    static BYTE parms[] = VTS_I4 VTS_I4;
    long result;
    // The DISPID is hard-coded here in the Invoke method
```

```
    InvokeHelper( 0x1, DISPATCH_METHOD,
                VT_I4, &result, parms,
                10p1, 10p2 );
    return result;
}
```

ATL also provides a wrapper generator called the *Connection Point wizard*. I cover it in detail in Chapter 7.

Early Binding Requirements

Early binding requires that a component provide type information and implement a dual interface. It is the most efficient binding technique and also the least flexible. As always, there is a trade-off. Early binding provides type checking because the client can use the type information to verify parameters and return types at compile time. The important point, though, is that method binding works directly through the Vtable so there are no DISPIDs or calls to GetIDsOfNames or Invoke. The Visual Basic code for early binding is the same as for ID binding:

```
Dim objMath as New Chapter6_Server.Math
Dim nResult as Integer
nResult = objMath.Add( 100, 55 )
```

The difference is that the component supports a dual interface and so Visual Basic queries for IID_IMath instead of IID_IDispatch and uses Vtable calls instead of IDispatch::Invoke. This C++ example demonstrates:

```
// Create an instance of the math component
// and QI for IID_IMath
IMath* pMath;
HRESULT hr = CoCreateInstance( CLSID_ATLMath,
                      NULL,
                      CLSCTX_SERVER,
                      IID_IMath,
                      (void**) &pMath );

// Direct Vtable access to the method
long lResult;
pMath->Multiply( 9, 99, &lResult );
cout << "9 * 99 = " << lResult << endl;
pMath->Relase();
```

This is the standard Vtable code that you have used all along. The trick is that the client can choose whatever type of binding it requires.

ATL's Support for Automation

ATL provides most of its automation support in terms of building components that implement an IDispatch. Built-in support for the client side in ATL is minimal. This follows from the design of ATL as a framework for building efficient components.

When building an ATL project, you have two options on the Attributes tab. You can choose to implement either a custom or a dual interface. As I've described, a dual interface adds IDispatch support to your Vtable implementation. Figure 6-3 shows the Object wizard's Attributes tab.

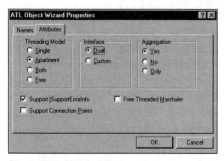

Figure 6-3: The Attributes tab

IDispatchImpl

When you choose the default dual option, your component implementation includes the IDispatchImpl class in its derivation hierarchy. The following code is from the chapter example that implements the math component using ATL's dual interface support:

```
class ATL_NO_VTABLE CMath :
      public CComObjectRootEx<CComSingleThreadModel>,
      public CComCoClass<CMath, &CLSID_Math>,
      public IDispatchImpl<IMath, &IID_IMath,
                     &LIBID_CHAPTER6_SERVERLib>
{
...
};
```

The IDispatchImpl template takes three parameters: the custom interface that describes the Vtable interface of the dual, the interface IID of the custom interface, and the GUID of the component's type library. When the template expands, you get this:

```
class ATL_NO_VTABLE IDispatchImpl : public IMath
{
public:
```

```
...
STDMETHOD(GetTypeInfoCount)(UINT* pctinfo)
{
    *pctinfo = 1;
    return S_OK;
}
STDMETHOD(GetTypeInfo)(UINT itinfo, LCID lcid,
                       ITypeInfo** pptinfo)
{
    return _tih.GetTypeInfo(itinfo, lcid, pptinfo);
}
STDMETHOD(GetIDsOfNames)(REFIID riid,
            LPOLESTR* rgszNames, UINT cNames,
            LCID lcid, DISPID* rgdispid)
{
    return _tih.GetIDsOfNames(riid, rgszNames,
                              cNames, lcid, rgdispid);
}
STDMETHOD(Invoke)(DISPID dispidMember, REFIID riid,
                  LCID lcid, WORD wFlags,
                  DISPPARAMS* pdispparams,
                  VARIANT* pvarResult,
                  EXCEPINFO* pexcepinfo,
                  UINT* puArgErr)
{
    return _tih.Invoke((IDispatch*)this, dispidMember, riid, lcid,
                       wFlags, pdispparams,
                       pvarResult, pexcepinfo, puArgErr);
}
protected:
    static CComTypeInfoHolder _tih;
    static HRESULT GetTI(LCID lcid, ITypeInfo** ppInfo)
    {
        return _tih.GetTI(lcid, ppInfo);
    }
};
```

ATL's IDispatchImpl implementation gets most of its functionality through the contained, static instance of CComTypeInfoHolder _tih. The CComTypeInfoHolder instance wraps the component's type library via the ITypeInfo interface.

CComTypeInfoHolder

ATL uses CComTypeInfoHolder to maintain an interface pointer to the type information for a component. As I mentioned earlier, COM provides APIs to make it easier to implement an IDispatch interface. These APIs, along with the ITypeInfo interface, enable a component to provide a default IDispatch implementation with only a little code. In other words, the component doesn't have to implement the standard IDispatch methods explicitly (such as Invoke).

The ITypeInfo interface provides a number of methods, many of which extract information about an associated component interface. Through the various ITypeInfo methods, you can determine the following:

◆ The set of member functions (methods and properties) implemented by the described interface

◆ Various data type descriptions, including enumerated types used in the interface's methods

◆ The general attributes of the types described – including structures, interfaces, and enumerators

There are two general uses of the ITypeInfo interface. Object browsers and development tools employ the interface to obtain method and property names and method parameters in order to display them or use them as part of the compile process. Also, a component can use the ITypeInfo interface to provide an implementation of IDispatch; this is precisely what ATL does.

The CComTypeInfoHolder maintains an ITypeInfo interface pointer and provides IDispatch support for any associated class. In your case, this is IDispatchImpl. IDispatchImpl delegates all the implementation details of IDispatch to that provided by the system through ITypeInfo. Table 6-6 describes some of the methods of ITypeInfo that CComTypeInfoHolder uses in its implementation.

TABLE 6-6 ITYPEINFO METHODS

Function	Description
GetIDsOfNames	Maps a member function to a specific DISPID. It's easy for ITypeInfo to implement this method because it knows the DISPIDs of the interface.
Invoke	Invokes a method, or accesses a property of an object, which implements the interface described by the type description. This method has one more parameter than IDispatch::Invoke – the actual instance on which to invoke the method.

The operating system primarily provides the implementation of CComTypeInfo Holder through ITypeInfo. Initially, on first access, the GetTI method loads the

type library of the component. Here's a condensed look at the CComTypeInfo
Holder::GetTI method:

```
HRESULT CComTypeInfoHolder::GetTI(LCID lcid, ITypeInfo** ppInfo)
{
    *ppInfo = NULL;
    HRESULT hRes;
    if ( m_pInfo == NULL )
    {
        ITypeLib* pTypeLib;
        hRes = LoadRegTypeLib(*m_plibid, m_wMajor,
                                m_wMinor, lcid, &pTypeLib);
        if (SUCCEEDED(hRes))
        {
            ITypeInfo* pTypeInfo;
            hRes = pTypeLib->GetTypeInfoOfGuid(*m_pguid, &pTypeInfo);
            if (SUCCEEDED(hRes))
                m_pInfo = pTypeInfo;
            pTypeLib->Release();
        }
    }
    *ppInfo = m_pInfo;
}
```

The LoadRegTypeLib function loads a component's type library based on the
TypeLib registry entry. The library is located using the provided GUID. Once the
library is loaded, ATL uses the ITypeLib::GetTypeInfoOfGuid method to retrieve
the ITypeInfo interface for your dual interface (IMath) and then stores it in the
m_pInfo member.

COM finally supplies the actual implementation of the IDispatch methods
through the ITypeInfo interface. Here's an example of the GetIDsOfNames method:

```
HRESULT CComTypeInfoHolder::GetIDsOfNames(REFIID riid,
                                            LPOLESTR* rgszNames,
                                            UINT cNames,
                                            LCID lcid,
                                            DISPID* rgdispid)
{
    ITypeInfo* pInfo;
    HRESULT hRes = GetTI(lcid, &pInfo);
    if (pInfo != NULL)
    {
        hRes = pInfo->GetIDsOfNames(rgszNames, cNames, rgdispid);
        pInfo->Release();
    }
```

```
    return hRes;
}
```

IDispatchImpl defers to CComTypeInfoHolder and CComTypeInfoHolder defers to the system-provided ITypeInfo implementation. ITypeInfo builds the IDispatch implementation based on the information provided in the component's type library.

CComVariant

ATL provides a thin wrapper class for automation's VARIANT structure. CCom Variant has just a handful of methods, most of which map directly to the underlying VARIANT API calls. The Chapter6_Server example uses CComVariant. Here's an excerpt:

```
CComVariant varOne( varOp1 );

// Coerce the variant into the desired type
HRESULT hr = varOne.ChangeType( VT_I4 );
if ( FAILED( hr ))
    return( DISP_E_TYPEMISMATCH );
```

The CComVariant class members map closely to the variant APIs. Table 6-7 describes the major members.

TABLE 6-7 CCOMVARIANT METHODS

Method/ Operator	Description
CComVariant(...)	Overloaded constructors are provided for most automation types.
ChangeType	Implements VariantChangeType.
Clear	Implements VariantClear.
Copy	Implements VariantCopy.
ReadFromStream, WriteToStream	Loads or saves a variant to a stream.
=	The equal operator is overloaded for most automation types.
==	Variant comparison.

The Visual C++ native COM support also provides the _variant_t type. (See the Appendix for details.)

Automation and Interface Versioning

Automation is a useful COM technology that is employed heavily in today's Windows development environments. However, straight dispinterfaces are slow because of the requirements of late binding. Dispinterfaces also require significantly more code within the client because of late binding requirements. Dual interfaces solve these problems by enabling a client to bind either early (to a Vtable) or late (via IDispatch); the only drawback is that the interface methods must use automation types.

Another drawback to automation is that it doesn't support COM's robust versioning necessarily. One of the most useful features of COM is the fact that you easily can add new functionality (for example, IMath2) to a component without breaking any existing clients. Robust versioning is handled through COM's support for multiple interfaces per component instance. Using IDispatch can make it more difficult to support multiple interfaces per component sometimes, at least when you factor in the various development tools (such as Visual C++, Visual Basic, and Visual J++).

The next few sections describe versioning with dispinterfaces and dual interfaces and discuss it in the context of adding an IMath2 interface to your Math component. You did this in Chapter 4, but this time you learn how dispinterfaces and duals affect the implementation.

Versioning IDispatch

If your component exposes only a dispinterface, then versioning is pretty easy to handle. When using a dispinterface, you can "upgrade" an interface by adding new members to the end of your dispatch map. Because each interface method is identified by a DISPID, you can add a new method by using a new DISPID. This technique of versioning does not break any existing client as long as you don't reorder the DISPIDs of the old methods. I've used this technique extensively when building automation servers with MFC.

The better technique for exposing a component's functionality is through a dual interface. By using duals, you get both late and early binding flexibility and, if the tool supports it, you can use the technique of multiple interfaces per component to handle versioning.

As described earlier, Visual Basic's CreateObject keyword creates an instance of a component and returns its IDispatch interface. However, a component can have only *one* default IDispatch; this is the one Visual

Basic uses. Visual Basic likes to view a component as having only one interface: its IDispatch identified by IID_IDispatch. Each dispinterface, though, has its own interface identifier (IID), so the QueryInterface implementation "decides" which dispinterface Visual Basic uses. So with automation components, you must expose the majority of your component's functionality on one dispinterface. That describes one of the most important COM design rules: Keep your interfaces discrete.

Versioning Duals

The addition of new DISPIDs works for a dispinterface, but this technique no longer works when you introduce the concept of a dual. Dual interfaces expose both an IDispatch and a custom interface. By definition, custom interfaces are immutable; in order to add members, you must declare a new interface. So you can't add a new DISPID to the IDispatch because you can't do the same with its associated custom interface.

The solution to this problem is to implement multiple dual interfaces when you need to update an existing dual. For example, here's how you use IDL to declare two dual interfaces in a component:

```
[
    object,
    uuid(DCA4F88E-4952-11D1-883A-444553540000),
    dual, helpstring("IMath Interface"),
    pointer_default(unique)
]
interface IMath : IDispatch
{
    [id(1), helpstring("method Add")]
            HRESULT Add([in] VARIANT varOp1,
                        [in] VARIANT varOp2,
                        [out,retval] VARIANT* pvarResult);
    // The rest of our IMath methods
    ...
};
[
    object,
    uuid(9F21BD41-4E25-11d1-883A-444553540000),
    dual, helpstring("IMath2 Interface"),
    pointer_default(unique)
]
interface IMath2 : IDispatch
{
```

```
    // Our IMath methods here
    ...
    // And our new method (Sum)
    [id(5), helpstring("method Sum")]
        HRESULT Sum([in] VARIANT varOp1,
                    [out, retval] long* plResult);
};
...
library CHAPTER6_SERVERLib
{
    importlib("stdole32.tlb");
    importlib("stdole2.tlb");
    [
        uuid(DCA4F88F-4952-11D1-883A-444553540000),
        helpstring("Math Class")
    ]
        coclass Math
        {
                [default] interface IMath;
                interface IMath2;
        };
};
```

Visual Basic uses the `coclass` name to indicate the default interface within a component. You can add an underscore to your `coclass` name so Visual Basic shows (in its Object Viewer) the default interface name instead, but this requires you to change all your ATL code that uses the `coclass` name when building symbols (for example, `CLSID_Math`). Still, this technique gives Visual Basic a cleaner view of your component's interfaces.

The MIDL compiler generates two interface classes. To employ them within an ATL implementation class, use the `IDispatchImpl` class twice in your derivation:

```
class ATL_NO_VTABLE CMath :
    public CComObjectRootEx<CComSingleThreadModel>,
    public CComCoClass<CMath, &CLSID_Math>,
    public ISupportErrorInfo,
    public IDispatchImpl<IMath, &IID_IMath,
                        &LIBID_CHAPTER6_SERVERLib>,
    public IDispatchImpl<IMath2, &IID_IMath2,
                        &LIBID_CHAPTER6_SERVERLib>
{
                    ...
};
```

You now have two interfaces that implement IDispatch. You must decide which IDispatch should be exposed through QueryInterface because many development tools query explicitly for IID_IDispatch instead of the IID of the dual.

When you develop a component that has just one dual interface (such as IMath), its COM map looks like this:

```
BEGIN_COM_MAP(CMath)
    COM_INTERFACE_ENTRY(IMath)
    COM_INTERFACE_ENTRY(IDispatch)
    COM_INTERFACE_ENTRY(ISupportErrorInfo)
END_COM_MAP()
```

Even though your component has just one dual interface (IMath), expose both IMath and IDispatch through ATL's QueryInterface implementation. Remember that your QueryInterface is special for a dual. It checks for both of the "interfaces" in the dual and returns either IDispatch or IMath through the same Vtable.

ATL uses the COM_MAP macros to specify which dual provides the default interface for any queries for IID_IDispatch. The preceding macros work fine if there is only one dual in a component. With multiple duals, the implementer must decide which interface provides the default IDispatch. ATL uses the COM_INTERFACE_ENTRY2 macro for this:

```
COM_INTERFACE_ENTRY2(IDispatch, IMath)
```

The COM_INTERFACE_ENTRY2 macro disambiguates multiple levels of inheritance. Instead of supplying only the interface that you want to expose, you also must supply the class through which to obtain the interface. For example, you can use the macro this way:

```
BEGIN_COM_MAP(CMath)
    COM_INTERFACE_ENTRY(IMath)
    COM_INTERFACE_ENTRY2(IDispatch, IMath)
    COM_INTERFACE_ENTRY(IAdvancedMath)
    COM_INTERFACE_ENTRY(ISupportErrorInfo)
END_COM_MAP()
```

You specify that ATL should return the IMath interface implementation when a client queries for IID_IDispatch. If you want to make the IAdvancedMath dual the default return from QI(IID_IDispatch) instead, do this:

```
BEGIN_COM_MAP(CMath)
    COM_INTERFACE_ENTRY(IMath)
    COM_INTERFACE_ENTRY(IAdvancedMath)
```

```
COM_INTERFACE_ENTRY2(IDispatch, IAdvancedMath)
COM_INTERFACE_ENTRY(ISupportErrorInfo)
END_COM_MAP()
```

The ENTRY2 macro makes it easy to implement components that have multiple dual interfaces.

Using multiple dual interfaces to solve the versioning problem works in nearly all cases. However, with Visual Basic (version 5.0), you still have one problem. Visual Basic doesn't support the concept of multiple dispinterfaces on one component, at least when using its late binding (for example, CreateObject) features. When using CreateObject, Visual Basic queries for IID_IDispatch and has only one default IDispatch interface on an object. You then must create an instance using its default interface and use the SET keyword to query for the newer interface. Visual Basic works great if you bind early (to any of the component's multiple duals) using its type library.

Implementing the Math Component Using Automation

In this example, I show you how to implement the math component using automation via a dual interface. I also demonstrate how to add an additional dual to support your IAdvancedMath functionality. The example, Chapter6_Server, contains three duals (IMath, IMath2, and IAdvancedMath), but I focus on the implementation of IMath and IAdvancedMath here. I've discussed most of the implementation of IMath2 already; it demonstrates the use of a safe array.

Step 1: Create the Math Component

Start Visual C++ and create a new project, selecting ATL COM AppWizard. Give it the name Chapter6_Server. In Step 1 of 1, select a type of DLL. Then select Finish and OK to generate the project. Using the ATL Object wizard, insert a simple component with the following options:

- Use a Short Name of Math.

- Make sure the interface name is IMath.

- Change the ProgID to Chapter6.Math.

- On the Attributes tab, enable the Support ISupportErrorInfo option and make sure that the Dual interface option is selected (as shown in Figure 6-4).

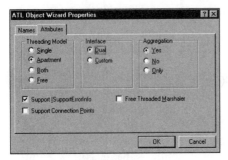

Figure 6-4: Math attributes

Step 2: Implement the IMath Interface

Using the Add Method option by right-clicking the ClassView tab, add the four methods from the previous IMath interface. This time, though, be sure to enter the parameter types as variants. (I employ variants in this example to demonstrate how they are used.) The implementation is as follows:

```
//
// Math.cpp : Implementation of CMath
//

#include "stdafx.h"
#include "Chapter6_Server.h"
#include "Math.h"

/////////////////
// CMath
/////////////////
...
STDMETHODIMP CMath::Add(VARIANT varOp1, VARIANT varOp2,
                        VARIANT *pvarResult)
{
    // Coerce the variant into the desired type
    // In this case we would like a long
    HRESULT hr = VariantChangeType( &varOp1,
                       &varOp1,
                       0,
                       VT_I4 );

    // If we can't get a long, return 'invalid argument' error
    if ( FAILED( hr ))
        return( DISP_E_TYPEMISMATCH );
```

```cpp
   // Coerce the variant into the desired type
   // In this case we would like a long
   hr = VariantChangeType( &varOp2,
                           &varOp2,
                           0,
                           VT_I4 );

   // If we can't get a long, return 'invalid argument' error
   if ( FAILED( hr ))
      return( DISP_E_TYPEMISMATCH );

   // Initialize the return value
   // If there isn't one, then just return
   if ( pvarResult )
   {
      VariantInit( pvarResult );
      pvarResult->vt = VT_I4;
      pvarResult->lVal = varOp1.lVal + varOp2.lVal;
   }
   return S_OK;
}

STDMETHODIMP CMath::Subtract(VARIANT varOp1, VARIANT varOp2,
                             VARIANT * pvarResult)
{
   CComVariant varOne( varOp1 );
   CComVariant varTwo( varOp2 );

   // Coerce the variant into the desired type
   HRESULT hr = varOne.ChangeType( VT_I4 );
   if ( FAILED( hr ))
      return( DISP_E_TYPEMISMATCH );

   // Coerce the variant into the desired type
   // In this case we would like a long
   hr = varTwo.ChangeType( VT_I4 );

   if ( FAILED( hr ))
      return( DISP_E_TYPEMISMATCH );

   // Initialize the return value
   // If there isn't one, then just return
   if ( pvarResult )
   {
      VariantInit( pvarResult );
```

```
        pvarResult->vt = VT_I4;
        pvarResult->lVal = varOne.lVal - varTwo.lVal;
    }
    return S_OK;
}
```

The implementation differs from what you've done before because you're using variant parameters. I show the implementations only for Add and Subtract. Add uses the variant APIs, and Subtract uses ATL's CComVariant class. The implementations of Multiply and Divide are similar.

Step 3: Set the IDL Attributes

Unless you included the method attributes when adding your method parameters in ClassView, you may have incorrect default IDL attributes for your component's methods. If necessary, modify the Chapter6_Server.IDL file to include the appropriate in/out/retval attributes:

```
//
// Chapter6_Server.idl : IDL source for Chapter6_Server.dll
//

...
[id(1), helpstring("method Add")] HRESULT
        Add( [in] VARIANT lOp1, [in] VARIANT lOp2,
             [out, retval] VARIANT* plResult);
[id(2), helpstring("method Subtract")] HRESULT
        Subtract( [in] VARIANT lOp1, [in] VARIANT lOp2,
                  [out, retval] VARIANT* plResult);
[id(3), helpstring("method Multiply")] HRESULT
        Multiply( [in] VARIANT lOp1, [in] VARIANT lOp2,
                  [out, retval] VARIANT* plResult);
[id(4), helpstring("method Divide")] HRESULT
        Divide([in] VARIANT lOp1, [in] VARIANT lOp2,
               [out, retval] VARIANT* plResult);
```

Step 4: Build the Project

That's it. Now build the Chapter6_Server project. You are finished building an ATL-based, automation-compatible version of the math component. As you can see, no additional work is required when implementing a dual with ATL.

Adding a Second IDispatch Interface

But what about the IAdvancedMath interface? Components can expose more than one IDispatch-based interface, but some automation-capable tools (such as Visual Basic) cannot take advantage of this. To demonstrate a component that contains multiple IDispatch-based interfaces, let's add another one to the component. The Visual C++ IDE doesn't have a quick way of adding interfaces to components, so you have to do it yourself. Here's the code for CHAPTER6_SERVER.IDL:

```
// Chapter6_Server.idl : IDL source for Chapter6_Server.dll
//
// The MIDL tool processes this file to
// produce the type library (Chapter6_Server.tlb) and marshaling
code.
import "oaidl.idl";
import "ocidl.idl";
...
[
   object,
   uuid(4B58EB8D-0B21-11D1-883A-444553540000),
   dual,
   helpstring("IAdvancedMath Interface"),
   pointer_default(unique)
]
interface IAdvancedMath : IDispatch
{
   [id(1), helpstring("method Factorial")] HRESULT
           Factorial( [in] short sOp,
                      [out, retval] long* plResult);
   [id(2), helpstring("method Fibonacci")] HRESULT
         Fibonacci( [in] short sOp, [out, retval] long* plResult);
};
...
library CHAPTER6_SERVERLib
{
...
coclass Math
{
   [default] interface IMath;
   interface IAdvancedMath;
};
```

You also must add the declarations and definitions for your methods to `MATH.H` and `MATH.CPP`.

```
// Math.h : Declaration of the CMath
#ifndef __MATH_H_
#define __MATH_H_

#include "resource.h"        // main symbols
...
/////////////////
// CMath
/////////////////
class ATL_NO_VTABLE CMath :
        public CComObjectRootEx<CComSingleThreadModel>,
        public CComCoClass<CMath, &CLSID_Math>,
        public ISupportErrorInfo,
        public IDispatchImpl<IMath, &IID_IMath,
                                    &LIBID_CHAPTER6_SERVERLib>,
        public IDispatchImpl<IAdvancedMath, &IID_IAdvancedMath,
                            &LIBID_CHAPTER6_SERVERLib>
{
...
BEGIN_COM_MAP(CMath)
   COM_INTERFACE_ENTRY(IMath)
   COM_INTERFACE_ENTRY2(IDispatch, IMath)
   COM_INTERFACE_ENTRY(IAdvancedMath)
   COM_INTERFACE_ENTRY(ISupportErrorInfo)
END_COM_MAP()

public:
   STDMETHOD(Factorial)( short sOp, long* plResult);
   STDMETHOD(Fibonacci)( short sOp, long* plResult);
};
```

As described earlier, your class derives from two `IDispatchImpl` classes, so you must use the `COM_INTERFACE_ENTRY2` macro. The interface specified in the second parameter becomes the interface returned when a client queries for `IDispatch`. Finally, here's the implementation of the methods, which should look familiar by now:

```
// IAdvancedMath interface
long calcFactorial( short n )
{
   if ( n > 1 )
      return n * calcFactorial( n - 1 );
   else
```

```
         return 1;
}
STDMETHODIMP CMath::Factorial( short sOp, long* plResult )
{
   *plResult = calcFactorial( sOp );
   return S_OK;
}
long calcFibonacci( short n )
{
   if ( n <= 1 )
      return 1;
   return calcFibonacci( n - 1 ) + calcFibonacci( n - 2 );
}
STDMETHODIMP CMath::Fibonacci( short sOp, long* plResult )
{
   *plResult = calcFibonacci( sOp );
   return S_OK;
}
```

When you're finished, build the project. You now have a math component that implements two dual interfaces.

Implementing a Third Dual Interface

The Chapter6_Server example actually implements three dual interfaces. The third is IMath2, which includes the Sum method to demonstrate how to work with safe arrays. By now, you should be able to add this new interface with the Sum method implementation. Here's a hint:

```
STDMETHODIMP CMath::Sum(VARIANT varOp1, long * plResult)
{
   if (! (varOp1.vt & VT_I4 ))
      return DISP_E_TYPEMISMATCH;

   if (! (varOp1.vt & VT_ARRAY ))
      return DISP_E_TYPEMISMATCH;

   SAFEARRAY* psa;
   if ( varOp1.vt & VT_BYREF )
      psa = *(varOp1.pparray);
   else
      psa = varOp1.parray;

   // Sum the elements of the array
```

```
long lLBound, lUBound;
SafeArrayGetLBound( psa,
                    1, &lLBound );
SafeArrayGetUBound( psa,
                    1, &lUBound );

long lSum = 0;
for( long i = lLBound; i <= lUBound; i++ )
{
    long lValue;
    SafeArrayGetElement( psa,
                         &i, &lValue );
    lSum += lValue;
}

*plResult = lSum;
return S_OK;
}
```

Both of your dual clients access this method to demonstrate client-side work with safe arrays.

Building a C++ Dual Interface Client

Your client application is again a simple Win32 console application. Using AppWizard, create the application and name it Chapter6_Client. Next, create a file called CHAPTER6_CLIENT.CPP and add the code in Listing 6-2.

Listing 6-2: Dual Interface Client code

```
//
// Chapter6_Client.cpp
//

#include <windows.h>
#include <tchar.h>
#include <iostream.h>

#include <initguid.h>
#include "..\Chapter6_Server\Chapter6_Server_i.c"
#include "..\Chapter6_Server\Chapter6_Server.h"

// For ATL's variant support
#include <atlbase.h>
```

```
int main( int argc, char *argv[] )
{
   cout << "Initializing COM" << endl;
   if ( FAILED( CoInitialize( NULL )))
   {
      cout << "Unable to initialize COM" << endl;
      return -1;
   }

   // Create the math component and return IUnknown
   IUnknown* pUnk;
   HRESULT hr = CoCreateInstance( CLSID_Math,
                      NULL,
                      CLSCTX_SERVER,
                      IID_IUnknown,
                      (void**) &pUnk );
   if ( FAILED( hr ))
   {
      cout.setf( ios::hex, ios::basefield );
      cout << "Failed to create server instance. HR = " << hr
                                                  << endl;
      CoUninitialize();
      return -1;
   }

   cout << "Instance created" << endl;

   // Here we demonstrate accessing a
   // dispinterface by first querying for
   // IDispatch (which returns the default)
   // and then using GetIDsOfNames and Invoke
   // to actually call the Add method
   IDispatch* pDispatch;
   hr = pUnk->QueryInterface( IID_IDispatch,
                           (void**) &pDispatch );
   pUnk->Release();
   if ( FAILED( hr ))
   {
      cout.setf( ios::hex, ios::basefield );
      cout << "Failed to create server instance. HR = " << hr
                                                  << endl;
      CoUninitialize();
      return -1;
   }
```

```
// Get the DISPID
LPOLESTR lpOleStr = L"Add";
DISPID dispid;
hr = pDispatch->GetIDsOfNames( IID_NULL,
                      &lpOleStr,
                      1,
                      LOCALE_SYSTEM_DEFAULT,
                      &dispid );
if (FAILED( hr ))
{
    cout.setf( ios::hex, ios::basefield );
    cout << "GetIDsOfNames failed. HR = " << hr << endl;
    CoUninitialize();
    return -1;
}

// Set up the parameters
DISPPARAMS dispparms;
memset( &dispparms, 0, sizeof( DISPPARAMS ));
dispparms.cArgs = 2;

// allocate memory for parameters
VARIANTARG* pArg = new VARIANTARG[dispparms.cArgs];
dispparms.rgvarg = pArg;
memset(pArg, 0, sizeof(VARIANT) * dispparms.cArgs);

// The parameters are entered right to left
// We are adding 123 to 456
dispparms.rgvarg[0].vt = VT_I4;
dispparms.rgvarg[0].lVal = 123;
dispparms.rgvarg[1].vt = VT_I4;
dispparms.rgvarg[1].lVal = 456;

// This method returns a value so we need a VARIANT to store it
VARIANTARG vaResult;
VariantInit( &vaResult );

// Invoke the method in the local server
hr = pDispatch->Invoke( dispid,
                      IID_NULL,
                      LOCALE_SYSTEM_DEFAULT,
                      DISPATCH_METHOD,
                      &dispparms,
```

```
                             &vaResult,
                             0,
                             NULL );

// Free up our variantargs
delete [] pArg;
if ( FAILED( hr ))
{
   cout.setf( ios::hex, ios::basefield );
   cout << "Unable to Invoke SetExpression. HR = " << hr << endl;
   CoUninitialize();
   return -1;
}

// Display the result
cout << "123 + 456 = " << vaResult.lVal << endl;

// Next, we demonstrate using the IMath
// dual interface. First QI then access
// the methods through the Vtable interface
IMath* pMath = 0;
pDispatch->QueryInterface( IID_IMath, (void**) &pMath );
pDispatch->Release();

// We're using variants in this chapter
CComVariant varResult;
CComVariant varOp1( 9 );
CComVariant varOp2( 99 );
pMath->Multiply( varOp1, varOp2, &varResult );
cout << "9 * 99 = " << varResult.lVal << endl;

// Because this is a dual interface we
// can access the IDispatch methods
// from IMath as well
lpOleStr = L"Multiply";
hr = pMath->GetIDsOfNames( IID_NULL,
                           &lpOleStr,
                           1,
                           LOCALE_SYSTEM_DEFAULT,
                           &dispid );
if (FAILED( hr ))
{
   cout.setf( ios::hex, ios::basefield );
   cout << "GetIDsOfNames (IMath) failed. HR = " << hr << endl;
```

```
      CoUninitialize();
      return -1;
   }

   cout << "The DISPID for Multiply is " << dispid << endl;

   // Get the IMath2 dual interface
   IMath2* pMath2;
   hr = pMath->QueryInterface( IID_IMath2,
                               (void**) &pMath2 );
   if ( FAILED( hr ))
   {
      cout.setf( ios::hex, ios::basefield );
      cout << "Unable to QI( IMath2 ). HR = " << hr << endl;
      CoUninitialize();
      return -1;
   }

   // Try calling our Sum method
   // We first have to build a safe array
   // It's an array of 10 longs with
   // the values 0,1,2,3,4...
   SAFEARRAY        *psaArray = 0;
   SAFEARRAYBOUND  rgsabound[1];
   rgsabound[0].lLbound = 0;
   rgsabound[0].cElements = 10;
   psaArray = SafeArrayCreate( VT_I4,
                               1, rgsabound );
   for( int i = 0; i < 10; i++ )
   {
     SafeArrayPutElement( psaArray,
                          (long *) &i, &i );
   }
   VARIANT varArray;
   VariantInit( &varArray );
   V_VT( &varArray ) = VT_ARRAY | VT_I4;
   V_ARRAY( &varArray) = psaArray;

   // Finally
   long lResult;
   pMath2->Sum( varArray, &lResult );
   cout << "The sum of 0,1,2,3...9 is " << lResult << endl;

   // Release the interfaces
```

```
pMath->Release();
pMath2->Release();

cout << "Shutting down COM" << endl;
CoUninitialize();
return 0;
}
```

The comments in the code explain what is going on, and I cover it earlier in the chapter. Basically, you now have more flexibility in accessing your component's functionality. You can choose its dispinterface or straight Vtable implementation.

Creating a Visual Basic Client

I've demonstrated the steps required to build Visual Basic clients. What makes this example a bit different is that you now have two ways of accessing the math component's functionality, just as with the C++ client.

I don't go into the details of building the Visual Basic form, but Figure 6-5 shows what it looks like.

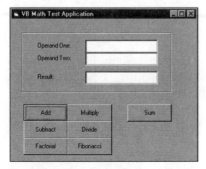

Figure 6-5: Your Visual Basic application

Late Binding

To demonstrate late binding, use the following code:

```
Dim objMath as Object
Sub Form_Load ()
    ' Create the component via its ProgID
    Set objMath = CreateObject("Chapter6.Math.1")
End Sub
```

When you load the form, you create an instance of the math component. In this case, Visual Basic queries for `IID_IDispatch`. Then when you call any of the four `IMath` methods, Visual Basic uses `GetIDsOfNames` and `Invoke`:

```
Private Sub cmdAdd_Click()
    txtResult = objMath.Add(txtOperand1, txtOperand2)
End Sub
Private Sub cmdDivide_Click()
    txtResult = objMath.Divide(txtOperand1, txtOperand2)
End Sub
Private Sub cmdMultiply_Click()
    txtResult = objMath.Multiply(txtOperand1, txtOperand2)
End Sub
Private Sub cmdSubtract_Click()
    txtResult = objMath.Subtract(txtOperand1, txtOperand2)
End Sub
```

How do you access `IAdvancedMath`? You can't access it — at least not through Visual Basic's late-binding support. Visual Basic's `Set` keyword does a `Query Interface`, but to do so it must bind to the interface at compile time. So Visual Basic supports late binding only on the primary dispatch of a component. You can get around this problem, but these ways involve additional work in the server.

Early Binding

Using late binding, as demonstrated in Chapter 4, is easy. Early binding requires you to use the Project→References menu option to import the type library, but it gives you the ability to use any of the three interfaces within the math component:

```
Dim objMath As New CHAPTER6_SERVERLib.Math

' The IMath2 interface is implemented in the Chapter6_Server example
' and is needed for the Sum method below
Dim objMath2 As CHAPTER6_SERVERLib.IMath2
Dim objAdvancedMath As CHAPTER6_SERVERLib.IAdvancedMath

Private Sub cmdAdd_Click()
    txtResult = objMath.Add(txtOp1, txtOp2)
End Sub

Private Sub cmdDivide_Click()
    txtResult = objMath.Divide(txtOp1, txtOp2)
End Sub

Private Sub cmdFactorial_Click()
```

```
    Set objAdvancedMath = objMath
    txtResult = objAdvancedMath.Factorial(txtOp1)
End Sub

Private Sub cmdFibonacci_Click()
    Set objAdvancedMath = objMath
    txtResult = objAdvancedMath.Fibonacci(txtOp1)
End Sub

Private Sub cmdMultiply_Click()
    txtResult = objMath.Multiply(txtOp1, txtOp2)
End Sub

Private Sub cmdSubtract_Click()
    txtResult = objMath.Subtract(txtOp1, txtOp2)
End Sub

Private Sub cmdSum_Click()
    Set objMath2 = objMath

    'Build a safe array of longs
    Dim longArray(-4 To 4) As Long
    For i = -4 To 4
        longArray(i) = i
    Next
    txtResult = objMath2.Sum(longArray)
End Sub
```

Summary

In this chapter, you learned the basics of COM's support for binding late to component functionality. In particular, you learned:

- How COM provides support for late-binding applications such as VBScript.

- That the IDispatch provides this capability.

- That a *dual interface* is a combination of both an IDispatch and custom Vtable interface.

- That there are several automation data types and that they map directly to the data types provided by Visual Basic.

- ATL's support for automation is provided through wizard-generated dual interfaces for your components.

In Chapter 7, I cover COM's techniques for implementing callbacks within components. Callbacks (or events) provide a way for two components to signal each other asynchronously. Asynchronous behavior is central to the development of efficient client/server applications; as you'll see, COM and ATL provide good support.

Chapter 7

Events and Connection Points

IN THE FIRST SIX CHAPTERS, I discuss various COM techniques for implementing and using interfaces. In all these examples, there is a clear delineation between the client (consumer) and the server (producer) of an interface's implementation. Client applications query for a specific interface and then call through that interface to access functionality in the server (a component). An important point is that the interaction between client and server is *synchronous*. The client invokes a method and waits until the call returns.

Today, this behavior is required because COM does not support explicit asynchronous method calls through its interfaces. However, COM provides pseudo-asynchronous behavior through its support for interface callbacks and connection points, also called *connectable objects*. These techniques enable a client application to pass an interface to the server; the server then can call back into the client and notify it of various events. By using this technique, a client becomes a server and a server becomes a client. The entities maintain a peer-to-peer relationship as opposed to the master-slave relationship of synchronous, one-way method calls. The trick is to pass an interface pointer from the client to the component; that's what I cover in this chapter.

With the release of Windows 2000 and COM+, COM now has explicit support for asynchronous method calls. However, if your applications work on Windows 9x and Windows NT 4.0 platforms, you must use the techniques described in this chapter as well as in Chapter 10.

Interface Callbacks

In this first section, I discuss a standard way of implementing component-to-client communication. So far, I have discussed only client-to-component communication through the interfaces implemented by the component. Now I show you how to open the communication channel and provide a richer environment. Follow these general guidelines to provide a component with callback (or notification) capabilities:

◆ The component describes several interfaces, some of which it implements (for example, IMath) and some of which a potential client implements (for example, ICallback).

◆ The client implements one of the interfaces described by the component (for example, ICallback), using its favorite technique.

◆ The component provides a method (for example, IMath::Advise) on one of its incoming interfaces through which the client can pass its implemented interface pointer (ICallback).

◆ The component then provides notifications to the client by calling methods through the interface implemented by the client.

Figure 7-1 illustrates this process.

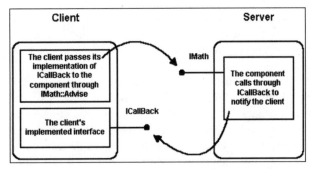

Figure 7-1: The math component with a callback interface

Incoming and Outgoing Interfaces

In the preceding scenario, the term *interface* does not describe what's going on sufficiently. COM uses the terms *incoming interface* and *outgoing interface* to describe the two types of interfaces that a component can support. An incoming interface is an interface implemented by the component. The IMath interface that you're familiar with is an incoming interface because your component implements it. An outgoing interface is described in the component's type library, but it actually is implemented by a client of the math component.

The client application must obtain a description of the component's outgoing interfaces and then implement them using whatever mechanism it chooses; for example, Visual Basic uses the `implements` keyword. After the interface is implemented, a pointer to it must be communicated to the component. The standard technique is to have the component expose an `Advise` method on one of its main incoming interfaces through which the client passes its pointer.

The Advise Method

The `Advise` method is easy to implement. It takes just one parameter: an interface pointer for the outgoing interface. Internally, the component stores this pointer so that it can use it at any time to "call back" the client. Note the IDL and implementation of a simple `Advise` method:

```
interface IMath : IUnknown
{
...
   [helpstring("method Advise")]
      HRESULT Advise([in] ICallBack* pCallBack);
...
};
STDMETHODIMP CMath::Advise(ICallBack * pCallBack)
{
   m_pCallBack = pCallBack;
   m_pCallBack->AddRef();
   return S_OK;
}
```

`Advise` takes the client's interface point and stores it. Later, when you need to notify the client of an event within the component, you call through the stored pointer. It works something like this:

```
STDMETHODIMP CMath::Subtract(long 10p1, long 10p2)
{
   long 1Result = 10p1 - 10p2;
   if ( m_pCallBack )
      m_pCallBack->ComputationComplete( 1Result );
   return S_OK;
}
```

There's only one problem with this implementation. How does the component determine when the callback pointer becomes invalid? In a simple case, the client and component can manage the callback pointer as part of their own lifetimes, so the callback pointer must remain valid until the component is destroyed. However, in more complex and useful cases, you should have a standard way of disconnecting an outgoing interface.

The Unadvise method is the standard way of breaking an interface connection between cooperating entities. Here's a simple implementation of Unadvise:

```
interface IMath : IUnknown
{
...
   [helpstring("method Unadvise")] HRESULT Unadvise();
};
STD METHODIMP CMath::Unadvise()
{
   m_pCallBack->Release();
   m_pCallBack = 0;
   return S_OK;
}
```

More complex implementations (which you see in a moment) add a cookie to both the Advise and Unadvise methods so that multiple connections can be managed at the same time.

Visual Basic's Implements Keyword

Visual Basic (version 5 and above) provides a new keyword that enables a client to implement COM interfaces described in a type library. First, you add the component's type library as a reference to the Visual Basic project. Next, you add a class module to the project and add the implements statement, specifying the interface that you want to implement. You then implement each public member using Visual Basic code. Here's a simple example:

```
// Code from the CallBack.CLS module
Implements CHAPTER7_CALLBACKSERVERLib.ICallBack
Private Sub ICallBack_ComputationComplete(ByVal lResult As Long)
    frmMain.txtResult = lResult
End Sub
```

Once an interface is implemented in a class module, you create an instance of the class and pass it to the component. It looks something like this:

```
Dim objCallBack As New CallBack
Private Sub Form_Load()
    objMath.Advise objCallBack
End Sub
```

Passing the objCallBack instance through the Advise method provides the component with a pointer to the ICallBack interface implemented in the Visual Basic class module.

Visual Basic is a worthy development tool for working with COM interfaces. I focus on ATL in this book, but (in many cases) Visual Basic applications are the target users of the components you build with ATL. The next section provides all the details of building an ATL/Visual Basic callback client and server.

The Callback Example

To demonstrate the callback technique of providing notifications to a client, let's modify the math component to describe a new interface through which it can notify a client when a computation is completed. This new interface, ICallback, is implemented by any client that wants to receive these notifications.

Step 1: Create the Chapter7_Server Project and Math Component

Start Visual C++ and create a new project, selecting ATL COM AppWizard. Give it the name Chapter7_CallbackServer. In Step 1 of 1, select a type of DLL. Then select Finish to generate the project. Using the ATL Object wizard, insert a simple object with the following options:

◆ Use a Short Name of Math.

◆ Make sure the interface name is IMath.

◆ Change the ProgID to Chapter7.CallbackMath.

◆ On the Attributes tab, make sure the Custom interface option is selected.

Step 2: Implement the IMath Interface

Using the Add Method option by right-clicking the ClassView tab, add the typical four methods for the IMath interface. The IDL signatures for each method are shown next. Notice that this time you don't return the result of the computation via an out parameter. Instead, you notify the client of the result through a callback method:

```
[helpstring("method Add")] HRESULT
     Add( [in] long lOp1, [in] long lOp2 );
[helpstring("method Subtract")] HRESULT
     Subtract( [in] long lOp1, [in] long lOp2 );
[helpstring("method Multiply")] HRESULT
     Multiply( [in] long lOp1, [in] long lOp2 );
[helpstring("method Divide")] HRESULT
     Divide([in] long lOp1, [in] long lOp2 );
```

Step 3: Add the Advise Methods

Next, you need to add two additional methods to the IMath interface: Advise and Unadvise. These two methods provide a way for the client to pass an interface pointer to the component. You then store this pointer as part of your implementation and "fire" notifications to the client through it. The Unadvise method enables the client to disconnect the notification interface. Following is the IDL and implementation:

```
// Chapter7_CallBackServer.IDL
interface IMath : IUnknown
{
...
   [helpstring("method Advise")]
      HRESULT Advise([in] ICallBack* pCallBack);
   [helpstring("method Unadvise")]
      HRESULT Unadvise();
};

// Math.H
...
class ATL_NO_VTABLE CMath :
     public CComObjectRootEx<CComSingleThreadModel>,
     public CComCoClass<CMath, &CLSID_Math>,
     public IMath
{
public:
   CMath()
   {
      m_pCallBack = 0;
   }
...
// IMath
public:
   STDMETHOD(Add)(long lOp1, long lOp2);
   STDMETHOD(Multiply)(long lOp1, long lOp2);
   STDMETHOD(Subtract)(long lOp1, long lOp2);
   STDMETHOD(Divide)(long lOp1, long lOp2);
   STDMETHOD(Advise)(ICallBack* pCallBack);
   STDMETHOD(Unadvise)();
private:
   ICallBack* m_pCallBack;
};

// Math.CPP
...
```

```
STDMETHODIMP CMath::Advise(ICallBack * pCallBack)
{
   m_pCallBack = pCallBack;
   m_pCallBack->AddRef();
   return S_OK;
}
STDMETHODIMP CMath::Unadvise()
{
   m_pCallBack->Release();
   m_pCallBack = 0;
   return S_OK;
}
```

Step 4: Define the Outgoing Interface

Next, you declare the outgoing interface in your component's IDL file. Name the interface ICallBack; it has just one method: ComputationComplete. You need to use GUIDGEN to create a unique GUID for the interface; then add it to the coclass entry so that it becomes part of the type library.

You also should mark the interface with the default and source attributes to signify that this is your component's default outgoing interface. However, to use it with Visual Basic's implements keyword, you cannot mark it as source. It's commented out in the following code:

```
// Chapter7_CallBackServer.IDL
...
[
   object,
   uuid(48CD3740-50A3-11d1-B5EC-0004ACFF171C),
   helpstring("ICallBack Interface"),
]
interface ICallBack : IUnknown
{
   [helpstring("method ComputationComplete")]
      HRESULT ComputationComplete( long lResult );
};


...


library CHAPTER7_CALLBACKSERVERLib
{
...
   coclass Math
   {
      [default] interface IMath;
```

```
        /* [source, default] Visual Basic doesn't like these */
        interface ICallBack;
    };
};
```

Step 5: Notify the Client

To receive the results of your math component's computations, clients must implement your outgoing ICallBack interface. To perform this notification, you need to add the callback code to each of the basic operation methods of IMath:

```
// IMath interface
STDMETHODIMP CMath::Add(long lOp1, long lOp2)
{
    long lResult = lOp1 + lOp2;
    if ( m_pCallBack )
        m_pCallBack->ComputationComplete( lResult );

    return S_OK;
}
STDMETHODIMP CMath::Subtract(long lOp1, long lOp2)
{
    long lResult = lOp1 - lOp2;
    if ( m_pCallBack )
        m_pCallBack->ComputationComplete( lResult );

    return S_OK;
}
STDMETHODIMP CMath::Multiply(long lOp1, long lOp2)
{
    long lResult = lOp1 * lOp2;
    if ( m_pCallBack )
        m_pCallBack->ComputationComplete( lResult );

    return S_OK;
}
STDMETHODIMP CMath::Divide(long lOp1, long lOp2)
{
    long lResult = lOp1 / lOp2;
    if ( m_pCallBack )
        m_pCallBack->ComputationComplete( lResult );

    return S_OK;
}
```

This design probably isn't the most flexible because it requires a client to provide a callback implementation if it wants to use your functionality. A better technique is to pass back a return value as well as fire the notification with the result. I use this approach in the next example, which uses connection points (COM's general notification technique).

A Visual Basic Client

To test the math component, let's write a Visual Basic application that supports result notifications. Again, the initial form is based on many of the previous Visual Basic examples. The form, shown in Figure 7-2, uses the same control names that you've used previously. Make sure you name the form frmMain.

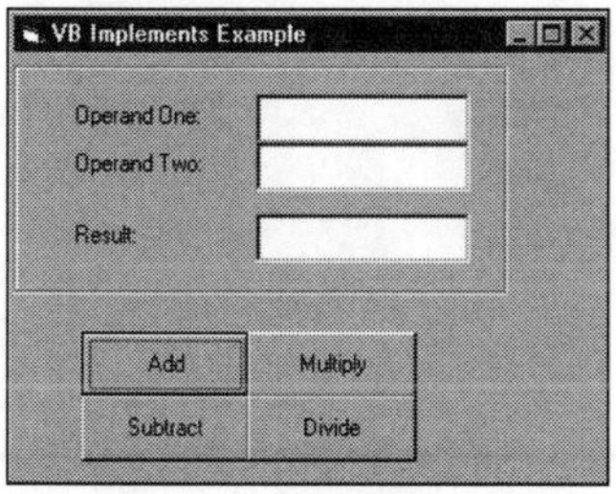

Figure 7-2: The Visual Basic form

Step 1: Reference the Type Library for Chapter7_CallBackServer

Once you build the form, add the type library of your math component using the Project → References menu. Figure 7-3 shows the math component and its interfaces. Then, add the following code to the form:

```
Dim objMath As New CHAPTER7_CALLBACKSERVERLib.Math
Private Sub cmdAdd_Click()
    objMath.Add txtOp1, txtOp2
End Sub
Private Sub cmdDivide_Click()
    objMath.Divide txtOp1, txtOp2
End Sub
Private Sub cmdMultiply_Click()
    objMath.Multiply txtOp1, txtOp2
End Sub
Private Sub cmdSubtract_Click()
    objMath.Subtract txtOp1, txtOp2
End Sub
```

This code slightly differs from the earlier examples because the methods do not return the result of the computation. To get the results, you must implement the ICallBack interface and pass the pointer to the component.

Figure 7-3 shows the math component and its interfaces.

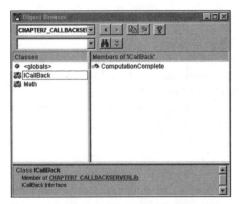

Figure 7–3: Math in Visual Basic's Object Browser

Step 2: Add the CallBack Class

Visual Basic supports the use of *class modules*, which behave just like the component classes that you develop using ATL. A Visual Basic class module is implemented using either an IDispatch- or IUnknown-based interface. By using Visual Basic's implements keyword, you can provide an implementation for an interface described in a type library (as long as it derives from IUnknown or IDispatch).

When you reference your math component's type library, the definition for ICallBack is added to Visual Basic's known types. Using the Project → Add Class Module, add a new class module to your project and give it the name CallBack, as shown in Figure 7-4.

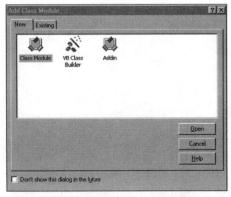

Figure 7–4: Visual Basic's Add Class Module dialog box

Next, use the `implements` keyword to indicate that the class implements the `Chapter7_CallBackServerLib.ICallBack` interface:

```
Implements CHAPTER7_CALLBACKSERVERLib.ICallBack
```

Figure 7-5 shows the interface.

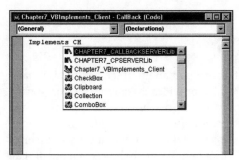

Figure 7-5: Using the `implements` keyword

After you use the `implements` keyword, the module's left combo box has `ICallBack` as an option. Choose `ICallBack`. This adds shell functions for each interface member. Add the following highlighted code:

```
Private Sub ICallBack_ComputationComplete(ByVal lResult As Long)
    frmMain.txtResult = lResult
End Sub
```

This code implements the `ComputationComplete` method of your `ICallBack` interface. After this interface is passed to the component, it "calls back," notifying the client of the result of any calculations. You then display the result in the result field on your form.

Step 3: Advise the Component

All that's left is to create an instance of your class that implements `ICallBack` and pass it into the component via the `IMath::Advise` method. You create an instance of the `CallBack` class and pass it to the component when the application is started (the form is loaded). On shutdown, you call the `Unadvise` method:

```
Dim objCallBack As New CallBack
Private Sub Form_Load()
    objMath.Advise objCallBack
End Sub
Private Sub Form_Unload(Cancel As Integer)
    objMath.Unadvise
End Sub
```

That's all there is to it. You now have an application that implements bidirectional communication using COM interfaces. This technique is very useful in many development situations and relatively easy to implement. However, both the client and the server need an understanding of the notification interface. COM also provides a more general technique for establishing outgoing interfaces in your components. This technique is more complex because of its generality, but technologies such as ActiveX controls use it extensively.

Connectable Objects

Implementing and passing interface pointers through an interface method is a basic technique for handling notifications. COM also provides a general solution for the notification problem; it's called *connection points*, or *connectable objects*. In the callback example, both the client and the server require some specific knowledge of the callback interface. Using connectable objects, which are based on a number of standard COM interfaces (for example, IConnectionPoint), a component can describe its outgoing interfaces in a general way and also provide a standard way for a client to implement and connect these interfaces to a component.

Connectable object technology supports the following set of features:

- ◆ It enables a component to define its outgoing interfaces.

- ◆ It provides a client with the capability to enumerate the outgoing interfaces supported by a component.

- ◆ It provides a client with the capability to connect (Advise) and disconnect (Unadvise) outgoing interfaces to a component.

- ◆ It provides a client with the capability to enumerate the connected, outgoing interfaces on a particular component instance.

The general flow of connectable object negotiation proceeds as follows:

1. The client queries for IConnectionPointContainer through a well-known interface on the component. If this succeeds, the component supports connection points.

2. The client uses one of two techniques to retrieve an IConnectionPoint interface, through which it sets up the connection. The client can use the FindConnectionPoint method to locate a specific connection point by its interface identifier (IID). This is the technique used most frequently. The second IConnectionPointContainer method, EnumConnectionPoints, returns a COM enumerator with a list of all IConnectionPoint interfaces implemented within a component. The client then can iterate through this list to determine which connection point (if any) that it wants to use.

3. If the client finds an acceptable outgoing interface, it must implement it. Otherwise, the process ends. Implementing the outgoing interface resembles your earlier treatment of the Visual Basic implements keyword. However, connection points are a more general technique, so in many cases the outgoing interface is derived from IDispatch.

4. Next, the client uses the IConnectionPoint::Advise method to pass an IUnknown pointer to its interface implementation. The interface implementation also is called a *sink*.

5. In the component's IConnectionPoint::Advise implementation, it uses QueryInterface to obtain the interface pointer to the client's implementation of the component's outgoing interface. Once this is performed, the connection is established. The component now can fire notifications by calling through this interface implemented within the client.

6. When the client no longer wants to be notified, it calls IConnectionPoint::Unadvise to shut down the connection.

IConnectionPointContainer

The component implements the IConnectionPointContainer interface; this interface is available from its main QueryInterface implementation. A client uses IConnectionPointContainer to determine whether a component supports connection points. If the QueryInterface succeeds, the client can use FindConnection Point to return an IConnectionPoint interface for a specific outgoing interface. The signature of FindConnectionPoint is as follows:

```
HRESULT FindConnectionPoint( REFIID riid,
                             IConnectionPoint **ppCP );
```

The client calls FindConnectionPoint, passing the GUID of the component's outgoing interface. There are at least two ways the client can obtain this GUID. The first is to look through the component's type library for its outgoing interfaces. The second approach requires the component to implement the IProvideClassInfo2 interface, which I discuss in a moment. The client can obtain the type information, as well as the GUID of the component's default outgoing interface, through the methods of IProvideClassInfo2.

The second method of IConnectionPointContainer returns a list of all the connection points within a component. Then the client can decide which specific connection point it wants to use. Here's its signature:

```
HRESULT EnumConnectionPoints( IEnumConnectionPoints **ppEnum );
```

IConnectionPoint

An IConnectionPoint interface acts as a point of connection for each outgoing interface supported in a component. It is through this interface that a client connects its
implementation of the component's outgoing interfaces. The GetConnection
Interface method passes back the interface identifier for the interface managed by
this specific connection point, and the GetConnectionPointContainer method provides the component's IConnectionPointContainer interface implementation:

```
Interface IConnectionPoint : IUnknown
{
    HRESULT GetConnectionInterface( IID *pIID );
    HRESULT GetConnectionPointContainer( IConnectionPointContainer
                                        **ppCPC )
    HRESULT Advise( IUnknown *pUnk, DWORD *pdwCookie );
    HRESULT Unadvise( DWORD dwCookie );
    HRESULT EnumConnections( IEnumConnections **ppEnum );
};
```

The more interesting IConnectionPoint methods are Advise, Unadvise, and
EnumConnections. Connectable object technology enables a component to maintain
multiple connections to its outgoing interfaces. In other words, a component may
have any number of clients connected to any one instance. To manage this, each
connection must have a unique identifier called a *cookie*. A cookie is a 32-bit value
that is unique in the context in which it is used. Cookies are employed throughout
the Win32 API.

The Advise method returns a cookie that uniquely identifies the client's connection. Then the cookie must be passed back to the Unadvise method. The
EnumConnections method returns a list of outstanding client connections on the specific connection point. In other words, it provides access to the IUnknown pointers
provided by the clients for this connection point.

Connection Points, Automation, and IProvideClassInfo2

The connection point technique of implementing notifications initially was
designed for and used in the development of ActiveX controls. As Chapter 8
reveals, ActiveX controls expose their functionality through automation — usually
with dual interfaces. Today, many development tools (such as Visual Basic) work
only with components that describe their outgoing interfaces as dispinterfaces. This
is because dispinterfaces are easier to implement at run time.

As described in Chapter 6, IDispatch-based interfaces only have to implement
IDispatch::GetIDsOfNames and IDispatch::Invoke. And in the case of connection points, in which the component already knows the DISPIDs and the
methods that it will call, the client doesn't need to implement anything other than
IDispatch::Invoke.

In situations in which a client implements an outgoing interface at run time, it is important to have an effective way for the client to identify a component's outgoing interfaces, methods, and parameters. COM specifies an additional interface for just this purpose. The IProvideClassInfo2 interface provides a simple mechanism whereby a client can obtain both the type information for a component and the interface identifier for its default, outgoing interface. You want this because you can use FindConnectionPoint to get a connection point for this interface, and then call Advise. Following is the definition of the IProvideClassInfo2 interface, as well as the GUIDKIND structure used to identify a default, outgoing interface:

```
interface IProvideClassInfo2 : IUnknown
{
   HRESULT GetClassInfo( ITypeInfo** ppTI );
   HRESULT GetGUID( DWORD dwGuidKind, GUID* pGUID );
);
typedef enum tagGUIDKIND
{
   GUIDKIND_DEFAULT_SOURCE_DISP_IID = 1,
} GUIDKIND;
```

IProvideClassInfo2Impl

ATL provides a basic implementation of IProvideClassInfo2 via its IProvide ClassInfo2Impl class. Those components that implement outgoing interfaces through connection points should provide the IProvideClassInfo2 interface. Using ATL, implementing this interface takes just a few lines of code:

```
class ATL_NO_VTABLE CMath :
   ...
   public IProvideClassInfo2Impl<&CLSID_Math, &IID_IMathEvents,
                                 &LIBID_CHAPTER7_CPSERVERLib>
{
...
BEGIN_COM_MAP(CMath)
   COM_INTERFACE_ENTRY(IProvideClassInfo2)
END_COM_MAP()
...
};
```

The first and third parameters provide information for ATL to load the type library, and the second parameter signifies the component's default, outgoing interface. The implementation of IProvideClassInfo2Impl is very similar to that of IDispatchImpl. It exposes the type library using an instance of CComType InfoHolder.

ATL and Connection Points

When you create an ATL component using the Object wizard, one option that appears is Support Connection Points. Figure 7-6 shows the Attributes tab with this option. If you select Support Connection Points, the wizard adds several lines of code to your component's header file. These lines add basic support for outgoing interfaces in your component, each of which is highlighted here:

```
class ATL_NO_VTABLE CMath :
    public CComObjectRootEx<CComSingleThreadModel>,
    public CComCoClass<CMath, &CLSID_Math>,
    public IDispatchImpl<IMath, &IID_IMath,
&LIBID_CHAPTER7_CPSERVERLib>,
    public IConnectionPointContainerImpl<CMath>
{
public:
...
BEGIN_COM_MAP(CMath)
    COM_INTERFACE_ENTRY(IMath)
    COM_INTERFACE_ENTRY(IDispatch)
    COM_INTERFACE_ENTRY(IConnectionPointContainer)
END_COM_MAP()
BEGIN_CONNECTION_POINT_MAP(CMath)
END_CONNECTION_POINT_MAP()
```

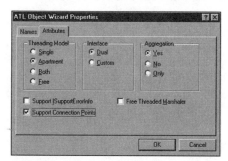

Figure 7-6: The Attributes tab

First, your component gets an implementation of the IConnectionPoint Container interface. This interface is added to your interface map. Finally, the wizard adds two macros that create a connection point map (which I discuss in a moment).

The wizard also adds an outgoing interface to your component's implementation via the IDL file. It names the interface by appending `Events` and prefixes the name with an underscore (_). Here's the code from the IDL file. The wizard adds the highlighted lines when you select the Support Connection Points option.

```
[
...
]
library CHAPTER7_CPSERVERLib
{
    importlib("stdole32.tlb");
    importlib("stdole2.tlb");

    [
        uuid(A4FA55EF-B221-11D2-97C1-00104BF7DE35),
        helpstring("_IMathEvents Interface")
    ]
    dispinterface _IMathEvents
    {
        properties:
        methods:
    };

    [
        uuid(A4FA55EE-B221-11D2-97C1-00104BF7DE35),
        helpstring("Math Class")
    ]
    coclass Math
    {
        [default] interface IMath;
        [default, source] dispinterface _IMathEvents;
    };
};
```

The new ATL Connection Point wizard provides additional support for implementing this outgoing interface.

The Implement Connection Point Wizard

ATL version 3.0 provides a new wizard called the *Implement Connection Point wizard* that generates wrapper classes based on an interface described in a type library. The wizard creates a wrapper class derived from `IConnectionPointImpl`. This wrapper class is used to "fire" events back to any connected clients.

To execute the Connection Point wizard, you first need a type library. With ATL projects, this means that you must add the interface declarations to your IDL file and build the project before you can utilize the wizard. Once you define a component's outgoing interface, you run the wizard to produce a class similar to this:

```
///////////////////////////
// CProxy_IMathEvents
///////////////////////////
template <class T>
class CProxy_IMathEvents :
    public IConnectionPointImpl<T, &DIID__IMathEvents,
CComDynamicUnkArray>
{
public:
    HRESULT Fire_ComputationComplete(LONG lResult)
    {
        CComVariant varResult;
        T* pT = static_cast<T*>(this);
        int nConnectionIndex;
        CComVariant* pvars = new CComVariant[1];
        int nConnections = m_vec.GetSize();
        for (nConnectionIndex = 0; nConnectionIndex < nConnections;
            nConnectionIndex++)
        {
            pT->Lock();
            CComPtr<IUnknown> sp = m_vec.GetAt(nConnectionIndex);
            pT->Unlock();
            IDispatch* pDispatch =
            reinterpret_cast<IDispatch*>(sp.p);
            if (pDispatch != NULL)
            {
                VariantClear(&varResult);
                pvars[0] = lResult;
                DISPPARAMS disp = { pvars, NULL, 1, 0 };
                pDispatch->Invoke(0x1, IID_NULL,
                                LOCALE_USER_DEFAULT,
                                DISPATCH_METHOD,
                                &disp,
                                &varResult,
                                NULL, NULL);
            }
        }
        delete[] pvars;
        return varResult.scode;
    }
};
```

The purpose of this proxy class is to provide the component with a convenient way to call through an interface pointer provided by a client application. Connection point technology enables multiple outgoing (or sink) interfaces per component instance. ATL manages these connections in a simple vector of IUnknown pointers. The vector class is implemented in the CComDynamicUnkArray class and is part of ATL.

When developing a connection point-based component, include the wrapper class in the implementation. The wizard does this for you, as shown here (the highlighted lines reflect the changes made by the Connection Point wizard):

```
// Our proxy class to fire events
#include "Chapter7_CPServerCP.h"
...
class ATL_NO_VTABLE CMath :
    ...
    public CProxy_IMathEvents<CMath>
{
...
BEGIN_CONNECTION_POINT_MAP(CMath)
   CONNECTION_POINT_ENTRY(DIID__IMathEvents)
END_CONNECTION_POINT_MAP()
...
};
```

To actually fire an event (that is, notify a client through its incoming interface), you use the methods provided by the proxy class:

```
STDMETHODIMP CMath::Add(long lOp1, long lOp2, long * plResult)
{
   *plResult = lOp1 + lOp2;
   Fire_ComputationComplete( *plResult );
   return S_OK;
}
```

A component can support any number of outgoing interfaces and ATL provides a set of macros to help in this implementation. These macros create something called a *connection map*. Remember, each outgoing interface supported by a component must provide a connection point (an object that implements IConnectionPoint) through which a client can pass its interface implementation.

Connection Maps

If your ATL component supports connection points, it must have a connection map. The connection map manages a table of connection points, one for each outgoing interface that a component supports. A component exposes only the IConnection PointContainer interface from its QueryInterface implementation and a client must obtain an outgoing interface's `IConnectionPoint` implementation through `IConnectionPointContainer`.

Here's a simple connection map declaration for a component that exposes one outgoing interface:

```
BEGIN_CONNECTION_POINT_MAP(CMath)
   CONNECTION_POINT_ENTRY(DIID__IMathEvents)
END_CONNECTION_POINT_MAP()
```

IConnectionPointImpl

For each outgoing interface that your component supports, you need an implementation of the `IConnectionPointImpl` class. In most cases, use the Connection Point wizard to create a class derived from `IConnectionPointImpl` for inclusion in your component's hierarchy. In other cases, you can create a connection point using a standard COM interface such as `IPropertyNotifySink`. This example component supports two outgoing interfaces using both of these techniques:

```
// Math.h : Declaration of the CMath
...
// Our proxy class to fire events
#include "Chapter7_CPServerCP.h"

class ATL_NO_VTABLE CMath :
    ...
    public IConnectionPointContainerImpl<CMath>,
    public CProxy_IMathEvents<CMath>,
    public CConnectionPointImpl<CMath, &IID_IPropertyNotifySink>
{
public:
...
BEGIN_COM_MAP(CMath)
    COM_INTERFACE_ENTRY_IMPL(IConnectionPointContainer)
    ...
END_COM_MAP()

BEGIN_CONNECTION_POINT_MAP(CMath)
    CONNECTION_POINT_ENTRY(DIID__IMathEvents)
    CONNECTION_POINT_ENTRY(IID_IPropertyNotifySink)
END_CONNECTION_POINT_MAP()
...
};
```

IConnectionPointContainerImpl

As expected, ATL's IConnectionPointContainerImpl class provides a default implementation of IConnectionPointContainer. To demonstrate how it works, I focus on the FindConnectionPoint method. The EnumConnectionPoint method uses similar techniques.

A client calls IConnectionPointContainer::FindConnectionPoint, passing in the IID of the outgoing interface for which it is looking. ATL's FindConnectionPoint implementation spins through the connection map looking for the associated IConnectionPoint implementation. Here's a concise version of the implementation:

```
template <class T>
class ATL_NO_VTABLE IConnectionPointContainerImpl
{
...
    STDMETHOD(FindConnectionPoint)(REFIID riid,
                                   IConnectionPoint** ppCP)
    {
        HRESULT hRes = CONNECT_E_NOCONNECTION;
        const _ATL_CONNMAP_ENTRY* pEntry = T::GetConnMap(NULL);
        IID iid;
        while (pEntry->dwOffset != (DWORD)-1)
        {
            IConnectionPoint* pCP =
                (IConnectionPoint*)((int)this+pEntry->dwOffset);
            if (SUCCEEDED(pCP->GetConnectionInterface(&iid)) &&
                        InlineIsEqualGUID(riid, iid))
            {
                *ppCP = pCP;
                pCP->AddRef();
                hRes = S_OK;
                break;
            }
            pEntry++;
        }
        return hRes;
    }
};
```

Other than using some difficult offset calculations, the implementation corresponds to what you already know about IConnectionPointContainer. ATL loops through the connection map until it finds a matching IID. If it finds a match, it returns the connection point implementation.

AtlAdvise

ATL provides the AtlAdvise method as a shortcut for clients that support connection points. AtlAdvise takes four parameters: the IUnknown* of the component, the IUnknown* of the client's outgoing interface implementation (for example, _IMath Events), the IID of the outgoing interface that it implements (for example, DIID_I MathEvents), and a variable to store the cookie returned by IConnection Point::Advise. Here's the implementation:

```
ATLAPI AtlAdvise(IUnknown* pUnkCP, IUnknown* pUnk,
                 const IID& iid, LPDWORD pdw)
{
   CComPtr<IConnectionPointContainer> pCPC;
   CComPtr<IConnectionPoint> pCP;
   HRESULT hRes = pUnkCP->
           QueryInterface(IID_IConnectionPointContainer,
                          (void**)&pCPC);
   if (SUCCEEDED(hRes))
      hRes = pCPC->FindConnectionPoint(iid, &pCP);

   if (SUCCEEDED(hRes))
      hRes = pCP->Advise(pUnk, pdw);

   return hRes;
}
```

Nothing difficult here. AtlAdvise performs the preceding, detailed steps. It queries for the IConnectionPointContainer interface, calls FindConnectionPoint with the provided IID, and finally calls the Advise method with the IUnknown* of the client's implemented interface. Here's how a C++ client can use AtlAdvise:

```
CComPtr<IMath> ptrMath;
HRESULT hr;
hr = CoCreateInstance( CLSID_Math, NULL, CLSCTX_SERVER,
                       IID_IMath, (void**) &ptrMath );

CComObject<CMathEvents>* ptrMathEvents = new CComObject<CMathEvents>;
CComPtr<IUnknown> ptrEventsUnk = ptrMathEvents;

DWORD dwCookie;
hr = AtlAdvise( ptrMath,
                ptrEventsUnk,
                DIID__IMathEvents,
                &dwCookie );
```

You see this again in a later example.

Visual Basic's WithEvents Keyword

Previous to release 5.0 of Visual Basic, only ActiveX controls enabled a Visual Basic developer to harness events through the connection point mechanism. With release 5.0 and above, however, Visual Basic has a new keyword that enables it to harness events fired from arbitrary COM components. The WithEvents keyword provides functionality similar to that provided by the AtlAdvise method discussed in the last section.

The WithEvents keyword requires early binding to components that support connection points, but this hardly is an issue. Now, hooking up events is as easy as adding one keyword to an object's dimension statement. For example:

```
Dim WithEvents objMath As CHAPTER7_CPSERVERLib.Math

Private Sub Form_Load()
    Set objMath = New CHAPTER7_CPSERVERLib.Math
End Sub

Private Sub objMath_ComputationComplete(ByVal lResult As Long)
    MsgBox "Computation result is " & lResult
End Sub
```

You use this technique later in the Visual Basic client example.

The Connection Point Example

In this example, I first implement the math component using a dual interface (like earlier in the chapter). This time, though, I use connection points to expose the outgoing notification interface. Once you implement the component, you then develop clients using both C++ and Visual Basic.

Step 1: Create the Math Component

Start Visual C++ and create a new project with the following characteristics:

1. ATL COM AppWizard.

2. Give it the name Chapter7_CPServer.

3. In Step 1 of 1, select a type of DLL.

4. Select Finish to generate the project.

5. Using the ATL Object wizard, insert a simple object with the following options.

6. Use a Short Name of Math.

7. Make sure the interface name is IMath.

8. Change the ProgID to Chapter7.CPMath.

9. On the Attributes tab, enable the Support Connection Points option and make sure the Dual interface option is selected. Figure 7-6 shows the Attributes tab.

Step 2: Implement the IMath Interface

Using the Add Method... option by right-clicking the ClassView tab, add the four methods for the IMath interface. The implementation is shown here:

```
// IMath interface
STDMETHODIMP CMath::Add( long lOp1, long lOp2, long* plResult )
{
    *pResult = lOp1 + lOp2;
    return S_OK;
}


STDMETHODIMP CMath::Subtract( long lOp1, long lOp2, long* plResult )
{
    *pResult = lOp1 - lOp2;
    return S_OK;
}


STDMETHODIMP CMath::Multiply( long lOp1, long lOp2, long* plResult )
{
    *pResult = lOp1 * lOp2;
    return S_OK;
}


STDMETHODIMP CMath::Divide( long lOp1, long lOp2, long* plResult )
{
    *pResult = lOp1 / lOp2;
    return S_OK;
}
```

You also should update the IDL file with the correct attributes for each method:

```
[helpstring("method Add")] HRESULT
        Add( [in] long lOp1, [in] long lOp2,
            [out, retval] long* plResult);
[helpstring("method Subtract")] HRESULT
```

```
      Subtract( [in] long lOp1, [in] long lOp2,
               [out, retval] long* plResult);
[helpstring("method Multiply")] HRESULT
     Multiply( [in] long lOp1, [in] long lOp2,
               [out, retval] long* plResult);
[helpstring("method Divide")] HRESULT
     Divide([in] long lOp1, [in] long lOp2,
            [out, retval] long* plResult);
```

Step 3: Define the Event Interface

Okay, you've seen all of that before. Next, you need to declare your outgoing interface in your component's IDL file. When you choose the Support Connection Points option, the wizard adds an outgoing interface to your IDL file with the name _IMathEvents. Most tools and environments require outgoing interfaces to be dispinterfaces; the wizard provides this by default. If you need a custom Vtable interface, just modify the IDL generated by the wizard. The wizard also adds the interface description to your coclass entry and marks it with the required default and source attributes to signify that this is your component's default outgoing interface. Here's a look at the IDL:

```
// Chapter7_CPServer.IDL
...
[
   uuid(6A38EE21-9A76-11D2-97C1-00104BF7DE35),
   version(1.0),
   helpstring("Chapter7_CPServer 1.0 Type Library")
]
library CHAPTER7_CPSERVERLib
{
   importlib("stdole32.tlb");
   importlib("stdole2.tlb");

   [
      uuid(AEB18821-53A3-11d1-883A-444553540000),
      helpstring("_IMathEvents Interface"),
   ]
   dispinterface _IMathEvents
   {
      properties:
      methods:
   };

   [
      uuid(6A38EE2E-9A76-11D2-97C1-00104BF7DE35),
```

```
    helpstring("Math Class")
]
coclass Math
{
    [default] interface IMath;
    [default, source] dispinterface _IMathEvents;
};
};
```

Next, you need to add the ComputationComplete method. You can do so by right-clicking in the ClassView tab on the _IMathEvents interface and selecting Add Method.... The signature of the method is as follows:

```
[id(1), helpstring("method ComputationComplete")]
            HRESULT ComputationComplete([in] long lResult);
```

Before executing the Connection Point wizard, you need to compile your IDL file to produce a type library. You must build the project (at least the IDL file) before continuing.

Step 4: Run the Implement Connection Point Wizard

As previously described, the Connection Point wizard creates a proxy or wrapper class that derives from ATL's IConnectionPointImpl class. You access the wizard by right-clicking your component class (for example, CMath) in the ClassView window. Figure 7-7 displays the Implement Connection Point wizard.

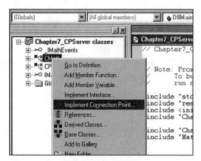

Figure 7-7: Invoking the Implement Connection Point wizard

After invoking the wizard, you see a dialog box like that shown in Figure 7-8. The Interfaces section contains all of the interfaces marked with the source attribute in your project's type library. In this case, you have but one — your _IMathEvents interface. Select the interface and click the OK button.

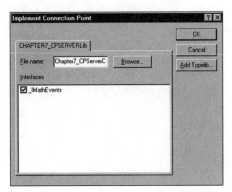

Figure 7-8: The Implement Connection Point wizard

The proxy implementation is provided in the default filename of `CHAPTER7_`
`CPSERVERCP.H`. The wizard automatically adds the `#include` for your proxy class and
makes sure your component class derives from the new class. Connection point
clients also may need access to the `IProvideClassInfo` interface, so add ATL's
`IProvideClassInfo2Impl` class:

```
// Math.h : Declaration of the CMath
...
// Our proxy class to fire events
// The wizard added this line for us
#include "Chapter7_CPServerCP.h"

class ATL_NO_VTABLE CMath :
   public CComObjectRootEx<CComSingleThreadModel>,
   public CComCoClass<CMath, &CLSID_Math>,
   public IDispatchImpl<IMath, &IID_IMath,
&LIBID_CHAPTER7_CPSERVERLib>,
   public IConnectionPointContainerImpl<CMath>,
   public CProxy_IMathEvents<CMath>,
   public IProvideClassInfo2Impl<&CLSID_Math, &DIID__IMathEvents,
                                 &LIBID_CHAPTER7_CPSERVERLib>
{
public:
...
BEGIN_COM_MAP(CMath)
   COM_INTERFACE_ENTRY_IMPL(IConnectionPointContainer)
   COM_INTERFACE_ENTRY(IMath)
   COM_INTERFACE_ENTRY(IDispatch)
   COM_INTERFACE_ENTRY(IProvideClassInfo2)
END_COM_MAP()
```

```
BEGIN_CONNECTION_POINT_MAP(CMath)
    CONNECTION_POINT_ENTRY(DIID__IMathEvents)
END_CONNECTION_POINT_MAP()
...
};
```

Next, update each method call to fire the `ComputationComplete` event. The proxy class provides the `Fire_ComputationComplete` method:

```cpp
//
// Math.cpp : Implementation of CMath
//
...
STDMETHODIMP CMath::Add(long lOp1, long lOp2, long * plResult)
{
    *plResult = lOp1 + lOp2;
    Fire_ComputationComplete( *plResult );
    return S_OK;
}

STDMETHODIMP CMath::Subtract(long lOp1, long lOp2, long * plResult)
{
    *plResult = lOp1 - lOp2;
    Fire_ComputationComplete( *plResult );
    return S_OK;
}

STDMETHODIMP CMath::Multiply(long lOp1, long lOp2, long * plResult)
{
    *plResult = lOp1 * lOp2;
    Fire_ComputationComplete( *plResult );
    return S_OK;
}

STDMETHODIMP CMath::Divide(long lOp1, long lOp2, long * plResult)
{
    *plResult = lOp1 / lOp2;
    Fire_ComputationComplete( *plResult );
    return S_OK;
}
```

Now, build the project so you can move on to accessing the connection point functionality with a couple of client examples.

Step 5: Build a C++ Connection Point Client

Your C++ client application is a bit different from those that you've developed previously. This time you use ATL on the client side. In order to use ATL, though, you need to create a simple Win32 application instead of the typical Win32 console application. The primary reason for this switch is because ATL requires an HINSTANCE; the best way to get access to this is by implementing WinMain.

Using AppWizard, create a Win32 application project and name it Chapter7_Client. On the Step 1 of 1 dialog box, choose the Empty Project option. Next, create a file called Chapter7_Client.cpp and add the following code:

```
//
// Chapter7_Client.cpp
//

#include <windows.h>

// Include ATL
#include <atlbase.h>
CComModule _Module;
#include <atlcom.h>
#include <atlimpl.cpp>

BEGIN_OBJECT_MAP(ObjectMap)
END_OBJECT_MAP()

#include "..\Chapter7_CPServer\Chapter7_CPServer.h"
#include "..\Chapter7_CPServer\Chapter7_CPServer_i.c"
...
```

Your client code now includes the ATL implementation files and declares a global CComModule instance. It also includes an empty ATL object map, which you need to initialize CComModule. Next, you have another global class and two helper functions to display messages as your application runs. Here they are:

```
...
class COMMModule
{
public:
   COMMModule()
   {
      CoInitialize( 0 );
   }
   ~COMMModule()
   {
```

```
        CoUninitialize();
    }
};

COMModule gModule;

void DisplayMessage( char* szMsg )
{
    MessageBox( 0, szMsg, "Chapter7_Client", MB_OK );
}

void HandleError( char*szMsg, HRESULT hr )
{
    char szMessage[128];
    sprintf( szMessage, "%s. HR = %x", szMsg, hr );
    DisplayMessage( szMessage );
}
...
```

The global COMModule class instance ensures that CoInitialize and CoUninitialize calls are made. This technique makes it easier to work with smart pointers because CoUninitialize isn't called until after all smart pointers go out of scope.

The other functions are simply for displaying a message box. However, they only support ANSI builds. Next you have an ATL class that implements the client side, outgoing interface for your math component. You use ATL's support for IUnknown, but you implement the IDispatch interface by hand. You're expecting only one Invoke call, so the implementation is rather easy:

```
...
class CMathEvents :
    public CComObjectRoot,
    public _IMathEvents
{
public:
    CMathEvents() {}

BEGIN_COM_MAP(CMathEvents)
        COM_INTERFACE_ENTRY(_IMathEvents)
END_COM_MAP()

// IMathEvents
public:
    STDMETHODIMP GetTypeInfoCount(UINT*)
    {
```

```
      return E_NOTIMPL;
}


STDMETHODIMP GetTypeInfo( UINT iTInfo,
                          LCID lcid,
                          ITypeInfo **ppTInfo)
{
   return E_NOTIMPL;
}


STDMETHODIMP GetIDsOfNames( REFIID riid,
                            LPOLESTR *rgszNames,
                            UINT cNames,
                            LCID lcid,
                            DISPID *rgDispId)
{
   return E_NOTIMPL;
}


STDMETHODIMP Invoke( DISPID dispIdMember,
                     REFIID riid,
                     LCID lcid,
                     WORD wFlags,
                     DISPPARAMS *pDispParams,
                     VARIANT *pVarResult,
                     EXCEPINFO *pExcepInfo,
                     UINT *puArgErr)
{
   switch( dispIdMember )
   {
      case 0x1:
         // Make sure there is just one argument
         if ( pDispParams->cArgs != 1 )
            return DISP_E_BADPARAMCOUNT;

         // We don't support named arguments
         if ( pDispParams->cNamedArgs )
            return DISP_E_NONAMEDARGS;

         // Coerce the argument into a long
         HRESULT hr;
         VARIANTARG var;
         VariantInit( &var );
         hr = VariantChangeTypeEx( &var,
                             &(pDispParams->rgvarg[0]),
```

```
                                              lcid, 0, VT_I4 );
            if FAILED( hr )
               return DISP_E_BADVARTYPE;

            ComputationComplete( var.lVal );
            break;
         default:
            DisplayMessage( "Error" );
            break;
      }
      return S_OK;
   }

   STDMETHODIMP ComputationComplete(long lResult)
   {
      char szMsg[128];
      sprintf( szMsg, "The result is %d", lResult );
      DisplayMessage( szMsg );
      return S_OK;
   }
};
...
```

You've seen code similar to this before. You have a dispinterface-based component that implements the _IMathEvents interface. Only implement the Invoke method and check for the DISPID for your single ComputationComplete method. When ComputationComplete is called, display a message box with the result of the computation.

Next, you have the implementation of WinMain. You initialize ATL by calling the CComModule::Init method, passing in the HINSTANCE of your app and the object map:

```
...
int WINAPI WinMain(HINSTANCE hInst, HINSTANCE, LPSTR, int)
{
   // Initialize the ATL module
   _Module.Init( ObjectMap, hInst );

   CComPtr<IMath> ptrMath;
   HRESULT hr;
   hr = CoCreateInstance( CLSID_Math,
                          NULL,
                          CLSCTX_SERVER,
                          IID_IMath,
                          (void**) &ptrMath );
```

```
    if ( FAILED( hr ))
    {
        HandleError( "Failed to create server instance", hr );
        return -1;
    }
...
```

After instantiating the math component, create an instance of your CMathEvents class to provide the _IMathEvents implementation. Here it is:

```
...
#ifdef NEED_FINAL_CONSTRUCT
    CComObject<CMathEvents>* ptrMathEvents;
    CComObject<CMathEvents>::CreateInstance( &ptrMathEvents );
#else
    CComObject<CMathEvents>* ptrMathEvents = new CComObject<CMathEvents>;
#endif
    CComPtr<IUnknown> ptrEventsUnk = ptrMathEvents;
...
```

I've provided two different techniques of instantiating CMathEvents to demonstrate their differences. By using the static CreateInstance method, you are assured that the component's FinalConstruct method is executed. (Chapter 3 covers Create Instance and Chapter 5 covers FinalConstruct). ATL's default implementation of FinalConstruct does nothing, so the second technique above works also. The second technique is the one that you typically use in C++ development, but you should use the first technique when working with ATL.

Another important point is that in the preceding instantiation code, the instance's reference count initially is zero. After the instantiation, you use an ATL smart pointer to query for IUnknown, which bumps the count to one:

```
...
// Set up the connection
DWORD dwCookie;
hr = AtlAdvise( ptrMath,
                ptrEventsUnk,
                DIID__IMathEvents,
                &dwCookie );
if (FAILED( hr ))
{
    HandleError( "Unable to set up the connection for IMathEvents",
                 hr );
    return -1;
}
...
```

The preceding code uses the `AtlAdvise` method to set up the connection with the math component. You have to pass in several things: pointers to both interfaces, the IID of the outgoing interface, and the address of a `DWORD` to receive the returned cookie.

```
...
// Access the IMath interface
long lResult;
ptrMath->Add( 300, 10, &lResult );
ptrMath->Subtract( 300, 10, &lResult );
ptrMath->Multiply( 300, 10, &lResult );
ptrMath->Divide( 300, 10, &lResult );
...
```

Next, you call the methods in the math component. As these execute, the math component notifies the client of the result through the `IMathEvents::ComputationComplete` method. This displays a message box similar to that in Figure 7-9.

Figure 7-9: The result of a computation

When you're finished, you shut down the connection:

```
...
// Shut down the event connection
AtlUnadvise( ptrMath,
             DIID__IMathEvents,
             dwCookie );

return 0;
}
```

That concludes your C++ client example. Next, do the same using Visual Basic.

Step 6: Write a Visual Basic Connection Point Client

As described earlier, Visual Basic provides native support for connection points via its `WithEvents` keyword. By using this keyword, writing a client with Visual Basic is nearly identical to your previous example that used Visual Basic's `implements` keyword.

To begin, start a Visual Basic executable project and build a form similar to the one in Figure 7-2. Next, using Visual Basic's Project → References dialog box, add the type library for your Chapter7_CPServer server. Finally, add this code:

```
Dim WithEvents objMath As CHAPTER7_CPSERVERLib.Math

Private Sub cmdAdd_Click()
    objMath.Add txtOp1, txtOp2
End Sub

Private Sub cmdDivide_Click()
    objMath.Divide txtOp1, txtOp2
End Sub

Private Sub cmdMultiply_Click()
    objMath.Multiply txtOp1, txtOp2
End Sub

Private Sub cmdSubtract_Click()
    objMath.Subtract txtOp1, txtOp2
End Sub

Private Sub Form_Load()
    Set objMath = New CHAPTER7_CPSERVERLib.Math
End Sub

Private Sub objMath_ComputationComplete(ByVal lResult As Long)
    txtResult = lResult
    MsgBox "Computation result is " & lResult
End Sub
```

Figure 7-10 shows the application in action.

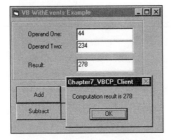

Figure 7-10: The Visual Basic connection point client

Summary

In this chapter, you learned the basics of COM's support for calling code in an associated client application. In particular, you learned:

◆ Asynchronous behavior can be simulated using interface callbacks.

◆ Interface callbacks provide an effective technique to notify client applications of changes within your components.

◆ COM provides a general callback mechanism called connectable objects or connection points.

◆ Both notification techniques are supported by the ATL framework.

In Chapter 8, I cover another important COM technology: ActiveX controls. An ActiveX control typically implements 20 or so COM interfaces. To this point, your components have implemented only a few interfaces; as you continue to add functionality, you must implement more and more interfaces. Frameworks such as ATL enable you to continue on this road of increased functionality by providing default implementations for the most important interfaces.

Chapter 8

Active X Controls

IN THIS CHAPTER

- ◆ ActiveX controls and containers
- ◆ ActiveX control functional categories
- ◆ Property persistence and property pages
- ◆ ATL's support for ActiveX controls
- ◆ The basic ATL ActiveX control classes

ACTIVEX CONTROLS PLAY a major role in Microsoft's component-based future. From a small start in 1993, ActiveX controls have grown into a tremendous demonstration of component-based software development. *ActiveX controls* are COM components that implement a number of standard interfaces. Some ActiveX controls implement only a handful of interfaces, whereas others implement more than 20.

It's hard to articulate what an ActiveX control is, primarily because the definition has changed frequently over the years. Today, ActiveX controls are used extensively in Microsoft's client-side (the Active Desktop) and server-side (for example, IIS) technologies. There are run-time and design-time controls, controls that work in Visual Basic, and controls that work only in Internet Explorer.

In this chapter, I investigate the requirements to implement a full ActiveX control that works in popular development environments such as Visual Basic. There are many available books on ActiveX controls, and in this chapter I only scratch the surface. My goal is to introduce you to as many ActiveX control interfaces as possible. That makes it easier to implement components based on their underlying functionality; in COM, this functionality is based on your ability to implement (or understand how to use) a series of COM interfaces.

 Are you tired of the math component example? You'll be happy to know that you're going to use a different example, finally. The next few chapters do not use it. However, when you get to the threading chapter, you once more have a look at the math component.

ActiveX Controls and Containers

ActiveX controls are discrete software elements similar to discrete hardware components. In most cases, a control must provide its functionality in conjunction with a cooperating software entity (called a container). *Control containers* (such as Visual Basic) make it easy to tie together various ActiveX controls into more complex and useful applications. One important feature of an ActiveX control container is the presence of a built-in language (such as VBScript) that can provide programmatic interaction with the various controls within the container.

ActiveX control containers resemble OLE *document containers* (such as Microsoft Word) in that they implement similar interfaces. Although OLE document containers and ActiveX control containers share many internal characteristics, the ultimate goals of each type of container differ. OLE document containers focus on the assembly of documents for viewing and printing; typically they are complete applications. ActiveX control containers are used as forms that contain controls tied together with a scripting language to create an application. Figure 8-1 shows a Visual Basic form that contains a number of ActiveX controls.

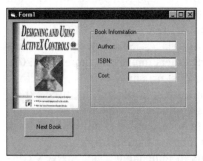

Figure 8-1: A Visual Basic form with some ActiveX controls

Container Modalities

In typical visual development environments, the container operates in various modes. When the developer designs the application or Web page, the control behaves differently than it does when the application executes. For example, when a Visual Basic developer needs a list box control, he or she clicks the list box icon on the tool palette, drags a representation of the list box control, and drops it on a form. The list box representation is merely a rectangle with a name in the upper-left corner. During design time, there is no need to create a window just to provide a representation of the control. When a user of the application executes the Visual Basic form and its associated code, the list box control window is created; therefore, it must behave like a list box and perform any special functions through its exposed properties, methods, and events. These two modes are described as *design-time mode* and *run-time mode.*

Control and Container Interfaces

An ActiveX control is an in-process server that supports a number of standard COM interfaces. An ActiveX control container also is a COM-based component that implements a set of standard COM interfaces. The trick is to hook up these interface implementations. In other words, when a control is embedded within a container, the container and control negotiate and exchange pointers to provide functionality.

A control container is really just a client of an ActiveX control, and at times a control is a client of the control container. As described in Chapter 7, a control and container maintain a peer-to-peer relationship by exchanging interface pointers. Controls and containers support incoming and outgoing interfaces.

When you drag-and-drop a control on a Visual Basic form, you use the typical COM instantiation technique. The container calls `CoCreateInstance` with the CLSID of the control. After instantiation, the container calls `QueryInterface` for those interfaces that it expects the control to implement. Some of these control interfaces provide methods through which the container can pass interface pointers for those interfaces that it implements. In this way, the control and container interact, providing significant functionality for users. This process becomes clearer as you work your way through the chapter. Figure 8-2 shows many of the interfaces that I discuss in this chapter.

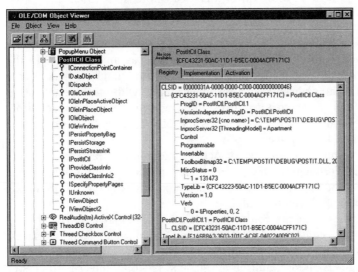

Figure 8-2: Control-implemented interfaces in `OLEVIEW`

What Is an ActiveX Control?

The definition of ActiveX has changed over the years. In late 1993, Microsoft introduced ActiveX controls (called OLE controls at the time) as a 32-bit replacement for the popular Visual Basic custom control (*VBX*) standard. The proprietary VBX specification was tied strongly to the 16-bit platform and was discarded for the new COM-based solution.

This initial version of the OLE control specification, now called the *OLE Controls '94 specification*, required that a control implement approximately 15 COM-based interfaces. Most of these interfaces were part of the OLE document specification; a control simply was an in-process OLE document server with a couple of new, control-specific interfaces.

In early 1996, after more than two years' experience with implementing and using OLE controls, Microsoft modified the specification significantly and released the *OLE Controls '96 specification*. (Shortly after this document was released, Microsoft coined the term ActiveX.) The new specification addressed a number of performance issues inherent in the earlier '94 specification controls. It also added significant new features and capabilities for controls and containers.

Along with the OLE Controls '96 specification, Microsoft released another document called *OLE Controls and Container Guidelines 2.0*. This document changed significantly the definition of the term ActiveX control. The next few sections cover these changes in more detail.

From this point, I use the term *ActiveX control* except when referring to document titles. However, the term *OLE control* was used before April 1996.

The OLE Controls '94 Specification

The original ActiveX control architecture was specified as an extension to the existing OLE document specification. An ActiveX control implemented all the interfaces required by an embedded OLE document server with in-place activation capabilities. Additionally, ActiveX controls implemented several new control-specific interfaces. In all, a control that meets the OLE Controls '94 specification implements more than 15 interfaces.

Implementing a component, such as an ActiveX control, that requires 15 interfaces is a lot of work. Fortunately, MFC provided an implementation for the majority of these interfaces so building ActiveX controls based on this early specification wasn't overwhelming as long as you used MFC.

One of the problems with the control specification was that it provided only guidelines as to how a control and container should implement their interfaces. Early on, several problems arose in getting controls to behave similarly in each of the available containers. (Most control developers say that this situation still exists.) To help with this situation, Microsoft released a document that described how a container and its controls should interact with one another.

Much of this coordination was described already via the OLE document specification, but there remained a need for a document to help developers understand the complex relationship between a control and its container. The resulting document was titled OLE Controls and Container Guidelines Version 1.1 (circa late 1995). The guideline puts forth the minimum requirements that a control or control container must meet. It describes the mandatory and optional interfaces.

OLE Controls '96 Specification

Although ActiveX controls provided a wonderful new technology that validated the concept of component-based development, they weren't perfect. The large number of interfaces and methods that a control had to implement, coupled with the requirement that most controls create a window when executing, made them somewhat "heavy."

Building an application with a large number of ActiveX controls could prove problematic. Also, some functionality holes needed to be filled. To address these issues, Microsoft released the OLE Controls '96 specification in early 1996. The changes to the existing control specification are embodied mostly in a series of new interfaces.

Controls and Container Guidelines

Along with the OLE Controls '96 specification, Microsoft released a new version of the controls and container guidelines document. By following the guidelines, developers can ensure that their controls and containers work reliably together. The ActiveX control is becoming ubiquitous within development tools and applications. The large number of controls and containers, with their specialized functionality, makes it imperative that you follow certain guidelines. By following the guidelines, a developer makes the control or container useful within the largest number of development environments.

One of the major changes in the guidelines is a new definition of an ActiveX control. The document states that an ActiveX control is any specialized COM object that supports the IUnknown interface and self-registration. The trouble with this definition is that every COM object fits it. In other words, every component that you develop in this book technically is an ActiveX control! The definition is so broad that it is useless. Most developers use the term ActiveX control to describe controls that work in most commercial ActiveX control containers (Visual Basic, Visual C++, and so on) — a definition that differs greatly from the one in this document.

Here is a list of the various control functional categories detailed in the guidelines:

◆ **A COM object:** An ActiveX control is just a specialized COM object. The only true requirement for a control is that it must support self-registration and the IUnknown interface. However, such a control cannot provide much functionality. According to the guidelines, a control developer should add only those interfaces that the control needs with the ultimate purpose of making the control as lightweight as possible.

◆ **Self-registration:** A control must support self-registration by implementing the `DllRegisterServer` and `DllUnregisterServer` functions. In addition, it must add the appropriate OLE document and automation server entries in the registry. A control must use the component categories API to indicate which services are required to host the control.

◆ **Interface support:** If a control supports an interface, it must support it at a basic level. The document provides guidelines for each potential ActiveX control and container interface. It describes which methods you must implement within each implemented interface.

◆ **Persistence support:** If a control needs to support persistence, it must implement at least one `IPersist*` interface and should support more than one. This arrangement makes it easier for a container to host the control. Support for `IPersistPropertyBag` is highly recommended because most of the major containers provide a Save as text capability.

◆ **Ambient properties:** If a control supports ambient properties (we'll discuss these in more detail later in this chapter) it must support a certain number of ambient properties exposed by the container. They are `LocalID`, `UserMode`, `UIDead`, `ShowGrabHandles`, `ShowHatching`, and `DisplayAsDefault`.

◆ **Dual interfaces:** ActiveX controls and containers are strongly encouraged to support dual interfaces. If you recall from Chapter 6, a component implements a dual interface by providing both an `IDispatch` interface and a custom interface for its methods and properties.

◆ **Miscellaneous:** ActiveX controls should not use the `WS_GROUP` or `WS_TABSTOP` window flags to avoid conflict with the container's use of these flags. A control should honor a container's call to `IOleControl::Freeze Events`. When events are frozen, a container discards event notifications from the control.

The control and containers guidelines document made a significant change in what is required for a COM object to be an ActiveX control. The only requirement for an ActiveX control is that it must support self-registration and `IUnknown`. That's it! This is quite a change from the earlier specification and guidelines, which required a control to implement at least 15 interfaces. Essentially, the document states that any COM object that provides self-registration is an ActiveX control.

This means that a control now has tremendous flexibility in choosing which interfaces it should implement. If you want your component to function as an ActiveX control, you usually need to implement a number of interfaces. The new guidelines basically put all the pressure on container developers. Because a control can pick and choose the interfaces it wants to implement, the container must be careful about what it assumes a control can do.

This new definition has caused much consternation in the developer community; as of this writing, this issue hasn't been resolved completely. Frameworks such as MFC and ATL make it easy to implement full-function controls, which implement the 20 or so interfaces that enable them to work in most containers. However, as described earlier, the guidelines detail what functionality a control can provide by describing those interfaces that actually provide the control's functionality. It's a good way to group the interfaces that a control should implement. I use this technique to guide you through the next few sections.

ActiveX Control Functional Categories

An ActiveX control is a COM object that supports those interfaces required to implement any desired functionality. In the next few sections, I cover each of these functional categories. At the end of this chapter, you implement a full-function ActiveX control; as you go through each functional category, you see code fragments from your control example.

Basic COM Support

An ActiveX control is first and foremost a COM object that must provide the most basic COM service: an implementation of the IUnknown interface. To create an instance of a control, the control housing (a DLL in this case) also must expose a class factory. I've discussed this process in detail already.

Self-Registration

A control must support self-registration. As I've discussed, ATL provides support for self-registration through its Registrar component. ATL provides a default .RGS file for a control, which adds several new registry entries that controls typically use. Following is the .RGS file for the example control:

```
HKCR
{
    PostItCtl.PostItCtl.1 = s 'PostItCtl Class'
    {
        CLSID = s '{CFC43231-50AC-11D1-B5EC-0004ACFF171C}'
    }
    PostItCtl.PostItCtl = s 'PostItCtl Class'
    {
        CurVer = s 'PostItCtl.PostItCtl.1'
    }
    NoRemove CLSID
    {
        ForceRemove {CFC43231-...-0004ACFF171C} = s 'PostItCtl Class'
        {
```

```
ProgID = s 'PostItCtl.PostItCtl.1'
VersionIndependentProgID = s 'PostItCtl.PostItCtl'
ForceRemove 'Programmable'
InprocServer32 = s '%MODULE%'
{
    val ThreadingModel = s 'Apartment'
}
ForceRemove 'Control'
ForceRemove 'Programmable'
ForceRemove 'Insertable'
ForceRemove 'ToolboxBitmap32' = s '%MODULE%, 202'
'MiscStatus' = s '0'
{
    '1' = s '131473'
}
'TypeLib' = s '{CFC43223-50AC-11D1-B5EC-0004ACFF171C}'
'Version' = s '1.0'
'Verb'
{
    '0' = s '&Properties, 0, 2'
}
            }
        }
    }
```

Control Registry Entries

Self-registration basically is the act of adding a number of registry keys and values to the Windows registry. As you can tell by the .RGS file, ActiveX controls have a number of special registry entries that you have not encountered before. Each of the following control entries is a subkey under \HKEY_CLASSES_ROOT\CLSID.

Control

The Control entry indicates that the component is an ActiveX control. This entry enables containers to identify the ActiveX controls available on the system easily by searching through the registry looking only for CLSIDs with a Control subkey. This mechanism for marking a control is obsolete now; you should use a specific component category (which I discuss in a moment). However, for compatibility with older containers such as Visual Basic 4.0, the Control entry should be added to the registry.

Programmable

The Programmable key specifies that the component supports automation. Most ActiveX controls support automation through an IDispatch or dual interface. This also was replaced with a new component category.

Insertable

The Insertable entry indicates that the component can be embedded within an OLE document container. OLE document containers such as Visio, Word, and Excel use this entry. They populate the Insert Object dialog box by spinning through the registry looking for components marked with the Insertable key. Controls should add this subkey only if they can provide functionality when embedded within an OLE document container.

MiscStatus

The MiscStatus entry specifies options of interest to the control container. You can query these values before the control is embedded. The value for this entry is an integer equivalent of a bit mask value composed of optional OLEMISC flags. Table 8-1 describes the MiscStatus values.

TABLE 8-1 CONTROL OLEMISC STATUS BITS

Name	Purpose
ACTIVATEWHENVISIBLE	Set to indicate that the control prefers to activate when visible. This option can be very expensive when there are a large number of controls. The new OLE Controls '96 specification makes it possible for controls to perform most functions even when not active. You should set this flag so that the control works in containers that do not support the new specification.
IGNOREACTIVATEWHENVISIBLE	Added by the OLE Controls '96 specification. If a control supports the new optimized control behavior, it should set this flag to inform new containers that they safely can use the OLE Controls '96 specification enhancements.

Continued

TABLE 8-1 CONTROL OLEMISC STATUS BITS *(Continued)*

Name	Purpose
INVISIBLEATRUNTIME	Indicates that the control should be visible only during the design phase. When running, the control should not be visible. Any control that provides only nonvisual services fits into this category.
ALWAYSRUN	The control should run always. Controls such as those that are invisible at run time may need to set this bit to ensure that they are loaded and running at all times. This enables their events to be communicated to the container.
ACTSLIKEBUTTON	The control is a button and so should behave differently if the container instructs the control to act as a default button.
ACTSLIKELABEL	The container should treat this control as a static label. For example, it always should set focus to the next control in the tab order.
NOUIACTIVE	Indicates that the control does not support UI activation. The control can be in-place activated but without a UI-active state.
ALIGNABLE	Indicates that the control wants the container to provide a way to align the control in various ways, usually along a side or at the top of the container
IMEMODE	Indicates that the control understands the input method editor mode. This is used for localization and internationalization within controls.
SIMPLEFRAME	The control uses the ISimpleFrameSite interface (if supported by the container). ISimpleFrameSite enables a control to contain instances of other controls. This is similar to group box functionality.
SETCLIENTSITEFIRST	Controls set this bit to indicate to the container that they want their site within the container set up before the control's construction. This enables the control to use information from the client site (particularly ambient properties) during loading.

Verb

A control should have the `Verb` key with a `Properties` entry. The `Properties` entry enables a container to display the control's property page.

ToolboxBitmap32

The `ToolboxBitmap32` entry value specifies the filename and resource ID of the bitmap used for the toolbar of the container. ATL does not provide a default bitmap for its controls, but you easily can add one yourself.

TypeLib

The `TypeLib` entry value specifies the GUID and actual location of the type library for the component. All components that have a type library should add this registry entry.

Component Categories

Early in the days of ActiveX controls, you only needed the preceding registry entries to specify the functionality of a control. The `Control` registry key indicated that a component was a control, and the `Insertable` key indicated whether the control could function as a simple OLE document server. Today, however, the functional capabilities of all COM-based components (especially controls) continue to expand rapidly. A more efficient and descriptive mechanism for categorizing the capabilities provided by these objects is needed. The control guidelines require that new controls support the new component categories feature discussed in Chapter 2.

OLE Document Interfaces

The technology that enables an ActiveX control to be embedded within a container has been around a long time. The OLE document standard (called *Compound Documents* at the time) was created in 1991 and comprised the major part of OLE. Actually, OLE was an acronym for *object linking and embedding*. When ActiveX controls came along, the OLE document standard was enhanced to allow document servers to expose programmatic functionality.

Today, if your control needs to provide a visual representation and basic interaction with the user through mouse clicks and similar means, it must support the basic OLE document interfaces: `IOleObject`, `IOleInPlaceObject`, `IOleInPlace ActiveObject`, `IDataObject`, and `IViewObject2`. Table 8-2 discusses each of these interfaces briefly. You see them again when I discuss ATL's control support classes.

TABLE 8-2 OLE DOCUMENT INTERFACES

Interface	Description
IOleObject	IOleObject provides the essence of the OLE document architecture. Through this interface, the container and component communicate to negotiate the size of the embedded object (the control, in your case), as well as to get the MiscStatus bits for the control.
IOleInPlaceObject	A control must implement IOleInPlaceObject to support the capability of activation and deactivation in place within the container. The interface also provides a method to notify the control when its size changes or it is moved within the container.
IOleInPlaceActiveObject	A control must implement IOleInPlaceActive Object to provide support for the use and translation of accelerator keys within the control. Many of IOleInPlaceActiveObject's methods are not required for ActiveX controls.
IOleControl	IOleControl is a new interface added to support ActiveX controls. It provides methods to enhance the interaction with the control's container. IOleControl primarily adds functionality to enable the control and container to work together when handling keyboard input.
IDataObject	A control implements this interface to provide graphical renderings to the container. IDataObject also provides a property set for its persistent properties.
IViewObject2	Controls that provide a visual aspect implement IViewObject2. It provides the container with methods to ask the control to render itself within the container's client area.

Automation Support: IDispatch

Chapter 6 discusses automation and the IDispatch interface in detail. An ActiveX control is required to expose its functionality (methods and properties) through an IDispatch-based interface. The guidelines recommend that controls implement IDispatch using duals because they provide the most efficient and flexible implementation.

Automation is used in other areas of ActiveX controls. An ActiveX control container exposes its ambient properties though a dispinterface. Also, control events are implemented with automation through COM's connectable object technology, which I cover in Chapter 7. I touch on this briefly in a moment.

Standard and Stock Properties

The ActiveX control specifications provide a set of standard properties that you should use when you implement a property that provides some common control functionality. This approach provides a uniform interface for the control user. Examples of such common properties include Font and BackColor. Table 8-3 lists the standard properties currently defined by the standard. You also encounter the term *stock property*. Frameworks such as MFC and ATL provide default implementations of most standard properties; when they do, they are termed stock properties.

TABLE 8-3 **STANDARD CONTROL PROPERTIES**

Property	Description
Appearance	Appearance of the control (such as 3-D).
AutoSize	If TRUE, the control should size to fit within its container.
BackColor	The background color of the control.
BorderStyle	The style of the control's border. A short that currently supports only two values. A 0 indicates no border, and 1 indicates a normal, single-line border around the control. More styles may be defined in the future.
BorderColor	The color of the border around the control.
BorderWidth	The width of the border around the control.
BorderVisible	Show the border.

Continued

TABLE 8-3 STANDARD CONTROL PROPERTIES *(Continued)*

Property	Description
DrawMode	The mode of drawing used by the control.
DrawStyle	The style of drawing used by the control.
DrawWidth	The width of the pen used for drawing.
FillColor	The fill color.
FillStyle	The style of the fill color.
Font	The font used for any text in the control.
ForeColor	The color of any text or graphics within the control.
Enabled	TRUE indicates that the control can accept input.
HWnd	The hWnd of the control's window.
ReadyState	Indicates the readiness state of a control. Used with data-bound or asynchronous properties.
TabStop*	The control's participation in the tab stop scheme.
Text, Caption	A BSTR that indicates the caption or text of the control. Both properties are implemented with the same internal methods. You can use only one of the two.

* Indicates non-stock implementation provided by ATL

When implementing properties in your controls, you should use one of the standard property names whenever possible. If you need a property that indicates the background color of your control, use the BackColor standard property. This makes things easier on the control user who already understands the purpose of the BackColor property.

Ambient Properties

ActiveX controls usually exist within the context of a control container. The container provides the environment through which the control supplies its functionality. A control, however, can learn a lot about this environment by communicating with the container. The control standard specifies that containers should expose a set of ambient properties, which enable the control to query for certain container characteristics. An example of an ambient property is UserMode. As discussed earlier, a container has two modes of operation: design-time mode and run-time mode. A control can determine the container's current mode by checking the UserMode ambient property.

The default `IDispatch` of the container provides ambient properties. As a control is loaded into the container, the ambient dispatch is passed to the control through `IOleObject::SetClientSite`. The control saves this pointer and, when it needs an ambient property value, it calls through the `IDispatch` pointer. Each of the ambient properties has a specified DISPID, so access to the property is easy. Table 8-4 lists the standard ambient properties. Note that containers do not have to expose all of these properties, although most of the good containers do.

TABLE 8-4 AMBIENT PROPERTIES

Property	Description
BackColor	Default background color for the control.
DisplayName	The name of the control as given by the container. This name should be used when the control needs to display information to the user.
Font	The default font for the control.
ForeColor	Foreground color for text.
LocaleID	The container's locale identifier.
MessageReflect	If this property is TRUE, the container supports reflecting messages back to the control.
ScaleUnits	A string name for the container's coordinate units (such as twips or cm).
TextAlign	Indicates how the control should justify any textual information 0: Numbers to the right, text to the left 1: Left justify 2: Center justify 3: Right justify 4: Fill justify
UserMode	Returns TRUE if the container is in run mode; otherwise, the container is in design mode.
UIDead	Indicates to the control that it should not accept or act on any user input directed to the control. Containers can use this property to indicate to the control that it is in design mode, or that it is running but the developer has interrupted processing during debugging.

Continued

TABLE 8-4 AMBIENT PROPERTIES *(Continued)*

Property	Description
ShowGrabHandles	If TRUE, the control should show grab handles when UI active.
ShowHatching	If TRUE, the control should show diagonal hatch marks around itself when UI active.
DisplayAsDefault	The container sets this property to TRUE for a button-style control when it becomes the default button within the container. This occurs when the user tabs to the specific control or when the control is the default button on the form and the focus is on a nonbutton control. The button should indicate that it is the default button by increasing the thickness of its border.
SupportsMnemonics	If TRUE, the container supports the use of mnemonics within controls.
AutoClip	If TRUE, the container automatically clips any portion of the control's rectangle that should not be displayed. If FALSE, the control should honor the clipping rectangle passed to it in the IOleInPlaceObject's SetObjectRects method.

ATL and Ambient Properties

The container's ambient properties are accessed by an ATL-based control through the GetAmbient* methods provided by the CComControl class. Each method name begins with GetAmbient and is followed by the appropriate ambient name. For example, the following code uses several ambient properties when a control draws its representation:

```
BOOL bUserMode = FALSE;
GetAmbientUserMode( bUserMode );
if ( bUserMode == FALSE )
{
   HFONT hOldFont = 0;
   IFont* pFont = 0;
   if ( SUCCEEDED( GetAmbientFont( &pFont )) && pFont )
   {
      HFONT hFont;
      pFont->get_hFont( &hFont );
      hOldFont = (HFONT) SelectObject( hdc, hFont );
```

```
        pFont->Release();
    }
    BSTR bstr = 0;
    if ( SUCCEEDED( GetAmbientDisplayName( bstr )))
    {
        DrawText( hdc,
                  OLE2A( bstr ),
                  -1,
                  &rc,
                  DT_TOP | DT_SINGLELINE );
    }
    if ( hOldFont )
        SelectObject( hdc, hOldFont );
}
```

The code first gets the ambient `UserMode`, which indicates whether the container is in the design phase or the run phase. When in design mode, most controls draw their ambient display name as part of the design-time representation. Next, you get the ambient font and ambient display name and render it using the `DrawText` Win32 API function.

Standard Control Methods

The ActiveX control specification recommends three standard methods that controls should implement if they provide the specific behavior. Table 8-5 shows each method.

TABLE 8-5 STANDARD CONTROL METHODS

Method	Description
AboutBox	Shows the About box for the control
Refresh	Forces a redraw of the control's representation
DoClick	Fires the standard `Click` event within the control

Connectable Objects and Control Events

To support events, an ActiveX control uses the connectable objects technology described in Chapter 7. A control's events are specified through its outgoing

IDispatch-based interface, just as with the Chapter 7 connection point example. Here's a look at your example control's event interface. Notice that it is marked with the source and default interface attributes.

```
[
    uuid(5010B641-6516-11d1-B5F7-0004ACFF171C),
    helpstring("_PostItCtlEvents Interface"),
]
dispinterface _PostItCtlEvents
{
    properties:
    methods:
        [id(DISPID_CLICK)] void Click();
};

[
    uuid(CFC43231-50AC-11D1-B5EC-0004ACFF171C),
    helpstring("PostItCtl Class")
]
coclass PostItCtl
{
    [default] interface IPostItCtl;
    [default, source] dispinterface _PostItCtlEvents;
};
```

A control also must implement the IConnectionPointContainer interface on its main QueryInterface. In addition, it provides a connection point object that implements IConnectionPoint. This enables the container to pass its implementation of the control's outgoing dispinterface.

Standard Events

Just as it does with properties and methods, the ActiveX control standard describes a set of standard events that a control can implement. The events primarily are for graphical controls. Table 8-6 lists each of the standard events.

TABLE 8-6 STANDARD EVENTS

Event	Description
Click	Fired by a BUTTONUP event for any mouse button
DblClick	Fired by a BUTTONDBLCLK message for any mouse button
Error	Fired by the control when an error occurs

Event	Description
KeyDown	Fired by the WM_SYSKEYDOWN or WM_KEYDOWN message
KeyPress	Fired by the WM_CHAR message
KeyUp	Fired by the WM_SYSKEYUP or WM_KEYUP message
MouseDown	Fired by the BUTTONDOWN event for any mouse button
MouseMove	Fired by the WM_MOUSEMOVE message
MouseUp	Fired by the BUTTONUP event for any mouse button

Property Pages

One of the most important areas of a control's functionality lies in its properties. ActiveX controls have the option of providing a series of control-specific property pages, which enable you to present control-specific information. The guidelines recommend that all controls that expose properties also implement property pages. *Property pages* typically are used during the design phase to provide a rich environment in which the control user manipulates the properties of the control. Figure 8-3 shows the property page for the control you will build at the end of the chapter.

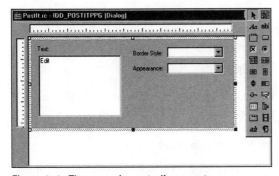

Figure 8-3: The example control's property page

Each property page is itself a COM component and is instantiated independently by the container application. Development frameworks may include certain standard property pages. For example, ATL provides an implementation of three common property pages: fonts, colors, and pictures. However, you typically implement a custom property page for each property control that does not fit the preceding types.

Most development tools (such as Visual Basic) provide a property window for showing and setting your control's properties, but this is not always the case. For this reason, always provide a complete set of property pages for your control.

During the application design process, the control user can modify a control's properties. When the user selects to edit a control's properties, the container asks the control for its list of property pages. The container instantiates each property page component individually and then merges all of them to form a property sheet. As property values are modified, the property page communicates directly with the control (through its IDispatch) to update any values. Figure 8-4 shows your complete control's property sheet; Table 8-7 describes each property page interface.

Figure 8-4: The control's property sheet

TABLE **8-7 PROPERTY PAGE INTERFACES**

Interface	Description
ISpecifyPropertyPages	A control implements this interface to provide the container with a list of its associated property pages. The GetPages method returns an array of CLSIDs, one for each property page.
IPropertyPageSite	IPropertyPageSite facilitates communication between the property page component and the property sheet frame as implemented by the container. An IPropertyPageSite pointer is provided to each property page after its instantiation through IPropertyPage::SetPageSite. The property page uses the OnStatusChange method to indicate to the frame that one or more properties have been modified.

Interface	Description
IPropertyPage2	IPropertyPage2 is implemented by each property page component and provides the container with methods to get the size of, move, create, destroy, activate, and deactivate the component's property page window. The container creates a frame for each property page and uses these methods to manage the display of the property sheet. This enables the property sheet to appear and behave as if driven by one application; in fact, a property sheet comprises individual components housed within a frame window created by the container.

Property Persistence

One of the most important aspects of ActiveX controls is the capability of their state to persist. As part of the design process, control users modify a control's state by manipulating its properties (through its property pages). A control embedded within a container is an instance of that control. Each control within the container has its own set of property values that makes the instance unique. For a control to maintain the state of its properties after the container shuts down, it must support a persistence mechanism.

Since its inception, the OLE document standard has provided support for component *persistence*. The container provides the environment whereby embedded servers (such as controls) can save and restore their internal states. Controls require assistance from the container because the container is in charge of the complete document or development environment. For example, when you use a Visual Basic form, the form itself maintains the state of any embedded controls in the .FRM file. The embedded controls have very little knowledge of how the form saves their states.

All this is done through a series of COM interfaces. There are a number of such interfaces because they have evolved over the years. For ActiveX controls, the three most important persistence interfaces are IPersistStream, IPersistStreamInit, and IPersistPropertyBag.

IPersistStream

IPersistStream is part of the OLE document specification. It provides a simple mechanism for a component to maintain the persistence of state. A *stream* is a simple file structure, defined by OLE, which provides binary, byte-by-byte data to the component. The component (a control) implements the IPersistStream interface, which contains methods such as Load and Save. The client application (your container) determines whether the component supports persistence by querying for one of the IPersist* interfaces. In our example, the control returns a pointer to its implementation of IPersistStream. The container then creates and opens a stream and passes it as a parameter to the IPersistStream::Load and IPersistStream:: Save methods.

IPersistStreamInit

The IPersistStreamInit interface was added with the ActiveX control specification. It provides a way for the control to initialize its state (that is, set any default property values) before the container initializes its properties. A new method, InitNew, was added to support this capability. By implementing InitNew, a control can initialize its state (as a constructor does) before any persistent information is loaded.

IPersistPropertyBag

A new persistence interface, IPersistPropertyBag, was added as part of the OLE Controls '96 specification (which now allows "*textual*" *persistence*). IPersist PropertyBag and the container-side interface, IPropertyBag, provide an efficient method of saving and loading text-based properties. The control implements IPersistPropertyBag, through which the container calls Load and Save. Instead of providing a stream for the control to write to, the container provides an implementation of the IPropertyBag interface. The control retrieves and saves its property values by calling IPropertyBag::Read and IPropertyBag::Write. The property bag persistence mechanism is very effective in a Web-based environment, where a control's property information must be stored within the HTML document.

When you use a control in Web environments, support for IPersistProperty Bag enables the control to use the HTML PARAM element. If a control implements IPersistStreamInit instead, the persistence of its properties is implemented using the HTML DATA element.

ATL's Support for ActiveX Controls

At this point, you understand a lot of what goes into developing an ActiveX control. A control is an in-process component that implements a series of Microsoft-defined interfaces, most of which I have described. ATL gives you significant support for developing controls because it provides default implementations for the majority of those interfaces a component must implement to be classified as a control.

In the next series of sections, I cover ATL's support for developing ActiveX controls. I begin with coverage of the ATL Object wizard. After that, I go over ATL's support classes for controls. I also look at each interface that a fully functional control must implement. After examining each of ATL's support classes, I walk you through the development of a complete ActiveX control.

ATL's ActiveX Control Support Files

The implementation of ATL's ActiveX control support appears in the ATLCTL.H and ATLCTL.CPP files in the ATL\INCLUDE directory. Both files are included in STDAFX.CPP. ATL's control implementation also depends on ATL's window support classes. These classes are similar to MFC's CWnd class; they provide basic windowing support with very little overhead. You can find the implementation of these classes in ATLWIN.H and ATLWIN.CPP.

ATL Object Wizard

I cover and use the ATL Object wizard in most of the preceding chapters. However, I haven't covered the Controls category of the wizard. Figure 8-5 shows the wizard's Controls category.

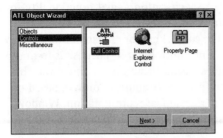

Figure 8-5: ATL Object wizard control types

Three component types are provided here. A full ActiveX control provides default implementations of nearly all control-related interfaces. An Internet Explorer control implements those interfaces required to be embedded within Internet Explorer along with a property page component, which most controls should provide. I describe the implementation of a full control because it demonstrates most of the interfaces implemented by a control.

The Names and Attributes Tabs

The Object wizard provides a series of four tabbed dialog boxes for setting the characteristics of an ActiveX control. Earlier chapters cover the options available on the first two tabs: Names and Attributes. When inserting a full control, you get two additional tabbed dialog boxes.

The Miscellaneous Tab

The Miscellaneous tab provides ActiveX control-specific information to the Object wizard. Only ActiveX controls use the various options presented here. The Miscellaneous dialog box appears in Figure 8-6. The following section describes each of the options on the Miscellaneous tab.

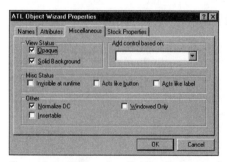

Figure 8-6: Object wizard's Miscellaneous tab

View Status and Transparent Controls

The View Status option indicates whether your control acts as an *opaque control* or as a *transparent control*. The OLE Controls '96 specification added functionality to make it easier to develop transparent controls, also described as *nonrectangular controls*. The gist is that the background of the control can be transparent.

For example, Visual Basic has long had a line control whose purpose is to draw a simple line. Developing a control that mimics Visual Basic's line control was difficult using the earlier OLE Controls '94 specification. Graphical controls based on this specification used a window to render their graphical representation. Windows are rectangular creatures, and difficulty arises when you try to draw items that do not "fill" a rectangle completely.

Controls based on the new specification typically do not require a window to do their work so the creation of nonrectangular controls is much easier. If your control's representation can be drawn in a rectangular space, you should choose the Opaque option; this option enables the container to draw the background quickly. It makes a `FillRect` call with the background color. On the other hand, if you develop a control that is transparent or nonrectangular, you should toggle off the Opaque option.

The Solid Background option is pertinent only when you choose the Opaque option. It indicates that your control has a solid background, as opposed to a hatched pattern. It also enables the container to render your control more quickly.

Misc Status Bits

When a control initially is embedded within a container, negotiation occurs between the two entities. As the control and container negotiate, the control provides the container with a set of bits that describes certain characteristics of the control. There are a number of these `MISC_STATUS` bits, but only a few of them pertain directly to ActiveX controls and their containers. Table 8-1 provides a list of those used by ActiveX controls.

The Object wizard's Misc Status frame enables you to specify three of these bits. Invisible at runtime indicates that your ActiveX control is invisible during the run-time phase. An invisible control typically provides some nonvisual service. A good example is the timer control, whose only purpose is to provide a series of events; it has no visual functionality. An invisible control, however, still provides some visual representation during the design phase.

The Acts like button and Acts like label bits are used by controls that provide functionality similar to that provided by buttons and labels. Because controls are small, independent components that have no knowledge of other controls in the container, they must rely on the container to provide container-wide information. For example, only the container knows whether a button is the current default button. Also, certain controls such as labels indicate to the container that they should receive special treatment in the container's tabbing order. You typically use these bits when implementing button-type and label-type controls.

Add Control Based On

The Add control based on option provides a skeletal project that superclasses an existing Windows control. You select the control to superclass from the drop-down list. Typically you *superclass* a control because you need functionality similar to that provided by a standard Windows control — for example, an edit field that accepts only numbers, a Windows 95 tree view that allows multiple selections, a list box that contains icons and text, and so on. By superclassing an existing control, you get some of the drawing code and control structures already implemented. Of course, if you owner-draw the control, you must do most of the drawing yourself.

When developing ActiveX controls using MFC, you can *subclass* an existing Windows control instead. The techniques are very similar. Both subclassing and superclassing enable you to modify the behavior of an existing window class. Superclassing gives you a bit more control over the process, but it also requires more work to implement.

Other

The Other section enables you to customize certain aspects of your control. Table 8-8 describes each of the three options.

TABLE 8-8 OTHER OPTIONS

Option	Description
Normalize DC	Checking this option causes ATL to pass a normalized device context to your control. This option makes drawing easier, but it is less efficient than managing the DC yourself.

Continued

TABLE 8-8 OTHER OPTIONS *(Continued)*

Option	Description
Insertable	When you check this option, ATL adds the Insertable registry entry for your control. This indicates that the control can be embedded within standard OLE containers such as Microsoft Word.
Windowed Only	Controls created using the ATL behave as windowless controls whenever possible. Windowless controls are more efficient than controls that create a window. However, older containers (such as Visual Basic 4.0) were created before the newer control specifications and they do not support windowless controls. By default, ATL creates a window for controls when embedded in older containers and does not create a window when instantiated in containers that support windowless controls. By checking this option, you specify that your control always requires the existence of a window.

The Stock Properties Tab

When you add an ActiveX control component with the Object wizard, an additional tab is provided to set up the control's initial properties. *Properties* are characteristics of the control that map to an attribute or data member of the underlying component implementation. ATL provides stock implementations for several standard properties. Table 8-3 shows the potential properties and their descriptions. Figure 8-7 displays the Stock Properties dialog box.

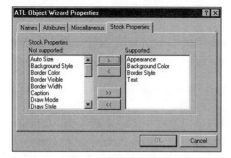

Figure 8-7: Adding stock properties

For each property selected, the Object wizard adds property accessor methods to your control's IDL file and a data member of the appropriate type. The CStockProp Impl class provides the implementation of the property methods, which I discuss in a moment.

Files Created by the ATL Object Wizard

Just as in the previous examples, the Object wizard creates a number of files for your control's implementation. However, as you can see by the abbreviated listing that follows, the implementation classes now include a number of interfaces that you've not encountered before. Controls that want to work in most commercial control containers (such as Visual Basic) must implement these interfaces. I cover most of these classes in the next few sections. The following code is generated by the Object Wizard:

```
class ATL_NO_VTABLE CPostItCtl :
    public CComObjectRootEx<CComSingleThreadModel>,
    public CComCoClass<CPostItCtl, &CLSID_PostItCtl>,
    public CComControl<CPostItCtl>,
    public CStockPropImpl<CPostItCtl, IPostItCtl,
                        &IID_IPostItCtl, &LIBID_POSTITLib>,
    public IProvideClassInfo2Impl<&CLSID_PostItCtl,
                                &DIID__PostItCtlEvents,
                                &LIBID_POSTITLib>,
    public IPersistStreamInitImpl<CPostItCtl>,
    public IPersistStorageImpl<CPostItCtl>,
    public IQuickActivateImpl<CPostItCtl>,
    public IOleControlImpl<CPostItCtl>,
    public IOleObjectImpl<CPostItCtl>,
    public IOleInPlaceActiveObjectImpl<CPostItCtl>,
    public IViewObjectExImpl<CPostItCtl>,
    public IOleInPlaceObjectWindowlessImpl<CPostItCtl>,
    public IDataObjectImpl<CPostItCtl>,
    public IConnectionPointContainerImpl<CPostItCtl>,
    public IPropertyNotifySinkCP<CPostItCtl>,
    public ISpecifyPropertyPagesImpl<CPostItCtl>,
{
...
BEGIN_COM_MAP(CPostItCtl)
    COM_INTERFACE_ENTRY(IPostItCtl)
    COM_INTERFACE_ENTRY(IDispatch)
    COM_INTERFACE_ENTRY_IMPL(IViewObjectEx)
    COM_INTERFACE_ENTRY_IMPL_IID(IID_IViewObject2, IViewObjectEx)
    COM_INTERFACE_ENTRY_IMPL_IID(IID_IViewObject, IViewObjectEx)
    COM_INTERFACE_ENTRY_IMPL(IOleInPlaceObjectWindowless)
    -COM_INTERFACE_ENTRY_IMPL_IID(IID_IOleInPlaceObject,
                                IOleInPlaceObjectWindowless)
    COM_INTERFACE_ENTRY_IMPL_IID(IID_IOleWindow,
```

```
                                    IOleInPlaceObjectWindowless)
    COM_INTERFACE_ENTRY_IMPL(IOleInPlaceActiveObject)
    COM_INTERFACE_ENTRY_IMPL(IOleControl)
    COM_INTERFACE_ENTRY_IMPL(IOleObject)
    COM_INTERFACE_ENTRY_IMPL(IQuickActivate)
    COM_INTERFACE_ENTRY_IMPL(IPersistStorage)
    COM_INTERFACE_ENTRY_IMPL(IPersistStreamInit)
    COM_INTERFACE_ENTRY_IMPL(ISpecifyPropertyPages)
    COM_INTERFACE_ENTRY_IMPL(IDataObject)
    COM_INTERFACE_ENTRY(IProvideClassInfo)
    COM_INTERFACE_ENTRY(IProvideClassInfo2)
    COM_INTERFACE_ENTRY_IMPL(IConnectionPointContainer)
END_COM_MAP()
...
};
```

Some of the interfaces, such as `IConnectionPointContainer` and `IProvide ClassInfo2`, should look familiar. The important point is that it requires quite a bit of work to implement an ActiveX control if you do not use a framework such as MFC or ATL. By examining the preceding code, you should see why.

CComControl

ATL provides a lot of its ActiveX control functionality via the `CComControl` class. This class is similar to MFC's `COleControl` implementation. By deriving your implementation class from `CComControl`, you get support for a number of COM interfaces, stock properties, property persistence, and basic windowing functionality. As you can see from the following code, though, the majority of `CComControl`'s behavior comes from `CComControlBase` and `CWindowImpl`:

```
template <class T>
class ATL_NO_VTABLE CComControl :
      public CComControlBase, public CWindowImpl<T>
{
...
};
```

CComControlBase

The `CComControlBase` class provides most of the functionality of `CComControl`. A control implements several COM interfaces, and many of these interfaces have subtle dependencies on one another. The `CComControlBase` class centralizes data members and functionality shared by several interface implementations (such as `IOleObject`, `IDataObject`, `IViewObjectEx`, and `IOleInPlaceObject`).

CWindowImpl

The `CWindowImpl` class derives from `CWindow`, which provides a thin wrapper around the Win32 windowing functions. It also derives from `CMessageMap`, which enables `CWindowImpl` to implement message mapping and chaining. `CWindowImpl` gives a control the capability to use a window in its implementation; however, the control does not have to use this functionality. If it does, though, it has a basic windowing class through which window messages can be mapped to member functions. This is similar to the functionality provided by MFC message maps.

For example, a control can trap window messages and act on them. Here's the message map from the example control:

```
BEGIN_MSG_MAP(CPostItCtl)
    MESSAGE_HANDLER(WM_PAINT, OnPaint)
    MESSAGE_HANDLER(WM_SETFOCUS, OnSetFocus)
    MESSAGE_HANDLER(WM_KILLFOCUS, OnKillFocus)
    MESSAGE_HANDLER(WM_LBUTTONDOWN, OnLButtonDown)
END_MSG_MAP()
```

The `MESSAGE_HANDLER` macro maps window messages to member functions. ATL message maps, like MFC message maps, allow an object to route or chain messages to other objects. This is useful if your controls comprise multiple windows.

CStockPropImpl

The `CStockPropImpl` class provides ATL's stock property implementation. This class resembles the `IDispatchImpl` class discussed in Chapter 6. In fact, if your control does not implement any stock properties, your implementation class derives from `IDispatchImpl` instead of `CStockPropImpl`.

The example control uses several stock properties. When the Object wizard's stock property dialog box adds the stock properties, it also adds accessor methods to the IDL file and data members to the implementation class. Here's a look at the `BackColor` property:

```
// PostIt.IDL
...
interface IPostItCtl : IDispatch
{
    [propput, id(DISPID_BACKCOLOR)]
        HRESULT BackColor([in]OLE_COLOR clr);
    [propget, id(DISPID_BACKCOLOR)]
        HRESULT BackColor([out,retval]OLE_COLOR* pclr);
...
};
// PostItCtl.h
...
```

```
public:
    OLE_COLOR m_clrBackColor;
```

When the BackColor property declaration is passed through the MIDL compiler, it outputs accessor methods of the form: get_PropertyName and put_Property Name. Take a look at the resulting header file:

```
// PostIt.h
...
IPostItCtl : public IDispatch
{
public:
    virtual HRESULT put_BackColor( OLE_COLOR clr) = 0;
    virtual HRESULT get_BackColor( OLE_COLOR *pclr) = 0;
...
};
```

The CStockPropImpl class uses a series of macros to produce the implementation of the preceding methods. The IMPLEMENT_STOCKPROP macro for BackColor expands to this:

```
//IMPLEMENT_STOCKPROP(OLE_COLOR, BackColor, clrBackColor,
//                    DISPID_BACKCOLOR)
// expands to this:
HRESULT STDMETHODCALLTYPE put_BackColor(OLE_COLOR clrBackColor)
{
    CPostItCtl* pT = (CPostItCtl*) this;
    if (pT->FireOnRequestEdit(DISPID_BACKCOLOR) == S_FALSE)
        return S_FALSE;
    pT->m_clrBackColor = clrBackColor;
    pT->m_bRequiresSave = TRUE;
    pT->FireOnChanged(DISPID_BACKCOLOR);
    pT->FireViewChange();
    return S_OK;
}
HRESULT STDMETHODCALLTYPE get_BackColor(type* pclrBackColor)
{
    CPostItCtl* pT = (CPostItCtl*) this;
    *pclrBackColor = pT->m_clrBackColor;
    return S_OK;
}
```

As you can see, the name of the stock property member variable is important because it is hard-coded into the implementation. Another important aspect of ATL's implementation of stock properties is that the ATL team uses a strange technique to save space. The macros in `CStockPropImpl` are there all the time, but your controls don't implement them always. Why, then, doesn't the compiler complain that the stock property data members (such as `m_clrBackColor`) are not defined?

Thanks to a technique of using a blind union to ensure that the symbols for all the stock properties are predefined, everything works – but it's confusing the first time you run into it. The following union is declared in the `CComControlBase` class, and the comments give you a hint as to what's really going on:

```
union
{
    // m_nFreezeEvents is the only one actually used
    int m_nFreezeEvents; // count of freezes versus thaws
    // These are here to make stock properties work
    IPictureDisp* m_pMouseIcon;
    IPictureDisp* m_pPicture;
    IFontDisp* m_pFont;
    OLE_COLOR m_clrBackColor;
    OLE_COLOR m_clrForeColor;
    ...
    BSTR m_bstrText;
    BSTR m_bstrCaption;
    long m_nBackStyle;
    long m_nBorderStyle;
    long m_nReadyState;
};
```

By placing the names of each stock property member in the union, the compiler is tricked into thinking that storage is allocated. However, only `m_nFreezeEvents` is used. Whenever the control developer implements a stock property such as `BackColor`, the real `m_clrBackColor` variable is declared within the implementation. Yes, this approach saves space – but it causes lots of gray hairs for those of us trying to figure out this stuff.

Initializing Stock and Stock Font Properties

When adding stock properties, the Object wizard provides only a default implementation of the `get` and `put` methods. You must initialize your properties to a default value. A good place to do this is in the control's constructors. It looks something like this:

```
CPostItCtl()
{
```

```
    m_nAppearance = 1;
    m_nBorderStyle = 0;
    // Backcolor is blue
    m_clrBackColor = RGB( 0, 255, 255 );
    // Foreground color is black
    m_clrForeColor = RGB( 0, 0, 0 );
}
```

Initialization of the stock font property requires a bit more work. When you work in COM environments, fonts are handled a bit differently than when you work with Win32 API calls. COM provides several APIs and interfaces to make a Windows font object serializable. The interfaces also enable a font to be marshaled across processes and machines:

```
static FONTDESC _fontDesc =
        { sizeof(FONTDESC), OLESTR("MS Sans Serif"),
          FONTSIZE( 12 ), FW_BOLD,
          ANSI_CHARSET, FALSE, FALSE, FALSE };
OleCreateFontIndirect( &_fontDesc,
                       IID_IFontDisp,
                       (void **)&m_pFont);
```

You initialize your stock font property to MS Sans Serif by creating a FONTDESC structure and passing it to the OleCreateFontIndirect API. COM implements a special font object that provides a mechanism to persist and marshal fonts. ActiveX controls use these fonts through the IFontDisp interface. Your control maintains an IFontDisp pointer to the current stock font object.

IOleObjectImpl

The IOleObject interface provides basic embedded object support so that the component can communicate with the container. IOleObject contains 21 methods; most of them are easy to implement, and only a few are of interest to an ActiveX control implementer. The SetExtent and GetExtent methods negotiate a control's extent or size and the GetMiscStatus method returns the OLEMISC status bits that I covered earlier.

ATL provides a functional implementation of IOleObject through its IOleObjectImpl class. The class provides the basic functionality that most controls need. Although the interface has 21 methods, a control only needs a few of them so ATL implements only that subset.

Restricting the Size of a Control

As an example of how you can modify a control's behavior, I demonstrate how to override one of IOleObject's methods. Certain controls may need to restrict their size or shape. When a control user changes the extents of a control, the container notifies the control of the new size through the IOleObject::SetExtent method. The SetExtent method takes as a parameter a SIZEL structure containing the new extents for the control. To restrict the size of the control, you override the default SetExtent method, check the new extents, and modify them if needed. Here's how to do it for your example control:

```
// PostItCtl.h
...
class ATL_NO_VTABLE CPPostItCtl :
...
    STDMETHOD(SetExtent)(DWORD dwDrawAspect, SIZEL *psizel)
    {
        ATLTRACE(_T("SetExtent sizing control to 1000x1000\n"));
        psizel->cx = psizel->cy = 1000;
        return IOleObjectImpl<CPostItCtl>::SetExtent(dwDrawAspect,
                                                     psizel);
    }
...
};
```

The SIZEL structure provides the extents in OLE's favorite unit: HIMETRIC. In your example, you force the control size to be a square of 1,000 HIMETRIC units.

The ATLTRACE macro resembles MFC's TRACE macro. When a project is compiled and executed in debug mode, ATLTRACE messages are displayed in Developer Studio's debug output window.

IViewObjectImpl

If a control expects to provide a visual representation, it should implement the IViewObjectEx interface. The IViewObject, IViewObject2, and IViewObjectEx interfaces are related; each interface is an extension of the others. The IViewObject interface provides a way for the container to ask a control to render itself. A control implements this interface and draws its representation onto a device context provided by the container. The initial version of this interface, IViewObject, was part of the original OLE document specification. The OLE

Controls '94 specification added GetExtent, which enabled the container to get a control's extents through this interface instead of IOleObject. Finally, as part of the OLE Controls '96 specification, IViewObject2 was enhanced to create IViewObjectEx. This interface includes five new methods that facilitate flicker-free drawing, nonrectangular objects, hit testing, and additional control sizing options.

ATL provides an implementation as well as support for all three of these view interfaces through its IViewObjectImpl class. The most important method of IViewObjectEx is the Draw method. Control containers call this method whenever they need the control to render itself. A number of parameters are passed, most of which deal with how and where to render the control's representation. ATL provides a simplification of the drawing process and ultimately calls the CComControl::OnDraw method.

CComControl::OnDraw

At both design time and run time, the container asks a control to draw its representation through this method. The Object wizard provides a simple implementation of this method that draws the text "ATL 2.0:"

```
HRESULT CNoteCtl::OnDraw(ATL_DRAWINFO& di)
{
    RECT& rc = *(RECT*)di.prcBounds;
    Rectangle(di.hdcDraw, rc.left, rc.top, rc.right, rc.bottom);
    DrawText( di.hdcDraw,
              _T("ATL 2.0"),
              -1,
              &rc,
              DT_CENTER | DT_VCENTER | DT_SINGLELINE );
    return S_OK;
}
```

The container passes a device context as well as the bounding rectangle in which the control should draw its representation.

IDataObjectImpl

Embedded servers use the IDataObject interface to provide the container with a method of rendering data to a device other than a device context. ActiveX controls typically use the IViewObject* interface instead of IDataObject, but it can be implemented if needed.

ATL provides a basic implementation of IDataObject in its IDataObjectImpl class. IDataObjectImpl implements the GetData method, which returns a metafile representation of the control that prints a view of the document. It also implements the DAdvise and DUnadvise methods. These methods set up a notification interface through which the control can notify the container if its representation needs updating.

IOleInPlaceObjectImpl

A control must implement the OLE document IOleInPlaceObject interface to support the capability of activation and deactivation in place within the container. The interface also provides a method to notify the control when its size changes or it is moved within the container.

IOleInPlaceActiveObjectImpl

A control must implement IOleInPlaceActiveObject to provide support for the use and translation of accelerator keys within the control. Many of IOleInPlace ActiveObject's methods are unnecessary for ActiveX controls.

IOleControlImpl

The IOleControl interface provides four methods through which the container gets information about a control's support for mnemonics (GetControlInfo, OnMnemonic), informs the control about any changes to the container's ambient properties (OnAmbientPropertyChange), and informs the control when it should and should not fire events (FreezeEvents).

ATL's implementation (IOleControlImpl) does nothing for the first three methods; the implementation of FreezeEvents is pretty basic. FreezeEvents maintains a member variable, m_nFreezeEvents, which contains the current freeze count. A control should not fire events if this count is greater than zero. However, there is no support in ATL for enforcing this rule; you must do it yourself.

If your control needs to be notified of any change in an ambient property, override OnAmbientPropertyChange:

```
// Demonstrate overriding OnAmbientPropertyChange
STDMETHOD(OnAmbientPropertyChange)(DISPID dispid)
{
    ATLTRACE(_T("An ambient property changed\n"));
    return S_OK;
}
```

IPersistStreamInitImpl and IPersistStorageImpl

If a control has property values that need to persist between instantiations, it must support one or more of COM's persistence interfaces. The control and container work together to store a control's property values in a file (such as FORM.FRM and PAGE.HTM) managed by the container. ATL provides default implementations for the IPersistStreamInit, IPersistStorage, and IPersistPropertyPage interfaces in their corresponding Impl classes.

The implementation of these classes is fairly straightforward. However, ATL has a series of macros that the control developer must use to indicate which properties in a control should persist. Four macros are employed: BEGIN_PROPERTY_MAP, PROP_ENTRY, PROP_PAGE, and END_PROPERTY_MAP. These macros combine to produce a property map.

Property Maps

The Object wizard adds a simple property map to your control's header file. The map is used for several things. It provides a list of properties that should persist, associates each property with its respective property page (if any), and also builds an array of CLSIDs for the ISpecifyPropertyPage::GetPages method described earlier. Here's an example of a property map:

```
BEGIN_PROPERTY_MAP(CPostItCtl)
    PROP_ENTRY( "Text", DISPID_TEXT, CLSID_PostItPpg )
    PROP_ENTRY( "Appearance", DISPID_APPEARANCE, CLSID_PostItPpg )
    PROP_ENTRY( "BorderStyle", DISPID_BORDERSTYLE, CLSID_PostItPpg )
    PROP_ENTRY( "BackColor", DISPID_BACKCOLOR, CLSID_StockColorPage)
    PROP_ENTRY( "ForeColor", DISPID_FORECOLOR, CLSID_StockColorPage )
    PROP_ENTRY( "Font", DISPID_FONT, CLSID_StockFontPage)
    PROP_PAGE(CLSID_StockFontPage)
    PROP_PAGE(CLSID_StockColorPage)
END_PROPERTY_MAP()
```

The PROP_ENTRY macro has three parameters: a description of the property, its DISPID, and the property page on which it resides. If there isn't an associated property page, the value CLSID_NULL is used. The PROP_PAGE macro specifies an ATL stock property page for inclusion when the container constructs the control's property sheet.

ATL's Support for Property Pages

A control's property pages are independent COM objects. ATL provides three stock property pages – one each for fonts, colors, and pictures. If your control has properties of these types, you easily can include them by adding them to your control's property map.

Controls also should implement a custom property page for those properties that are not one of the three stock property page types. ATL provides an Object wizard, included in the Controls tab, for adding custom property pages. To add a custom property page in your control, insert this component into your control project.

A property page simply is a Windows dialog box that supports one COM interface: IPropertyPage. The Object wizard creates a component that derives from both CDialogImpl and IPropertyPageImpl. Here's the initial header file:

```
// PostItPpg.h : Declaration of the CPostItPpg
...
class ATL_NO_VTABLE CPostItPpg :
   public CComObjectRootEx<CComSingleThreadModel>,
   public CComCoClass<CPostItPpg, &CLSID_PostItPpg>,
   public IPropertyPageImpl<CPostItPpg>,
   public CDialogImpl<CPostItPpg>
{
public:
   CPostItPpg()
   {
      m_dwTitleID = IDS_TITLEPostItPpg;
      m_dwHelpFileID = IDS_HELPFILEPostItPpg;
      m_dwDocStringID = IDS_DOCSTRINGPostItPpg;
   }
   enum {IDD = IDD_POSTITPPG};

DECLARE_REGISTRY_RESOURCEID(IDR_POSTITPPG)

BEGIN_COM_MAP(CPostItPpg)
    COM_INTERFACE_ENTRY_IMPL(IPropertyPage)
END_COM_MAP()

BEGIN_MSG_MAP(CPostItPpg)
   CHAIN_MSG_MAP(IPropertyPageImpl<CPostItPpg>)
END_MSG_MAP()
};
```

Most of the preceding code should look familiar to you. The new classes are CDialogImpl and IPropertyPageImpl.

CDialogImpl

ATL's `CDialogImpl` class provides a basic implementation of a Windows dialog box. The dialog box can be modeless or modal, and it uses an associated dialog box resource. `CDialogImpl` derives from both `CWindow` and `CMessageMap` and so has all the methods provided by these classes. Most important is the capability to route Windows messages via ATL's message map mechanism. (I discuss this earlier in the chapter).

When inserting the property page component, the Object wizard also inserts a dialog box resource into your project's `.RC` file. The next step is to add controls to the dialog box. You also must add a significant amount of code to manage moving property values to and from the dialog box controls.

When the property page is loaded initially, you must retrieve and set the control's property values in the dialog box. If any properties have enumerated types, you also must handle this. The best place to do all this is in the `WM_INITDIALOG` message. Here's some code from the example:

```
LRESULT CPostItPpg::OnInitDialog( UINT, WPARAM wParam, LPARAM
lParam, BOOL& )
{
   USES_CONVERSION;
   if ( m_nObjects > 0 )
   {
      CComQIPtr<IPostItCtl, &IID_IPostItCtl> pPostItCtl( m_ppUnk[0]
                                                               );

      BSTR bstrText = 0;
      if SUCCEEDED( pPostItCtl->get_Text( &bstrText ))
         SetDlgItemText( IDC_TEXT, W2A( bstrText ));

      // Initialize the Appearance combo box
      SendDlgItemMessage( IDC_APPEARANCE,
                          CB_ADDSTRING,
                          0,
                          (long) "0 - Flat" );
      SendDlgItemMessage( IDC_APPEARANCE,
                          CB_ADDSTRING,
                          0,
                          (long) "1 - 3D" );

      // Get the current value of the Appearance property
      long lAppearance;
      if SUCCEEDED( pPostItCtl->get_Appearance( &lAppearance ))
         ::SendMessage( GetDlgItem( IDC_APPEARANCE ),
                    CB_SETCURSEL,
                    lAppearance,
```

```
                        0 );
    ...
    }
    return 1;
}
```

IPropertyPageImpl

As expected, the IPropertyPageImpl class implements the IPropertyPage inter-face. ATL also provides the IPropertyPage2Impl class, but it does not implement the extra method (EditProperty) added via IPropertyPage2 so it isn't used. The IPropertyPage interface has 11 methods. The most important methods are SetObjects, which passes an array of IDispatch interfaces for the associated con-trols; Show, which forces the page to display; and Apply, which is called when the user moves to another page or clicks the Apply button.

ATL doesn't provide a nice data exchange facility like MFC's *DDX (dialog data exchange)*, so you must write a lot of Win32 code when developing property pages for your ATL controls. As an example, here is the code needed to update one prop-erty in a control when the user presses the Apply button on the page:

```
STDMETHODIMP CPostItPpg::Apply(void)
{
    USES_CONVERSION;
    for (UINT i = 0; i < m_nObjects; i++)
    {
        CComQIPtr<IPostItCtl, &IID_IPostItCtl> pPostItCtl( m_ppUnk[i]
                                                        );
        BSTR bstrText = 0;
        if ( GetDlgItemText( IDC_TEXT, bstrText ) )
        {
            if FAILED( pPostItCtl->put_Text( bstrText ))
            {
                HandleError();
                return E_FAIL;
            }
        }
    }
    m_bDirty = FALSE;
    return S_OK;
}
```

The code obtains an interface pointer to the control's custom interface (remem-ber, it implements a dual interface), extracts the property value from the dialog box's control, and calls the appropriate put method to update the control's property. These steps must be performed for each property on the property page.

Building an Example Control

That concludes my whirlwind coverage of the ActiveX control specifications and ATL's support for building controls. Next I demonstrate the requirements to develop an ActiveX control with ATL. I build a basic control that uses most of the control functionality provided by ATL. It's hard to cover everything you can do with ATL and ActiveX controls in one chapter, but I try. By learning the basics of how controls work and how ATL implements the various control interfaces, you should have a solid foundation on which to develop your own controls. Also, visit www.WidgetWare.com and check out the ActiveX control FAQ area when you encounter problems developing your own controls. There, you can find answers to more than 100 questions on COM, OLE, and ActiveX development.

Create the Control's Housing

Start Visual C++ and create a new project, selecting ATL COM AppWizard. Give it the name PostIt. In Step 1 of 1, select a type of DLL. Then select Finish and OK to generate the project.

Use ATL Object Wizard

Using the ATL Object wizard, insert a full control component into your server's housing. Then fill out the four tabbed dialog boxes with the information provided next.

Use the Names and Attributes Tabs

Take the default settings after giving the control a name of PostItCtl. Figure 8-8 shows the finished Names tab. On the Attributes tab, be sure to enable the Support Connection Points option because you need to add an event to your control.

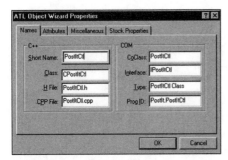

Figure 8-8: The Names dialog box

Use the Miscellaneous Tab

The Miscellaneous tab provides ActiveX control-specific information to the Object wizard. Take the defaults for each of the options. The Miscellaneous tab appears in Figure 8-6.

Use the Stock Properties Tab

When you add an ActiveX control component with the Object wizard, an additional tab is provided to set up the control's initial stock properties. The potential properties and their descriptions appear in Table 8-3.

For your example control, add the following properties on the Stock Properties tab (the resulting dialog box is shown in Figure 8-9):

- ◆ Appearance
- ◆ Background Color
- ◆ Border Style
- ◆ Font
- ◆ Foreground Color
- ◆ Text

After filling out the four tabbed dialogs, click OK.

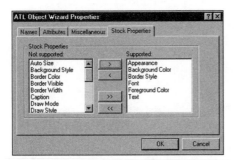

Figure 8-9: Adding stock properties

Creating a Basic Control

Your control isn't functional right out of the box, but that gives you an opportunity to learn as you add functionality. The ATL Object wizard creates a control that implements 17 interfaces. As described, a control that implements the majority of these control interfaces should work in almost any container that supports ActiveX controls. However, a control developer doesn't have to implement all these interfaces. The new control standards stipulate that a control must implement only those interfaces that it needs to supply its functionality. This is just fine, but most of today's containers expect a number of them to be there. That's why I'm choosing to implement a control that implements them all.

Initializing Your Stock Properties

When you add your control's stock properties through the ATL Object wizard, it basically does one thing: it creates data members within your class to hold the values of your properties. Here's a look at the code:

```
// PostItCtl.H
...
class ATL_NO_VTABLE CPostItCtl :
    public CComObjectRootEx<CComSingleThreadModel>,
{
...
// IPostItCtl
public:
    HRESULT OnDraw(ATL_DRAWINFO& di)
    {
        RECT& rc = *(RECT*)di.prcBounds;
        Rectangle(di.hdcDraw, rc.left, rc.top, rc.right, rc.bottom);
        SetTextAlign(di.hdcDraw, TA_CENTER|TA_BASELINE);
        LPCTSTR pszText = _T("ATL 3.0 : PostItCtl");
        TextOut(di.hdcDraw,
                (rc.left + rc.right) / 2,
                (rc.top + rc.bottom) / 2,
                pszText,
                lstrlen(pszText));
        return S_OK;
    }

    short m_nAppearance;
    OLE_COLOR m_clrBackColor;
    LONG m_nBorderStyle;
    CComPtr<IFontDisp> m_pFont;
    OLE_COLOR m_clrForeColor;
    CComBSTR m_bstrText;
};
```

However, that's all it does. You still need to set the initial values for the properties because the default ATL implementation doesn't do that for you. A good place to do this is in the control's constructor:

```
CPostItCtl()
{
    m_nAppearance = 1;
    m_nBorderStyle = 0;
    m_clrBackColor = RGB( 0, 255, 255 );
    m_clrForeColor = RGB( 0, 0, 0 );
    static FONTDESC _fontDesc =
         { sizeof(FONTDESC), OLESTR("MS Sans Serif"),
           FONTSIZE( 12 ), FW_BOLD,
           ANSI_CHARSET, FALSE, FALSE, FALSE };
    OleCreateFontIndirect( &_fontDesc,
                           IID_IFontDisp,
                           (void **)&m_pFont);
}
```

Remember the discussion on initialization of properties from earlier in this chapter? In the preceding code, you set the background color to blue, the foreground color to black, and the font to MS Sans Serif. Table 8-9 details the meaning of your integer properties.

TABLE 8-9 PROPERTY VALUES

Property	Values
Appearance	0: Flat 1: 3D
BorderStyle	0: None 1: Single Line

CComControl::OnDraw

Most ActiveX controls provide some sort of visual representation. Your PostIt control basically is an expensive Windows label control. Drawing text on the screen provides the majority of its functionality, but the control demonstrates much of what you can do within an ActiveX control.

When your control is embedded, the container instantiates the control instance, loads any property values, and tells the control to render itself again. Whenever the control's region needs redrawing, the container again tells the control to render itself. The nice thing about all this is that the control always is notified through the OnDraw method. However, the default code provided by the Object wizard doesn't do much.

The first thing you need to do is add some drawing code. When the container asks the control to render itself, the container provides a device context on which to render. In most cases, the container provides a DC that is part of its own window. With older tools, such as MFC, a control gets its own window. Today, though, that isn't always the case. It's not a big deal; all you need is a device context on which to draw. Replace the wizard-provided code with this:

```
HRESULT OnDraw(ATL_DRAWINFO& di)
{
    USES_CONVERSION;
    COLORREF  colBack, colFore;
    HBRUSH    hOldBrush = 0;
    HBRUSH    hBackBrush = 0;
    HDC       hdc = di.hdcDraw;
    RECT& rc = *(RECT*)di.prcBounds;
    // Convert the OLE_COLOR types into COLORREFs
    OleTranslateColor( m_clrBackColor, NULL, &colBack );
    OleTranslateColor( m_clrForeColor, NULL, &colFore );

    // Create a brush using the background color
    // and select it into the DC
    hBackBrush = (HBRUSH) CreateSolidBrush( colBack );
    hOldBrush = (HBRUSH) SelectObject( hdc, hBackBrush );

    // Fill the background with our new brush
    FillRect( hdc, &rc, hBackBrush );

    // If the BorderStyle is 1, draw
    // a border around the control
    if ( m_nBorderStyle )
    {
        HPEN hPen = (HPEN) CreatePen( PS_SOLID, 1, RGB( 0, 0, 0 ));
        HPEN hOldPen = (HPEN) SelectObject( hdc, hPen );
        Rectangle( hdc, rc.left, rc.top, rc.right, rc.bottom );
        if ( hOldPen )
            SelectObject( hdc, hOldPen );
        DeleteObject( hPen );
    }

    // If the appearance is 3-D, draw an edge
    if ( m_nAppearance )
    {
        DrawEdge( hdc, &rc, EDGE_SUNKEN, BF_RECT );
        // Adjust our rectangle
        rc.left += 2;
```

```
   rc.top += 2;
   rc.bottom -= 2;
   rc.right -= 2;
}

// Get the user-selected font and select
// it into our device context.
CComQIPtr<IFont, &IID_IFont> pFont( m_pFont );
HFONT hOldFont = 0;
HFONT hFont = 0;
if ( pFont )
{
   pFont->get_hFont( &hFont );
   pFont->AddRefHfont( hFont );
   hOldFont = (HFONT) SelectObject( hdc, hFont );
}

// Check to see if we're in design mode or
// run-time mode. If in design mode, get the
// ambient display name and draw it within
// the control.
BOOL bUserMode = FALSE;
GetAmbientUserMode( bUserMode );
if ( bUserMode == FALSE )
{
   BSTR bstr = 0;
   if ( SUCCEEDED( GetAmbientDisplayName( bstr )))
   {
      SetBkMode( hdc, TRANSPARENT );
      SetTextColor( hdc, colFore );
      DrawText( hdc,
                W2A( bstr ),
                -1,
                &rc,
                DT_TOP | DT_SINGLELINE );
   }
}

// Draw the user-specified text
if ( m_bstrText.Length() )
{
   SetBkMode( hdc, TRANSPARENT );
   SetTextColor( hdc, colFore );
   DrawText( hdc,
             W2A( m_bstrText ),
```

```
                     -1,
                     &rc,
                     DT_CENTER | DT_VCENTER | DT_WORDBREAK );
      }

      // Release the IFont object. We don't
      // delete the font because the OLE font
      // object manages this
      if ( pFont )
         pFont->ReleaseHfont( hFont );

      // Restore the old font
      if ( hOldFont )
         SelectObject( hdc, hOldFont );

      // Restore the old brush and delete
      // the one we created earlier
      if ( hOldBrush )
      {
         SelectObject( hdc, hOldBrush );
         DeleteObject( hBackBrush );
      }
      return S_OK;
}
```

That's a lot of code, but it's commented liberally so that you don't have to go over every line. Basically, you're using the stock properties that you set up to render the control. After adding the preceding code, rebuild the project and insert the control in Visual Basic; now you have a functional control.

Implementing Persistence of Your Control's Properties: Property Maps

For your control's properties to persist, they must be added to ATL's property map. However, the ATL Object wizard adds the appropriate macro entries automatically, so you just take a look at them here.

For each property that you want to make persistent, you must add a PROP_ENTRY macro with a textual description of the property, the property's DISPID, and any associated property page. Your control doesn't have any property pages yet, which is why you see the use of CLSID_NULL instead. The following highlighted code implements persistence for your standard properties, as added by the wizard:

```
//
// PostItCtl.h : Declaration of the CPostItCtl
//
```

```
...
class ATL_NO_VTABLE CPostItCtl :
    public CComObjectRootEx<CComSingleThreadModel>,
...
BEGIN_PROPERTY_MAP(CPostItCtl)
    PROP_DATA_ENTRY("_cx", m_sizeExtent.cx, VT_UI4)
    PROP_DATA_ENTRY("_cy", m_sizeExtent.cy, VT_UI4)
    PROP_ENTRY("Appearance", DISPID_APPEARANCE, CLSID_NULL)
    PROP_ENTRY("BackColor", DISPID_BACKCOLOR, CLSID_StockColorPage)
    PROP_ENTRY("BorderStyle", DISPID_BORDERSTYLE, CLSID_NULL)
    PROP_ENTRY("Font", DISPID_FONT, CLSID_StockFontPage)
    PROP_ENTRY("ForeColor", DISPID_FORECOLOR, CLSID_StockColorPage)
    PROP_ENTRY("Text", DISPID_TEXT, CLSID_NULL)
    // Example entries
    // PROP_ENTRY("Property Description", dispid, clsid)
    // PROP_PAGE(CLSID_StockColorPage)
END_PROPERTY_MAP()
```

Adding Stock Property Pages

As described earlier, ATL provides three stock property pages for standard, often-used property types such as font, color, and picture. The stock property pages have standard CLSIDs, and you can use them directly within your control. Again, the wizard makes these entries for use in the property map, as shown in the highlighted code:

```
BEGIN_PROPERTY_MAP(CPostItCtl)
    PROP_DATA_ENTRY("_cx", m_sizeExtent.cx, VT_UI4)
    PROP_DATA_ENTRY("_cy", m_sizeExtent.cy, VT_UI4)
    PROP_ENTRY("Appearance", DISPID_APPEARANCE, CLSID_NULL)
    PROP_ENTRY("BackColor", DISPID_BACKCOLOR, CLSID_StockColorPage)
    PROP_ENTRY("BorderStyle", DISPID_BORDERSTYLE, CLSID_NULL)
    PROP_ENTRY("Font", DISPID_FONT, CLSID_StockFontPage)
    PROP_ENTRY("ForeColor", DISPID_FORECOLOR, CLSID_StockColorPage)
    PROP_ENTRY("Text", DISPID_TEXT, CLSID_NULL)
    // Example entries
    // PROP_ENTRY("Property Description", dispid, clsid)
    // PROP_PAGE(CLSID_StockColorPage)
END_PROPERTY_MAP()
```

By launching the control's custom property sheet, you see something like Figure 8-10.

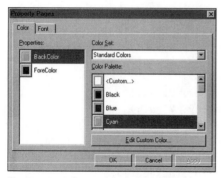

Figure 8-10: Custom property pages

A control also should implement a custom property page for any properties not handled by the stock property pages. You have stock property pages for three of your six properties; you need a custom page for the remaining three.

Adding a Custom Property Page

Early in this example when you added the PostIt control to your project using the ATL Object wizard, only the control component was added. As you now understand, a property page is an independent COM object used by the container to interact with a control. To add a custom property page to the control, you use the Object wizard again. Fire it up by pressing the Insert → New ATL Object menu item. Select Controls and Property Page and click Next. You see something like that in Figure 8-11.

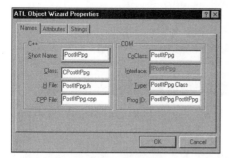

Figure 8-11: Property page properties

Enter a short name of PostItPpg and take the defaults for the rest of the Names tab. Also take the defaults for the Attributes tab, and enter the appropriate information in the Strings tab. When finished, click OK. The ATL Object wizard creates the files listed in Table 8-10.

TABLE 8-10 PROPERTY PAGE FILES

File	Description
PostItPpg.h	The header file for your new property page class: CPostItPpg
PostItPpg.cpp	The CPostItPpg class implementation
PostItPpg.rgs	The registry script for your property page object
PostIt.rc	A resource is added for the property page dialog box.

The ATL Object wizard adds several new files to support the custom property page for your control. First, edit the dialog box resource and add controls for each of your three properties. Table 8-11 details the control types and identifiers. Figure 8-12 shows you how to build the dialog box with the Visual C++ resource editor.

TABLE 8-11 PROPERTY PAGE CONTROLS AND IDS

Control Type	Identifier
Multi-line entry field	IDC_TEXT
Drop-list combo box	IDC_APPEARANCE
Drop-list combo box	IDC_BORDERSTYLE

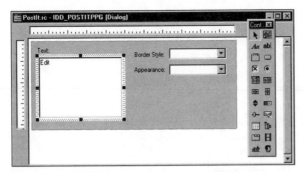

Figure 8-12: Building the property page dialog box

After you build the dialog box, you need to populate the controls with valid property values. As the property page loads, you must retrieve the current property values from the associated control instance. The best time to do this is when the dialog box is being created. Override WM_INITDIALOG by adding the following PostItPpg.H and PostItPpg.CPP files:

```
// PostItPpg.h : Declaration of the CPostItPpg
#include "resource.h"
#include "PostIt.h"

class ATL_NO_VTABLE CPostItPpg :
    public CComObjectRootEx<CComSingleThreadModel>,
    public CComCoClass<CPostItPpg, &CLSID_PostItPpg>,
...
BEGIN_MSG_MAP(CPostItPpg)
   MESSAGE_HANDLER( WM_INITDIALOG, OnInitDialog )
   CHAIN_MSG_MAP(IPropertyPageImpl<CPostItPpg>)
END_MSG_MAP()

LRESULT OnInitDialog( UINT, WPARAM wParam, LPARAM lParam, BOOL& );
...
};

// PostItPpg.CPP
...
LRESULT CPostItPpg::OnInitDialog( UINT, WPARAM wParam,
                                  LPARAM lParam, BOOL& )
{
   USES_CONVERSION;
   if ( m_nObjects > 0 )
     {
      CComQIPtr<IPostItCtl, &IID_IPostItCtl> pPostItCtl( m_ppUnk[0]
                                                       );
      BSTR bstrText = 0;
      if SUCCEEDED( pPostItCtl->get_Text( &bstrText ))
         SetDlgItemText( IDC_TEXT, W2A( bstrText ));

      // Initialize the Appearance combo box
      SendDlgItemMessage( IDC_APPEARANCE,
                          CB_ADDSTRING,
                          0,
                          (long) "0 - Flat" );
      SendDlgItemMessage( IDC_APPEARANCE,
                          CB_ADDSTRING,
                          0,
                          (long) "1 - 3D" );
```

```
        // Get the current value of the Appearance property
        short sAppearance;
        if SUCCEEDED( pPostItCtl->get_Appearance( &sAppearance ))
          ::SendMessage( GetDlgItem( IDC_APPEARANCE ),
                    CB_SETCURSEL,
                    sAppearance,
                    0 );

        // Initialize the BorderStyle combo box
        SendDlgItemMessage( IDC_BORDERSTYLE,
                    CB_ADDSTRING,
                    0,
                    (long) "0 - None" );
        SendDlgItemMessage( IDC_BORDERSTYLE,
                    CB_ADDSTRING,
                    0,
                    (long) "1 - Single Line" );

        // Get the current value of the BorderStyle property
        long lBorderStyle;
        if SUCCEEDED( pPostItCtl->get_BorderStyle( &lBorderStyle ))
          ::SendMessage( GetDlgItem( IDC_BORDERSTYLE ),
                    CB_SETCURSEL,
                    lBorderStyle,
                    0 );
    }
    return 1;
}
```

When the dialog box (property page) initially is created, you are performing two basic functions. First, you query for the control's dual interface – IPostItCtl. Once you have a pointer to this interface, you pull property values from the control. Also, you're populating your drop-list combo boxes with valid property values. Once populated, you retrieve the value from the control and set the current selection.

The preceding code initially sets up the property page. However, if a user changes a value on the property page, you must pass the new value to the associated control. You also must enable the Apply button on the property sheet whenever a value changes. First, you must trap the EN_CHANGE and CBN_CHANGE events so that you're notified every time the entry field or one of the combo boxes is modified:

```
// PostItPpg.h
...
BEGIN_MSG_MAP(CPostItPpg)
    COMMAND_HANDLER( IDC_TEXT, EN_CHANGE, OnPropertyChange )
    COMMAND_HANDLER( IDC_APPEARANCE, CBN_SELCHANGE, OnPropertyChange )
```

```
    COMMAND_HANDLER( IDC_BORDERSTYLE, CBN_SELCHANGE, OnPropertyChange )
    MESSAGE_HANDLER( WM_INITDIALOG, OnInitDialog )
    CHAIN_MSG_MAP(IPropertyPageImpl<CPostItPpg>)
END_MSG_MAP()

LRESULT OnPropertyChange( WORD wNotify, WORD wID, HWND hWnd,
                          BOOL& bHandled );
```

The following snippet of code sets the dirty flag for the page (thus enabling the Apply button) and notifies any attached property browsers (such as Visual Basic) that the property value has changed:

```
// PostItPpg.Cpp
...
LRESULT CPostItPpg::OnPropertyChange( WORD wNotify, WORD wID, HWND hWnd,
                                      BOOL& bHandled )
{
    SetDirty( TRUE );
    m_pPageSite->OnStatusChange( PROPPAGESTATUS_DIRTY |
                                 PROPPAGESTATUS_VALIDATE );
    return 0;
}
```

All that remains is to implement the functionality of the Apply button. Here's what you need to add:

```
// PostItPpg.h
...
class ATL_NO_VTABLE CPostItPpg :
    public CComObjectRootEx<CComSingleThreadModel>,
{
...
STDMETHOD(Apply)(void);
private:
    void HandleError();
};
// PostItPpg.cpp
...
void CPostItPpg::HandleError()
{
    USES_CONVERSION;
    CComPtr<IErrorInfo> pError;
    CComBSTR strError;
    GetErrorInfo( 0, &pError );
    pError->GetDescription( &strError );
```

```
        MessageBox( OLE2T(strError),
                    _T("Error"),
                    MB_ICONEXCLAMATION );
}
STDMETHODIMP CPostItPpg::Apply(void)
{
    USES_CONVERSION;
    for (UINT i = 0; i < m_nObjects; i++)
    {
        CComQIPtr<IPostItCtl, &IID_IPostItCtl> pPostItCtl( m_ppUnk[i]
                                                          );

        BSTR bstrText = 0;
        if ( GetDlgItemText( IDC_TEXT, bstrText ) )
        {
            if FAILED( pPostItCtl->put_Text( bstrText ))
            {
                HandleError();
                return E_FAIL;
            }
        }
        enum enumAppearance eAppearance;
        eAppearance = (enum enumAppearance)
                        SendDlgItemMessage( IDC_APPEARANCE,
                                            CB_GETCURSEL,
                                            0, 0 );
        if FAILED( pPostItCtl->put_Appearance( eAppearance ))
        {
            HandleError();
            return E_FAIL;
        }
        long lBorderStyle;
        lBorderStyle = SendDlgItemMessage( IDC_BORDERSTYLE,
                                           CB_GETCURSEL,
                                           0, 0 );
        if FAILED( pPostItCtl->put_BorderStyle( lBorderStyle ))
        {
            HandleError();
            return E_FAIL;
        }
    }
    m_bDirty = FALSE;
    return S_OK;
}
```

Now you must go back to the code for your control and update it with your new property page. You modify your property map to include the CLSID of your custom property page:

```
BEGIN_PROPERTY_MAP(CPostItCtl)
    PROP_DATA_ENTRY("_cx", m_sizeExtent.cx, VT_UI4)
    PROP_DATA_ENTRY("_cy", m_sizeExtent.cy, VT_UI4)
    PROP_ENTRY("Appearance", DISPID_APPEARANCE, CLSID_PostItPpg)
    PROP_ENTRY("BackColor", DISPID_BACKCOLOR, CLSID_StockColorPage)
    PROP_ENTRY("BorderStyle", DISPID_BORDERSTYLE, CLSID_PostItPpg)
    PROP_ENTRY("Font", DISPID_FONT, CLSID_StockFontPage)
    PROP_ENTRY("ForeColor", DISPID_FORECOLOR, CLSID_StockColorPage)
    PROP_ENTRY("Text", DISPID_TEXT, CLSID_PostItPpg)
    // Example entries
    // PROP_ENTRY("Property Description", dispid, clsid)
    // PROP_PAGE(CLSID_StockColorPage)
END_PROPERTY_MAP()
```

You've made a lot of changes. Go ahead and rebuild the project. Fire up Visual Basic and check out the new functionality. The custom property page enables you to change any of the control's properties. As soon as you press the Apply button, the control redraws.

Adding Events to a Control

Controls implement events using COM's connectable object technology. (Chapter 7 covers connection points and events in detail.) The following steps demonstrate the requirements to add an outgoing interface to an ActiveX control. Your example control already has the default implementation of IConnectionPointContainer and IProvideClassInfo2 provided by the Object wizard. You need to define your interface, use the Connection Point wizard to create a wrapper class, and then fire the event through the client's interface implementation.

A control's outgoing event interface must be a dispinterface for most containers; it also must be declared within the library section of your control's IDL file. Your example control implements the stock Click event. First, define it. The wizard adds the interface declaration. All you need to do is add the specific method, Click:

```
// PostIt.IDL
...
library POSTITLib
{
    importlib("stdole32.tlb");
    importlib("stdole2.tlb");
```

```
[
    uuid(BF31419F-B661-11D3-8391-0060081AEB5F),
    helpstring("_IPostItCtlEvents Interface")
]
dispinterface _IPostItCtlEvents
{
    properties:
    methods:
        [id(DISPID_CLICK)] void Click();
};

[
    uuid(CFC43231-50AC-11D1-B5EC-0004ACFF171C),
    helpstring("PostItCtl Class")
]
coclass PostItCtl
{
    [default] interface IPostItCtl;
    [default, source] dispinterface _PostItCtlEvents;
};
...
};
```

You declare a dispinterface that has one method, Click. You need to generate the preceding GUID manually using the GUIDGEN utility.

Using the Connection Point Wizard

Build the project to update the type library and then use the Connection Point wizard to generate a wrapper class for the outgoing interface. Chapter 7 outlines the steps to do this. Accept the default name of CPPostIt.CPP. Next, include the file in your control's header file, update the IProvideClassInfo2Impl declaration, and add the class to the connection map. These steps are highlighted in the code:

```
//
// PostItCtl.h : Declaration of the CPostItCtl
//
...
#include "PostitCP.h"

class ATL_NO_VTABLE CPostItCtl :
    public CComObjectRootEx<CComSingleThreadModel>,
    public CComCoClass<CPostItCtl, &CLSID_PostItCtl>,
    public CComControl<CPostItCtl>,
```

```
    public CStockPropImpl<CPostItCtl, IPostItCtl,
                          &IID_IPostItCtl, &LIBID_POSTITLib>,
    public IProvideClassInfo2Impl<&CLSID_PostItCtl,
                                  &DIID__PostItCtlEvents,
                                  &LIBID_POSTITLib>,

    ...

    public CProxyIPostItCtlEvents<CPostItCtl>
{
...
BEGIN_CONNECTION_POINT_MAP(CPostItCtl)
    CONNECTION_POINT_ENTRY(IID_IPropertyNotifySink)
    CONNECTION_POINT_ENTRY(DIID__PostItCtlEvents)
END_CONNECTION_POINT_MAP()
```

All that's left is to trap the WM_LBUTTONDOWN message and fire the event through the outgoing interface. You add a message map entry and implement the method:

```
// PostItCtl.H
...
class ATL_NO_VTABLE CPostItCtl :
    public CComObjectRootEx<CComSingleThreadModel>,
{
...
BEGIN_MSG_MAP(CPostItCtl)
    ...
    MESSAGE_HANDLER(WM_LBUTTONDOWN, OnLButtonDown)
END_MSG_MAP()
...
private:
    LRESULT OnLButtonDown(UINT uMsg, WPARAM wParam,
                          LPARAM lParam, BOOL& bHandled);
    ...
};

// PostItCtl.CPP
...
LRESULT CPostItCtl::OnLButtonDown(UINT uMsg, WPARAM wParam,
                                  LPARAM lParam, BOOL& bHandled)
{
    Fire_Click();
    return 0;
}
```

Your control now supports the Click event. Build the project and you have a control that implements nearly every aspect of ATL's control support. Chapter 9 covers any remaining steps.

The Visual Basic project included with the downloadable examples demonstrates the use of the example control. You also can use it in Visual C++ applications, Internet Explorer, and most other ActiveX control containers.

Summary

In this chapter, you learned the basics of ActiveX controls. In particular, you learned:

- ◆ ActiveX controls are just specialized COM components
- ◆ ActiveX controls depend on an ActiveX control container for much of their functionality
- ◆ That ActiveX controls use many of the COM technologies that we've covered in previous chapters
- ◆ ATL provides significant support for building ActiveX controls

In Chapter 9, I cover COM's support for managing lists of common data items through enumerators and collections.

Chapter 9

COM Enumerators and Collections

IN THIS CHAPTER

- ◆ Iteration with COM enumerators
- ◆ Accessing list of items in COM
- ◆ ATL's support for enumerator-based components
- ◆ Iteration with COM collections
- ◆ ATL's support for building collection components

MANAGING A LIST OF related items is a common aspect of software development. COM provides a standard technique for inserting and iterating a list of items through its concept of an enumerator object. Certain languages and tools, such as Visual Basic, expand this idea to include the concept of a collection, which exposes an enumerator object in a standard way. In this chapter, I cover both techniques.

COM Enumerators

COM provides a standard interface type for iterating over a list of specifically typed items. COM itself provides several implementations of this standard interface for various COM data types. Of course, you can design your own iterator interface using your specific type by adhering to this standard. The standard iterator interface is described in the documentation as the IEnumXXXX interface. Of course, the IEnumXXXX interface doesn't exist really because the XXXX always gets replaced with a distinct type such as VARIANT, a CLSID, a BSTR, and so on. Here is the definition of the basic IEnumXXXX interface:

```
interface IEnumXXXX : IUnknown
{
    virtual HRESULT Next(unsigned long celt,
                    XXXX*  rgelt,
                    unsigned long *pceltFetched) = 0;
    virtual HRESULT Skip(unsigned long celt) = 0;
```

```
    virtual HRESULT Reset() = 0;
    virtual HRESULT Clone(IEnumXXXX **ppenum) = 0;
};
```

Built-in Enumerator Interfaces

COM provides a number of ready-to-use iterator interfaces based on the `IEnumXXX` definition(as shown in Table 9-1). I use the `IEnumCLSID`, `IEnumString`, and `IEnumVariant` interfaces in the chapter examples.

TABLE 9-1 STANDARD COM ENUMERATOR INTERFACES

Interface	Description
IEnumCLSID	Iterates a list of common CLSIDs
IEnumString	Iterates a list of BSTRs
IEnumUnknown	Iterates a list of IUnknown interface pointers
IEnumVariant	Iterates a list of data stored in a VARIANT
IEnumFORMATETC	Iterates a list of FORMATETC data structures
IEnumOLEVERB	Iterates a list of OLEVERB elements. Each item describes operations that can be performed on a given OLE object.

The IEnumString Interface

The standard enumerator interfaces each contain the same four methods, all of which deal with iteration of the underlying data type. To make your discussion more concrete, let's use an existing standard enumerator interface: `IEnumString`. Here is its definition:

```
interface IEnumString : IUnknown
{
    virtual HRESULT Next(unsigned long celt,
                         LPOLESTR *rgelt,
                         unsigned long *pceltFetched) = 0;
    virtual HRESULT Skip(unsigned long celt) = 0;
    virtual HRESULT Reset() = 0;
    virtual HRESULT Clone(IEnumString **ppenum) = 0;
};
```

The Next method retrieves the next series of elements. The celt parameter specifies how many to return via the rgelt parameter, which is a pointer to an array. If there are fewer items than requested, the pceltFetched parameter contains the actual number of elements returned.The Skip method skips over the specified number of elements in the sequence. The Reset method sets the enumeration sequence back to the beginning element. The Clone method creates another enumeration object that contains the same state (for example, position) as the current one. This enables a client application to maintain multiple positions within a given enumeration.

Client Enumerator Access

Client applications access enumerator interfaces just as they do all other COM interfaces. Component applications can expose the various IEnumXXXX interfaces directly through an enumerator object or indirectly through the concept of a *collection object*. I talk about the collection technique in the next section. You can demonstrate a simple example of accessing an enumerator object with the system-provided Component Categories Manager component:

```
HRESULT hr;
ICatInformation* pci = 0;

// Create an instance of the CCM and ask for ICatInformation
hr = CoCreateInstance( CLSID_StdComponentCategoriesMgr,
                       NULL,
                       CLSCTX_INPROC_SERVER,
                       IID_ICatInformation,
                       (void**) &pci );

// We're looking for components that implement the 'Control'
category
CATID catidImpl[1];
catidImpl[0] = CATID_Control;
IEnumCLSID* pEnum = 0;

// The list of controls is passed back via IEnumCLSID
hr = pci->EnumClassesOfCategories( 1, catidImpl, 0, 0, &pEnum );

// Spin through the list components
GUID guids[1];
ULONG ulNum;
hr = pEnum->Next( 1, guids, &ulNum );
while(  hr == S_OK )
{
   // Look up the ProgID
```

```
WCHAR* pProgID = 0;
ProgIDFromCLSID( guids[0], &pProgID );

WCHAR* pCLSIDString = 0;
StringFromCLSID( guids[0], &pCLSIDString );

// Display controls ProgID and CLSID
USES_CONVERSION;
cout << W2A( pProgID ) << " - " << W2A( pCLSIDString ) <<endl;

// Free up any memory
CoTaskMemFree( pProgID );
CoTaskMemFree( pCLSIDString );

hr = pEnum->Next( 1, guids, &ulNum );
}
```

The preceding code creates an instance of the Component Categories Manager and asks for the `ICatInformation` interface. This interface provides a series of methods that enable the user to retrieve lists of components that meet certain criteria. In the previous example, you use the `EnumClassesOfCategories` method to get a list of components that implement the Control category. In other words, you want a list of all ActiveX controls on the machine.

The `EnumClassesOfCategories` method returns an enumerator interface of type CLSID, or `IEnumCLSID`, which provides a way to *iterate* the list of returned components. The remainder of the code demonstrates using the `IEnumCLSID::Next` method to fetch the component CLSIDs one at a time. As you retrieve the CLSIDs, they are converted to the appropriate ProgID and written to the display. Figure 9-1 shows the output from this code.

Figure 9-1: Output of the `IEnumCLSID` example

ATL's Enumerator Support

Client access to enumerator objects is straightforward. However, building a COM object that supports enumeration is a bit more difficult. For that reason, ATL provides several support classes that make building enumerator objects easier. Table 9-2 summarizes each of these classes. When developing components that support enumerators, you typically use ATL's CComEnum class. The other ATL classes primarily are support classes used by CComEnum.

TABLE 9-2 ATL ENUMERATOR CLASSES

Class	Description
CcomIEnum	Abstract class that defines the enumeration (IEnumXXXX) interface
CcomEnumImpl	Implements the IEnumXXXX interface. This class assumes the underlying data is stored in an array.
CComEnumOnSTL	Implements the actual enumerator object using the *Standard Template Library (STL)*
CcomEnum	Implements the actual enumerator object using CComEnumImpl

Using CComEnum

Enumerator objects are created through a client request, which typically is a method call on a given component. ATL's templated CComEnum class implements a basic COM object that exposes a specified IEnumXXXX interface. After instantiation using standard ATL techniques, the object is initialized with data through its Init method. Then the enumerator interface can be returned to the client application. The following code demonstrates dynamically creating an enumerator object and returning an IEnumString interface pointer to the client application:

```
STDMETHODIMP CBasicEnum::get_Enum(IEnumString **ppUnk)
{
    // Create a simple definition for an enumerator of type
    // IEnumString
    typedef CComObject<CComEnum< IEnumString, &IID_IEnumString,
                       LPOLESTR, _Copy<LPOLESTR> > >
                                            enumString;
```

```
// Use the creator class to create the instance
enumString* pEnum = 0;
enumString::CreateInstance( &pEnum );

// Initialize the enumerator with data from our
// internal vector of strings
HRESULT hr = pEnum->Init( m_vecStrings.begin(),
                          m_vecStrings.end(),
                          0,
                          AtlFlagCopy );

// If everything works, query for the IEnumString interface
// and return it to the client application
if (SUCCEEDED( hr ))
    hr = pEnum->QueryInterface( IID_IEnumString,
                                (void**) ppUnk );

if (FAILED( hr ))
{
    delete pEnum;
    return hr;
}

return S_OK;
}
```

I've commented the previous code so little explanation is necessary. The only tricky parts are the typedef that makes it easier to specify the resulting templated class and the call to pEnum->Init that populates the enumerator object with elements from your internal vector of strings. The AtlFlagCopy parameter specifies that a complete copy of each element is made. The other two options, AtlFlagNoCopy and AtlFlagTakeOwnership, determine who is responsible for the lifetime management of the underlying elements.

Building a Simple Enumerator Client Application

Using AppWizard, create a Win32 application project and name it Chapter9_ EnumClient. On the Step 1 of 1 dialog box, choose the Empty Project option. Next, create a file called Chapter9_EnumClient.cpp and add the code in Listing 9-1. The preceding section discusses the significant code fragments.

Listing 9-1: Chapter9_EnumClient.cpp

```cpp
//
// Chapter9_EnumClient.cpp
//

#include <windows.h>
#include <tchar.h>
#include <iostream.h>

// Include component category support
#include <comcat.h>

// Include basic ATL support for its conversion macros
#include <atlbase.h>

int main(int argc, char* argv[])
{
   cout << "Initializing COM" << endl;

   if ( FAILED( CoInitialize( NULL )))
   {
      cout << "Unable to initialize COM" << endl;
      return -1;
   }

   HRESULT hr;
   ICatInformation* pci = 0;
   hr = CoCreateInstance( CLSID_StdComponentCategoriesMgr,
                          NULL,
                          CLSCTX_INPROC_SERVER,
                          IID_ICatInformation,
                          (void**) &pci );

   CATID catidImpl[1];
   catidImpl[0] = CATID_Control;
   IEnumCLSID* pEnum = 0;
   hr = pci->EnumClassesOfCategories( 1,
                                      catidImpl,
                                      0, 0,
                                      &pEnum );

   // Spin through the list
   GUID guids[1];
```

```
ULONG ulNum;
hr = pEnum->Next( 1, guids, &ulNum );
while(  hr == S_OK )
{
    // Look up the ProgID
    WCHAR* pProgID = 0;
    ProgIDFromCLSID( guids[0], &pProgID );

    WCHAR* pCLSIDString = 0;
    StringFromCLSID( guids[0], &pCLSIDString );

    // Display controls ProgID and CLSID
    USES_CONVERSION;
    cout << W2A( pProgID ) << " - " << W2A( pCLSIDString ) <<endl;

    // Free up any memory
    CoTaskMemFree( pProgID );
    CoTaskMemFree( pCLSIDString );

    hr = pEnum->Next( 1, guids, &ulNum );
}


// Release the interface pointers
pEnum->Release();
pci->Release();


CoUninitialize();
return 0;
}
```

Implementing a Simple Enumerator Object

Exposing a simple enumerator from a component is relatively easy using ATL's CComEnum class. The following steps describe how to build a component that implements a get_Enum method off its main interface. This method returns an IEnumString interface pointer through which client applications can iterate a simple list of strings.

Step 1: Create the ATL Server Project

Start Visual C++ and create a new project with the following characteristics:

1. Use the ATL COM AppWizard.

2. Give it the name `Chapter9_EnumServer`.

3. In Step 1 of 1, select a type of DLL.

4. Select Finish to generate the project.

5. Using the ATL Object Wizard, insert a simple object with the following options:

6. Use a short name of `BasicEnum`.

7. Make sure the interface name is `IBasicEnum`.

8. On the Attributes page, enable the Support `ISupportErrorInfo` option and make sure the Custom interface option is selected.

9. After the project is created, add a method called `get_Enum` to the `IBasicEnum` interface. The method takes the following form:

```
STDMETHOD(get_Enum)(/*[out, retval]*/ IEnumString  **ppVal);
```

Step 2: Implement the Enumerator Object

Your component maintains an internal list of strings in an STL-based vector. These strings are placed in the vector on creation. Later, when the client requests an enumerator on this collection, you build the enumerator object in the call to `get_Enum`. Here is the code from `BASICENUM.H`:

```
//
// BasicEnum.h : Declaration of the CBasicEnum
//

#ifndef __BASICENUM_H_
#define __BASICENUM_H_

#include "resource.h"        // main symbols

#include <vector>

class ATL_NO_VTABLE CBasicEnum :
    public CComObjectRootEx<CComSingleThreadModel>,
    public CComCoClass<CBasicEnum, &CLSID_BasicEnum>,
    public ISupportErrorInfo,
```

```
            public IBasicEnum
{
public:
    CBasicEnum()
    {
        // Put some items in the vector
        m_vecStrings.push_back( L"StringOne" );
        m_vecStrings.push_back( L"StringTwo" );
        m_vecStrings.push_back( L"StringThree" );
        m_vecStrings.push_back( L"StringFour" );
        m_vecStrings.push_back( L"StringFive" );
    }

...


// IBasicEnum
public:
        STDMETHOD(get_Enum)(/*[out, retval]*/ IEnumString  **ppVal);

private:
    std::vector<LPOLESTR> m_vecStrings;
};

#endif //__BASICENUM_H_
```

As you can see, the previous code includes the STL vector support classes and uses a vector of type LPOLESTR to store a series of Unicode strings. The following code demonstrates creating an enumerator object, filling it with the strings from your vector and finally returning the IEnumString interface pointer to the client:

```
//
// BasicEnum.cpp : Implementation of CBasicEnum
//

#include "stdafx.h"
#include "Chapter9_EnumServer.h"
#include "BasicEnum.h"


...

STDMETHODIMP CBasicEnum::get_Enum(IEnumString **ppUnk)
{
    // Create an enumerator of type IEnumString
    typedef CComObject<CComEnum< IEnumString, &IID_IEnumString,
                            LPOLESTR, _Copy<LPOLESTR> > >
```

```
                                            enumString;

    enumString* pEnum = 0;
    enumString::CreateInstance( &pEnum );

    HRESULT hr = pEnum->Init( m_vecStrings.begin(),
                              m_vecStrings.end(),
                              0,
                              AtlFlagCopy );
    if (SUCCEEDED( hr ))
       hr = pEnum->QueryInterface( IID_IEnumString,
                                   (void**) ppUnk );

    if (FAILED( hr ))
    {
       delete pEnum;
       return hr;
    }

    return S_OK;
}
```

After adding this code, build the project. The next section describes modifying your simple client application to access the above enumerator functionality.

Step 3: Access Your Simple Enumerator Server

To access the functionality in the simple server application, use the following code:

```
HRESULT hr;
IBasicEnum* pbe = 0;
hr = CoCreateInstance( CLSID_BasicEnum,
                       NULL,
                       CLSCTX_INPROC_SERVER,
                       IID_IBasicEnum,
                       (void**) &pbe );

IEnumString* pEnum = 0;
hr = pbe->get_Enum( &pEnum );
if ( SUCCEEDED( hr ))
{
   LPOLESTR string[1];
   ULONG ulNum;
   hr = pEnum->Next( 1, string, &ulNum );
   while(  hr == S_OK )
   {
```

```
        // Display string
        USES_CONVERSION;
        cout << W2A( string[0] ) << endl;

        hr = pEnum->Next( 1, string, &ulNum );
    }
    pEnum->Release();
}
pbe->Release();
```

In the preceding code, you access the custom IBasicEnum::get_Enum method to retrieve the IEnumString interface.

COM Collections

COM's automation technology has provided for a high-level collection object since the early days of COM. Initially, the Visual Basic development environment used this collection technique; now it is a well-known aspect of COM development. Creating a collection object in Visual Basic requires just one line of code:

```
Dim colMovies as New Collection
```

This collection object provides basic collection operations such as Add, Remove, and Count. You retrieve items in the collection through a default Item property, which can take an integer index, a unique key string, or both. Here is a simple example of using the Visual Basic collection object to create a collection of movie objects:

```
Dim colMovies As New Collection

Private Sub Form_Load()
    Dim objMovie As clsMovie

    ' Add a movie to the collection
    Set objMovie = New clsMovie
    objMovie.Title = "Saving Private Ryan"
    objMovie.Director = "Steven Spielberg"
    colMovies.Add objMovie, objMovie.Title

    ' Add a movie to the collection
    Set objMovie = New clsMovie
    objMovie.Title = "Star Wars"
    objMovie.Director = "George Lucas"
    colMovies.Add objMovie, objMovie.Title
```

```
' Add a movie to the collection
Set objMovie = New clsMovie
objMovie.Title = "Jurassic Park"
objMovie.Director = "Steven Spielberg"
colMovies.Add objMovie, objMovie.Title

' Retrieve a director given a title
txtDirector = colMovies("Star Wars").Director

' Iterate over the collection and put the movies in a listbox
' This syntax uses the IEnumVariant interface
For Each objMovie In colMovies
    lbxMovies.AddItem objMovie.Title & " - " & objMovie.Director
Next

' Iterate over the collection and put the movies in a listbox
' This syntax just uses the Count and Item properties
Dim iCount As Integer
For iCount = 1 To colMovies.Count
    Set objMovie = colMovies(iCount)
    lbxMovies.AddItem objMovie.Title & " - " & objMovie.Director
Next

' Remove the items from the collection
For iCount = colMovies.Count To 1 Step -1
    colMovies.Remove iCount
Next

End Sub
```

The preceding code uses a simple Visual Basic class (clsMovie) to encapsulate movie data. Instances of this class are added to your collection object. The example demonstrates using the basic Add, Remove, Item, and Count methods of the collection object. The Item property uses a DISPID of zero, indicating that it is the default property of the collection object.

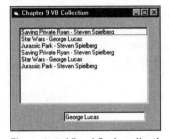

Figure 9-2: Visual Basic collection object example

Implementing Collections

Collection objects provide iteration capabilities like enumerator objects, but do so at a higher level. The collection technique basically is typeless, so you can use it in late-binding, IDispatch-based environments (for example, VBScript).

In general, collection-based objects implement the following properties and methods through a dispatch-only or dual interface component:

- ◆ Add method: Adds an item to the collection. The developer decides the actual parameters for this method. Typically, it is a VARIANT that contains the IDispatch* of the item being added. However, it may contain the actual item data and the implementation of Add itself creates the item object internally. The Add method typically returns the IDispatch* of the added item.

- ◆ Count property: A read-only property of type long that contains the number of items in the collection.

- ◆ Remove method: Removes an item from the collection. The developer defines the parameters. A typical implementation is to pass in the index value for the item to remove.

- ◆ Item property: A read-only, default property that returns the specified item in the collection. The return type is of IDispatch* and the developer defines the input parameters. The input typically is a VARIANT that supports a numerical index or some string-based key value for the item.

- ◆ NewEnum property: A read-only property used by certain development tools (for example, Visual Basic). This property returns an IEnumXXXX interface that enables the client to iterate over the collection.

The items stored in the collection are small COM objects that implement a dispatch-only or dual interface. The following ATL examples demonstrate the basics of building an ATL application that uses collection objects.

ATL's Collection Support

Collection objects, and the items they contain, are just simple COM objects. That said, ATL's support for collections is provided by its basic COM object support. The only special consideration is support for the _NewEnum method that returns an enumerator interface (which I cover earlier in the chapter).

When implementing collections in ATL, you need to create several different COM components. Each item is a small COM object that contains mostly data properties. Here is the code for a simple movie item:

```
class ATL_NO_VTABLE CMovie :
    public IDispatchImpl<IMovie, &IID_IMovie, ...>,
    public CComObjectRoot
```

```
{
public:
   CMovie() {};

BEGIN_COM_MAP(CMovie)
   COM_INTERFACE_ENTRY(IDispatch)
   COM_INTERFACE_ENTRY(IMovie)
END_COM_MAP()

// IMovie
public:
   STDMETHOD(get_Title)(BSTR *pVal);
   STDMETHOD(put_Title)(BSTR newVal);
   STDMETHOD(get_Director)( BSTR* );
   STDMETHOD(put_Director)( BSTR );

private:
   CComBSTR m_bstrDirector;
   CComBSTR m_bstrTitle;
};
```

As you can see, the object has two properties that expose details about the movie it represents. The item implements this functionality through a dual interface, which is important if it is to support working within a collection.

The collection component implements the methods and properties described earlier. The collection must store the items; it usually is handled via some sort of vector structure such as the STL vector implementation. Here's a piece of code from the example:

```
class ATL_NO_VTABLE CMovieCollection :
   public IDispatchImpl<IMovieCollection,
                        &IID_IMovieCollection>,
   public CComObjectRoot
{
public:
   CMovieCollection() {};

BEGIN_COM_MAP(CMovieCollection)
   COM_INTERFACE_ENTRY(IDispatch)
   COM_INTERFACE_ENTRY(IMovieCollection)
END_COM_MAP()

public:
   STDMETHODIMP Add(IMovie* pMovie );
   STDMETHODIMP Remove(long lIndex );
```

```
    STDMETHODIMP get_Count(long* plCount);
    STDMETHODIMP get_Item(long lItem, IMovie** ppIMovie );
    STDMETHODIMP get__NewEnum(IUnknown** ppUnk);

private:
    std::vector<CComVariant> m_vecMovies;
};
```

Collection objects typically are exposed through an appropriately named property. This example has a high-level application object with a `Movies` property. The collection object is created internally when the application object is created. Then, individual movie items are added to the collection.

When completed, our example requires three distinct components to implement this basic collection functionality. You can implement most collection components in much the same way, so the collection code shown in this chapter can function for nearly all collection-based objects that you create.

Implementing a Collection of Movies

To demonstrate the techniques in this module, you're going to build an ATL-based component that implements a collection of movie objects. The initial steps should look familiar to you. You use a DLL house and implement the collection as an externally creatable component. Each individual movie object, however, is a small, non-creatable COM object.

Step 1: Create the ATL Collection Server Project

Start Visual C++ and create a new project with the following characteristics:

1. Use the ATL COM AppWizard.

2. Give it the name `Chapter9_CollectionServer`.

3. In Step 1 of 1, select a type of DLL.

4. Select Finish to generate the project.

5. Using the ATL Object Wizard, insert a simple object with the following options:

6. Use a short name of `Application`.

7. Make sure the interface name is `IApplication`.

8. Change the ProgID to `Chapter9_Collection.Application`.

9. On the Attributes page, enable the Support `ISupportErrorInfo` option and make sure the Dual interface option is selected.

Step 2: Implement the Movie Component

Create the MOVIES.H and MOVIES.CPP files using the following code. This demonstrates using the ATL classes to create a simple COM object that exposes some simple properties. You can use the wizards if you need to, but the code demonstrates doing it all without the wizards. When finished typing in the code, add the files to the Chapter9_CollectionServer project:

```
//
// Movies.h
//

#include <vector>

class ATL_NO_VTABLE CMovie :
    public IDispatchImpl<IMovie, &IID_IMovie,
                        &LIBID_CHAPTER9_COLLECTIONSERVERLib>,
    public CComObjectRoot
{
public:
    CMovie() {};

BEGIN_COM_MAP(CMovie)
    COM_INTERFACE_ENTRY(IDispatch)
    COM_INTERFACE_ENTRY(IMovie)
END_COM_MAP()

DECLARE_NOT_AGGREGATABLE(CMovie)

// IMovie
public:
    STDMETHOD(get_Title)(BSTR *pVal);
    STDMETHOD(put_Title)(BSTR newVal);
    STDMETHOD(get_Director)( BSTR* );
    STDMETHOD(put_Director)( BSTR );

private:
    CComBSTR m_bstrDirector;
    CComBSTR m_bstrTitle;
};

//
// Movies.cpp
//
```

```
#include "stdafx.h"
#include "Chapter9_CollectionServer.h"
#include "Movies.h"

// CMovie
STDMETHODIMP CMovie::get_Director( BSTR* pbstr )
{
   *pbstr = m_bstrDirector.Copy();
   return S_OK;
}


STDMETHODIMP CMovie::put_Director( BSTR bstr )
{
   m_bstrDirector = bstr;
   return S_OK;
}


STDMETHODIMP CMovie::get_Title(BSTR * pbstr)
{
   *pbstr = m_bstrTitle.Copy();
   return S_OK;
}


STDMETHODIMP CMovie::put_Title(BSTR bstr)
{
   m_bstrTitle = bstr;
   return S_OK;
}
```

The previous code implements a simple COM object that represents a movie. It contains two properties: Title and Director. Your implementation also uses the STD vector class; however, you need to enable C++ exception handling under Settings → C++ → C++ Language for your project.

Step 3: Modify the IDL File

You also must modify the IDL file to include the definition of the IMovie interface. Reference the interface definition in the type library section of your IDL file:

```
//
// Chapter9_CollectionServer.IDL
//
```

```
...
[
    object,
    uuid(F579C5C1-3777-11d2-883A-444553540000),
    dual,
    helpstring("IMovie Interface"),
    pointer_default(unique)
]
interface IMovie : IDispatch
{
    [propget, id(1), helpstring("property Director")]
        HRESULT Director([out, retval] BSTR *pVal);
    [propput, id(1), helpstring("property Director")]
        HRESULT Director([in] BSTR newVal);
    [propget, id(2), helpstring("property Title")]
        HRESULT Title([out, retval] BSTR *pVal);
    [propput, id(2), helpstring("property Title")]
        HRESULT Title([in] BSTR newVal);
}
...
[
    uuid(55D7F7E1-2447-11D3-82C2-0060081AEB5F),
    version(1.0),
    helpstring("CollectionServer 1.0 Type Library")
]
library CHAPTER9_COLLECTIONSERVERLib
{
    importlib("stdole32.tlb");
    importlib("stdole2.tlb");

    interface IMovie;

    [
        uuid(55D7F7EE-2447-11D3-82C2-0060081AEB5F),
        helpstring("Application Class")
    ]
    coclass Application
    {
        [default] interface IApplication;
    }
}
```

Step 4: Implement the Movie Collection Component

Next you need to implement the movie collection component. Add the following to
MOVIES.H as it contains the complete implementation:

```
//
// Movies.h
//
...
//
// CMovieCollection
//
class ATL_NO_VTABLE CMovieCollection :
    public IDispatchImpl<IMovieCollection, &IID_IMovieCollection,
                         &LIBID_CHAPTER9_COLLECTIONSERVERLib>,
    public CComObjectRoot
{
public:
    CMovieCollection() {};

BEGIN_COM_MAP(CMovieCollection)
    COM_INTERFACE_ENTRY(IDispatch)
    COM_INTERFACE_ENTRY(IMovieCollection)
END_COM_MAP()

DECLARE_NOT_AGGREGATABLE(CMovieCollection)

public:
    STDMETHODIMP RemoveAll()
    {
        m_vecMovies.erase( m_vecMovies.begin(),
                           m_vecMovies.end() );
        return S_OK;
    }
    STDMETHODIMP Add(IMovie* pMovie )
    {
        // Add the variant (dispatch) to the collection
        m_vecMovies.push_back(CComVariant( pMovie ));
        return S_OK;
    }
    STDMETHODIMP Remove(long lIndex )
    {
        // Make sure the index is within range (index is 1-based)
        if (lIndex < 1 || lIndex > m_vecMovies.size())
            return E_INVALIDARG;
```

```
    m_vecMovies.erase( m_vecMovies.begin() + lIndex - 1 );

    return S_OK;
}

STDMETHODIMP get_Count(long* plCount)
{
    *plCount = m_vecMovies.size();
    return S_OK;
}

STDMETHODIMP get_Item(long lItem, IMovie** ppIMovie )
{
    if ( lItem < 1 || lItem > m_vecMovies.size())
        return E_INVALIDARG;

    // Get the item
    CComVariant& var = m_vecMovies[lItem - 1];

    HRESULT hr = var.pdispVal->QueryInterface( IID_IMovie,
                                (void**) ppIMovie );
    if (FAILED( hr ))
        return E_UNEXPECTED;

    return S_OK;
}
STDMETHODIMP get__NewEnum(IUnknown** ppUnk)
{
    typedef CComObject<CComEnum<IEnumVARIANT, &IID_IEnumVARIANT,
                            VARIANT, _Copy<VARIANT> > >
                                                enumVariant;

    enumVariant* pEnum = new enumVariant;

    HRESULT hr = pEnum->Init( m_vecMovies.begin(),
                            m_vecMovies.end(),
                            0,
                            AtlFlagCopy );
    if (SUCCEEDED( hr ))
        hr = pEnum->QueryInterface( IID_IEnumVARIANT,
                                (void**) ppUnk );

    if (FAILED( hr ))
        delete pEnum;
```

```
        return S_OK;
    }

private:
    std::vector<CComVariant> m_vecMovies;
};
```

Step 5: Define the IMovieCollection Interface

In addition, you must modify the IDL file to include the definition of the IMovie interface. Again, you must include a reference to the interface in the library section. This ensures that the interface definition is included in your type library. Use the following code:

```
//
// Chapter9_CollectionServer.IDL
//
...
// Add this after the IMovie definition
[
    object,
    uuid(F579C5C4-3777-11d2-883A-444553540000),
    dual,
    helpstring("IMovieCollection Interface"),
    pointer_default(unique)
]
interface IMovieCollection : IDispatch
{
    [propget, id(1)] HRESULT Count([out, retval] long *pVal);
    [id(2)] HRESULT Add([in] IMovie* pMovie );
    [id(3)] HRESULT Remove([in] long inIndex);
    [id(4)] HRESULT RemoveAll();
    [propget, id(DISPID_VALUE)]
        HRESULT Item([in] long inIndex,[out, retval] IMovie** ppMovie );
    [propget, id(DISPID_NEWENUM)]
        HRESULT _NewEnum([out, retval]LPUNKNOWN *pVal);
}
 [
    uuid(55D7F7E1-2447-11D3-82C2-0060081AEB5F),
    version(1.0),
    helpstring("CollectionServer 1.0 Type Library")
]
library CHAPTER9_COLLECTIONSERVERLib
{
```

```
    importlib("stdole32.tlb");
    importlib("stdole2.tlb");

    interface IMovie;
    interface IMovieCollection;
    [
        uuid(55D7F7EE-2447-11D3-82C2-0060081AEB5F),
        helpstring("Application Class")
    ]
    coclass Application
    {
        [default] interface IApplication;
    };
}
```

Step 6: Implement the IApplication Interface

Using the Add Property. . . option by right-clicking the ClassView tab, add a read-only Movies property of type IDispatch** and a CreateMovie method that returns an IDispatch** (that is, [out, retval]).

Now add the implementation of the property and method. You create an instance of the collection object upon application creation through the FinalConstruct method. You also add two movies to your collection to demonstrate how you can populate a collection object on startup:

```
//
// Application.h : Declaration of the CApplication
//
...
#include "movies.h"
#include "resource.h"
...
class ATL_NO_VTABLE CApplication :
    public CComObjectRootEx<CComSingleThreadModel>,
    public CComCoClass<CApplication, &CLSID_Application>,
    public ISupportErrorInfo,
    public IDispatchImpl<IApplication, &IID_IApplication,
                        &LIBID_CHAPTER9_COLLECTIONSERVERLib>
{
public:
    CApplication() {}
    HRESULT FinalConstruct()
    {
        HRESULT hr;
```

```
        // Create our movies collection
        hr = CComObject<CMovieCollection>::CreateInstance( &m_pMovies );
        if (FAILED( hr ))
            return hr;

        // Bump the reference count to 1
        m_pMovies->GetUnknown()->AddRef();

        // Create some movies and add them
        // to the collection
        AddMovies( m_pMovies );

        return S_OK;
    }
...
// IApplication
public:
    STDMETHOD(CreateMovie)(/*[out,retval]*/ IDispatch** ppMovie);
    STDMETHOD(get_Movies)(/*[out, retval]*/ IDispatch** ppVal);

private:
    CComObject<CMovieCollection>* m_pMovies;
    void AddMovies( CComObject<CMovieCollection>* pMovies );
};
//
// Application.cpp : Implementation of CApplication
//

#include "stdafx.h"
#include "Chapter9_CollectionServer.h"
#include "movies.h"
#include "Application.h"
...
void CApplication::AddMovies( CComObject<CMovieCollection>* pMovies
)
{
    CComObject<CMovie>* pMovie;
    IMovie* pIMovie;
    {
        CComObject<CMovie>::CreateInstance( &pMovie );
        pMovie->QueryInterface( IID_IMovie,
                                (void**) &pIMovie );
```

```
        CComBSTR bstrDir( "George Lucas" );
        pIMovie->put_Director( bstrDir );
        CComBSTR bstrTitle( "Star Wars" );
        pIMovie->put_Title( bstrTitle );
        pMovies->Add( pIMovie );
    }
    {
        CComObject<CMovie>::CreateInstance( &pMovie );
        pMovie->QueryInterface( IID_IMovie,
                                (void**) &pIMovie );
        CComBSTR bstrDir( "Steven Spielberg" );
        pIMovie->put_Director( bstrDir );
        CComBSTR bstrTitle( "Jurassic Park" );
        pIMovie->put_Title( bstrTitle );
        pMovies->Add( pIMovie );
    }
}


STDMETHODIMP CApplication::get_Movies(IDispatch** ppVal)
{
    // Pass back a movies collection
    // Return the IDispatch* of the collection
    m_pMovies->QueryInterface( IID_IDispatch,
                               (void**) ppVal );
    return S_OK;
}

STDMETHODIMP CApplication::CreateMovie(IDispatch** ppMovie)
{
    CComObject<CMovie>* pCMovie;
    CComObject<CMovie>::CreateInstance( &pCMovie );
    pCMovie->AddRef();
    pCMovie->QueryInterface( IID_IMovie,
                             (void**) ppMovie );
    return S_OK;
}
```

Step 7: Build the Project

That's it. Now build the project.

Creating a Visual Basic Client

Next, to test your collection, you need to create a simple Visual Basic application. Create a form that looks something like Figure 9-3.

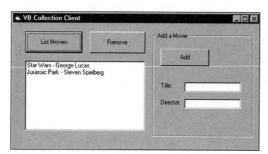

Figure 9-3: Visual Basic client form

Name the command buttons cmdList, cmdRemove, and cmdAdd. Name the list box lstMovies and the two entry fields txtTitle and txtDirector. Next, add this code to the form:

```
Dim objApp As Object

Private Sub cmdAdd_Click()
    Dim obj As Object
    Set obj = objApp.CreateMovie
    obj.Director = txtDirector
    obj.Title = txtTitle
    objApp.Movies.Add obj
    cmdList_Click
End Sub

Private Sub cmdList_Click()
    lstMovies.Clear
    For Each obj In objApp.Movies
        lstMovies.AddItem obj.Title & " - " & obj.Director
    Next
End Sub

Private Sub cmdRemove_Click()
    If lstMovies.ListIndex > -1 Then
        objApp.Movies.Remove lstMovies.ListIndex + 1
        cmdList_Click
    End If
End Sub
```

```
Private Sub Form_Load()
   Set objApp = CreateObject("Chapter9_Collection.Application.1")
End Sub
```

Building a C++ Client

Next, let's build a client application in C++. Again, the application is a simple Win32 console application. Using AppWizard, create a Win32 console application and name it Chapter9_CollectionClient. Next, create a file named Chapter9_CollectionClient.CPP and add the following code:

```
//
// Chapter9_CollectionClient.cpp
//

#include <windows.h>
#include <tchar.h>
#include <iostream.h>
#include <initguid.h>

#include <atlbase.h>

#include
"..\Chapter9_CollectionServer\Chapter9_CollectionServer_i.c"
#include "..\Chapter9_CollectionServer\Chapter9_CollectionServer.h"

int main( int argc, char *argv[] )
{
   cout << "Initializing COM" << endl;
   if ( FAILED( CoInitialize( NULL )))
   {
      cout << "Unable to initialize COM" << endl;
      return -1;
   }

   // Get the class factory
   IApplication* pApp;
   HRESULT hr = CoCreateInstance( CLSID_Application,
                      NULL,
                      CLSCTX_SERVER,
                      IID_IApplication,
                      (void**) &pApp );
   if ( FAILED( hr ))
   {
```

```
        cout.setf( ios::hex, ios::basefield );
        cout << "Failed to create server instance. HR = " << hr << endl;
        return -1;
    }

    cout << "Instance created" << endl;

    IMovieCollection *pMovies;
    pApp->get_Movies( (IDispatch**) &pMovies );

    long lCount;
    pMovies->get_Count( &lCount );
    for ( int i = 0; i < lCount; i++ )
    {
        USES_CONVERSION;
        IMovie* pMovie = 0;
        pMovies->get_Item( i + 1, &pMovie );

        BSTR bstr = 0;
        pMovie->get_Title( &bstr );
        cout << W2A( bstr ) << " - ";
        SysFreeString( bstr );
        pMovie->get_Director( &bstr );
        cout << W2A( bstr ) << endl;
        SysFreeString( bstr );

        pMovie->Release();
    }
    pMovies->Release();
    cout << "Shutting down COM" << endl;
    CoUninitialize();
    return 0;
}
```

Summary

In this chapter, you learned the basics of how to implement components that support built-in iteration through COM's enumerator interfaces and COM collection objects. In particular, you learned:

◆ COM provides a standard technique for exposing iteration techniques in your components.

- ◆ ATL provides support for enumerator interfaces through a set of CComEnum classes.

- ◆ Collection objects are primarily used by client development tools such as Visual Basis.

- ◆ ATL also supports the development of high-level collection objects through its CComEnum classes.

The next chapter takes a look at one of the more complicated areas of COM-based development – threading.

Chapter 10

COM Threading

IN THIS CHAPTER

- ◆ The COM threading models
- ◆ The COM apartment concept
- ◆ Moving interface pointers between threads
- ◆ ATL's support for the various COM threading models

WHEN I TEACH my five-day COM course, the students anxiously await the COM threading module discussion. It seems that COM threading is one of the most misunderstood (and feared) COM topics. There's no doubt that multithreading is a difficult topic in itself, and introducing COM into the equation makes it even more difficult. There are those who will tell you that COM threading is easy, but that's because they've been working with COM a long time.

This chapter first covers the basics of COM threading and then moves into a discussion of ATL's support for the various COM threading models. The chapter ends with an example of a multithreaded math component. I haven't used the math component example since Chapter 7, and I'm sure you missed it. This chapter is, however, the last time you see it.

A Quick Summary of COM Threading

Let's begin with a summary of COM threading to introduce you to the many terms and lay the groundwork for the coming sections. Before the release of Windows NT 3.51, COM did not support the concept of multiple threads accessing a COM object. When creating components, developers did not have to worry about concurrency issues. In other words, the components did not require thread safety. All component access occurred on the process's main (or primary) thread, so concurrency support was not required. Many components exist that are not thread-safe; the need to support this legacy code contributes to the complexity of the various threading models.

 I use the term *COM object* to indicate an instance of a COM component somewhere in a process.

The Single-Threaded Apartment

Windows NT 3.51 (and Windows 95) introduced the *single-threaded apartment (STA)*, which enables COM objects to exist in different threads in the same process. The primary reason for introducing this new model was to improve the performance of applications that use several COM objects.

Before the release of the STA model, all component access proceeded through the main thread of an application – typically through the process's message pump. Consider an out-of-process server managing 100 clients via 100 instances of a component. Client access to an instance is serialized (through the message pump) because it must occur on the main thread. This arrangement is useful for component developers because they need not trouble themselves with concurrency issues; but in large client/server applications, this performance hit (forcing all client requests through a single queue) is unacceptable.

STA enables a client to create any number of threads to house COM objects. It also enables the development of components that use multiple threads in their implementation. Each thread that uses COM in any way becomes its own STA. An STA is an abstract entity that makes it easier to discuss relationships among clients and component instances. It also enables you to put forth rules that users must follow when working in COM multithreaded environments.

In your example of 100 clients, your out-of-process server can create an STA for each COM object. This requires the creation of 100 threads within your server, but it gives each client the appearance of multiple, simultaneous accesses to its component instance. In other words, you enable the development of higher-performance components.

One of the benefits of the STA model is that COM handles most of the details, so building a component that supports running in an STA is relatively painless. You still do not have to worry about concurrency when implementing your components.

The Multithreaded Apartment

The STA model provided good performance improvements, but there was room for more. With the release of Windows NT 4.0 (and the Windows 95 DCOM upgrade), a new threading model was introduced: the *multithreaded apartment (MTA)*. The MTA model enables COM objects in different threads to access one another directly.

In the STA model, cross-thread calls must be marshaled; this is an expensive process. COM uses marshaling to synchronize access to those components that don't support concurrency. A COM object that resides in an STA must marshal its interface pointers when passed to another apartment (an STA or MTA).

This means that two COM threading models exist today: the STA model and the MTA model. The purpose of these models is to give component developers freedom in the way they develop components. If they want very efficient components, they ensure concurrency support so that they can code to the MTA model. If component developers are more concerned with functionality and less about concurrency, they can code to the STA model. Above all, though, the purpose of the two models is to enable both component types to work together regardless of the model chosen by a client application.

The Apartment

The COM *apartment* is a conceptual entity that enables you to think about components and their clients in a logical way. The term apartment indicates that some sort of separation (or wall) exists between the software entities within an apartment. An apartment is not a thread, but a thread belongs to only one apartment. An apartment is not an instance of a COM object, but each COM instance belongs to only one apartment. The wall that exists between apartments is the set of rules by which COM clients and components must abide. If either one breaks the rules, your application pays — usually by faulting.

A process can have one or more apartments, depending on its implementation. Apartments are created or entered by calling the `CoInitialize` or `CoInitializeEx` function. Each thread that calls `CoInitialize(0)` or `CoInitializeEx( 0, COINIT_APARTMENTTHREADED )` creates a new STA. Each thread that calls `CoInitializeEx ( 0, COINIT_MULTITHREADED )` either creates or enters the MTA. A process can have only one MTA, and each MTA thread enters this apartment. Figure 10-1 shows a process with four threads and three apartments. You must follow COM's threading rules when you cross apartments (as indicated by the lines in the figure).

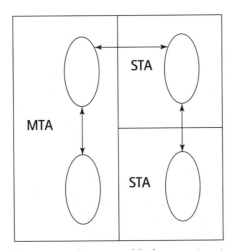

Figure 10-1: A process with three apartments

Threading rule: You must call `CoInitialize` or `CoInitializeEx` for each thread (including your main thread) that uses COM. This call informs COM of your intentions and places your thread in a new STA (or you can create or enter the

MTA). Subsequently, when you create an instance of a component, COM compares your threading model with that of the component and places it in the appropriate apartment – hopefully your own apartment. If the client and component threading models are not compatible, cross-apartment calls will be required, which will have a significant impact on your component's performance.

In-Process Components

In-process components are loaded into an existing apartment when a client calls `CoCreateInstance`. The in-process component does not have an opportunity to call `CoInitializeEx` to instruct COM which apartment model it supports. Instead, in-process components indicate their threading model support through a new registry entry. The `ThreadingModel` entry is a named value stored under the component's `\HKCR\CLSID\InProcServer32` key. It can have one of the following four values:

- ◆ `None`: The absence of the value indicates that the component does not support any of the threading models. Thus, you must create and access it only on the client's primary thread (the first STA).

- ◆ `Apartment`: The component can execute in any STA in the client process – not just the primary STA. By marking your component as supporting the apartment-threading model, you indicate that its class factory is thread-safe and that you protect any global data. This approach enables the client to load the component into any STA. It also provides the client with direct access to your component's interfaces as long as it accesses them from within the same STA in which it was created.

- ◆ `Free`: The component must reside in the MTA. Your component is thread-safe in every way and it can handle direct, simultaneous access by multiple threads. The component can pass interface pointers directly to other threads, including STA threads. COM, however, ensures marshaling of interface pointers when moving from the MTA to the STA.

- ◆ `Both`: The component is thread-safe in every way and can reside in either an STA or MTA. The component understands that it may run in an STA and so it marshals interface pointers to other apartments when necessary. However, at run time it doesn't know whether it's in an MTA or STA so it should aggregate with the free-threaded marshaler, marshal its pointers manually, and let COM make the decision.

Threading rule: You must inform COM of your in-process component's threading model by adding a `ThreadingModel` value to the `HKCR\CLSID\InProcServer32` registry key.

Single-Threaded Apartments (STA)

An STA contains one thread on which all its components are created. The component instances that reside within the STA may not be thread-safe so COM must synchronize access to each of them within the STA. COM does this by creating a hidden window for every STA within a process. If the client and component instance reside within the same thread, everything is fine because the thread itself ensures synchronization. However, if an interface pointer is passed to another thread (be it an STA or MTA), you must ensure synchronized access to the instances within the STA. COM handles this task in nearly all cases.

Through its marshaling process, COM ensures serialized access to components that don't support concurrency. COM's marshaling process uses the message pump of an STA to perform this task. Every external call into an instance within an STA goes through the message pump. Just as window messages are serialized via a message pump, so is access to STA components. Components used within an STA must meet the *reentrancy* requirement. In other words, a critical section, semaphore, and so on must protect all global variable use and local variables must be allocated on the stack.

 Threading rule: The reason COM needs to know your threading model is so that it can ensure synchronized access to those components that do not support concurrency. COM ensures thread-safe access through marshaling. If your component does not support concurrency — but protects its global data — it should use the STA model.

The Primary STA

The very first STA created in a process is special. You must create and access older components that have no knowledge of threading models on the primary STA. COM must assume that the components do not support concurrent access. In other words, all interaction with these components must occur on the primary STA even when accessing the component's class factory (for example, `DllGetClassObject`).

STA Component Requirements (Summary)

Here are the component requirements for supporting execution in any STA:

1. Because a component's class factory can be accessed simultaneously by multiple STAs, its exposed entry points (such as `DllGetClassObject`) must be thread-safe. In most cases, a component housing creates a unique class factory instance for each client request, thereby making the entry point safe. If only one instance of the factory supports all creation requests, however, it must be made thread-safe.

2. The component must protect access to any global data.

3. The internals of the component need not be thread-safe because COM ensures serialized access to each component instance while in the STA.

4. If the component implements custom interfaces, it should provide a proxy/stub DLL (through standard or universal marshaling) to enable marshaling of cross-apartment calls.

5. In-process components should mark themselves as supporting the "any-STA" model by setting the `ThreadingModel` value to `Apartment`.

These requirements apply to in-process components except where noted. Out-of-process components are accessed through COM's marshaling code and are much easier to implement. For this reason, this chapter concerns itself primarily with the workings of in-process components.

 Threading rule: In-process components need a proxy/stub DLL for their custom interfaces if they expect to function in multithreaded environments. Moving an interface pointer from one apartment to another requires marshaling.

Multithreaded Apartments (MTA)

Windows NT 4.0 introduced the multithreaded apartment model. Its primary purpose was to give component developers better performance and flexibility in their implementations. A process can have only one MTA, but this apartment can have any number of threads with each thread possessing a number of component instances. The STA model requires the marshaling of interface pointers between apartment threads—something that reduces performance considerably. MTA enables each thread direct access to component instances in other MTA threads. Direct pointer access is much faster than marshaling.

However, this freedom comes at a price. For a component to operate in the MTA, it must be thread-safe in every way. In the MTA, multiple clients can access a COM object simultaneously. These clients may or may not be in the same thread in which the component was created.

MTA Component Requirements (Summary)

Here are the component requirements for supporting execution in the MTA of a process:

1. COM does not synchronize calls to a component, so the component must support simultaneous access by multiple clients. In other words, the component must be thread-safe.

2. The component can pass direct pointers to other threads in the MTA. This typically is performed when a component creates MTA-based worker threads. The component should use COM's marshaling APIs and let COM decide whether the pointers can be passed directly.

3. The component's class factory must be thread-safe and global data must be protected, just as in the STA case.

4. The components should mark themselves as supporting the free threading model by setting the ThreadingModel value to Free.

These requirements apply to in-process components.

Mixed-Model Component Requirements

A component can choose to support both the STA and MTA models. This gives COM flexibility when deciding in which apartment to create a component instance. An out-of-process component explicitly indicates its threading model to COM via the CoInitializeEx call, so only in-process components need to deal with supporting both models.

 Threading rule: To use the CoInitializeEx function, you must run NT 4.0, Windows 2000, Windows 98, or Windows 95 with the DCOM upgrade. To use the new MTA functions (for example, CoInitializeEx) in your code, you must define the _WIN32_DCOM preprocessor symbol.

The Free-Threaded Marshaler

The *free-threaded marshaler* is a system component provided by COM to help those in-process components that support both threading models (via the Threading Model=Both registry entry). The free-threaded marshaler aggregates with any client accessing the component and custom marshals direct pointers to all apartments within the process.

 Threading rule: If your in-process component supports both STA and MTA, it should aggregate with the free-threaded marshaler via the CoCreate FreeThreadedMarshaler API. Take care, though, if your component maintains direct pointers to objects in other STAs. See Microsoft Knowledge Base article Q150777 for more details.

CoMarshallnterThreadInterface InStream

One of the primary rules that you must follow when working in multithreaded COM environments is that you must marshal interface pointers when passed to another apartment. Luckily, COM handles this marshaling in most cases, as with `QueryInterface` and `CoCreateInstance` as well as when you move interface pointers through a COM method call. As a developer, though, you sometimes must marshal interface pointers between apartments manually, primarily when COM isn't involved in the cross-apartment call. In other words, you move the pointer across apartments yourself.

Manually marshaling an interface pointer is as easy as using two COM API calls. The first one, `CoMarshalInterThreadInterfaceInStream`, takes an interface pointer, marshals it into a stream, and returns the `IStream` pointer. Then you can move this pointer directly across an apartment boundary. In the other apartment, the `CoGetInterfaceAndReleaseStream` function extracts the marshaled interface pointer from the stream. Through this process, COM ensures synchronization of calls on the associated object.

Later in this chapter, you develop a math component that uses a thread to perform its calculations. Each time the client calls one of `IMath`'s methods (such as `Add` or `Multiply`), the component creates a secondary thread to do the calculation. One of the parameters to the thread is a callback (`ICallBack`) interface pointer through which the thread notifies the client when the calculation is complete. This example represents a scenario in which you must marshal an interface pointer manually from one apartment to another.

The `Add` method should look familiar to you. This time it calls `SimulateLong Computation`, which starts a thread. Here's a bit of the code:

```
STDMETHODIMP CMath::Add(long lOp1, long lOp2)
{
    SimulateLongComputation( mathAdd, lOp1, lOp2 );
    return S_OK;
}
...
HRESULT CMath::SimulateLongComputation( mathOPERATOR op,
                                        long lOp1, long lOp2)
{
    // Marshal the ICallBack interface into a stream
    IStream* pStream = 0;
    HRESULT hr = CoMarshalInterThreadInterfaceInStream(
                                        IID_ICallBack,
                                        m_pCallBack,
                                        &pStream );
```

```
if( SUCCEEDED( hr ))
{
    // Create the thread parameters object and
    // fill it out with our parameters
    ThreadParameters* pTP = new ThreadParameters;
    pTP->op = op;
    pTP->lOp1 = lOp1;
    pTP->lOp2 = lOp2;
    pTP->pStream = pStream;

    // Create the thread
    HANDLE   hThread;
    DWORD    dwThreadID;
    hThread = CreateThread( 0, 0,
                            PerformComputation,
                            pTP,
                            0,
                            &dwThreadID);

    ...
}
    ...
    return hr;
}
```

Just as in the Chapter 7 CallBack example, the client implements an ICallBack interface and passes it to the component via the IMath::Advise method. The component stores the interface in the m_pCallBack member. The preceding code first marshals the ICallBack pointer into a stream. Next, it populates a thread parameters structure with the operator, operands, and IStream pointer. This structure is passed to the thread via the CreateThread call.

The PerformComputation function provides the code for execution by the thread. The first thing you do is call CoInitialize with a NULL parameter, which creates a new STA. Interface pointers must be marshaled between apartments. In this case, you move the ICallBack pointer from the initial client apartment to the STA created directly by your component:

```
DWORD WINAPI PerformComputation( void *p )
{
    // Initialize COM for this thread
    CoInitialize( 0 );

    // Get the thread parameters
    ThreadParameters* pTP = (ThreadParameters*) p;
```

```
// Unmarshal the ICallBack pointer
ICallBack* pCallBack = 0;
HRESULT hr = CoGetInterfaceAndReleaseStream( pTP->pStream,
                                IID_ICallBack,
                                (void**) &pCallBack );
// We successfully retrieved the ICallBack interface
if( SUCCEEDED( hr ))
{
    // Perform the calculation
    long lResult;
    switch( pTP->op )
    {
        case mathAdd:
            lResult = pTP->lOp1 + pTP->lOp2;
            break;
        ...
    }

    // Delay, but not too long, to simulate
    // doing some real work
    Sleep( min( lResult, 5000 ));

    // Notify the client with the result of the computation
    pCallBack->ComputationComplete( lResult );
}
// Delete our thread parameters structure
delete pTP;
CoUninitialize();
return hr;
}
```

You extract the calculation parameters and stream from the thread structure and then use the CoGetInterfaceAndReleaseStream API to unmarshal the ICallBack interface pointer from the stream. After performing the calculation and delaying a bit for effect, you notify the client with the result through ICallBack. Finally, you shut down COM before the thread exits.

Threading rule: You must marshal interface pointers between apartments. The easiest way is to use the marshaling APIs CoMarshalInterThreadInterface InStream and CoGetInterfaceAndReleaseStream. In a few cases you can get around this rule, but it's best to manually marshal every time and use the free-threaded marshaler in your components (marked as Both) to ensure the best performance.

Code-Based Examples

In all the examples so far, the client applications create STAs by using the CoInitialize API with a NULL parameter. After initializing COM, you then call CoCreateInstance to create an instance of the component. It looks something like this:

```
int WINAPI WinMain(HINSTANCE hInst; HINSTANCE, LPSTR, int)
{
    // This creates the main STA
    CoInitialize( 0 );
    CComPtr<IMath> ptrMath;

    // By default, ATL components are marked as Apartment if in-process
    HRESULT hr = CoCreateInstance( CLSID_Math,
                    NULL,
                    CLSCTX_SERVER,
                    IID_IMath,
                    (void**) &ptrMath );

    ...
}
```

This process has only one thread, but you still must initialize COM to use its services. This creates a process with a single, primary STA. When you call CoCreateInstance, COM compares your threading model (STA) with that of the component. If the component is out-of-process, you can view it as another STA because COM marshals the calls in every case anyway. If the component is in-process, COM looks in the registry to determine which threading model the component supports. In your case, the math component supports the STA model so COM creates the instance directly within the apartment. Access to the component (through its interfaces) is direct. There is no need for marshaling because you have only one thread and threads are self-synchronizing.

The following code again demonstrates an application that initially creates an STA. This time, however, the math component can run only in the MTA. In other words, the registry is marked with ThreadingModel=Free:

```
int main( int argc, char *argv[] )
{
    // Create an STA
    CoInitializeEx( 0, COINIT_APARTMENTTHREADED );
    CComPtr<IMath> ptrMath;
```

```
    // The component is in-process and marked as "Free"
    // COM will create an MTA for the component
    HRESULT hr = CoCreateInstance( CLSID_Math,
                        NULL,
                        CLSCTX_SERVER,
                        IID_IMath,
                        (void**) &ptrMath );
    ...
}
```

COM recognizes that the component can reside only in an MTA so it creates an MTA explicitly for the component. In this case, the math component requires a proxy/stub DLL for the `IMath` interface because the interface pointer must be marshaled from the MTA to the STA. The STA thread gets a pointer to an interface proxy through the `CoCreateInstance` call.

Here's another example of the client creating an STA. This time, the math component can run in any STA or the MTA because it marks the registry with `ThreadingModel=Both`:

```
int main( int argc, char *argv[] )
{
    // Create an STA
    CoInitializeEx( 0, COINIT_APARTMENTTHREADED );
    CComPtr<IMath> ptrMath;

    // The component is in-process and marked as "Both"
    // COM will create the component in our STA,
    // so no marshaling is necessary
    HRESULT hr = CoCreateInstance( CLSID_Math,
                        NULL,
                        CLSCTX_SERVER,
                        IID_IMath,
                        (void**) &ptrMath );
    ...
}
```

As the comments indicate that the component supports both threading models, COM creates the instance directly within the STA of the client. No proxy is needed for this example. Now, let's look at some MTA examples. Your code examples now demonstrate how the client creates an MTA with various math component configurations:

```
int main( int argc, char *argv[] )
{
    // Create or join the MTA
    CoInitializeEx( 0, COINIT_MULTITHREADED );
```

```
CComPtr<IMath> ptrMath;

// The math component is now marked as ThreadingModel=Apartment
// COM must therefore create an STA for the component
// The interface must be marshaled from the STA to the
// MTA and so we need a proxy/stub DLL
HRESULT hr = CoCreateInstance( CLSID_Math,
                               NULL,
                               CLSCTX_SERVER,
                               IID_IMath,
                               (void**) &ptrMath );

    ...
}
```

In the preceding CoCreateInstance call, COM creates an STA for the math component because it supports only the STA model. The component requires a proxy/stub DLL because COM must marshal the pointer from the STA back to the client's MTA. Here's one more:

```
int main( int argc, char *argv[] )
{
    // Create or join the MTA
    CoInitializeEx( 0, COINIT_MULTITHREADED );
    CComPtr<IMath> ptrMath;

    // The math component is now marked as ThreadingModel=Free
    // COM creates the math component directly in the MTA
    // No marshaling support is required
    HRESULT hr = CoCreateInstance( CLSID_Math,
                                   NULL,
                                   CLSCTX_SERVER,
                                   IID_IMath,
                                   (void**) &ptrMath );

    ...
}
```

You should know by now what happens. The client creates or joins the already existing MTA; the component itself supports running in an MTA and so is created in the same thread as the client. No marshaling code is required.

You've gone over several examples of STA/MTA interaction, but there are several more. Table 10-1 outlines all the possible configurations. The important point is that COM manages these relationships. As developers, we just need to be aware of what's going on. If you follow the COM threading rules outlined in this chapter, your applications will behave appropriately.

TABLE **10-1 COMPONENT ACCESS AND CREATION BASED ON THREADING MODEL**

Client Apartment*	Server Marked As**	Pointer Access/Result
Primary STA	Single	Direct access. Component is created in the primary STA.
Non-primary STA	Single	Proxy access. Component is created in the primary STA.
MTA	Single	Proxy access. Component is created in the primary STA. COM creates an STA if necessary.
Primary STA	Apartment	Direct access. Component is created in the primary STA.
Non-primary STA	Apartment	Direct access. Component is created in the client's STA.
MTA	Apartment	Proxy access. Component is created in an STA created by COM.
Primary STA	Free	Proxy access. Component is created in the MTA, which may require creation by COM.
Non-primary STA	Free	Proxy access. Component is created in the MTA, which may require creation by COM.
MTA	Free	Direct access. Component is created in the MTA.
Primary STA	Both	Direct access. Component is created in the primary STA.
Non-primary STA	Both	Direct access. Component is created in client's STA.
MTA	Both	Direct access. Component is created in the MTA.

*Primary STA indicates the first STA created in the process

**-Single indicates that a server supports running only in the primary STA. This is indicated by the absence of the ThreadingModel registry value.

ATL and COM Threading

ATL currently supports all of COM's threading models and is the first framework to do so. MFC supports only the single-STA and multiple-STA models because its classes are thread-safe only at the class level. When you initially create an ATL component using the ATL Object wizard, the Attributes tab presents you with several threading model options (see Figure 10-2).

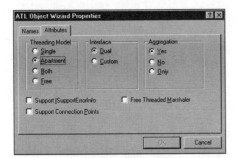

Figure 10-2: The Attributes tab

Single and Apartment

Selecting either Single or Apartment instructs the Object wizard to use the `CComSingleThreadModel` class as the template parameter for the `CComObject RootEx` class. Both options use the same ATL implementation. A component that supports execution in the primary STA of a client is a subset of a component that supports any-STA execution:

```
class ATL_NO_VTABLE CMath :
    public CComObjectRootEx<CComSingleThreadModel>,
    public CComCoClass<CMath, &CLSID_Math>,
    public IMath
{
...
};
```

CComSingleThreadModel

Components that support the single or multiple STA model do not have to be thread-safe, and ATL uses this fact to make these components more efficient. In Chapter 3, I discuss how `CComObjectRootEx` takes a template parameter that indicates what level of threading support a component requires. Here's a concise look at its implementation:

```
template <class ThreadModel>
class CComObjectRootEx : public CComObjectRootBase
{
public:
    typedef ThreadModel _ThreadModel;
    typedef _ThreadModel::AutoCriticalSection _CritSec;
    ULONG InternalAddRef()
    {
        return _ThreadModel::Increment(&m_dwRef);
    }
    ULONG InternalRelease()
    {
        return _ThreadModel::Decrement(&m_dwRef);
    }
void Lock() {m_critsec.Lock();}
    void Unlock() {m_critsec.Unlock();}
private:
    _CritSec m_critsec;
};
```

The ThreadModel class provides the implementation of a component's AddRef and Release methods as well as its Lock and Unlock methods, which manage the housing's global instance count. CComSingleThreadModel provides simple or no-op implementations of these methods because the component developer states that multiple-threading support is not required. Here's a look at the CComSingle ThreadModel class:

```
class CComSingleThreadModel
{
public:
    static ULONG WINAPI Increment(LPLONG p) {return ++(*p);}
    static ULONG WINAPI Decrement(LPLONG p) {return-(*p);}
    typedef CComFakeCriticalSection AutoCriticalSection;
    typedef CComFakeCriticalSection CriticalSection;
    typedef CComSingleThreadModel ThreadModelNoCS;
};
```

As you can see, the Increment and Decrement methods perform simple operations and the critical section class is "typedefed" to use ATL's CComFakeCriticalSection class. As you can guess, CComFakeCriticalSection does nothing. If you use the CComSingleThreadModel implementation, your component's code is efficient but it does not support the MTA model.

The only difference between selecting the Single or the Apartment option is that the Object wizard adds the `ThreadingModel=Apartment` string to the Apartment option component's `.RGS` file.

Free and Both

If you choose the Free or Both option, the Object wizard adds the appropriate RGS entry for you and also adds the `CComMultiThreadModel` class to your component's `CComObjectRootEx` implementation:

```
class ATL_NO_VTABLE CMath :
   public CComObjectRootEx<CComMultiThreadModel>,
   public CComCoClass<CMath, &CLSID_Math>,
   public IMath
{
...
};
```

The `CComMultiThreadModel` class provides implementations of the thread-safe reference counting methods. Again, though, this provides thread safety only for the component's `IUnknown` and class factory implementations. The component developer must ensure the thread safety of the component's internal implementation:

```
class CComMultiThreadModel
{
public:
   static ULONG WINAPI Increment(LPLONG p)
        {return InterlockedIncrement(p);}
   static ULONG WINAPI Decrement(LPLONG p)
        {return InterlockedDecrement(p);}
   typedef CComAutoCriticalSection AutoCriticalSection;
   typedef CComCriticalSection CriticalSection;
   typedef CComMultiThreadModelNoCS ThreadModelNoCS;
};
```

Free-Threaded Marshaler

The Free-Threaded Marshaler option automatically aggregates the free-threaded marshaler with your component. You should select this option only if you mark your in-process component as supporting both the any-STA and MTA threading models (the Both option). The Object wizard adds the following highlighted code:

```
// Math.h
...
class ATL_NO_VTABLE CMath :
   public CComObjectRootEx<CComMultiThreadModel>,
```

```
   public CComCoClass<CMath, &CLSID_Math>,
   public IMath
{
public:
   CMath()
   {
      m_pUnkMarshaler = NULL;
   }
BEGIN_COM_MAP(CMath)
   COM_INTERFACE_ENTRY(IMath)
   COM_INTERFACE_ENTRY_AGGREGATE(IID_IMarshal, m_pUnkMarshaler.p)
END_COM_MAP()

   DECLARE_GET_CONTROLLING_UNKNOWN()
   HRESULT FinalConstruct()
   {
      return CoCreateFreeThreadedMarshaler(
         GetControllingUnknown(), &m_pUnkMarshaler.p);
   }
   void FinalRelease()
   {
      m_pUnkMarshaler.Release();
   }
   CComPtr<IUnknown> m_pUnkMarshaler;
   ...
};
```

You've seen this code before. It resembles the aggregation example from Chapter 5.

CComObjectRoot

ATL enables you to specify a global threading model for every component within a housing. You do this by defining one of three preprocessor symbols and then deriving all your components from CComObjectRoot. CComObjectRoot is a simple typedef of CComObjectRootEx with a parameter of CComObjectThreadModel:

```
typedef CComObjectRootEx<CComObjectThreadModel> CComObjectRoot;
```

The CComObjectThreadModel parameter is defined via one of three preprocessor symbols:

```
// From ATLBASE.H
#if defined(_ATL_SINGLE_THREADED)
```

```
    typedef CComSingleThreadModel CComObjectThreadModel;
    typedef CComSingleThreadModel CComGlobalsThreadModel;
#elif defined(_ATL_APARTMENT_THREADED)
    typedef CComSingleThreadModel CComObjectThreadModel;
    typedef CComMultiThreadModel CComGlobalsThreadModel;
#else
    typedef CComMultiThreadModel CComObjectThreadModel;
    typedef CComMultiThreadModel CComGlobalsThreadModel;
#endif
```

By default, the ATL AppWizard defines _ATL_APARTMENT_THREADED in your project's STDAFX.H file. This has an effect only if you use CComObjectRoot instead of CComObjectRootEx when implementing your components.

The technique of defining the global preprocessor symbol was used in the initial versions of ATL. Today, however, you should define the threading model for your components at the component level using either the CComSingleThreadModel or CComMultiThreadModel parameter to CComObjectRootEx — unless, of course, you need the older technique.

The _ATL_ThreadingModel_ symbols also control certain global thread safety aspects of ATL's implementation. By defining the _ATL_APARTMENT_THREAD symbol, which ATL does by default, your components can function properly. However, if you define the _ATL_SINGLE_THREAD symbol, none of your components get support for thread-safe class factories or module lock counts so be careful.

The Threading Example

For this example, you use the math component one more time. I discuss asynchronous behavior in Chapter 7, where I develop a math component example that uses either a callback or a connection point interface to simulate asynchronous behavior through a COM interface. The example in this chapter extends this notion by using a thread to perform the math calculations. This technique provides true asynchronous behavior, but you do most of the work. (In Windows 2000, COM does the work instead.) You first develop the component, and then you use the multithreaded component from a C++ client.

Step 1: Create the Math Component

Start Visual C++ and create a new project, selecting ATL COM AppWizard. Give it the name Chapter10_Server. In Step 1 of 1, select a type of DLL. Select Finish and then OK to generate the project. Using the ATL Object wizard, insert a simple component with the following options:

◆ Use a short name of Math.

◆ Make sure the interface name is IMath.

◆ Change the ProgID to Chapter10.Math.

◆ On the Attributes page, make sure the Custom interface option is selected.

Step 2: Implement the IMath Interface

Using the Add Method option, by right-clicking the IMath interface in Developer Studio's ClassView tab, add the following six methods for the IMath interface. If you include the IDL attributes in the Add Method dialog box, Developer Studio adds them only to the IDL file. Figure 10-3 shows how to add the Add method.

```
STDMETHOD(Add)(/*[in]*/ long l0p1, /*[in]*/ long l0p2);
STDMETHOD(Subtract)(/*[in]*/ long l0p1, /*[in]*/ long l0p2);
STDMETHOD(Multiply)(/*[in]*/ long l0p1, /*[in]*/ long l0p2);
STDMETHOD(Divide)(/*[in]*/ long l0p1, /*[in]*/ long l0p2);
STDMETHOD(Advise)(/*[in]*/ ICallBack* pCallBack);
STDMETHOD(Unadvise)();
```

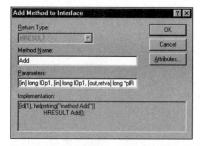

Figure 10-3: Adding methods with attributes

Step 3: Define the Event Interface

Just as in the Chapter 7 CallBack example, here you define an outgoing interface for your math component. The client implements the ICallBack interface and passes the pointer to the component through IMath::Advise. Your outgoing interface has two methods. The component calls ComputationComplete when a client computation is finished. The Error method is called if an error occurs while the computation is being processed. In any event, the client is notified asynchronously of the result. Here is the code:

```
// Chapter10_Server.IDL
...
[
    object,
    uuid(9029D3B0-67FE-11d1-B5F9-0004ACFF171C),
    helpstring("ICallBack Interface"),
    pointer_default(unique)
]
interface ICallBack : IUnknown
{
    [helpstring("method ComputationComplete")]
        HRESULT ComputationComplete( [in] long lResult );
    [helpstring("method Error")]
        HRESULT Error( [in] BSTR bstrDescription );
};
...
library CHAPTER10_SERVERLib
{
    importlib("stdole32.tlb");
    importlib("stdole2.tlb");
[
        uuid(EBFEC173-67FA-11D1-B5F9-0004ACFF171C),
        helpstring("Math Class")
    ]
    coclass Math
    {
        [default] interface IMath;
        [default, source] interface ICallBack;
    };
};
```

Step 4: Implement the Advise Methods

The Advise and Unadvise methods provide a way for the client to pass an interface pointer to the component. You then store this pointer as part of your implementation and fire notifications to the client through it. The Unadvise method enables a client to disconnect the notification interface. Here is the IDL and implementation:

```
// Math.H
...
class ATL_NO_VTABLE CMath :
    public CComObjectRootEx<CComSingleThreadModel>,
```

```
    public CComCoClass<CMath, &CLSID_Math>,
    public IMath
{
public:
    CMath()
    {
        m_pCallBack = 0;
    }
...
// IMath
public:
    STDMETHOD(Add)(/*[in]*/ long lOp1, /*[in]*/ long lOp2);
...
private:
    ICallBack* m_pCallBack;
};

// Math.CPP
...
STDMETHODIMP CMath::Advise(ICallBack * pCallBack)
{
    m_pCallBack->AddRef();
    m_pCallBack = pCallBack;
    return S_OK;
}

STDMETHODIMP CMath::Unadvise()
{
    m_pCallBack->Release();
    m_pCallBack = 0;
    return S_OK;
}
```

Step 5: Perform the Computation in a Thread

To demonstrate how to build a multithreaded COM component, you start a thread for each computation that the math component performs. For your simple computations, this isn't necessary; but you can imagine a method called `Calculate_PI_To_x_Digits` that might require a significant amount of time. What you're demonstrating here is that a COM method call can return immediately, and the actual work performed by the method can run in a background thread. When the work is done (the thread completes), the client is notified through its callback interface.

Performing the computation in a different thread adds complexity to the implementation, but not very much. You need a function that can execute as a thread, a thread parameter structure to pass thread-specific information, and a method to start the whole process. First, let's examine the header file:

```
//
// Math.h : Declaration of the CMath
//
...
typedef enum mathOPERATOR
{
    mathAdd,
    mathSubtract,
    mathMultiply,
    mathDivide
} mathOPERATOR;

struct ThreadParameters
{
    mathOPERATOR    op;
    long            lOp1;
    long            lOp2;
    IStream*        pStream;
};
class ATL_NO_VTABLE CMath :
    public CComObjectRootEx<CComSingleThreadModel>,
    public CComCoClass<CMath, &CLSID_Math>,
    public IMath
{
...
private:
    ICallBack* m_pCallBack;
    HRESULT SimulateLongComputation( mathOPERATOR op,
                                     long lOp1,
                                     long lOp2 );
};
```

You need an enumerated type to indicate the type of computation that the thread performs; the ThreadParameters structure contains everything the thread needs to carry out the computation. The IStream* parameter contains your marshaled interface pointer through which the client is notified. The SimulateLongComputation method actually starts the thread:

```
//
// Math.cpp : Implementation of CMath
//
...
```

```
STDMETHODIMP CMath::Add(long l0p1, long l0p2)
{
    SimulateLongComputation( mathAdd, l0p1, l0p2 );
    return S_OK;
}
STDMETHODIMP CMath::Subtract(long l0p1, long l0p2)
{
    SimulateLongComputation( mathSubtract, l0p1, l0p2 );
    return S_OK;
}
STDMETHODIMP CMath::Multiply(long l0p1, long l0p2)
{
    SimulateLongComputation( mathMultiply, l0p1, l0p2 );
    return S_OK;
}
STDMETHODIMP CMath::Divide(long l0p1, long l0p2)
{
    SimulateLongComputation( mathDivide, l0p1, l0p2 );
    return S_OK;
}
```

As you can see from the implementation, a thread is created each time the client calls one of the four computation methods. Here is the `SimulateLongComputation` method:

```
//
// Math.cpp : Implementation of CMath
//
...
HRESULT CMath::SimulateLongComputation(mathOPERATOR op,
                                       long l0p1, long l0p2)
{
    // Marshal the ICallBack interface into a stream
    IStream* pStream = 0;
    HRESULT hr = CoMarshalInterThreadInterfaceInStream(
                                              IID_ICallBack,
                                              m_pCallBack,
                                              &pStream );

    if( SUCCEEDED( hr ))
    {
        // Create the thread parameters object and
        // fill it with our parameters
        ThreadParameters* pTP = new ThreadParameters;
        pTP->op = op;
        pTP->l0p1 = l0p1;
```

```
            pTP->lOp2 = lOp2;
            pTP->pStream = pStream;
            // Create the thread
            HANDLE  hThread;
            DWORD   dwThreadID;
            hThread = CreateThread( 0, 0,
                                    PerformComputation,
                                    pTP,
                                    0,
                                    &dwThreadID);
            // If we have a handle, then everything
            // worked so close the handle
            if( hThread )
            {
                CloseHandle( hThread );
            }
            else
            {
                // Thread creation failed. Destroy
                // our parameters and release the stream
                delete pTP;
                pStream->Release();
                // Notify the client that an error occurred
                CComBSTR bstrMsg( "Unable to start computation thread" );
                m_pCallBack->Error( bstrMsg );
            }
        }
        else
        {
            // If the marshaling fails, we probably don't have
            // the proxy/stub registered
            CComBSTR bstrMsg( "Unable to marshal the ICallBack interface.
\
                              Make sure the proxy/stub is registered" );
            m_pCallBack->Error( bstrMsg );
        }
        return hr;
    }
```

Because each thread becomes a single-threaded apartment, you marshal the
ICallBack interface pointer into a stream. If this succeeds, create and initialize a
ThreadParameters structure containing the operator, the operands, and the
IStream pointer. Next, create the thread, passing the address of your thread function
and the ThreadParameters structure. If the thread creation fails, clean up your
structure, release the stream, and notify the client of the error through the

ICallBack::Error method. If all goes well, the thread executes the code specified in the PerformComputation function:

```cpp
//
// Math.cpp : Implementation of CMath
//
...
DWORD WINAPI PerformComputation( void *p )
{
    CoInitialize( 0 );

    // Get the thread parameters
    ThreadParameters* pTP = (ThreadParameters*) p;

    // Unmarshal the ICallBack pointer
    ICallBack* pCallBack = 0;
    HRESULT hr = CoGetInterfaceAndReleaseStream( pTP->pStream,
                                    IID_ICallBack,
                                    (void**) &pCallBack );
    // We successfully retrieved the ICallBack interface
    if( SUCCEEDED( hr ))
    {
        // Perform the calculation and delay
        // to simulate doing some real work
        long lResult;
        switch( pTP->op )
        {
            case mathAdd:
                lResult = pTP->lOp1 + pTP->lOp2;
                break;
            case mathSubtract:
                lResult = pTP->lOp1 - pTP->lOp2;
                break;
            case mathMultiply:
                lResult = pTP->lOp1 * pTP->lOp2;
                break;
            case mathDivide:
                lResult = pTP->lOp1 / pTP->lOp2;
                break;
        }

        // Delay, but not too long
        Sleep( min( lResult, 5000 ));
```

```
        // Notify the client with the result of the computation
        pCallBack->ComputationComplete( lResult );
    }

    // Delete our thread parameters structure
    delete pTP;
    CoUninitialize();
    return hr;
}
```

The preceding code implements the thread. First you initialize COM. The CoInitialize call creates a single-threaded apartment and interface pointers are marshaled between STAs, as demonstrated in this example. If an interface pointer crosses an STA through a COM API (such as CoCreateInstance) or interface method (such as QueryInterface), COM does the marshaling automatically. However, in your case, you pass the pointer without COM's help, so you must marshal the pointer manually.

First get the thread parameters and unmarshal the ICallBack pointer. If this succeeds, simulate a long computation and finally notify the client of the result through the ICallBack::ComputationComplete method.

Step 6: Build the Project

That's all there is to building a multithreaded component. This example demonstrates the requirements to build a component that moves an interface pointer among threads. In other words, the component itself contains multiple threads. In many cases, the clients also are multithreaded, but this example demonstrates some of the useful techniques. Build the project, and next develop a C++ client application.

A C++ Client Application

In your C++ client example, you use ATL on the client side (as in Chapter 7). In fact, the client application closely resembles the Chapter 7 C++ connection point example. This time, instead of using connection points you use a callback interface. In other words, you implement the Chapter 7 Visual Basic CallBack example in C++.

Use a Win32 application because you need an HINSTANCE for initializing ATL. You also need a message loop in this example because you must wait for the math component to complete its operations. A message loop is perfect for handling this asynchronous behavior. And already described earlier in this chapter, COM uses the message queue to implement much of its functionality anyway so it's best to have one around.

Using AppWizard, create a Win32 application project and name it `Chapter10_Client`. Next, create a file called `Chapter10_Client.cpp` and add the following code. You step through the code in sequential order:

```
//
// Chapter10_Client.cpp
//
#include <windows.h>

// Include ATL
#include <atlbase.h>

CComModule _Module;
#include <atlcom.h>
#include <atlimpl.cpp>

BEGIN_OBJECT_MAP(ObjectMap)
END_OBJECT_MAP()

#include "..\Chapter10_Server\Chapter10_Server.h"
#include "..\Chapter10_Server\Chapter10_Server_i.c"
...
```

Your client code includes the ATL implementation files and declares a global `CComModule` instance. It also includes an empty ATL object map, which you need to initialize `CComModule`. Next, you have two helper functions to display messages as the application runs:

```
...
void DisplayMessage( char* szMsg )
{
    MessageBox( 0, szMsg, "Chapter10_Client", MB_OK | MB_TOPMOST );
}
void HandleError( char*szMsg, HRESULT hr )
{
    char szMessage[256];
    sprintf( szMessage, "%s. HR = %x", szMsg, hr );
    DisplayMessage( szMessage );
    CoUninitialize();
}
...
```

These functions are simple, but they support only ANSI builds. Next, you have an ATL class that implements the client-side, outgoing interface for your math component:

```
...
class CCallBack :
   public CComObjectRoot,
   public ICallback
{
public:
   CCallBack() {}

BEGIN_COM_MAP(CCallBack)
   COM_INTERFACE_ENTRY(ICallBack)
END_COM_MAP()

// ICallBack
public:
   STDMETHODIMP ComputationComplete(long lResult)
   {
      char szMsg[128];
      sprintf( szMsg, "The result is %d", lResult );
      DisplayMessage( szMsg );

      // Terminate the application when we
      // get the result of the last computation
      if ( lResult == 3000 )
         PostQuitMessage( 0 );

      return S_OK;
   }
   STDMETHODIMP Error(BSTR bstrMessage)
   {
      USES_CONVERSION;
      DisplayMessage( W2A( bstrMessage ));
      return S_OK;
   }
};
...
```

You've seen similar code before. Your component, based on a custom interface, implements the ICallBack interface. You implement the two methods in ICallBack: ComputationComplete and Error. Both implementations display a message box.

Next you implement WinMain, call CoInitialize, and initialize ATL by calling the CComModule::Init method, passing the HINSTANCE of your app and the object map:

```
...
int WINAPI WinMain(HINSTANCE hInst, HINSTANCE, LPSTR, int)
{
   CoInitialize(0);

   // Initialize the ATL module
   _Module.Init( ObjectMap, hInst );

   // Create an instance of our math component
   CComPtr<IMath> ptrMath;
   HRESULT hr;
   hr = CoCreateInstance( CLSID_Math,
                          NULL,
                          CLSCTX_SERVER,
                          IID_IMath,
                          (void**) &ptrMath );

   if ( FAILED( hr ))
   {
      HandleError( "Failed to create server instance", hr );
      return -1;
   }
...
```

After instantiating the math component, you next create an instance of the CCallBack component, which provides the ICallBack implementation:

```
...
   // Create an instance of our CallBack component
   CComObject<CCallBack>* pCallBack;
   CComObject<CCallBack>::CreateInstance( &pCallBack );

   // QueryInterface for ICallBack and pass
   // it to the component
   CComPtr<ICallBack> ptrCallBack;
   pCallBack->QueryInterface( IID_ICallBack,
                              (void**) &ptrCallBack );
   ptrMath->Advise( ptrCallBack );
...
```

After creating the instance, you query the interface for `ICallBack`, which bumps the reference count on the component to 1. Next, you pass the `ICallBack` interface implementation to the math component:

```
...
    // Access the IMath functionality
    // As the computations complete, the callback
    // implementation will display a message box

    ptrMath->Add( 300, 10 );
    ptrMath->Subtract( 300, 10 );
    ptrMath->Divide( 300, 10 );
    ptrMath->Multiply( 300, 10 );
...
```

Finally, you call the methods in the math component. As they execute, the math component creates a thread to handle the computation. When the computation completes, the component notifies the client through `ICallBack::Computation Complete`. Figure 10-4 shows the result of the four computations.

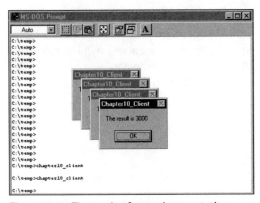

Figure 10-4: The result of several computations

Because you've implemented asynchronous behavior, you need a message loop so that you can wait for the notifications to arrive. STAs are required to pump messages:

```
...
    // Sit in a message loop until the
    // last notification is fired
    MSG    msg;
    while (GetMessage( &msg, NULL, 0, 0 ))
    {
```

```
        TranslateMessage( &msg );
        DispatchMessage( &msg );
    }
...
```

When you're finished, shut down the connection, release your pointers, and uninitialize COM just as you've done in the past:

```
...
    // Shut down the connection
    ptrMath->Unadvise();

    // Release our interfaces
    if ( ptrMath )
        ptrMath = 0;
    if ( ptrCallBack )
        ptrCallBack = 0;

    CoUninitialize();
    return 0;
}
```

That completes my coverage of COM threading. I hope that you now have a better handle on the various threading models and the requirements to build components that conform to them. As you can see, ATL does much of the hard work for you. The important point is to understand and obey the rules. Here are more resources for understanding COM threads:

- Microsoft Knowledge Base article Q150777

- Microsoft's DCOM Architecture white paper

- Don Box's COM/ActiveX Q&A articles in *Microsoft Systems Journal (MSJ)*

- David Platt's threading articles in the February 1997 and August 1997 editions of *MSJ*

Summary

In this chapter, you learned the basics of how COM manages concurrency in both client and component applications. In particular, you learned:

- There are several COM threading models.

- When developing components, you need to be aware of what environments it will execute in.

◆ The COM apartment is an important abstraction used to describe how
clients and component instances interact.

◆ ATL provides basic support for all COM threading models.

In Chapter 11, I take a look at ATL's support for basic window and dialog box development. Currently, support is limited when compared with MFC. However, future versions will continue to build on the existing message map architecture.

Chapter 11

OLE DB and ATL

IN THIS CHAPTER

- ◆ LearnOLE DB terminology and the interfaces that comprise this technology
- ◆ Discover the new ATL classes provided with Developer Studio 98
- ◆ Use ATL to develop an OLE DB Provider for a simple text file
- ◆ Use ATL in an MFC project to develop an OLE DB Consumer
- ◆ Use ADO in an HTML page to interact with the OLE DB Provider

AS I SIT IN a deck chair on the balcony of the Island Hotel in Cedar Key, FL, I can't help but feel lucky in life. On a moment's notice, I am able do things like paddle a kayak through the narrow channels of these islands, interact with the bottlenose dolphins and manatees that frequent these waters, and develop an OLE DB Provider to access data from a proprietary data source. A nerd in paradise is still a nerd.

One of the more powerful Microsoft technologies supported by the latest version of ATL is *OLE DB*. With the overwhelming success of Web-based e-commerce applications, OLE DB (with the help of ADO) has become the standard on which Microsoft developers have based their data access future. The latest version of ATL provides a plethora of new classes that enable developers to implement a generalized data access method to a proprietary data source based on OLE DB.

You may ask yourself, "Why did Microsoft create another data access paradigm?" Microsoft continues to improve the data access methodologies for the same reason Ford continued making Mustangs after the 64 1/2. The point is that very seldom does a company come up with the best way of doing something right off the bat, regardless of what the marketing department says. As I explain in the remainder of this chapter, OLE DB is an evolution in data access that utilizes technologies popularized since ODBC. Hopefully, by the end of this chapter you will agree that OLE DB provides the flexibility and ease of use necessary to build commercial-quality database applications.

This chapter covers the relationship between OLE DB and ATL as I see it. Do not read this chapter as the definitive guide to OLE DB. I don't spend a lot of time going over the OLE DB specification mostly because a number of books – as well as your compiler's online help – do this already. Instead, I choose to outline some of the key concepts of OLE DB and how it relates to ATL. I give you enough information here that you easily can find more information if necessary. I spend the rest of the chapter showing you how to build a generic provider for a proprietary data source, as well as consumers that can access it. With this knowledge, I feel that you can investigate areas on your own that are specific to your implementation.

A Brief History of Microsoft Data Access Technologies

Microsoft developers recognized very early in their quest for OS dominance that it would be very important to provide a standard method for accessing data contained in databases. They wanted a programming abstraction to databases, much like the Windows *Graphical Device Interface (GDI)* provides abstraction to output devices. This, in theory, would lessen the application developer's commitment to the underlying database and allow for programs to be built without database dependency. This idea particularly appealed to software development companies that relied on databases because they could claim support for a large number of back-end databases without maintaining code littered with `#ifdef ORACLE` preprocessor directives.

ODBC

Microsoft's first offering was *open database connectivity (ODBC)*. ODBC defines a standard for developing drivers or DLLs, which export a defined set of functions that enable a client application to "generically" request data from a variety of databases typically without regard for the underlying database. The *structured query language (SQL)* is the agreed-upon language for ODBC drivers. If the underlying database does not support SQL (`BTRIEVE`, text files, and so on), then the driver assumes responsibility for parsing the SQL into something understandable by the underlying engine.

As with most new standards, ODBC suffered from major acceptance in the early days. Most Research and Development departments recognized the usefulness of such a standard right away, but the performance of early ODBC drivers left plenty to be desired. In some cases, data access times were doubled over proprietary access to the same database. Everyone agreed that it was a good idea, but Microsoft had some work to do before many Windows development groups migrated to this standard.

Let's fast forward to now (circa September 1999). ODBC certainly has come a long way. It is supported in 16-bit and 32-bit applications. I challenge you to find a database vendor of any significance that does not provide access to its data through ODBC. Microsoft provides a development kit that assists database developers in creating ODBC drivers for their databases. These drivers are really just DLLs that export a number of C functions. Microsoft has published the standard for support by other operating systems – including various flavors of UNIX.

All is good, right? Wrong! Microsoft recognized that ODBC must evolve to adapt to the ever-changing technical environment around us. Evolution of ODBC presented some problems. For example, ODBC was created before the widespread acceptance of the Internet.

Everything I have talked about so far is related to accessing data from a database. A number of sources that contain data don't really fit with what you typically think of as a database. For example, consider e-mail systems, spreadsheets, unstructured data, COM components, proprietary data sources, and so on.

The SQL needed to support only the core ODBC implementation may offer more than is necessary in a nontraditional data source. It is important to realize that any new standard should be flexible enough to allow for the data source that may not choose to implement SQL.

Enter OLE DB?

Microsoft introduced OLE DB as the new standard for accessing data from *DBMS (database management system)*, as well as non-DBMS, architectures almost three years ago. OLE DB simplifies the requirements for implementation of a data source provider by only requiring the data provider to return the data in tabular form. This simple requirement satisfies the need for a generic access mechanism for diverse data sources. The only requirement of nontraditional data sources is that they must be capable of expressing their contents in a tabular form.

The primary components, shown in Figure 11-1, in an OLE DB application are *consumers* and *providers*. An *OLE DB Provider* is an application that responds to queries and provides data from a data source in a tabular form by implementing a set of COM interfaces. An *OLE DB Consumer* is an application that communicates with an OLE DB Provider through COM interfaces to provide application-level access to an underlying data source. ADO is an example of a data consumer and Microsoft's first consumer implementation of OLE DB. I discuss ADO later in this chapter.

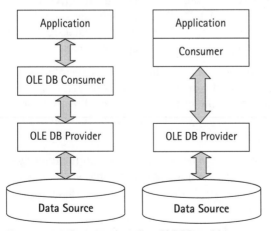

Figure 11-1: Components of an OLE DB architecture

OLE DB defines objects that the provider implements and the consumer utilizes to communicate with the provider. The following objects are defined in the OLE DB Object Model, which is depicted in Figure 11-2:

- **Enumerators:** provide the ability to enumerate existing data sources. An enumerator object searches the registry for registered providers and exposes the ISourcesRowset interface, which returns a rowset describing all data sources and enumerators visible to this enumerator.

- **Data Source:** used by the consumer to establish a connection to the data provider. This object encapsulates the connection information such as user name, password, and so on. These objects act as the factory for session objects. To access a data source object, a consumer must call CoCreateInstance to create the object. The data source object exposes the IDBProperties interface that (among other things) enables the consumer to set user and password properties. Support for IDBCreateSession, IDBInitialize, IDBProperties, and IPersist interfaces is mandatory in a data source object.

- **Session:** provides support for transactions, generations of data sets, and commands. The session object is generated from data source objects. These objects act as a factory for transactions, command objects, and rowset objects. Support for IGetDataSource, IOpenRowset, and ISessionProperties is mandatory in a session object.

- **Command:** processes commands. This object is considered optional for the provider to support. If the consumer queries for an interface to this object and does not receive one, then the consumer can assume that the provider does not support commands. Command objects can query or modify a data source and can return multiple rowsets. Support for command objects is optional for OLE DB Providers. If an OLE DB Provider implements the command object, support for the IAccessor, IColumnInfo, ICommand, ICommand Properties, ICommandText, and IConvertType interfaces is mandatory.

- **Rowset:** represents the data source's data in tabular form. Executing a command against a command object can create a rowset object. If a command object is not implemented, a rowset can be acquired directly from the data provider. Support for IAccessor, IColumnsInfo, IConvertType, IRowset, and IRowsetInfo interfaces is mandatory for rowset objects.

- **Index:** a special type of rowset that enables ordered access to the underlying rowset. Support of this object by the provider is optional. Index objects must support the IAccessor, IColumnsInfo, IConvertType, IRowset, IRowsetIndex, and IRowsetInfo interfaces.

- **Transaction:** typically buffers modifications to a data source giving the application the opportunity to roll back in the event of catastrophic failure. OLE DB Providers can support distributed transactions, enabling multiple OLE DB consumers to participate in shared transactions.

♦ **Error:** encapsulates errors associated with data access. This object can provide extended return codes and status information to provide richer information to the consumer application in the event an error occurs. Support of this object by the provider is optional.

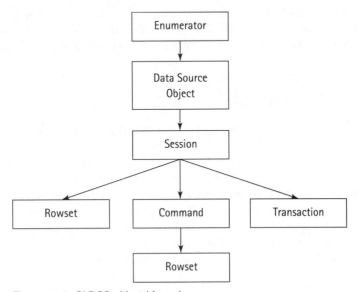

Figure 11-2: OLE DB object hierarchy

If your OLE DB Provider supports any of the preceding objects, then you are responsible for implementing the mandatory interfaces for each. If you choose ATL as a starting point for your provider, you find that the mandatory interfaces are provided for you. Obviously, you have to provide the code that communicates with your specific data source.

To reiterate, the provider provides implementations for the required interfaces listed previously. Here are the steps a consumer takes to connect to a data source object:

1. Create the Data Source object by calling `CoCreateInstance` with the CLSID of the data source object.

2. Query the data source object for the `IDBInitialize` interface.

3. Create and initialize variants that contain login properties such as user ID and password.

4. Query the data source object for the `IDBProperties` interface and call the `SetProperties` method to initialize the properties. Don't forget to release the `IDBProperties` interface.

5. Call the `Initialize` method of the `IDBInitialize` interface to log on to the data source.

6. Assuming that the initialization succeeds, the consumer can begin querying for other interfaces that potentially execute commands and generate rowsets.

7. When finished, the `Uninitialize` method of the `IDBInitialize` interface is called and the interface is released.

It sounds easy enough, but there is more code here than most people want to write – especially if it's not necessary. As you see later in the chapter, ATL and ADO provide a significant amount of the boilerplate code to access the provider.

ATL and OLE DB

ATL 3.0 provides significant support for creating OLE DB Providers and Consumers. Creating providers and consumers is as simple as executing a wizard to create any other ATL COM object. Once the object is generated, ATL makes development easier by providing template classes that implement all of the required, and some of the optional, OLE DB interfaces. Developers need only to concern themselves with filling in the translation layer between OLE DB requests and data source manipulation.

In this section, I discuss the provider and consumer classes defined in ATL 3.0. Although I spend more time laying out the pieces here than with OLE DB, it is important to point out that I easily could write a book on this topic. If I don't adequately address your particular interest and you are too shy to send e-mail, please feel free to look in the `ATLDB.H` header file for all of the answers.

ATL OLE DB Provider Templates

The provider template implementations provided by ATL conform to the OLE DB version 1.1 specification. With ATL, you easily can generate a read-only provider with no commands. With some extra effort, you can create a read/write provider. The OLE DB Provider class templates provide support for data source, session, command, and rowset OLE DB objects.

Data Source Classes

After using the wizard to create your provider, you have a class that provides implementations for the OLE DB interfaces that make up the data source object. This class inherits from the template implementation classes of ATL. These classes provide default support for the mandatory interfaces of an OLE DB data source object. Here is an overview of the purpose of each of these implementation classes; keep in mind that, as the developer, you are free to override the implementations provided by ATL:

◆ `IDBInitializeImpl`: provides an implementation of the `IDBInitialize` interface. The default implementation manages the creation and deletion of a connection with the consumer. This is a mandatory interface for data source objects.

◆ `IDBPropertiesImpl`: provides an implementation of the `IDBProperties` interface. This interface manages the properties associated with the data source. Properties of a data source object can consist of initialization properties such as user ID and password, or data source information such as support for transactions. This is a mandatory interface for all data source objects.

◆ `IDBCreateSessionImpl`: provides an implementation for the `IDBCreate Session` interface. The default implementation creates an instance of the wizard-generated session class and returns the interface for that session object. This is a mandatory interface for all data source objects.

The most frequently asked question by new ATL developers is, "What do I override and how do I do it?" I save the latter question for the example. What you override depends entirely on the implementation and what you are trying to accomplish. If you depend on any of the initialization properties, such as user ID and password, you override `IDBProperties::IsValidValue`. This method is called when a consumer initializes the data source through the `IDBProperties::SetProperties` method. At this point, you typically squirrel the values away in data source member variables for use when the consumer requests a session object. To provide your own custom authentication or connection-specific logic, simply override the `IDBCreateSession:CreateSession` method.

Session Classes

Like the data source class, the wizard generates a session class. This class inherits from the implementation wrappers of the mandatory interfaces of a session object, as well as a template used to create command objects. Here I list all of the interface implementations that the wizard provides free of charge:

◆ `IGetDataSourceImpl`: provides an implementation of the `IGetDataSource` interface. This method provides the consumer with a mechanism of communicating with the data source object that created the session. There is only one method called `GetDataSource`. This is a mandatory interface for all session objects.

◆ `IOpenRowsetImpl`: provides an implementation of the `IOpenRowset` interface. The wizard generates the source for the method `OpenRowset`. This method creates an instance of the generated rowset class and calls the `CreateRowset` method defined in `ATLDB.H`. This is a mandatory interface for all session objects.

◆ `ISessionPropertiesImpl`: provides an implementation of the `ISession Properties` interface. This interface is similar to the `IDBProperties` interface. It enables the consumer to query and modify session properties through the `GetProperties` and `SetProperties` methods. This is a mandatory interface for all session objects.

- ◆ `IDBCreateCommandImpl`: provides an implementation of the `IDBCreate Command` interface. This class has one method called `CreateCommand`. This method creates an instance of the class identified by the second argument to the template. By default, this argument is the wizard-generated command object. This interface is optional for session objects. I've run into some consumer applications (guilty party's name available upon request) that assume if this interface is supported, then the data source understands SQL. Support for SQL is determined by querying for the `SQLSUPPORT` property of the data source object.

As with the wizard-generated data source, the developer can override functionality in the session class.

Rowset Classes

Once again, the wizard is involved in creating a default class that supports all of the mandatory interfaces of the rowset object. With this class, the developer must provide data from the source in a tabular format. Here is a brief overview of each of the template implementations that make up the rowset class:

- ◆ `CRowsetImpl`: the class containing the inherited interface implementations that make up the rest of this list. It is provided to prevent the multiple inheritance of a lengthy set of interfaces. The developer of the provider in most cases should provide only an implementation for the `Execute` method. One of the arguments to this template class is the array type to use. By default, it is set to `CSimpleArray<Storage>`. This class works fine for static schema, but does not work at all for dynamic schema like the one you create in the next example.

- ◆ `IRowsetImpl`: provides an implementation of the `IRowset` interface

- ◆ `CSimpleRow`: abstracts the row handle needed to access the table rows in the rowset. The *row handle* is an alias used by `IRowsetImpl` to uniquely identify a row.

- ◆ `IAccessorImpl`: provides an implementation of the `IAccessor` interface. This interface manages a set of `DBBINDING` structures using an `HACCESSOR`. In the ATL implementation, the `HACCESSOR` is simply the address of the `DBBINDING` or `ATLBINDING` structure for that column.

- ◆ `IRowsetInfoImpl`: implements the `IRowsetInfo` interface. This interface gives the consumer access to all properties defined in the command class of the project.

◆ `IColumnsInfoImpl`: implements the `IColumnsInfo` interface. When the ATL OLE DB Provider wizard generates a provider, the implementation of this class (by default) simply calls a static function implemented in the class that contains the hard-coded schema information. It is not always obvious to new users of the provider templates how to change this, but rest assured that we do exactly that in the example.

◆ `IConvertTypeImpl`: implements the `IConvertType` interface. This interface provides information about the availability of type conversion on a given command or rowset. The ATL implementation delegates this call to OLE DB's conversion object.

◆ `IDBSchemaRowsetImpl`: implements the `IDBSchemaRowset` interface. This interface provides information about the data (metadata) to interested consumers.

When the ATL OLE DB Provider wizard generates your provider, you notice several rowset classes. The primary rowset class is for returning data. The remaining three return metadata relating to tables (`DBSCHEMA_TABLES`), columns (`DBSCHEMA_COLUMNS`), and provider types (`DBSCHEMA_PROVIDER_TYPES`).

Command Classes

The ATL-generated command class abstracts an OLE DB command object. This object typically expects *data definition language (DDL)* or *data manipulation language (DML)* statements. However, as the examples show, it does not have to support DDL or DML to work. If you develop the provider, then you must determine the language that you understand. Here is a brief overview of each of the template implementations that make up the command class:

◆ `ICommandTextImpl`: implements the `ICommandText` interface. This interface has two methods responsible for getting and setting the command text.

◆ `ICommandImpl`: implements the `ICommand` interface. This interface defines three methods. The first method, `GetDBSession`, returns the current session object. The return value can be `NULL` if the provider does not have an object that creates this command object. Another method, `Execute`, simply executes the command text. The final method, `Cancel`, enables the currently executing command to be cancelled in a separate thread before the `Execute` method returns.

◆ `ICommandPropertiesImpl`: implements the `ICommandProperties` interface. This interface sets and gets properties associated with the command object.

ATL OLE DB Consumer Templates

Now that you've seen the ATL OLE DB Provider templates, let's move right along to the ATL-provided consumer templates. You can categorize these templates into four areas:

◆ General Data Source Support

◆ Rowset and Binding Support

◆ Table and Command Support

◆ User Records

 You can use these classes in MFC projects as well as in ATL projects.

General Data Source Support

These classes provide the plumbing for connecting to and accessing data sources. Here is a general description of the classes that offer data source support in consumer applications:

◆ CDataSource: manages the connection between the consumer and the data source of the provider. It provides methods to open and close the data source. To specify an initialization string, use the OpenFromInitialization method.

◆ CEnumerator: enables you to browse the available data sources via the ISourceRowset interface. You can use the Find method of this class to determine if a data source is registered on the machine.

◆ CSession: represents a single database access session. Each connection to the data source can have multiple sessions. The session class provides methods to manage transactions against a data source.

Rowset and Binding Support

These templates and classes enable you to set and retrieve data. You can divide these classes into groups of accessors and rowsets:

◆ CAccessorBase: the base class for the other accessor classes. In addition to allowing multiple accessors for a single rowset, this class provides binding for parameter and output columns.

- ◆ CAccessor: used when you statically bind to the data source. It is only useful if you know the layout of the data you want to access. If you use the ATL wizard to generate your consumer, you must specify the table with which you intend to bind. The wizard generates the necessary column definition macros to bind you to that table statically.

- ◆ CDynamicAccessor: allows for dynamic access to providers (unlike the sibling CAccessor class). The class uses IColumnInfo::GetColumnInfo to gather column information. It has methods to access column information such as type, size, and so on. You can use the GetValue method to get the value of a column by specifying the ordinal position of the column.

- ◆ CDynamicParameterAccess: derived from CDynamicAccessor and very similar to it. However, CDynamicParameterAccess provides access to command parameters. The provider must support ICommandWithParameters in order to use this class successfully.

- ◆ CManualAccessor: provided for those that know the best way to talk to the consumer. This class enables you to use whatever data types you wish, as long as the provider is capable of converting it. It handles result columns and command parameters.

- ◆ CRowset: the base class for the rowset classes. This class represents an OLE DB rowset object. It encapsulates the IRowset interface. Among other methods, this class enables you to move around in a rowset.

- ◆ CBulkRowset: provides the ability to fetch and manipulate data in bulk. It is capable of retrieving multiple row handles with a single call.

- ◆ CArrayRowset: gives you the ability to access records through an array syntax by overriding the [ ] operator.

Table and Command Support

These classes are derived from the CAcccessorRowset template class. The parameters to the template specify which accessor and rowset class to use. CTable and CCommand derive from CAccessorRowset and provide support for, you guessed it, tables and commands.

CTable provides support for directly accessing a simple rowset in a data source. The only method provided is Open, which enables you to open the rowset given a table name.

CCommand sets and executes a command. You can use this class when you need to set or retrieve parameters from the rowset. This class also provides support for commands that return multiple rowsets.

User Records

If you build a static accessor, then your consumer needs to define a user record. If you use the ATL wizard, a user record class is created for you. This class specifies the physical layout and column information of a specific table in the data source. Macros are provided to specify output columns and parameter bindings.

Active Data Objects

Active Data Objects (ADO) is the generalized data consumer offered by Microsoft. ADO provides a very simplistic set of objects that encapsulate the details of general data access. It quickly is becoming the data access method of choice among developers. Part of the reason for this is that it is available on so many different development languages such as C++, Visual Basic, and Delphi. ADO is based on the COM architecture so it is accessible from any language that can speak COM. All interfaces are automation interfaces, making it available from VBScript-ing languages also. Visual Interdev's design-time controls are integrated tightly with ADO. Microsoft provides a generic OLE DB Provider for ODBC data sources, which enables ADO not only to use OLE DB Providers but also to use any ODBC driver.

ADO's object model is very simple and is depicted in Figure 11-3. The objects are as follows:

◆ `Connection`: kind of a cross between the OLE DB data source and session objects. Connection objects handle user authentication through user name and password, as well as provide transaction support. Another useful feature of the connection object is exposed through the execute method. This method enables you to specify a command that returns a set of data. Using this method simplifies the process of connecting to a data source and retrieving data.

◆ `Command`: encapsulates a command that the data source can interpret. This command can be a SQL command, a stored procedure, or anything that the underlying data source understands. A neat thing about this object — as with most ADO objects — is that it can be created independently of the connection object.

◆ `Recordset`: represents the tabular data returned from a data source. It supports the ability to navigate a collection of records, update records in batch, and add and delete new records. Using this object, you also can access column information such as type and size.

◆ `Field`: encapsulates a column of a recordset object. Through the field object, you can access the column information of a field. This object can be accessed only through the recordset object's fields collection.

◆ `Parameter`: encapsulates a command parameter. This object can be input, output, or both. Input parameters are marshaled into ADO. Output parameters are returned, typically by a stored procedure, from ADO. This object typically is used with stored procedures and parameterized queries.

◆ `Error`: encapsulates an ADO error. This object is very similar to the OLE DB error object.

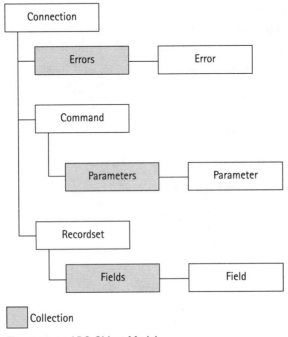

Figure 11-3: ADO Object Model

This obviously is a very limited introduction to ADO. The documentation provided with the latest version of ADO gives you more detailed information including the methods and properties of the preceding objects. In the examples section of this chapter, I show you how to develop ADO clients to access the OLE DB Provider that you also build.

In the Lab: Examples

Now it's time for the fun stuff. I welcome the managers and those of you that skipped right past the overview and went to the examples. In this section, you put all of this dry technical reading to use by implementing a provider and a consumer. Further, you use ADO as a consumer to access the provider you create.

General Project Overview

In the example, you design a custom data source and a read-only OLE DB Provider that can access this proprietary data source. This relationship is shown in Figure 11-4. Your data source is a file that contains the full path of the *comma-delimited files* (tables) that make up the data source. The provider has a very limited command set that consists of the name of the comma-delimited file (table) that you intend to access.

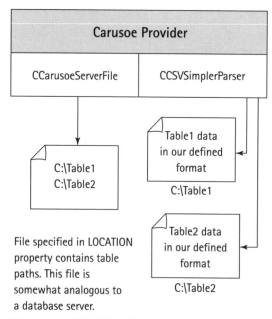

Figure 11-4: OLE DB Provider/data source relationship

The Data Source File

To begin with, you need to design your proprietary data source. For simplicity, your data source is a flat text file that contains the full path of the comma-delimited files. Here is an example of the contents of the data source file:

```
d:\my documents\temperatures.txt
d:\my documents\orders.txt
```

As you can see, this file contains the location or filenames of the tables of the data source. Carriage returns separate the tables.

I develop a simple class that is capable of reading this file. Since this really lies outside the scope of this chapter, I only outline the interface rather than go into the gory details. Feel free to look at the source code for this class if you are interested in how it is done. You can find the implementation for this class in `CrusoeServerFile.cpp` and `CrusoeServerFile.h`. The interface to the class is:

- ◆ `Initialize`: expects the full path of the file that contains the full paths of the comma-delimited table files. This method must be called before calling any other methods in the class.

- ◆ `GetTableCount`: returns the number of tables identified in the file, specified in initialization.

- ◆ `GetTableAt`: given a location between 0 and the table count minus 1, returns the name of the table at that location.

The Table Files

These tables are comma-delimited files that conform to a particular proprietary layout of my design. The first line of the comma-delimited file describes the table by providing some combination of column name, column type, column size, and precision. All of the examples I have seen previously have the data source schema built right into the provider. This works fine if you have a static schema, but does not for most commercially acceptable applications that ask the data source for schema information. In my example, I show you how to provide schema information dynamically based on the data source.

Without further ado, let's define the comma-delimited file. As I said before, the data exists in the form of a text file with comma-separated values. The first row is special because it contains the schema information. In my design, colons separate the schema information. The syntax is as follows:

```
Column Name:Column Type[:Column Size][:Column Precision][,]
```

Where:

- ◆ **Column name** is the name by which you address the column.

- ◆ **Column type** is the data type associated with the column. This value can be string, integer, float, or date. All date-type values are expected to be in the form of MM/DD/YYYY. Feel free to implement time, as it is very similar to date.

- ◆ **Column size** is the size of the column for string column types.

- ◆ **Column precision** is the precision of decimal places for float-type values.

Here is an example of a data file that the parser is capable of dealing with; this file is the `temperatures.txt` file referenced in the data source:

```
City:string:25,High:integer,Low:integer,Precipitation:float:2
Daytona,88,73,0.00
```

```
Fort Myers,91,75,0.00
Ft. Lauderdale,90,75,0.00
Homestead,90,73,0.04
Jacksonville,88,70,0.00
Key West,89,77,0.00
Lakeland,91,71,0.00
Miami,91,76,0.13
Orlando,91,73,0.00
Pensacola,89,70,0.00
Sarasota,89,73,0.00
Tallahassee,92,70,0.00
Tampa,90,74,0.00
West Palm Beach,90,74,0.03
```

Now you have defined how your data should look. The next step is to build a parser that is capable of understanding data in this format. Parser development is certainly out of the scope of this book, not to mention entirely off the topic, so I merely outline the interface here. The provided source contains the implementation of this very simple parser for those of you that are interested. For everyone else, suffice it to say that as long as the data follows the preceding format then this parser should be capable of reading it.

Your parser will have a very simple interface capable of:

◆ Storing the filename of the comma-delimited file representing the server through the `Initialize` method

◆ Moving to the first record in a set through the `MoveFirst` method

◆ Moving to the next record in a set through the `MoveNext` method

◆ Moving to the previous record in a set through the `MovePrev` method

◆ Moving to the last record in a set through the `MoveLast` method

◆ Moving to a specific record in a set through the `GotoRow` method

◆ Returning the number of columns in the recordset through the `GetColumnCount` method

◆ Returning the number of rows in the recordset through the `GetRowCount` method

◆ Accessing the underlying data at a record position

So there you have it. None of the movement functions can be called unless the parser is initialized with a data file. The source for the parser is located in the `CSVParser.cpp` and `CSVParser.h` files.

Creating the Provider Project

In this part of the example, you create an OLE DB Provider. You also create an ATL-based project with the AppWizard. I call my project ATL_OLEDB_Prov (see Figure 11-5).

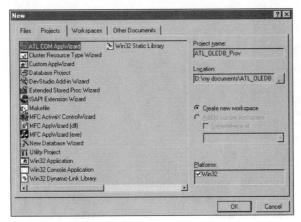

Figure 11-5: AppWizard

All OLE DB Providers are COM DLLs at heart so the server type should be Dynamic Link Library. I am fond of the MFC CString class so I also check Support MFC from the additional options on Step 1 of the wizard (see Figure 11-6).

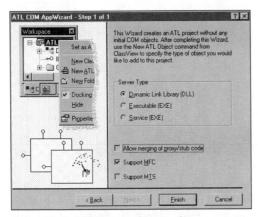

Figure 11-6: AppWizard – Step 1 of 1

ADD OLE DB PROVIDER SUPPORT OBJECTS

Now you use the ATL Object wizard to add OLE DB Provider support. The initial wizard dialog window is shown in Figure 11-7.

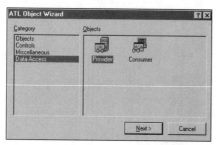

Figure 11-7: Object wizard - Provider

After you click the Next button, the ATL Object wizard Properties screen is displayed as shown in Figure 11-8. I call my provider `CrusoeProv` in tribute to the primary character of the classic book by Daniel Defoe. Fill in the short name; the remainder of the fields is defaulted for you. I accept the defaults here.

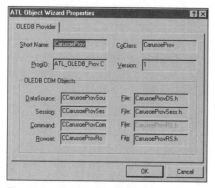

Figure 11-8: Object wizard - Provider Properties

When you click OK here, your project is populated with classes for source, session, command, rowset, schema rowsets, and a column definition object. I've discussed them all except the column definition object. If you follow my directions earlier in this section, this class is named `CCrusoeProvWindowsFile`. This class provides data and column information to the rowset object. By default, it is hard-wired to columns that represent files on a supplied file system directory. Later, you change this so it is provided dynamically from the table of your choosing.

ADD CUSTOM INTERFACES TO OLE DB PROVIDERS

Now you add a custom interface to your provider. This particular interface provides the data source location to interested clients. It contains one method called GetServerFileName that takes a BSTR* parameter, which contains the data source location specified upon connection to the OLE DB Provider.

For the purpose of this example, you use the interface from the schema objects to query the data source object for this information. However, if you develop a custom consumer, nothing prevents you from querying for this interface from the consumer. In this case, the information probably is irrelevant because the consumer provides this information anyway. The point is that you can provide custom interfaces that custom consumers can access.

To begin with, you add a new interface to your IDL file. My IDL file is ATL_OLEDB_Prov.idl. Add the following code to your IDL file:

```
[
    object,
    uuid(8DFCA8E0-791B-11d3-9D83-D79826594133),
    helpstring("IDBCrusoeProvSource Interface"),
    pointer_default(unique)
]
interface IDBCrusoeProvSource : IUnknown
{
    [helpstring("GetServerFile Method")]
        HRESULT GetServerFileName([out]BSTR* pBSTRFileName);
};
```

Next, you need to implement the interface in your data source object. In this case, the object name is CCrusoeProvSource and it is located in the Crusoe ProvDS.h file. Open this file and add support for the new interface by:

◆ Adding IDBCrusoeProvSource to the classes that CCrusoeProvSource inherits from

◆ Adding IDBCrusoeProvSource to the COM interface map

◆ Adding a protected member variable to the class called m_strServerFile that is used to hold the value of the server file

◆ Implementing the GetServerFileName method to return the current value of the m_strServerFile variable when called

Your data source class should look something like this when complete (for convenience, I highlighted the areas that you should change from the default):

```
class ATL_NO_VTABLE CCrusoeProvSource :
    public CComObjectRootEx<CComSingleThreadModel>,
    public CComCoClass<CCrusoeProvSource, &CLSID_CrusoeProv>,
```

```
   public IDBCreateSessionImpl<CCrusoeProvSource,
CCrusoeProvSession>,
   public IDBInitializeImpl<CCrusoeProvSource>,
   public IDBPropertiesImpl<CCrusoeProvSource>,
   public IPersistImpl<CCrusoeProvSource>,
   public IInternalConnectionImpl<CCrusoeProvSource>,
   public IDBCrusoeProvSource
{
protected:
   CString m_strServerFile;

public:
   HRESULT FinalConstruct()
   {
       return FInit();
   }

   // IDBCrusoeProvSource
   STDMETHODIMP GetServerFileName(BSTR* pBSTRFileName)
   {
       *pBSTRFileName = m_strServerFile.AllocSysString();
       return S_OK;
   }

DECLARE_REGISTRY_RESOURCEID(IDR_CRUSOEPROV)
BEGIN_PROPSET_MAP(CCrusoeProvSource)
   BEGIN_PROPERTY_SET(DBPROPSET_DATASOURCEINFO)
       PROPERTY_INFO_ENTRY(ACTIVESESSIONS)
       PROPERTY_INFO_ENTRY(DATASOURCEREADONLY)
       PROPERTY_INFO_ENTRY(BYREFACCESSORS)
       PROPERTY_INFO_ENTRY(OUTPUTPARAMETERAVAILABILITY)
       PROPERTY_INFO_ENTRY(PROVIDEROLEDBVER)
       PROPERTY_INFO_ENTRY(DSOTHREADMODEL)
       PROPERTY_INFO_ENTRY(SUPPORTEDTXNISOLEVELS)
       PROPERTY_INFO_ENTRY(USERNAME)
   END_PROPERTY_SET(DBPROPSET_DATASOURCEINFO)
   BEGIN_PROPERTY_SET(DBPROPSET_DBINIT)
       PROPERTY_INFO_ENTRY(AUTH_PASSWORD)
       PROPERTY_INFO_ENTRY(AUTH_PERSIST_SENSITIVE_AUTHINFO)
       PROPERTY_INFO_ENTRY(AUTH_USERID)
       PROPERTY_INFO_ENTRY(INIT_DATASOURCE)
       PROPERTY_INFO_ENTRY(INIT_HWND)
       PROPERTY_INFO_ENTRY(INIT_LCID)
       PROPERTY_INFO_ENTRY(INIT_LOCATION)
       PROPERTY_INFO_ENTRY(INIT_MODE)
```

```
        PROPERTY_INFO_ENTRY(INIT_PROMPT)
        PROPERTY_INFO_ENTRY(INIT_PROVIDERSTRING)
        PROPERTY_INFO_ENTRY(INIT_TIMEOUT)
    END_PROPERTY_SET(DBPROPSET_DBINIT)
    CHAIN_PROPERTY_SET(CCrusoeProvCommand)
END_PROPSET_MAP()
BEGIN_COM_MAP(CCrusoeProvSource)
    COM_INTERFACE_ENTRY(IDBCreateSession)
    COM_INTERFACE_ENTRY(IDBInitialize)
    COM_INTERFACE_ENTRY(IDBProperties)
    COM_INTERFACE_ENTRY(IPersist)
    COM_INTERFACE_ENTRY(IInternalConnection)
    COM_INTERFACE_ENTRY(IDBCrusoeProvSource)
END_COM_MAP()

public:
};
```

You may wonder where the variable that you added gets filled in. In your implementation, you use the DBPROP_INIT_LOCATION property to house the location of your data source file. The OLE DB Consumer specifies this property in the connection string. You write the code to get this information in the next section.

ADD SECURITY TO THE DATA SOURCE

The next step is to provide a level of security to your provider. My authentication scheme is very simple. I provide access to a single user with an ID of rpatton and a password of password. I think it would be a much happier world if all authentication schemes were this simple. Think of all the sticky notes that end users could save if they didn't need to write their IDs and tricky passwords down and attach them to their monitors.

All of the properties provided by the consumer are passed through a method called IsValidValue. To squirrel away values, or even validate them immediately, all you need to do is override this method. In your case, you are interested in three values:

- ◆ DBPROP_INIT_LOCATION is the location of the data source file that contains full paths to your comma-delimited files or tables.

- ◆ DBPROP_AUTH_USERID is the user ID specified during the connection.

- ◆ DBPROP_AUTH_PASSWORD is the password specified during the connection.

The code below adds a userID and password pair to our class, and provides a method to populate these member variables.

```
protected:
    CString m_strServerFile;
```

```
    CString m_strUserId;
    CString m_strPassword;

public:

    HRESULT FinalConstruct()
    {
        return FInit();
    }
    HRESULT IsValidValue(ULONG iCurSet, DBPROP* pDBProp)
    {
        ATLASSERT(pDBProp != NULL);
        CComVariant var = pDBProp->vValue;

        switch (pDBProp->dwPropertyID)
        {
        case DBPROP_INIT_LOCATION:
            m_strServerFile = var.bstrVal;
            break;
        case DBPROP_AUTH_USERID:
            m_strUserId = var.bstrVal;
            break;
        case DBPROP_AUTH_PASSWORD:
            m_strPassword = var.bstrVal;
            break;
        default:
            break;
        }

        return

IDBPropertiesImpl<CCrusoeProvSource>::IsValidValue(iCurSet,
                                                   pDBProp);
    }
...
```

Notice that I refer all calls to IsValidValue to the base class implementation. This call eventually ends up in a call to CUtlProps::IsValidValue. This method doesn't do much, but it is always a good idea to call it. It checks the return value of VT_BOOL type properties. If the property variant type is VT_BOOL and the value isn't VARIANT_TRUE or VARIANT_FALSE, the return value is S_FALSE. Otherwise, S_OK is returned.

Now you have all of the properties that you need. The next steps for authentication are:

1. Override CreateSession to provide security checks before allowing the creation of a session.

2. Create a method called `AuthenticateLogonInfo` that is responsible for validating the user ID and password supplied by the consumer.

3. Let the consumer know that you do not support SQL by setting a property of the data source.

And here is the code:

```
...
STDMETHODIMP CreateSession(IUnknown* pUnkOuter,
                              REFIID riid, IUnknown** ppDBSession)
{
   HRESULT hr = S_OK;

   // Make sure we have a server file
   if (m_strServerFile.IsEmpty())
      hr = E_FAIL;

   // Make sure we have valid logon information
   if (SUCCEEDED(hr))
      hr = AuthenticateLogonInfo();

   // Create the Session
   if (SUCCEEDED(hr))
      hr = IDBCreateSessionImpl<CCrusoeProvSource,
                                 CCrusoeProvSession>
                  ::CreateSession(pUnkOuter, riid, ppDBSession);
      return hr;
}

HRESULT AuthenticateLogonInfo()
{
   HRESULT hr = E_ACCESSDENIED;
   if (m_strUserId == CString("rpatton"))
      if (m_strPassword == CString("password"))
         hr = S_OK;

   return hr;
}

// IDBCrusoeProvSource
STDMETHODIMP GetServerFileName(BSTR* pBSTRFileName)
{
   *pBSTRFileName = m_strServerFile.AllocSysString();
   return S_OK;
}
```

```
DECLARE_REGISTRY_RESOURCEID(IDR_CRUSOEPROV)
BEGIN_PROPSET_MAP(CCrusoeProvSource)
  BEGIN_PROPERTY_SET(DBPROPSET_DATASOURCEINFO)
    PROPERTY_INFO_ENTRY(ACTIVESESSIONS)
    PROPERTY_INFO_ENTRY(DATASOURCEREADONLY)
    PROPERTY_INFO_ENTRY(BYREFACCESSORS)
    PROPERTY_INFO_ENTRY(OUTPUTPARAMETERAVAILABILITY)
    PROPERTY_INFO_ENTRY(PROVIDEROLEDBVER)
    PROPERTY_INFO_ENTRY(DSOTHREADMODEL)
    PROPERTY_INFO_ENTRY(SUPPORTEDTXNISOLEVELS)
    PROPERTY_INFO_ENTRY(USERNAME)
    PROPERTY_INFO_ENTRY_EX(SQLSUPPORT, VT_I4, 0,
                           DBPROPVAL_SQL_NONE,
                           DBPROPOPTIONS_REQUIRED)
  END_PROPERTY_SET(DBPROPSET_DATASOURCEINFO)
  BEGIN_PROPERTY_SET(DBPROPSET_DBINIT)
    PROPERTY_INFO_ENTRY(AUTH_PASSWORD)
    PROPERTY_INFO_ENTRY(AUTH_PERSIST_SENSITIVE_AUTHINFO)
    PROPERTY_INFO_ENTRY(AUTH_USERID)
    PROPERTY_INFO_ENTRY(INIT_DATASOURCE)
    PROPERTY_INFO_ENTRY(INIT_HWND)
    PROPERTY_INFO_ENTRY(INIT_LCID)
    PROPERTY_INFO_ENTRY(INIT_LOCATION)
    PROPERTY_INFO_ENTRY(INIT_MODE)
    PROPERTY_INFO_ENTRY(INIT_PROMPT)
    PROPERTY_INFO_ENTRY(INIT_PROVIDERSTRING)
    PROPERTY_INFO_ENTRY(INIT_TIMEOUT)
  END_PROPERTY_SET(DBPROPSET_DBINIT)
  CHAIN_PROPERTY_SET(CCrusoeProvCommand)
END_PROPSET_MAP()
```

The `CreateSession` method implementation checks that the `m_strServerFile` variable is set. In your implementation, this is simply a full path to a file in the file system. For this particular example, I don't validate that this file exists (just to keep things simple). In a production-quality provider, you would want to put as many checks here as possible before allowing the creation of a session.

If the `m_strServerFile` is not empty, the `CreateSession` method calls a method of your creation called `AuthenticateLogonInfo`. This method simply verifies that the user ID is `rpatton` and the password is `password`. As I mentioned earlier, your authentication scheme probably needs to be much more complicated than this, but you capture the consumer-supplied properties in the same fashion.

Finally, you specify in the property map that you do not support SQL by initializing the OLE DB-defined `DBPROP_SQLSUPPORT` property. In all of these examples, you provide the command but some consumers graphically depict the tables that a given provider serves. If the provider doesn't set this property, the consumer likely sends a SELECT statement to the provider. If your provider doesn't support SQL and can't parse this statement, your provider does not work with this consumer. So it is always a good idea to set this property if your provider doesn't understand SQL.

That's all you need to do to this class. In summary, you add support for a new interface called IDBCrusoeProvSource, which enables other objects to get the contents of the LOCATION property specified by the consumer during connection. You also add a rudimentary authentication mechanism to your data source. Finally, you let potential consumers know that you do not understand SQL by setting a data source property designed for this purpose. At this point, your provider should build cleanly.

Providing Schema Information

Upon connecting to the data source and creating a session, most consumers query for schema information from the provided schema objects. When you generate an ATL consumer later in the section, the ATL wizard shows you all tables in the provided data source location using the table row schema object. After you select a table, the wizard uses the column schema object to retrieve the columns supported by the selected table.

The classes you modify now are located in the CrusoeProvSess.h file. Follow these steps to add the supplied data source and comma-delimited file parsers to your project.

1. Copy the CrusoeServerFile.h, CrusoeServerFile.cpp, SimpleCSVParser.h, and SimpleCSVParser.cpp files to the directory in which you created the OLE DB Provider.

2. Go to the File View of Developer Studio, right-click the project file, and choose "Add Files to Project..." from the context menu.

3. Select the four new files that you moved in Step 1 to add them to your project.

When the session object is created, the consumer uses it to query for the schema rowsets. In the ATL-generated session class, you have a set of macros that define the classes (also generated), which manage providing schema data to the consumer in the form of a rowset. The schema map macro generated for your project is in the CCrusoeProvSession class and looks like this:

```
BEGIN_SCHEMA_MAP(CCrusoeProvSession)
    SCHEMA_ENTRY(DBSCHEMA_TABLES, CCrusoeProvSessionTRSchemaRowset)
    SCHEMA_ENTRY(DBSCHEMA_COLUMNS, CCrusoeProvSessionColSchemaRowset)
    SCHEMA_ENTRY(DBSCHEMA_PROVIDER_TYPES,
                 CCrusoeProvSessionPTSchemaRowset)
END_SCHEMA_MAP()
```

The generated `CCrusoeProvSessionTRSchemaRowset` class provides table information from the data source in a rowset. In your implementation, you open the data source file and read the contents that make up your tables. You then add this information to an array. ATL manages returning this data as a set. All you need to do is stock the array with data.

Replace the generated `Execute` method of the `CCrusoeProvSessionTRSchemaRowset` class with code that works with your data source to gather the information:

```
HRESULT Execute(LONG* pcRowsAffected, ULONG, const VARIANT*)
{
    USES_CONVERSION;
    CTABLESRow trData;
    HRESULT hr = S_OK;
    long rowsAffected = 0;

    IGetDataSource* pDataSource = NULL;
    IDBCrusoeProvSource* pDBCrusoeProvSource = NULL;

    try
    {
        hr = m_spUnkSite->QueryInterface(IID_IGetDataSource,
                                        (void**)&pDataSource);
        if (FAILED(hr))
            throw hr;

        hr = pDataSource->GetDataSource(IID_IDBCrusoeProvSource,
                                   (LPUNKNOWN*)
                                        &pDBCrusoeProvSource);
        if (FAILED(hr))
            throw hr;

        BSTR bstrServerName;
        hr = pDBCrusoeProvSource>GetServerFileName(&bstrServerName);
        if (FAILED(hr))
            throw hr;

        CString fileName(bstrServerName);
        ::SysFreeString(bstrServerName);

        lstrcpyW(trData.m_szType, OLESTR("TABLE"));
        lstrcpyW(trData.m_szDesc, OLESTR("Crusoe Server File"));

        CCrusoeServerFile serverFile;
        serverFile.Initialize(fileName);
        for (long l = 0; l < serverFile.GetTableCount(); l++)
        {
```

```
        CComBSTR tableName;
        serverFile.GetTableAt(1, tableName);
        lstrcpyW(trData.m_szTable, tableName.m_str);
        if (!m_rgRowData.Add(trData))
            throw E_OUTOFMEMORY;
        rowsAffected++;
      }
   }
   catch(HRESULT errorCode)
   {
      TRACE("Error %X thrown in
             CCrusoeProvSessionTRSchemaRowset::Execute()\n",
             errorCode);
   }

   if (pDBCrusoeProvSource)
      pDBCrusoeProvSource->Release();
   if (pDataSource)
      pDataSource->Release();

   *pcRowsAffected = rowsAffected;
   return hr;
}
```

The m_spUnkSite member variable is the CCrusoeProvSource object. You can use this variable to get the interface pointer to the custom interface you create in the data source object. Once you have that interface, you can query the data source object for the location of the file that contains the references to the tables of your source object.

The ATL-defined CTABLESRow structure provides data about the tables contained in a data source. I use the provided CCrusoeServerFile class to parse the data source file. This class can tell me how many tables exist in the file, as well as the names of each table. For each table in the file, I create an element in the m_rgRowData array. This array then creates a rowset that is returned to the interested consumer.

Similar to the table schema provided, you need to provide schema information for the columns of the tables. To do this, you enlist the help of your CSimple CSVParser class to get the column information.

Replace the Execute method of the CCrusoeProvSessionColSchemaRowset with this code:

```
HRESULT Execute(LONG* pcRowsAffected, ULONG, const VARIANT*)
{
   USES_CONVERSION;
   CCOLUMNSRow trData;
   HRESULT hr = S_OK;
```

```
long rowsAffected = 0;

IGetDataSource* pDataSource = NULL;
IDBCrusoeProvSource* pDBCrusoeProvSource = NULL;

try
{
    hr = m_spUnkSite->QueryInterface(IID_IGetDataSource,
                                     (void**)&pDataSource);
    if (FAILED(hr))
        throw hr;

    hr = pDataSource->GetDataSource(IID_IDBCrusoeProvSource,
                            (IUnknown**) &pDBCrusoeProvSource);
    if (FAILED(hr))
        throw hr;

    BSTR bstrServerName;
    hr = pDBCrusoeProvSource->GetServerFileName(&bstrServerName);
    if (FAILED(hr))
        throw hr;

    CString fileName(bstrServerName);
    ::SysFreeString(bstrServerName);

    CCrusoeServerFile serverFile;
    serverFile.Initialize(fileName);
    for (long l = 0; l < serverFile.GetTableCount(); l++)
    {
        CSimpleCSVParser parser;
        CComBSTR bstrTableName;
        serverFile.GetTableAt(l, bstrTableName);
        parser.Initialize(OLE2T(bstrTableName));

        lstrcpyW(trData.m_szTableName, bstrTableName);

        for (int cols = 0; cols < parser.GetColumnCount(); cols++)
        {
            CColumnDefinition* pColDef =
                        parser.GetColumnDefinition(cols);
            trData.m_ulOrdinalPosition = cols + 1;
            trData.m_bIsNullable = VARIANT_TRUE;
            trData.m_bColumnHasDefault = VARIANT_FALSE;
            trData.m_ulCharMaxLength = pColDef->GetColumnSize();
            trData.m_ulColumnFlags = 0;
            lstrcpyW(trData.m_szColumnName,
```

```
                        T2OLE(pColDef->GetColumnName()));

        switch (pColDef->GetColumnType())
        {
        case stringType:
            trData.m_nDataType = DBTYPE_STR;
            trData.m_ulCharMaxLength +=  sizeof(TCHAR);
            break;

        case intType:
            trData.m_nDataType = DBTYPE_UI4;
            trData.m_ulCharMaxLength = sizeof(long);
            break;

        case floatType:
            trData.m_nDataType = DBTYPE_R8;
            trData.m_ulCharMaxLength = sizeof(double);
            break;

        case dateType:
            trData.m_nDataType = DBTYPE_DBDATE;
            trData.m_ulCharMaxLength = sizeof(DBDATE);
            break;
        }

        // Add to the row data
        m_rgRowData.Add(trData);
      }
    }
  }
  catch(HRESULT errorCode)
  {
    TRACE("Error %X thrown in
          CCrusoeProvSessionTRSchemaRowset::Execute()\n",
          errorCode);
  }

  if (pDBCrusoeProvSource)
    pDBCrusoeProvSource->Release();

   if (pDataSource)
    pDataSource->Release();

   return hr;
}
```

Much like in the tables schema class, you need to get the location of the data source file because this file tells you the locations of your comma-delimited files (tables). Once you have this information, you use the CSimpleCSVParser class to open these tables by passing the table name – which just happens to be a full path to the file.

The ATL-defined CCOLUMNSRow structure defines an available column. For each column in each table, you must define an entry into the m_rgRowData array. The underlying rowset implementation manages the conversion between this array to a rowset. I briefly describe the important members of this structure here:

- m_szTableName: contains the name of the table that contains this column.

- m_ulOrdinalPosition: the 1-based index of the column in the table.

- m_szColumnName: contains the name of this column.

- m_nDataType: the OLE DB-defined data type of the object. Notice that my proprietary data source must map the proprietary type to one defined by OLE DB. This typically is the case for proprietary data sources.

- m_ulCharMaxLength: the size of the column. I always add room for the NULL character for types of DBTYPE_STR.

The only thing that remains for this file is some declarations. It's not considered good programming etiquette to wait for the compiler to remind you that you used classes such as CSimpleCSVParser and CCrusoeServerFile without declaring them. The final step is to include the header files for each of these classes:

```
#include "CrusoeServerFile.h"
#include "SimpleCSVParser.h"
```

That completes your work in this file. To summarize, you modify the generated Execute methods of both the CCrusoeProvSessionTRSchemaRowset and CCrusoe ProvSessionColSchemaRowset classes to provide table and column information respectively. At this point, your provider should build cleanly.

Building the Data Manager

Your ATL OLE DB Provider needs to have a class that can manage retrieving the data. The wizard generates a class called CCrusoeProvWindowsFile that is capable of doing this if your provider is bound statically to the underlying source. The one in these examples is not, so you have to do some major surgery on this class. To be honest, I don't like the generated name, so I completely rewrite this class to do my bidding.

Follow the steps below to remove the generated CCrusoeProvWindowsFile class:

1. Find the CCrusoeProvWindowsFile class in the CrusoeProvRS.h file.

2. Select this class and remove it. Be careful not to remove the other classes declared in this file.

3. Build the provider, but don't freak out when you get build errors. Feel free to freak out if you don't get build errors.

The error that I want you to pay special attention to is (approximately) on line 67. It resides in the template parameters of the CRowsetImpl object. If you look at the help for this class, you find that this parameter is for the storage class of the user record. So your rowset object is connected to the new data manager class that you create. If you look in the ATLDB.h file, you find that this storage class builds an array of items of that type called m_rgRowData.

Now you create the data manager class, as shown in Listing 11-1.

Listing 11-1: The data manager class

```
class CCrusoeProvTextFile
{
public:
    CCrusoeProvTextFile()
    {
        m_cacheNdxStart = -1;
        m_cacheRows = 0;
        m_nRowSize = 0;
        m_pData = NULL;
    }
    ~CCrusoeProvTextFile()
    {
        RemoveAll();
    }

    void LoadCache(long nStart)
    {
        if (m_pData == NULL)
            return;

        memset(m_pData, NULL,
                (int)(m_cacheRows*(m_nRowSize+1)*sizeof(TCHAR)));

        if (nStart < 0 || nStart > m_parser.GetRowCount())
            return;

        m_parser.GotoRow(nStart);
        long rows = min(m_cacheRows, m_parser.GetRowCount() - nStart);
        LPBYTE pLoc = m_pData;
        long tmpLong;
```

```
double tmpDouble;
CString tmpString;

for (long i = 0; i < rows; i++)
{
   for (long j = 0; j < m_parser.GetColumnCount(); j++)
   {
      CColumnDefinition* pColDef =
                   m_parser.GetColumnDefinition(j);
      if (pColDef)
      {
         switch (pColDef->GetColumnType())
         {
            case stringType:
               _tcscpy((LPTSTR) pLoc, pColDef->
                                     GetColumnValue());
               pLoc += pColDef->GetColumnSize() +
                        sizeof(TCHAR);
               break;

            case intType:
               tmpLong = atol(pColDef->GetColumnValue());
               memcpy(pLoc, (void*)&tmpLong, sizeof(long));
               pLoc += sizeof(long);
               break;

            case floatType:
               tmpDouble = atof(pColDef->GetColumnValue());
               memcpy(pLoc, &tmpDouble, sizeof(double));
               pLoc += sizeof(double);
               break;

            case dateType:
               tmpString = pColDef->GetColumnValue();
               DBDATE dbDate;
               ConvertStringToDate(tmpString.GetBuffer(0),
                                 &dbDate);
               memcpy(pLoc, &dbDate, sizeof(DBDATE));
               pLoc += sizeof(DBDATE);
               break;
         }
      }
   }
   m_parser.MoveNext();
}
```

```
      m_cacheNdxStart = nStart;
}


// Assumption: The Parser ALWAYS gives us date in MM/DD/YYYY
// format
void ConvertStringToDate(LPTSTR str, DBDATE* pDBDate) const
{
   char strSep[2];
   strcpy(strSep, "/");

   // Extract First Item
   LPTSTR  token;
   unsigned short number;
   token = strtok(str, strSep);
   if (token)
   {
      number = (unsigned short) atoi(token);
      pDBDate->month = number;
   }

   token = strtok(NULL, strSep);
   if (token)
   {
      number = (unsigned short) atoi(token);
             pDBDate->day = number;
   }

   token = strtok(NULL, strSep);
   if (token)
   {
      number = (unsigned short) atoi(token);
      pDBDate->year = number;
   }                            '

}


HRESULT Initialize(CComBSTR& strTableLocation,
                   CSimpleArray<ATLCOLUMNINFO>& rgColInfo)
{
   USES_CONVERSION;

   if (!m_parser.Initialize(_bstr_t(strTableLocation.m_str)))
      return E_FAIL;

   // Calculate the row size
```

```
m_nRowSize = 0;
int offset = 0;
for (long i = 0; i < m_parser.GetColumnCount(); i++)
{
    CColumnDefinition* pColDef = m_parser.GetColumnDefinition(i);
    if (pColDef)
    {
        ATLCOLUMNINFO colInfo;
        memset(&colInfo, 0, sizeof(ATLCOLUMNINFO));
        colInfo.pwszName =
            ::SysAllocString(T2OLE(pColDef->GetColumnName()));
        colInfo.iOrdinal = i+1;
        colInfo.dwFlags = NULL;
        colInfo.bPrecision = 0xFF;
        colInfo.bScale = 0xFF;
        colInfo.columnid.uName.pwszName = colInfo.pwszName;

        switch (pColDef->GetColumnType())
        {
            case stringType:
                colInfo.wType = DBTYPE_STR;
                m_nRowSize += pColDef->GetColumnSize()
                                    + sizeof(TCHAR);
                colInfo.ulColumnSize =
                        pColDef->GetColumnSize() + sizeof(TCHAR);
                break;

            case intType:
                colInfo.wType = DBTYPE_I4;
                m_nRowSize += sizeof(long);
                colInfo.ulColumnSize = sizeof(long);
                break;

            case floatType:
                colInfo.wType = DBTYPE_R8;
                colInfo.bPrecision =
                    (BYTE) pColDef->GetColumnPrecision();
                m_nRowSize += sizeof(double);
                colInfo.ulColumnSize = sizeof(double);
                break;

            case dateType:
                colInfo.wType = DBTYPE_DBDATE;
                m_nRowSize += sizeof(DBDATE);
```

```
                colInfo.ulColumnSize = sizeof(DBDATE);
                break;
        }

        colInfo.cbOffset = offset;
        offset += colInfo.ulColumnSize;
        rgColInfo.Add(colInfo);
    }
}

if (m_nRowSize > 0)
{
    // calculate to use 500K for cache space
    m_cacheRows = 500000/m_nRowSize;

    m_pData = new BYTE[(int)(m_cacheRows*(m_nRowSize+1))];
    if ( m_pData )
            memset(m_pData, NULL,
                   (int)(m_cacheRows*(m_nRowSize+1) *
                                sizeof(TCHAR)));
}
else
    return E_FAIL;

return S_OK;
}

template <class T>
static ATLCOLUMNINFO* GetColumnInfo(T* pT, ULONG* pcCols)
{
    CComQIPtr<ICommand> spCommand = pT->GetUnknown();
    if (spCommand == NULL)
    {
        if (pcCols != NULL)
            *pcCols = pT->m_rgColInfo.GetSize();
        return pT->m_rgColInfo.m_aT;
    }
    CComPtr<IRowset> pRowset;
    if (pT->m_rgColInfo.m_aT == NULL)
    {
        LONG cRows;
        HRESULT hr = spCommand->Execute(NULL, IID_IRowset,
                           NULL, &cRows, (IUnknown**)&pRowset);
    }
```

```
            if (pcCols != NULL)
                *pcCols = pT->m_rgColInfo.GetSize();

            return pT->m_rgColInfo.m_aT;
        }

        LONG GetSize() const
        {
            return (m_parser.GetRowCount());
        }

        BYTE& operator[] (long nIndex)
        {
            long lowRange = m_cacheNdxStart;
            long highRange = m_cacheNdxStart + m_cacheRows - 1;

            // If the row isn't in the cache then reload the cache
            if ((m_cacheNdxStart == -1) ||
                (nIndex < lowRange || nIndex > highRange))
            {
                LoadCache(nIndex);
                m_cacheNdxStart = nIndex;
            }

            return  m_pData[(nIndex - m_cacheNdxStart)*(m_nRowSize)];
        }

        void RemoveAll()
        {
            if (m_pData)
            {
                delete [] m_pData;
                m_pData = NULL;
            }
        }

protected:
    CSimpleCSVParser m_parser;
    LPBYTE m_pData;

    long m_cacheNdxStart;
    long m_cacheRows;
    long m_nRowSize;
};
```

Because the rowset class depends on this connection, it also expects that certain methods be defined in the class. Here's a commented list of these methods:

- `Initialize`: You use this method in the rowset class to initialize your array with data. Of the methods listed, it is the only one not used in `ATLDB.h`. In other words, I use the array class `m_rgRowData` declared in the rowset class and call this method. I can call it anything, but `Initialize` seems appropriate. When it is called, the rowset passes the location of the comma-delimited file and an array to put column information. The comma-delimited file is parsed with the help of `CSimpleCSVParser` and the column information is extracted and placed in the array. Afterwards, I reserve 500K of RAM to cache away up to 500K of records. None of these examples use this much space, but if they did, this would provide a big performance boost over handling one at a time.

- `GetColumnInfo`: If you really paid attention to the compiler errors you received when you built the project earlier, you would have noticed that a number of these errors are related to this method. This is a static method responsible for providing column information to the caller. The caller of this function needs to provide the class of an object as a template parameter. If you study the code, you can see that the class needs to have a variable declared called `m_rgColInfo` that has a method called `GetSize`. In your case, declare a variable of this type in both the command and rowset classes.

- `GetSize`: This method is called to retrieve the number of rows in the set of data.

- `operator []`: This method is called when data is needed. The index parameter specified corresponds to the zero-based row in the set. In my implementation, I look at the index and see if it is in my cache. If it is, I simply return the address of that row in the cache. If it isn't, I reload the cache beginning with the row at the specified index and then return the address of that row in the cache.

- `RemoveAll`: This method is called when the rowset is finished with the class. This is a good place to clean up any allocated data or release any interfaces you may have used to acquire data. In my implementation, I simply clean up the allocated data.

The remaining two methods are utility functions that the class uses internally:

- `LoadCache`: This method simply loads the cache with data from the table beginning with the index supplied by the caller. It loads until it is out of space in the cache or until there are no records left.

- `ConvertStringToDate`: This method accepts a string that contains a date in the form of MM/DD/YYYY and converts it to a `DBDATE` structure.

I need to do a few more things to complete work on the data manager:

- I changed the name of the data manager file, so I need to do a global replace of `CCrusoeProvWindowsFile` with `CCrusoeProvTextFile`.

- I need to add the include files for the `CSimpleCSVParser` class to this file.

- I need to include `comdef.h`, which defines the `bstr_t` helper classes.

MODIFY THE COMMAND AND ROWSET CLASSES

Now that you have a data manager class, you need to invoke it from the rowset's `Execute` method.

Add a template parameter to the rowset class's `CRowsetImpl` template parameter list:

```
class CCrusoeProvRowset
: public CRowsetImpl< CCrusoeProvRowset, CCrusoeProvTextFile,
CCrusoeProvCommand, CCrusoeProvTextFile>
```

Replace the `Execute` method of the rowset class with this code:

```
HRESULT Execute(DBPARAMS * pParams, LONG* pcRowsAffected)
{
    USES_CONVERSION;

    ObjectLock lock(this);

    if (m_strCommandText.Length() <= 0)
        return E_FAIL;

    HRESULT hr = m_rgRowData.Initialize(m_strCommandText,
                                        m_rgColInfo);

    if (pcRowsAffected != NULL)
        *pcRowsAffected = 1;

    return hr;
}
```

Finally, you need to add member variables to each class that enable the data manager to provide column information. Add the following member variable to both the `CCrusoeProvRowset` and `CCrusoeProvCommand` classes:

```
CSimpleArray<ATLCOLUMNINFO> m_rgColInfo;
```

Compile the provider and with any luck you won't have any errors to fix. Testing the provider has to wait until you develop something capable of talking to it. Read on.

Accessing OLE DB Providers through ADO

In this example, you build an HTML page that uses client-side VBScript to access the OLE DB Provider you created in the last example. You can move this code with little modification to an Active Server Page (ASP) that uses server-side scripting to access your provider. However, I think a larger part of the audience is more familiar with client-side scripting, so I elect to access the provider on the client. The client-side scripting language is VBScript, so it is important that your browser support VBScript. (I tested the code with Internet Explorer 5.0.)

This example uses ADO to dynamically discover tables from a provided data source location. You populate a select control (list box) with the tables. You also add a button to the page that enables the user to get the data from the selected table.

CREATE THE PAGE

Create an HTML page on your file system called OLEDBPage.htm and type in the code from Listing 11-2.

Listing 11-2: OLEDBPage.htm

```
<html>

<head>
<title>Using OLE DB Providers in HTML Pages</title>
</head>
<script language=vbscript>
sub GetData_OnClick()
    Call LoadDataFromSelectedTable
end sub

sub LoadDataFromSelectedTable
    dim conn
    dim rs
    dim strHTML
    dim txtRangeObj

    ' Initialize the text range object to point to our span tag
    ' below
    set txtRangeObj = document.body.CreateTextRange()
    txtRangeObj.MoveToElementText(tableData)

    ' Open the Server File
    set conn = CreateObject("ADODB.Connection")
    conn.Open "Provider=CrusoeProv OLE DB Provider;_
        LOCATION=d:\my documents\serverfile.txt", "rpatton", "password"

    ' This will be the table name selected from the list box
```

```
set rs = conn.Execute(tables.value)

' Build an HTML String that will contain the complete table of
' data
strHTML = "<h2 align=center>Table: " & tables.value & "</h2>"

' Put the results in a table
strHTML = strHTML & "<table border=1 align=center>"
strHTML = strHTML & "<tr>"

' Create a heading column for each field in the record
for each field in rs.Fields
    strHTML = strHTML & "<th>" & field.Name & "</th>"
next

strHTML = strHTML & "</tr>"

while not rs.EOF
    strHTML = strHTML & "<tr>"

    for each field in rs.Fields
        strHTML = strHTML & "<td"

        ' We want to align all numbers and dates to the right
        ' 200 is adVarChar which is the type our strings
        ' will return as
        if field.type <> 200 then
            strHTML = strHTML & " align=right>"
        else
            strHTML = strHTML & ">"
        end if

        ' Put the contents of the field for this
        ' record into the table
        strHTML = strHTML & field.Value
        strHTML = strHTML & "</td>"
    next

    strHTML = strHTML & "</tr>"
    rs.MoveNext
wend

strHTML = strHTML & "</table>"
document.all("tableData").innerHTML =  strHTML
```

```vbscript
    set txtRangeObj = nothing
    set rs = nothing
    set conn = nothing
end sub
</script>

<body bgcolor="#D5CCBB">
<h1 align="center">Defined Tables in ServerFile.txt Data Source</h1>
<center>
<SCRIPT LANGUAGE=VBScript>

    ' We are going to dynamically discover the tables
    ' of a data source. This is accomplished by getting
    ' the tables schema from the data source. At that
    ' point it is a recordset and information provided
    ' by the provider for the table is available

    dim conn
    dim rs
    dim bSelected

    bSelected = false

    set conn = CreateObject("ADODB.Connection")
    conn.Open "Provider=CrusoeProv OLE DB Provider;LOCATION=d:\my
    documents\serverfile.txt", "rpatton", "password"

     ' adSchemaTables = 20; Opens the Tables Schema Rowset
    set rs = conn.OpenSchema(20)

    document.write "<select size=5 name=tables id=tables>"
    while not rs.EOF
        document.write "<option value=""" & rs("TABLE_NAME")

        ' Select the first table in the set
        if not bSelected then
            document.write """ selected>"
            bSelected = true
        else
            document.write """>"
        end if

        document.write rs("TABLE_NAME")
        document.write "</option>"
```

```
        rs.MoveNext
    wend

    document.write "</select>"

    set rs = nothing
    set conn = nothing

</SCRIPT>
<br><br>
<input type=button id=GetData name=GetData value="Get Data">
</center>
<br><br>

<span id=tableData name=tableData>
<SCRIPT LANGUAGE=VBScript>
    ' Load the data from the initialized table above
    Call LoadDataFromSelectedTable
</SCRIPT>
</table>
</span>
</body>

</html>
```

To test the page:

- ◆ Make sure the location portion of the string matches the location of your data source file.

- ◆ Make sure that the user and password match the authentication scheme that you build into the provider.

- ◆ Make sure that the execution string matches the location of the comma-delimited file.

- ◆ Finally, load the page in Internet Explorer or in any other VBScript-enabled browser.

This page gives you a pretty good idea of the power of ADO. It is very easy to access from any language, scripting or otherwise. It also provides the client with the ability to dynamically determine not only the structure of the data but also the structure of table and data source. It doesn't take a significant amount of effort to turn this example into a full-blown query front end for ADO that can talk to any OLE DB Provider.

MFC/ATL Consumer Example

In this example, you embed an ATL consumer within an MFC application to provide access to the OLE DB Provider you created. One of the real niceties of the latest version of Developer Studio is the ability to incorporate ATL objects into MFC projects. That is exactly what you do next. This is a very simple example, but it should give you the knowledge necessary to build a custom consumer for any OLE DB Provider.

Without further ado, first create a dialog-based MFC project called `ATL_OLEDB_Consumer`. Make sure that the Automation checkbox on Step 2 of the AppWizard is selected. If you forget to do this, make sure you make a call to `AfxOleInit` in the `InitInstance` method of the application object. The defaults are acceptable for the remaining application properties.

ADD ATL CONSUMER SUPPORT

The first thing you need to do is add consumer support to the project. This is as easy as adding a new ATL object to an ATL project. The IDE will display a dialog reminder that you are adding an ATL object to an MFC project and ATL support is added.

Follow these steps to add ATL support to your project:

1. Choose Insert → New ATL Object... from the main menu of Developer Studio.

2. Click the Yes button of the dialog box that asks whether you want to add ATL support to this project.

You now should be in the ATL Object wizard as shown in Figure 11-9. Add a consumer to bind to your OLE DB Provider following these steps:

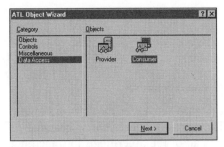

Figure 11-9: Object wizard - consumer

1. Select Data Access from the Category list.

2. Select Consumer from the Objects list.

3. Click the Next button.

4. From the ATL Object Wizard Properties dialog box click the Select Datasource... button and you will see a dialog like Figure 11-10.

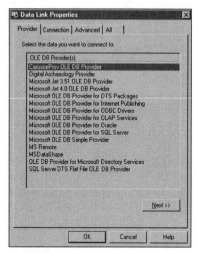

Figure 11-10: Data link properties

5. Select the `CrusoeProv` OLE DB Provider from the list of providers on the Provider tab of the Data Link Properties property sheet.

6. Select the Connection tab, this is shown in Figure 11-11, and fill in the Location, User name, and Password fields. Make sure these fields correspond with the location of the data source and authentication scheme you build into your provider.

7. Select the OK button.

8. Select the Temperatures table from the Select Database Table dialog box shown in Figure 11-12.

9. Click the OK button to select the Temperatures table.

10. Now you are back to the ATL Object Wizard Properties dialog box shown in Figure 11-13. Notice that the short name is not very short. I changed mine to `Temperatures`, which shortens all of the other fields to something more memorable.

11. Click the OK button to add the new classes to your project.

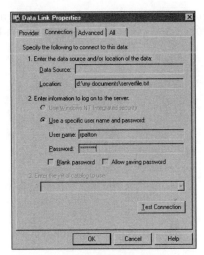

Figure 11-11: Data link properties – connection

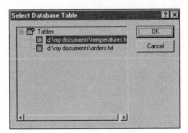

Figure 11-12: Select Database Table

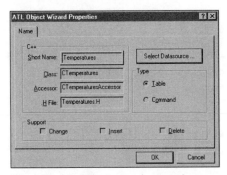

Figure 11-13: Object wizard properties – name

Notice the two new classes in your project. If you follow the preceding naming conventions, they are called CTemperatures and CTemperaturesAccessor. Listing 11-3 shows what is generated in my project.

Listing 11-3: Temperatures.h

```
// Temperatures.H : Declaration of the CTemperatures class

#ifndef __TEMPERATURES_H_
#define __TEMPERATURES_H_

class CTemperaturesAccessor
{
public:
    TCHAR m_City[27];
    unsigned long m_High;
    unsigned long m_Low;
    double m_Precipitation;
    unsigned long m_customerid;
    unsigned long m_orderid;
    DBDATE m_orderdate;
    double m_Amount;

BEGIN_COLUMN_MAP(CTemperaturesAccessor)
    COLUMN_ENTRY(1, m_City)
    COLUMN_ENTRY(2, m_High)
    COLUMN_ENTRY(3, m_Low)
    COLUMN_ENTRY(4, m_Precipitation)
END_COLUMN_MAP()


    // You may wish to call this function if you are
    // inserting a record and wish to
    // initialize all the fields, if you are not going
    // to explicitly set all of them.
    void ClearRecord()
    {
        memset(this, 0, sizeof(*this));
    }
};

class CTemperatures : public CTable<CAccessor<CTemperaturesAccessor>
>
{
public:
    HRESULT Open()
```

```
    {
        HRESULT hr;

        hr = OpenDataSource();
        if (FAILED(hr))
            return hr;

        return OpenRowset();
    }
    HRESULT OpenDataSource()
    {
        HRESULT hr;
        CDataSource db;
        CDBPropSet dbinit(DBPROPSET_DBINIT);

        dbinit.AddProperty(DBPROP_AUTH_PASSWORD, OLESTR("password"));
        dbinit.AddProperty(DBPROP_AUTH_PERSIST_SENSITIVE_AUTHINFO,
                           false);
        dbinit.AddProperty(DBPROP_AUTH_USERID, OLESTR("rpatton"));
        dbinit.AddProperty(DBPROP_INIT_DATASOURCE, OLESTR(""));
        dbinit.AddProperty(DBPROP_INIT_LCID, (long)0);
        dbinit.AddProperty(DBPROP_INIT_LOCATION,
                           OLESTR("d:\\my
                                  documents\\serverfile.txt"));
        dbinit.AddProperty(DBPROP_INIT_MODE, (long)0);
        dbinit.AddProperty(DBPROP_INIT_PROMPT, (short)2);
        dbinit.AddProperty(DBPROP_INIT_PROVIDERSTRING, OLESTR(""));
        dbinit.AddProperty(DBPROP_INIT_TIMEOUT, (long)0);
        hr = db.Open(_T("ATL_OLEDB_Prov.CrusoeProv.1"), &dbinit);

        if (FAILED(hr))
            return hr;

        return m_session.Open(db);
    }
    HRESULT OpenRowset()
    {
        return CTable<CAccessor<CTemperaturesAccessor> >
        ::Open(m_session,
                            _T("d:\\my
                            documents\\temperatures.txt"));
    }
    CSession m_session;
};

#endif // __TEMPERATURES_H_
```

These are two very simple classes that use intrinsic ATL OLE DB Consumer support to provide bound access to a command or table in an OLE DB Provider. The class `CTemperaturesAccessor` is bound statically to the table that you select from the list of tables in the wizard. Notice that it contains a variable for each column of every table in the provider, but it only creates entries in the column map for the ones contained in the selected table. I'm not sure why that is, but I can tell you that it doesn't hurt to remove the extraneous variables if they annoy you as much as they do me.

The `CTemperatures` class is derived from the `CTable` template class. This class provides support for opening the data source and moving around as well as for other table-related functionality. You can see that the `OpenDataSource` method has the properties supplied and defaulted from the wizard that generated the class. In case it isn't obvious, you can provide the login information as a variable from information supplied by the user rather than hard-coded from information supplied to the wizard.

ADD UI ELEMENTS TO THE MAIN DIALOG BOX

Now you add some UI to the main dialog box that shows the contents of the table you just selected. This consists of a multicolumn list control. Follow these steps to alter the main dialog box to look like Figure 11-14:

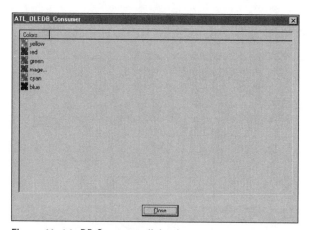

Figure 11-14: DB Consumer dialog box

1. Delete the Cancel button from the dialog box.

2. Set the text of the OK button to `&Close` and move it to the bottom center of the dialog box.

3. Insert a list control onto the dialog box and size it appropriately.

4. Change the control ID of the list control to `IDC_TEMPERATURESLIST`.

5. Change the view style of the list control to Report.

WRITE CODE TO POPULATE UI ELEMENTS FROM CONSUMER

Now you have a dialog box worthy of displaying your data. The next step is to write the code that glues your back-end data access to your front-end UI. For simplicity, I choose to do this work in the `OnInitDialog` method of the dialog box. Follow these steps:

1. Use the class wizard to add a variable called `m_temperaturesList` for the list control of the dialog box.

2. Add a variable to `CATL_OLEDB_ConsumerDlg` called `m_temperatures` of type `CTemperatures`. Make sure you include the `Temperatures.h` header file.

3. Add the boldface code to your `InitDialog` method:

```
BOOL CATL_OLEDB_ConsumerDlg::OnInitDialog()
{
   CDialog::OnInitDialog();

   // Add "About..." menu item to system menu.

   // IDM_ABOUTBOX must be in the system command range.
   ASSERT((IDM_ABOUTBOX & 0xFFF0) == IDM_ABOUTBOX);
   ASSERT(IDM_ABOUTBOX < 0xF000);

   CMenu* pSysMenu = GetSystemMenu(FALSE);
   if (pSysMenu != NULL)
   {
      CString strAboutMenu;
      strAboutMenu.LoadString(IDS_ABOUTBOX);
      if (!strAboutMenu.IsEmpty())
      {
         pSysMenu->AppendMenu(MF_SEPARATOR);
         pSysMenu->AppendMenu(MF_STRING, IDM_ABOUTBOX, strAboutMenu);
      }
   }

   // Set the icon for this dialog.
   //  when the application's main window is not a dialog
   SetIcon(m_hIcon, TRUE);
   SetIcon(m_hIcon, FALSE);
```

```
// Create the columns to display the temperatures in the list control
m_temperaturesList.InsertColumn(0, "City", LVCFMT_LEFT, 150);
m_temperaturesList.InsertColumn(1, "High", LVCFMT_RIGHT, 70);
m_temperaturesList.InsertColumn(2, "Low", LVCFMT_RIGHT, 70);
m_temperaturesList.InsertColumn(3, "Precipitation",
                                   LVCFMT_RIGHT, 70);

// Add the data from the data source
HRESULT hr = m_temperatures.Open();
if (SUCCEEDED(hr))
{
    CString tmpString;
    int i = 0;
    while (m_temperatures.MoveNext() == S_OK)
    {
      // City
      int ndx = m_temperaturesList.InsertItem(i,
                                  m_temperatures.m_City);

      // High Temperature
      tmpString.Format("%d", m_temperatures.m_High);
      m_temperaturesList.SetItemText(ndx, 1, tmpString);

      // Low Temperature
      tmpString.Format("%d", m_temperatures.m_Low);
      m_temperaturesList.SetItemText(ndx, 2, tmpString);

      // Precipitation
      tmpString.Format("%0.2lf", m_temperatures.m_Precipitation);
      m_temperaturesList.SetItemText(ndx, 3, tmpString);
      i++;
    }
}

return TRUE;
}
```

Build and execute your application; you should see the records of the temperatures text file in the list control. That pretty much covers how to develop a simple consumer class to access OLE DB Providers.

Summary

In this chapter, you learned the basics of how ATL provides support for building OLE DB consumers and providers. In particular, you learned:

◆ That OLE DB is Microsoft's most recent data access technology.

◆ How ATL implements support for OLE DB consumer and provider components.

◆ How to implement a simple OLE DB provider using ATL.

◆ That ADO is a high-level data access technique that makes it easier to work with the new OLE DB technologies.

Initially, the ATL framework focused mostly on providing non-GUI support for building COM components. If, as a developer, you were interested in building an application that required extensive windowing support, you most likely would use the Microsoft Foundation Class (MFC) library or Visual Basic. However, with each new version of ATL, Microsoft continues to add MFC-like GUI functionality. In the next chapter, I briefly discuss the window and dialog box support provided by ATL.

Chapter 12

Dialog Boxes and Windows

IN THIS CHAPTER

◆ ATL's Windowing classes

◆ CWindow and message handling

◆ Implementing windows using ATL

◆ Implementing dialog boxes using ATL

INITIALLY, THE ATL framework focused mostly on providing nonvisual support for building COM components. If, as a developer, you were interested in building an application that required extensive GUI support, you most likely would use the Microsoft Foundation Class (MFC) library or Visual Basic. However, with each new version of ATL, Microsoft continues to add MFC-like GUI functionality. In this chapter, I briefly discuss the window and dialog box support provided by ATL.

ATL Windowing Classes

ATL provides several windowing classes that encapsulate a window handle and the functionality that a window can provide. These classes are very similar to those provided by the MFC libraries. Although the functionality provided by the ATL windowing classes isn't as feature-rich as those provided by MFC, the long-term goal of the ATL team is to provide MFC-like functionality via ATL. Table 12-1 lists the basic ATL windowing classes.

TABLE 12-1 ATL WINDOWING CLASSES

Class Name	Description
CWindow	Encapsulates a window handle (HWND) and exposes those Win32 API functions that work with an HWND
CWindowImpl	Derives from CWindow to provide a framework for handling window messages within your code

Continued

TABLE 12-1 ATL WINDOWING CLASSES *(Continued)*

Class Name	Description
CDialogImpl	Also derives from CWindow, but provides support for modal and modeless dialog box capabilities
CContainedWindow	A class that expects to be contained as a child of another window. This class is useful when managing several child windows within a main parent window.
CAxDialogImpl	Similar to CDialogImpl, but also provides support for directly *embedding* (hosting) ActiveX controls
CSimpleDialog	A simple dialog box class that provides support for simple modal dialog boxes. This is a specialization of the CDialogImpl class.
CAxWindow	A class similar to CWindow, but one that supports direct embedding (hosting) of ActiveX controls
CWndClassInfo	Maintains specific window class information. Used internally by several of the preceding classes
CWinTraits	Specifies default styles to use during window creation

CWindow

The CWindow class is a very thin wrapper around the Win32 API functions that deal with windows. The class has a single data member, an HWND, and its methods map directly to an underlying Win32 API call.

You can use the CWindow class independently if a lightweight HWND wrapper is all you need. However, ATL primarily uses CWindow in its implementation of higher level classes such as CWindowImpl, CSimpleDialog, and CDialogImpl.

The following example code demonstrates using the CWindow class to create a simple button control. This technique works well, but it doesn't provide a mechanism for acting on or using the actual capabilities of the control. In order to do that, you need to have a look at the CWindowImpl class.

```
CWindow simpleWindow;
RECT rect = { 0, 0, 100, 100 };
simpleWindow.Create( "Button",
                     NULL,
                     &rect,
                     "Click Here");
simpleWindow.ShowWindow( SW_SHOWNORMAL );
```

CWindowImpl and Message Maps

The CWindowImpl class derives from CWindow, and so it exposes all of the basic windowing functionality. The primary difference with CWindowImpl, though, is that it also provides the ability to handle window messages within any deriving class. CWindowImpl uses the same technique that MFC uses, namely the concept of message maps.

You use the CWindowImpl class by deriving your own class from it. You also must specify your deriving class as a template parameter. Here's a simple example:

```
class CMainWindow : public CWindowImpl< CMainWindow >
{
   BEGIN_MSG_MAP( CMainWindow )
      MESSAGE_HANDLER( WM_CREATE, OnCreate )
      MESSAGE_HANDLER( WM_PAINT, OnPaint )
      MESSAGE_HANDLER( WM_DESTROY, OnDestroy )
   END_MSG_MAP()

   LRESULT OnCreate( UINT, WPARAM, LPARAM, BOOL& )
   {
      return 0;
   }

   LRESULT OnPaint( UINT, WPARAM, LPARAM, BOOL& )
   {
      PAINTSTRUCT ps;
      HDC hdc = GetDC();
      BeginPaint( &ps );

      RECT rc;
      GetClientRect( &rc );

      HBRUSH hbr = CreateSolidBrush( RGB( 0x00, 0xFF, 0xFF ));
      HBRUSH hOldBr = (HBRUSH) SelectObject( hdc, hbr );
      FillRect( hdc, &rc, hbr );

      SelectObject( hdc, hOldBr );
      DeleteObject( hbr );

      EndPaint( &ps );
      return 0;
   }

   LRESULT OnDestroy( UINT, WPARAM, LPARAM, BOOL& )
   {
      PostQuitMessage( 0 );
```

```
        return 0;
    }
};
```

Your `CMainWindow` class intercepts the `WM_CREATE`, `WM_PAINT`, and `WM_DESTROY` window messages and modifies the behavior of the window. You don't do anything special on creation, but you do paint the client area with a light blue brush and post a `WM_QUIT` message to the dispatch loop when the window is destroyed.

Here's how you create a window using the `CMainWindow` class:

```
CMainWindow window;
RECT rectPos = { 0, 0, 300, 300 };
window.Create( NULL,
               rectPos,
               "Main Window",
               WS_VISIBLE | WS_OVERLAPPEDWINDOW );
```

This code creates the window in the upper-left corner with a title bar caption of "Main Window" and uses the `OVERLAPPEDWINDOW` style. Most frame windows use this style because it displays the system menu as well as the Minimize and Maximize buttons. Figure 12-1 shows the window created with the preceding code.

Figure 12-1: A simple window using `CWindowImpl`

CWinTraits

Window styles such as `WS_VISIBLE` and `WS_CHILD` can be specified when a window is created through the call to `CreateWindow` or `CreateWindowEx` (as shown in the preceding example). ATL also enables you to specify window traits through a template parameter of type `CWinTraits`. You also can create the aforementioned window using this technique:

```
class CMainWindow : public CWindowImpl< CMainWindow, CWindow,
            CWinTraits< WS_VISIBLE | WS_OVERLAPPEDWINDOW, 0 > >
```

```
{
....
};

CMainWindow window;
RECT rectPos = { 0, 0, 300, 300 };
window.Create( NULL,
               rectPos,
               "Main Window" );
```

CSimpleDialog

Dialog boxes are used extensively in Windows programming; ATL provides two classes that make creating dialog boxes easier, at least when compared with building them by hand with the API. The `CSimpleDialog` class provides basic support for constructing modal dialog boxes from templates stored in your application's resource file. The class is very easy to use because you only need to provide the dialog box resource identifier as a template parameter. Here's an example:

```
CSimpleDialog<IDD_SIMPLEDIALOG> simpleDialog;
simpleDialog.DoModal();
```

That's all there is to creating a modal dialog box in ATL. When the call to `DoModal` returns, the dialog box is dismissed.

CDialogImpl

For more complicated dialog box handling, ATL provides the `CDialogImpl` class, which is similar to `CWindowImpl`. In order to create modeless dialog boxes, you must derive your own class from `CDialogImpl`. You specify the dialog box resource identifier using a named enum in your derived class. Here's an example of how to do it:

```
class CModelessDialog : public CDialogImpl< CModelessDialog >
{
public:
   enum { IDD = IDD_MODELESS_DIALOG };

   BEGIN_MSG_MAP( CModelessDialog )
      MESSAGE_HANDLER( WM_INITDIALOG, OnInitDialog )
      MESSAGE_HANDLER( WM_CLOSE, OnClose )
   END_MSG_MAP()

   LRESULT OnInitDialog( UINT, WPARAM, LPARAM, BOOL& )
   {
```

```
        return 0;
    }

    LRESULT OnClose( UINT, WPARAM, LPARAM, BOOL& )
    {
        DestroyWindow();
        return 0;
    }
};
```

Your dialog box class also intercepts the WM_INITDIALOG and WM_CLOSE messages using the message map macros described in the CWindowImpl section. Because you are creating a modeless dialog box, you need to make sure the window is destroyed when the dialog box ultimately is closed. This is handled in the WM_CLOSE message handle via a call to DestroyWindow.

Building a Simple Window GUI

To demonstrate using the ATL window classes, you now build a simple Win32 *GUI (graphical user interface)* application. This example demonstrates using ATL to create non-COM applications that use the GUI services of the Windows operating system. Previously, you used the AppWizard to create Win32 console applications. However, Windows-based applications need access to the HINSTANCE parameter provided by the Windows WinMain entry point.

Using AppWizard, create a Win32 application project and name it Chapter12_ATLWindows. On the Step 1 of 1 dialog box, choose the simple Win32 application option. After clicking Finish, add the following code:

```
//
// Chapter12_ATLWindows.cpp
//

#include "stdafx.h"

#include <atlbase.h>
CComModule _Module;
#include <atlwin.h>

int APIENTRY WinMain(HINSTANCE hInstance,
                     HINSTANCE hPrevInstance,
                     LPSTR     lpCmdLine,
                     int       nCmdShow)
{
```

```
_Module.Init( 0, hInstance );

_Module.Term();
return 0;
}
```

This code pulls in the ATL support classes for windowing. You also need to initialize the global _Module class with the hInstance passed in via WinMain.

Step 1: Create a Simple Window

To begin the example, use the CWindowImpl class to create the main window for the application:

```
#include <atlbase.h>
CComModule _Module;
#include <atlwin.h>

class CMainWindow : public CWindowImpl< CMainWindow >
{
   BEGIN_MSG_MAP( CMainWindow )
      MESSAGE_HANDLER( WM_CREATE, OnCreate )
      MESSAGE_HANDLER( WM_PAINT, OnPaint )
      MESSAGE_HANDLER( WM_RBUTTONDOWN, OnRButtonDown )
      MESSAGE_HANDLER( WM_LBUTTONDOWN, OnLButtonDown )
      MESSAGE_HANDLER( WM_DESTROY, OnDestroy )
   END_MSG_MAP()

   LRESULT OnLButtonDown( UINT, WPARAM, LPARAM, BOOL& )
   {
      return 0;
   }

   LRESULT OnRButtonDown( UINT, WPARAM, LPARAM, BOOL& )
   {
      return 0;
   }

   LRESULT OnCreate( UINT, WPARAM, LPARAM, BOOL& )
   {
      return 0;
   }
```

```
    LRESULT OnPaint( UINT, WPARAM, LPARAM, BOOL& )
    {
        PAINTSTRUCT ps;
        HDC hdc = GetDC();
        BeginPaint( &ps );

        RECT rc;
        GetClientRect( &rc );

        HBRUSH hbr = CreateSolidBrush( RGB( 0x00, 0xFF, 0xFF ));
        HBRUSH hOldBr = (HBRUSH) SelectObject( hdc, hbr );
        FillRect( hdc, &rc, hbr );

        SelectObject( hdc, hOldBr );
        DeleteObject( hbr );

        EndPaint( &ps );
        return 0;
    }

    LRESULT OnDestroy( UINT, WPARAM, LPARAM, BOOL& )
    {
        PostQuitMessage( 0 );
        return 0;
    }
};
```

Using message maps, you add handlers for five different messages. For now, you are dealing with only the WM_PAINT and WM_DESTROY messages. You add code to the other handlers later. The OnPaint handler fills the client area with a light blue brush and the OnDestroy handler forces the application to close by sending a WM_QUIT message to the dispatch loop.

Next, you need to add code to create an instance of your window class as well as add a message pump for your application.

```
int APIENTRY WinMain(HINSTANCE hInstance,
                     HINSTANCE hPrevInstance,
                     LPSTR     lpCmdLine,
                     int       nCmdShow)
{
    _Module.Init( 0, hInstance );
```

```
CMainWindow window;
RECT rectPos = { 0, 0, 300, 300 };
window.Create( NULL,
               rectPos,
               "Main Window",
               WS_OVERLAPPEDWINDOW | WS_VISIBLE );

MSG msg;
while( GetMessage( &msg, 0, 0, 0 ))
{
   TranslateMessage( &msg );
   DispatchMessage( &msg );
}

_Module.Term();

return 0;
}
```

Next, build and execute the application. You should see a window like that shown in Figure 12-1.

Step 2: Create a Modal Dialog Box

To demonstrate creating a simple modal dialog box, you need to add a dialog box resource. Using the Insert→Resource... option, add a resource of type `Dialog`. Figures 12-2 and 12-3 show this process. Be sure to give the dialog box a resource ID of `IDD_SIMPLEDIALOG`.

Figure 12-2: Inserting a dialog box resource template

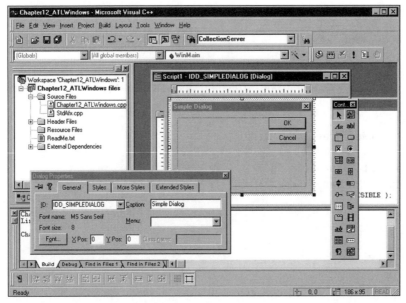

Figure 12-3: Your simple dialog box template

After modifying the dialog box, you need to save the resource script file. Give it a name of RESOURCE.RC. You also need to add RESOURCE.RC to your project and include RESOURCE.H, which was created when you inserted the resource into your project:

```
//
// Chapter12_ATLWindows.cpp
//

#include "stdafx.h"
#include "resource.h"

#include <atlbase.h>
CComModule _Module;
#include <atlwin.h>
```

Now, to actually display the dialog box you need to create an instance of the CSimpleDialog class. You do this by clicking the left button in the client area of your main application window. Here's the code:

```
LRESULT OnLButtonDown( UINT, WPARAM, LPARAM, BOOL& )
{
    CSimpleDialog<IDD_SIMPLEDIALOG> simpleDialog;
    simpleDialog.DoModal();
```

```
    return 0;
}
```

Build and run the application. By left-clicking your application's client area, you should see something like that in Figure 12-4.

Figure 12-4: Your modal dialog box

Step 3: Create a Modeless Dialog Box

Implementing a modeless dialog box requires that you derive your own class from CDialogImpl. However, you also need to associate a dialog box resource template with this class. Insert another basic dialog box into your project and give it a resource identifier of IDD_MODELESS_DIALOG. You also should check the Visible style on the More Styles tab under Properties for the dialog box. To distinguish the modeless dialog box from your modal one, you can change the size or add a static label like you see in Figure 12-5.

After adding the new dialog box , add the following code to your .CPP file:

```
//
// Chapter12_ATLWindows.cpp
//

#include "stdafx.h"
#include "resource.h"

#include <atlbase.h>
CComModule _Module;
#include <atlwin.h>

class CModelessDialog : public CDialogImpl< CModelessDialog >
{
public:
    enum { IDD = IDD_MODELESS_DIALOG };
```

```
BEGIN_MSG_MAP( CModelessDialog )
    MESSAGE_HANDLER( WM_INITDIALOG, OnInitDialog )
    MESSAGE_HANDLER( WM_CLOSE, OnClose )
END_MSG_MAP()

LRESULT OnInitDialog( UINT, WPARAM, LPARAM, BOOL& )
{
    return 0;
}

LRESULT OnClose( UINT, WPARAM, LPARAM, BOOL& )
{
    DestroyWindow();
    return 0;
}
};

class CMainWindow : public CWindowImpl< CMainWindow >
{
    BEGIN_MSG_MAP( CMainWindow )
    ...
    END_MSG_MAP()
    ...
    LRESULT OnRButtonDown( UINT, WPARAM, LPARAM, BOOL& )
    {
        CModelessDialog* pDlg = new CModelessDialog;
        pDlg->Create( 0 );
        return 0;
    }
...
};
```

Now, build and run the project one more time. By right-clicking the main window, you can launch as many modeless dialog boxes as you want. Figure 12-5 shows the final application with a number of modeless dialog boxes.

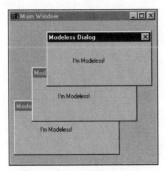

Figure 12-5: The application with three modeless dialog boxes

Summary

In this chapter, you learned the basics of implementing basic windows and dialog boxes using ATL's windowing support classes. In particular, you learned:

- ATL has basic support for building GUI applications

- ATL's basic windowing support is provided through the CWindow and CWindowImpl classes

- ATL provides higher-level classes that allow you to create simple widows and dialog boxes with just a few lines of code

- Handling window messages in ATL uses a concept called message mapping, which is similar to the technique used by MFC

Future versions of ATL will continue to build on this basic window support. In the next chapter, you take a look at the future of COM development in Windows 2000.

Chapter 13

COM+ Fundamentals

IN THIS CHAPTER

- ◆ An introduction to the COM+ services provided by Windows 2000
- ◆ Coverage of COM+ Events
- ◆ Overview of COM+ Queue Components
- ◆ Details on the new COM+ Component Load Balancing (CLB) service
- ◆ A peek at a future version of Visual C++

 This chapter is based on an article I wrote titled "COM + MTS = COM+: Next Step in the Microsoft Component Strategy," originally published in the February/March 1999 issue of *Visual C++ Developer's Journal*.

IN OCTOBER 1997, Microsoft previewed the future of COM with the announcement of COM+ at the 1997 *Professional Developer's Conference (PDC)*. COM+ was described as a new run time that would make it easier to develop COM-based components, address many of the issues of deploying components, and provide several new services for the COM developer. Mary Kirtland of Microsoft presented at the conference and authored two COM+ articles for the November and December 1997 issues of *Microsoft Systems Journal* in which she described these changes.

This early view of COM+ produced lots of speculation and anxiety as to what the future held for COM developers, primarily because Kirtland's article focused on major changes to the languages and tools that developers use every day. The changes were based on a new COM+ run time that would move most of the COM grunge code (for example, IUnknown and class factory implementations) into the OS, making it easier for tool vendors to present a unified view of COM-based development.

Over two years have passed and COM+ is quite different from its original description in 1997. In fact, Kirtland opened her 1998 PDC *COM+ Internals* presentation with the words, "Forget everything I said last year about COM+." Actually, though, Kirtland's articles certainly are worth reading. The general ideas remain valid and many are incorporated into the next release of Visual C++. However, be warned that many of the details are inaccurate.

I'm not criticizing Microsoft. I'm pointing out that the real view of COM+ has changed significantly in the intervening years. As developers, we know this happens on projects. Our enthusiasm and optimism overwhelm the business requirements or man-hours available for the project. Microsoft sometimes enables us to participate in the development process, which leads to these problems. However, I've always been an advocate for too much information instead of too little – even if I have to backtrack now and then.

Above all, COM+ is a major upgrade of Microsoft's long-term component strategy. The production release of COM+ is packaged in the final release of Windows 2000. In this chapter, I first discuss where COM+ fits into Microsoft's long-term application development strategy. After that, I go into detail as to what COM+ is and what services it adds to the existing COM and MTS technologies. I then conclude with a look at what's coming in the next release of Visual C++ to help the COM developer.

Windows DNA

Before I discuss the details of COM+, I'd like to provide a quick look at a broader technology called the *Windows Distributed interNet Applications Architecture*, or *Windows DNA*. Windows DNA is Microsoft's latest acronym that describes its move from workstation-based to enterprise-level application development. Windows DNA describes those Microsoft technologies that provide a complete, integrated n-tier development model.

Windows DNA is the set of services provided by the operating system, which enables application developers to effectively build distributed Windows applications. In a nutshell, Windows DNA describes those services that developers require to build scalable and dependable enterprise-level systems on the Windows platform.

Figure 13-1 depicts Windows DNA from a technology perspective as it stands today. When building an application, a developer uses several different Windows and Internet technologies based on the targeted user of the application. Rich client applications are written using the Win32 API and distributed as executables in the typical fashion. Thin client applications, or those that target a browser, use either straight HTML or dynamic HTML at the presentation tier.

At the middle tier, developers use DCOM, MTS, IIS, and Active Server Pages to handle business logic and other application services. Components executing on the middle tier access back-end data using Active Data Object (ADO) or OLE DB. Microsoft also provides tools to access data on non-Windows platforms. ODBC, COM services on UNIX, and the new *COM Transaction Integrator (COMTI)* are examples of this.

Figure 13-2 depicts the long-term goal of Windows DNA: a technology called Forms+ at the GUI level, COM+ at the middle tier, and Storage+ on the data tier. Details on *Forms+* and *Storage+* are sketchy, but the majority of COM+ is delivered with Windows 2000.

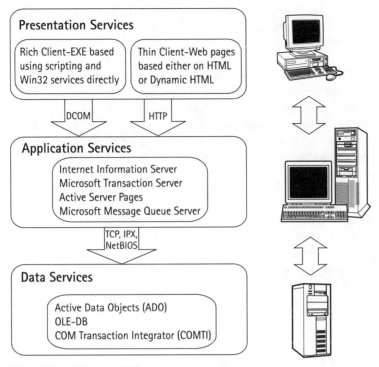

Figure 13-1: Windows DNA

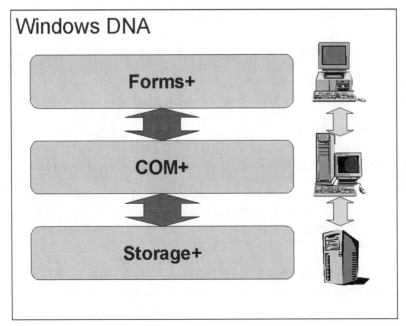

Figure 13-2: The future of Windows DNA

The goal of the Forms+ initiative is to merge the Win32 GUI and Web APIs. Forms+ is Microsoft's answer to the difficulties developers face today when deciding what presentation platform to target in developing an application. Today, developers have to choose either to target Windows using the Win32 API or to target the browser and use HTML or dynamic HTML. Forms+ is a move away from Win32 API and a move toward DHTML for Windows presentation development. Spend some time with the architecture of Internet Explorer 5 for a glimpse of where Forms+ is headed.

The details on Storage+ are even sketchier. Storage+ is the future of the Windows file system and probably will look a lot like OLE DB with the addition of several new features. Storage+ is the most distant technology of Windows DNA and you won't see much on this front until well after Windows 2000 ships.

What all of this means is that Microsoft understands the software market is moving faster and faster toward the Internet. All of the future "killer applications" will be developed for the Web environment, be it an intranet or the Internet. In order to proliferate in this new market, Microsoft is making it easier for developers to build applications without a dependency on the Win32 API.

However, this chapter isn't about Windows DNA specifically; it's about the core service of Windows DNA: COM+. As you can see from Figure 13-2, COM+ is at the heart of Microsoft's DNA architecture. Let's move on to answer the question, "What is COM+?"

COM + MTS = COM+

What exactly is COM+? COM+ is many things, but the basic answer is quite simple. *COM+* is the merging of the COM and MTS programming models with the addition of several new features.

COM was created long ago as a workstation-level component technology. With the release of Distributed COM in NT 4, the technology was expanded to support distributed applications via remote component instantiation and method invocations. Then, MTS was created to provide server-side component services and to fix some of the deficiencies of DCOM (for example, its handling of security issues, complete lack of a component management and configuration environment, and so on). COM+ now comes along to unify COM, DCOM, and MTS into a coherent, enterprise-worthy component technology. Figure 13-3 depicts this relationship.

COM+ takes the COM and MTS programming models to the next level. At the same time, COM+ fixes many of the deficiencies associated with COM and DCOM development. Some examples of deficiencies that COM+ fixes include: a much better component administration environment, support for load balancing and object pooling, and an easier-to-use event model.

Here's another way to look at COM+: It is the maturation of Microsoft's component architecture. Developers always had difficulty understanding COM, at least initially. Developing COM-based applications requires a change in mindset. You have to think about your applications in a different way, which is hard for developers. It's almost as difficult as moving from C to C++ programming. You must think differently. COM+ doesn't change this completely, but it does move many of the tedious, grungy details into the operating system so developers can focus on higher-level problems and their solutions.

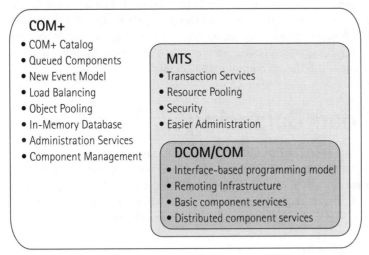

COM+
- COM+ Catalog
- Queued Components
- New Event Model
- Load Balancing
- Object Pooling
- In-Memory Database
- Administration Services
- Component Management

MTS
- Transaction Services
- Resource Pooling
- Security
- Easier Administration

DCOM/COM
- Interface-based programming model
- Remoting Infrastructure
- Basic component services
- Distributed component services

Figure 13-3: COM+ services

COM+ Services

Because COM+ is the merging of COM, DCOM, and MTS with all of its new features, it covers a lot of territory. In this chapter, I only focus on those major services that are new with COM+ and those that will be incorporated into the final release of Windows 2000. Of course, each of these technologies could consume a large chapter by itself, so I have to move quickly.

The COM+ Catalog

Today, COM and MTS components place all of their configuration information in the Windows registry. With COM+, however, most component information is stored in a new database currently called the *COM+ Catalog*. The COM+ Catalog unifies the COM and MTS registration models and provides an administrative environment for components. As a developer, you interact with the COM+ Catalog using either the COM+ Explorer or a series of new COM interfaces that expose its capabilities.

One of the features of COM+ is its support for *declarative programming*. What this means is that you can develop components in a generic way and defer many of the details until the time of deployment. For example, you can develop a component that supports working in a load-balanced environment. However, the decision of whether or not to use load balancing is deferred. Some applications may want to use load balancing; others may not want to use it. You indicate support by setting an attribute or *declaring* to use its support for load balancing. You accomplish this at an administrative level using the COM+ Explorer, which is similar to the MTS Explorer. The MTS declarative security model represents another example. Instead of handling security programmatically, you enable the administrators to do it through MTS packages and the MTS administration model.

COM+ Load Balancing

Today, one of the deficiencies of DCOM/MTS is that it doesn't intrinsically support the notion of load balancing. To create an instance of a remote component, a client application must specify explicitly — either through the COSERVERINFO structure or via the RemoteServerName registry entry — the name of the machine on which to create the instance. This is shown in the following code snippet:

```
typedef struct _COSERVERINFO
{
    DWORD dwReserved1;
    LPWSTR pwszName;
    COAUTOINFO *pAutoInfo;
    DWORD dwReserved2;
} COSERVERINFO;
...
COSERVERINFO si;
ZeroMemory( &si, sizeof( si ));
si.pwszName = L"RemoteMachine";
CoCreateInstanceEx( CLSID_MyComponent,
                    NULL,
                    CLSCTX_REMOTE_SERVER,
                    &si,
                    ... );
```

The problem with this approach is that it doesn't scale. It works fine if you have only 40 or so clients (depending on the application) accessing the remote server; but as the number of clients increases, you may want to add additional servers to support them. However, the remote machine name is a static element in the client application, so all instantiation requests go to the same machine. There are ways around this, but you have to write code. This includes configuration tools that enable administrators to specify that this set of 40 clients direct to this machine, that set of 40 direct to that machine, and so on.

What DCOM really needs is some way to route the remote creation request to the machine that has the lightest load at that time. COM+ solves this problem by providing a load-balancing service that is transparent to client applications. To enable load balancing for your components, you first define an *application cluster*, which is a series of machines (up to eight) having your server-side components installed. You then must configure a *load-balancing router* machine to route the creation requests to one of the machines in the application cluster.

COM+ load balancing is implemented as an NT service that executes on the router node. As remote creation requests are received, it works with the local SCM (Service Control Manager) to route the request to the machine with the lightest load (as depicted in Figure 13-4). Of course, one of the more difficult aspects of load balancing lies in determining which machine in the application cluster has the lightest load.

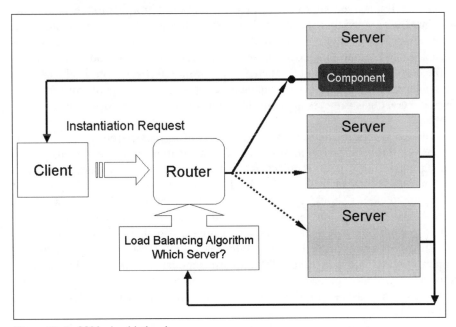

Figure 13-4: COM+ load balancing

Each component capable of load balancing has associated with it a *load-balancing engine*, which works with the router to determine which machine to route the request. The default COM+ load-balancing engine uses a response-time algorithm in which the response time is calculated by timing each method call through each interface on every instance on a given machine. This may not be the best technique for your application, but it is general enough to work in many circumstances. If you don't like the default algorithm, you can replace it by writing your own load-balancing engine, which is just a COM+ component.

To support load balancing, your client code just passes the creation request to the router node like this:

```
COSERVERINFO si;
ZeroMemory( &si, sizeof( si ));
si.pwszName = L"RouterMachineName";
CoCreateInstanceEx( CLSID_MyComponent,
                    NULL,
                    CLSCTX_REMOTE_SERVER,
                    &si,
                    ... );
```

The router looks in the COM+ Catalog to see if the request is for a load-balanced component. If it is, the router works with the local SCM to route it to the appropriate machine. Once routed to a specific node in the application cluster, the remote object is created and the reference is passed directly back to the client. Once the instance is created, a direct connection exists between it and the client application.

The techniques for building components that work effectively with load balancing are similar to those of any MTS component. Design your components for short life-times and don't make any assumptions that your component will execute on a specific machine.

Although COM+ load balancing was written to be transparent to client applications, certain client-side approaches can make it more effective. Instead of explicitly creating a remote object on a specific machine, you pass the router's machine name instead. Also, COM+ load balancing is used only at component activation so clients should create instances only when needed and release them when finished. This recommendation contradicts the MTS base client recommendation to grab object references early and hold on to them. This programming model inconsistency will be fixed in a later release of COM+ when load balancing supports the MTS *just-in-time (JIT)* activation model. When designing applications today, you must choose either the MTS client model of "bind early and hang on as long as possible" or the load-balancing client model of "bind late and release early."

There are still some issues with COM+ load balancing including the fact that the router node is a single point of failure, but it takes a big step in the right direction by providing your distributed applications with additional support for scalability.

COM+ IMDB

Another COM+ service that helps you build scalable applications is the COM+ *In-Memory Database (IMDB)*. We all know that one of the best ways to speed up a data-intensive application is to make sure as much of its data is loaded into physical memory as possible. The IMDB is a robust, transient, and transacted database system that operates only on physical memory. The IMDB was written primarily for Web environments in which you have thousands of users accessing database information, but you can use it in any application that needs rapid access to large amounts of data.

The IMDB implements a DB-oriented caching system optimized for lookups and retrievals. The IMDB can load tables from an existing back-end database or can house transient data as part of your application. An example in which the IMDB is useful is in a large Web application where servicing thousands of requests per minute for data within a relational database is an expensive proposition. By using the IMDB for those tables that are read frequently, the application can support many more requests with only the addition of physical memory, which gets cheaper every day. Also, all requests for data from those tables are handled on the application tier where IIS and its components reside, eliminating a network trip for the data. Figure 13-5 depicts this scenario.

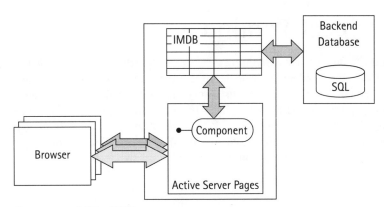

Figure 13-5: COM+ IMDB

Components access the IMDB using either its OLE DB provider interfaces or through ADO, which sits atop OLE DB. The IMDB service is implemented on a per-machine basis and currently it does not support distribution. In other words, you cannot load the same tables on multiple IMDB machines. In order for components to share information using the IMDB, they must execute on the same machine.

The IMDB runs as a Windows service. On startup, the IMDB service reads whole tables from any back-end databases that you specify and caches them in shared memory. The IMDB service only supports reading whole tables. If there isn't enough physical memory to load the complete table, an error occurs. Components then access the IMDB tables through an in-process proxy object, which provides very efficient access to data within the IMDB.

One important difference with IMDB is that you do not access the data using typical SQL commands. The primary goal of the IMDB was to make data access as fast as possible; to achieve this, a SQL query processor was not implemented. Access to IMDB data occurs through standard *indexed sequential access method (ISAM)* techniques, which means you must associate an index with those columns you use for searching and filtering.

The IMDB is great for caching database tables for fast access. However, it also is useful for managing transient state data within your applications. Today, MTS components use the *Shared Property Manager (SPM)* to share transient information. The IMDB provides support for transacted operations and eventually will support distribution. If your application has components that execute on several machines and these components need to share information, the IMDB is the long-term solution for sharing transient state information.

 The COM+ IMDB service was removed from the final release of Windows 2000. However, the facility may be released in the future as an add-on product.

COM+ Object Pooling

Object pooling is the process of maintaining a set of component instances loaded in memory so that they are available immediately for use by client applications. Object pooling is another important feature required to build large, scalable applications. Today, when developing components for the MTS environment, your components implement the IObjectControl interface. When the component is instantiated within MTS, MTS provides activation and deactivation notifications through the IObjectControl interface. Its declaration is this:

```
interface IObjectControl : public IUnknown
{
    HRESULT Activate();
    void Deactivate();
    BOOL CanBePooled();
};
```

After deactivating an instance, MTS calls CanBePooled() to see if the instance can be placed in a pool of objects standing ready for use by the next client request. At least that's what would happen if MTS 2.0 supported object pooling. Today, MTS doesn't provide support for object pooling and the CanBePooled() method is never called. With the release of COM+, object pooling is supported. The big question, then, is should my components support being pooled?

The answer to this question in most cases is no. Because of the design of MTS — which is very efficient at caching component information — there are only a few cases in which you need to develop components that support object pooling.

There are two general rules for determining whether your components should support pooling. First, you should use pooling only when you predict that the construction time for your object will be longer than the actual "use" time of the object. Second, you should use pooling if your component accesses a limited resource such as a database, mainframe, or socket connection. Pooling is a good idea for this second reason because the size of a pool of objects can be limited. So, if your application has access to only 10 mainframe connections, then you can configure the object pool to support only 10 instances of the component. This ensures that only 10 connections exist at any given time.

Object pooling support is needed for building large, scalable applications. However, in most cases, the COM+ system already provides these system-level objects for you (for example, ODBC resource objects) so you can focus on providing application-level components.

COM+ Queued Components

Today, COM's development model is based on procedural interactions. A client connects to a component, queries for the appropriate interface, and makes synchronous method calls through the returned interface. The lifetimes of the client and the component instance are coupled tightly, and information is retrieved from the component via [out] parameters.

RPC-based services, like those provided with COM, are necessary for building distributed applications. However, certain applications can benefit from another development technique called *messaging*. A message-based application decouples the execution lifetimes of the client and its components. The new COM+ Queued Components service provides a solution for this type of application.

Let's begin with a simple example. The following code creates an instance of an order component, sets some properties such as client number and order quantity, and then calls Submit(). The Submit() method takes the information, validates it, and probably creates a row in an Orders table of a database:

```
IOrder* pOrder = 0;
CoCreateInstance( CLSID_Order,
                  ...
                  IID_IOrder,
                  (void**) &pOrder );

pOrder->put_Customer( 2000 );
pOrder->put_Quantity( 2 );
CComBSTR bstrSKU( "3535-2334" );
pOrder->put_SKU( bstrSKU );

long lOrderNumber;
pOrder->Submit( &lOrderNumber );
pOrder->Release();
```

This is an example of how you use COM services today. The lifetime of the client is coupled tightly with the component, and an RPC connection is maintained between the two until the IOrder interface pointer is released. The model is easy to program, the client assumes that the component is loaded and running throughout the interaction, and information is returned from the component through [out] parameters as shown by the return of the order number.

In a message-based application, the client and component are separated by time and, therefore, their lifecycles are decoupled. The *decoupling* is achieved by using an underlying messaging system instead of direct RPC connections. In the case of COM+ Queued Components, this underlying system is *Microsoft's Message Queue Server (MSMQ)*. Figure 13-6 shows the client and component separated by a queuing mechanism.

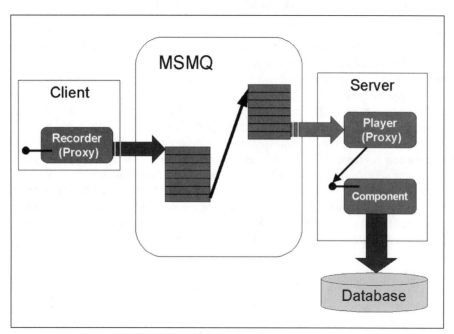

Figure 13-6: COM+ queued components

This gives the application developer additional flexibility in the areas of scalability and availability. If the component isn't available, the client application can still execute. If you have a scenario in which there are thousands of clients and only a few servers, the client applications can place their requests into the queue (which is hidden from the client application), thereby providing a way to balance and serialize the server load. Applications with volatile load demands, such as Web applications that can see their usage rocket or plummet based on some external event, also can benefit from a message-based approach.

Today, of course, both RPC- and message-based distributed application services are needed. With COM+ Queued Components, application developers can choose the technology that fits their requirements. Let's take a quick look at how the COM+ Queued Component service works and what is required to implement a queued component.

As in most COM+ services, the primary goal is to hide as many of the underlying details from the application developer as possible. The actual queuing mechanism is hidden and you develop your clients and components in the same way that you always do – with two primary exceptions. First, your component interfaces can have only [in] parameters because they are passed by value via an MSMQ message. Second, your component's interface methods cannot return application-specific HRESULTs because there is no client application to accept them.

Here's how the process works. When the client instantiates a queued component, the run time actually creates a local proxy object called a *recorder*. As the client makes method calls, the recorder proxy serializes the calls into an MSMQ message. When the client commits the object by releasing all references to it, the message is passed to the server via MSMQ. A special service running on the server then dequeus the messages and instantiates the component using another proxy called the *player*. The player interacts with the component as if it were the actual client by playing the stored method calls. If anything fails, the message is placed back into the queue. Then you have several options based on the services provided by MSMQ.

The most difficult aspect of message-based development is determining how to get information back to the client. There are several techniques that you can use. First, some applications don't need a response. Second, you can implement the client application using response queues and report back asynchronously. Third, Queued Components supports pass-by-value interface references, which enable the component to fire back information to the client without having a direct connection.

There is a lot to talk about with queued components, and I only cover the basics here. Queued components add significantly to what you can do with your distributed Windows applications. They provide decoupled, asynchronous processing – something that certainly is needed in Microsoft's enterprise development model.

COM+ Events

Today, COM provides two techniques for handling events or callbacks among a component and any associated clients. The first technique uses an interface callback mechanism in which the client implements an interface described by the component. Then by calling through the client's interface, events or notifications are fired. A simple example is shown below. The Advise() and Unadvise() methods set up the connection:

```
// Our event interface
interface IMyEvents : IUnknown
{
```

```
    HRESULT SomethingHappened( BSTR bstrWhat );
}


// An interface on our component
interface ISomeInterface : IUnknown
{
    ...
    HRESULT Advise( IMyEvents* pIEvents );
    HRESULT Unadvise();
}
```

The second technique, called connectable objects, uses the standard COM IConnectionPoint interfaces. This technique is similar to the preceding one, but it provides a more general (and complex) way of connecting the cooperating entities. It also includes run-time discovery and minimal multicasting capabilities.

Actually, the whole concept of client and component blurs when talking about events. In reality, the component becomes a client and the client becomes a component – at least in the conventional sense. What you really have are two cooperating software entities that want to share information. From this point on, I use the term *publisher* to indicate a module that publishes or provides information; I use the term *subscriber* for the module that wants to receive such information. These also are the terms used by the COM+ Events service.

The older COM event model has several drawbacks, some of which include:

- ◆ The architecture only describes a series of interfaces. COM does provide the interface remoting infrastructure, but that's it. As a developer, you still have to write the code to implement these interfaces.

- ◆ Implementing a complex application that makes heavy use of events may require complex coding to handle multiplexing events, multiple connected clients, circular references, deadlock situations, and so on.

- ◆ The client and component lifetimes are coupled tightly through the exchanged interface pointer. The interface pointer, which provides very limited information, is the only binding point between the entities.

- ◆ There is no activation model. The client must be running and connected in order to receive events from a component.

- ◆ The connection point interfaces were developed without regard to distributed environments and are not very efficient in those scenarios.

- ◆ It is hard to get in between a component instance and its clients in order to monitor the connection, provide trace information, and so on.

Of course, one solution to the preceding problems is to fix them by writing additional code. As COM developers, we're used to doing just that. What the COM+ Events service does is provide built-in code for handling the grungy details of how a producer of information advertises it for consumption and how a consumer of information locates and subscribes to it.

The COM+ event model (see Figure 13-7) significantly upgrades the existing COM event model. The COM+ Events service still supports the older techniques, as all legacy code is still supported, but it provides much broader and intrinsic support for publish-subscribe scenarios. Hooking up two or more cooperating entities so that they can share information is a classic problem in distributed environments and the COM+ Events service makes this problem a lot easier to manage.

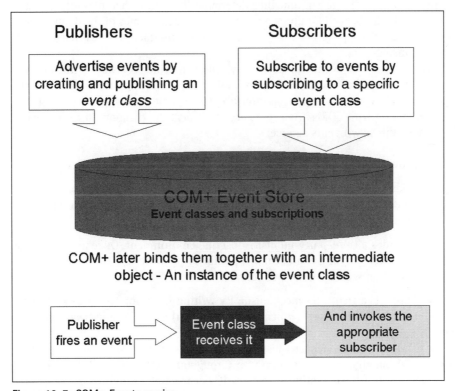

Figure 13-7: COM+ Events service

The COM Events service decouples the tight binding between the publisher and subscriber by introducing an intermediary object called the event class. Any entity that wants to publish information must do so through an event class object. Interacting with the COM+ events subsystem through the IEventClass interface, which is abbreviated here, creates the event class:

```
struct IEventClass : public IDispatch
{
    HRESULT put_EventClassID( BSTR bstrEventClassID );
```

```
    HRESULT put_EventClassName( BSTR bstrEventClassName );
    HRESULT put_FiringInterfaceID( BSTR bstrFiringInterfaceID );
    ...
};
```

An event class is a component implemented by the run time that sits between the publisher and its subscribers. The event class actually implements the event interface and so it looks like a subscriber to the publisher. When a publisher wants to fire an event, it creates an instance of the event class, calls the appropriate method, and then releases the interface. The run time then determines how and when to notify any subscribers. As in the Queued Components service case, the lifetimes of the publisher and subscribers are decoupled. For this reason, all event interfaces are restricted to only [in] parameters.

Subscribing to an event is just as easy. The subscriber registers with the COM Events service by creating a subscription object, again through the help of the run time and the IEventSubscription interface. Once created, the subscriber registers the subscription with COM+. As events are published, the component is notified.

In short, this new Events service:

♦ Provides a publish-subscribe scenario that decouples the entity lifecycles.

♦ Adds an activation model to the event system. If a subscriber is not active when an event occurs, the event run time can activate the subscriber and pass it the event information.

♦ Provides a third-party publish-subscribe environment. Once an event class is created, anyone can become a publisher or subscriber of the events (based on security issues, of course).

♦ Supports a rich filter mechanism. By writing filter objects, you can filter at the publisher level (which is very efficient) or at the subscriber level.

The COM+ Events service isn't just for application developers. It is used internally to handle debugging and trace messages throughout COM+ as well as within the implementation of the operating system itself. For example, Windows 2000 uses the COM+ event subsystem in the implementation of the new *System Event Notification Server (SENS)*. SENS is a COM+ event publisher that provides notifications of system-level events such as a user logging in and out, network connections, plug-and-play events, and so on. You easily can receive these events by creating and registering a subscription to the SENS.

COM+ Security

Another significant enhancement that COM+ provides is in the area of security. Years ago, when COM was only a local machine technology, developers didn't concern themselves with security. Later, with the release of DCOM as part of Windows NT 4.0, security became a real issue for component developers. While DCOM's support for remote method calls enabled true distributed development, it came with a cost. Yes, the programming model stayed the same, but the effort required to build a secure application increased significantly. Developers spent an excessive amount of time thinking about low-level security details when developing distributed applications.

MTS provided some assistance in this area by introducing the concept of role-based security. *Role-based security* enables the application developer to create various classes of authority, or roles. Then each potential user of the application is assigned to one or more authority classes. For example, in a banking environment, you can envision several authority classes. The bank president may have ultimate authority over financial decisions, branch managers have certain authorities, and so on. Each bank customer has a certain authority level as well. As long as you remember your PIN, you have access to your own accounts via an ATM.

Given the preceding example, a banking application can set up the MTS roles: President, Manager, Teller, and Customer. Every user of the banking application then is assigned to a specific role or authority level. Of course, under Windows NT, this means each user identity (UserID/Password) is assigned a given role because the underlying implementation still depends on NT's security system. The benefit of this approach is that application developers can write their components in terms of high-level roles. You can protect access to application functionality, such as the ability to approve an account withdrawal of greater than $10,000, by checking the role of the caller. Here is some abbreviated MTS-based code that demonstrates this checking for role membership:

```
STDMETHODIMP CSomeComponent::Withdrawal(double dAmount)
{
   // Get the MTS context object
   IObjectContext* pObjectContext = 0;
   GetObjectContext( &pObjectContext )

   // If the withdrawal is over $10,000, make sure it's a manager
   if ( dAmount > 10000.00 )
   {
      BOOL bInRole;
      CComBSTR bstrRole( "Manager" );
      hr = pObjectContext->IsCallerInRole( bstrRole, &bInRole );
      if (! bInRole )
      {
         // Not in role
         return E_FAIL;
      }
   }
   // Perform the withdrawal...
   return S_OK;
}
```

When running in the MTS environment, each component instance has an associated context object. This object contains information about the execution context. The previous code obtains the client's role by interrogating this context object. If the withdrawal amount is greater than $10,000 and the caller is not a manager, the transaction fails.

As introduced with MTS, role-based security enables the developer to focus on application-level security issues instead of low-level, platform-specific ones. However, MTS provides only modest support when compared to that offered by COM+.

Like MTS, the COM+ security services are provided through the concept of roles. Of course, if this does not meet your application requirements, you can continue to write low-level NT or Windows 2000 security code within your applications. There are situations in which role-based security is not effective (for example, per-instance security), but COM+ does provide extensive support for impersonation and cloaking to help in these situations.

The goal of the COM+ security architecture is to isolate, as much as possible, the low-level security issues from your application. When developing a secure COM+ application, you begin by establishing an authorization policy. This policy describes the various roles and what each role can do in terms of accessing code within your applications. In other words, the policy describes who can do what to the resources within your application.

After establishing an application security policy, you then factor your application into its separate components. Each user of the application is assigned one or more roles indicating their level of authorization, or access. Using COM+, you can assign roles to specific components, interfaces, and methods within your application. The COM+ run time controls client access to each one of these entities. If a client in role "Teller" tries to access the DeleteAccount method – which is marked with role "Manager" – COM+ fails the call before invoking the method within your component.

This is a powerful technique in that COM+ enforces the access policy for your application. Another important point is that the setup and maintenance of this policy is handled declaratively (that is, outside of your component's code). COM+ handles the access control details, so the policy can be managed administratively long after you develop your application. Users are given roles; components, interfaces, and methods are assigned roles; and COM+ ensures that the access policy is enforced by implicitly performing membership checks as calls are made across security boundaries. COM+ has abstracted yet another implementation detail!

Use of declarative, role-based security works in many application scenarios. In cases where it does not, you can add security logic to your components just as in the preceding MTS code example. Programmatic, role-based security is enhanced in COM+ through its security call context object. A call context object is associated with each call and contains information about the number of callers in the call chain as well as the identity of each caller.

The COM+ security architecture contains other useful features that make it easier to build secure applications, but most applications take advantage of the built-in support for role-based security. When designing your COM+ applications, make sure you develop an access policy, and then factor your application based on how different clients will access your application resources. If you perform these small steps, COM+

can handle the majority of the security issues that you face when developing a secure, distributed application.

Future Changes to Visual C++

That wraps up my coverage of some of the new COM+ features. Next, let's take a quick look at what changes are being added to Visual C++ to make developing COM+ applications easier. These changes are similar to what Kirtland discussed in her MSJ articles last year. However, instead of implementing these features in the COM+ run time and exposing them to tools such as Visual C++, a short-term solution was used. I describe the solution in this section.

The COM+ features I've discussed are great, but as C++ developers we still need some way to harness all these features. Writing COM components in C++ is still a bit tedious, although ATL has made it much better. Developing COM components with C++ is hard because the COM and C++ programming models don't "mesh" exactly. Frameworks such as ATL make development easier, but they still require some knowledge of low-level COM. The Visual C++ and ATL teams have joined together to make COM development easier through something called attributed-based programming.

Attribute-Based Programming

Attributed-based programming is the technique of using declarative instructions in your code to guide its implementation. To put it another way, instead of writing system-level COM code (mostly the same in all components), you direct the development tool to implement this "glue" code for you.

Attributes encapsulate domain-specific (for example, COM) concepts and provide this information to the compiler. The attributes do not change the underlying semantics of the C++ code. In fact, through a collaborative process with something called an attribute provider, the embedded attributes produce standard C++ code.

Attribute Syntax

The syntax for using these attributes in your C++ code is simple. All attributes are enclosed in brackets and you can apply attributes to any declaration. An important point is that attributes always apply to declarations and not to types or instances. The following code gives you an example of how you use attributes:

```
[
   coclass,
   progid("TechPreview.Math.1" ),
   uuid("21091111-7A3F-11d2-81D6-0060081AEB5F")
]
class Math
{
public:
```

```
    HRESULT Add( [in] long, [in] long, [out,retval] long* );
    ...
}
```

The `coclass` attribute specifies that the `Math` class is a COM component and the `progid` and `uuid` attributes provide the ProgID and CLSID for the resulting component. Eventually these attributes produce ATL and IDL code, but you won't see it. If you've done much programming with ATL, you should recognize that the C++ attributes look a lot like the attributes in your component's IDL file because the attribute syntax is based heavily on IDL. You can have simple names, name-value pairs, and names with sets of properties. Here are some examples:

```
// Just a name
[ coclass ]
class X {...};

// A name with a value
[ uuid("21091110-7A3F-11d2-81D6-0060081AEB5F") ]
    interface IFoo {...}

// A name with a set of properties
[ module(dll, name="MyComponent", version="1.0") ]
```

The *VC++ Technology Preview* defines a small number of attributes, most of which I list in Table 13-1. In this release, all of the attributes are related to COM development. However, this probably will change to include future technologies.

TABLE 13-1 COM ATTRIBUTES

Attribute	Description
coclass	Adds COM support to the class and to the underlying IDL file
dual	Marks the interface as supporting both Vtable and `IDispatch` access
emitidl	Indicates that all subsequent attributes should be emitted to the component's IDL file
id	Specifies the DISPID for methods in interfaces that support `IDispatch`
in/out	Indicates the direction of the parameter in a method
progid	Specifies the ProgID for the component
retval	Indicates that the parameter is the return value from a method
threading	Specifies the threading model for the component

Attribute	Description
uuid	Specifies a GUID for a class, type library, or interface
module	Specifies information about the component housing (for example, DLL or EXE). Items such as housing name, type library GUID, and so on

Compiler Changes

The C++ compiler wasn't changed to intrinsically support the building of COM components. Instead, a mechanism that supports the addition of language attributes (like the ones in Table 13-1) was added to the compile process. The compiler group at Microsoft doesn't need to be aware of COM or ATL and the ATL group doesn't need to know how compilers work. They just got together and created a component-based solution that is pretty cool.

Attributes are handled by an extension to the C++ build process. As the compiler encounters attributes in the source, it passes them to an attribute provider. The provider then converts the attributes into C++ code and passes them back to the compiler, which then compiles them into the resultant object code. Currently, there is only an ATL provider, but Microsoft may allow others to extend the compiler using this architecture in the future. Providers also can generate their own inputs (for example, IDL) to the build process. Figure 13-8 shows the complete process.

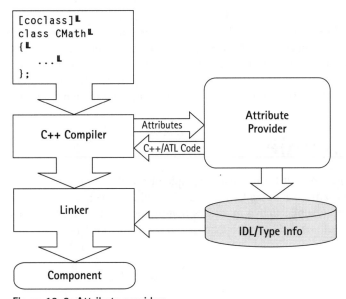

Figure 13-8: Attribute providers

Language purists don't like the fact that Microsoft is extending the C++ language, but the neat part is that eventually anyone can add functionality to the language by writing his or her own attribute providers. This strategy also decouples the compiler and ATL versions. The ATL team can upgrade its ATL provider without waiting for the next release of Visual C++. Exactly what component development is all about!

The Interface Keyword

Actually, one new keyword was added to the base compiler implementation. The `interface` keyword is similar to the `struct` keyword, but it is restricted by the following conditions. The interface can inherit only from another interface, the interface can contain only methods, and these methods must be public, pure virtual, and declared. In other words, the `interface` keyword indicates an abstract class that contains only pure public methods. For example, the following code:

```
interface IMath
{
    HRESULT Add();
};
```

is equivalent to this:

```
struct IMath
{
    virtual HRESULT Add() = 0;
};
```

As you know, COM interfaces are just abstract classes like the preceding one and so the `interface` keyword makes your code easier to read and understand. In fact, if you look at the Java language, you can see that it has an `interface` keyword that operates in a similar way. The `interface` keyword is not COM specific; it just moves the concept of an abstract interface into Microsoft's C++ language implementation.

A Final Example

I'm running out of space, so next I provide an example of a COM component that is developed using the new attribute-based C++ syntax. Following is the header file for a simple math component. It supports two interfaces that provide basic math functionality. At first glance, you think you're looking at an IDL file but you are not:

```
//
// math.hdr
```

```
//
...
[ emitidl ];

[
   uuid("FA5FEDA2-7900-11d2-BDC6-000000000000"),
   helpstring("IMath Interface"),
]
interface IMath : IUnknown
{
  [helpstring("Add Method")] HRESULT
      Add( [in] long l0p1, [in] long l0p2,
          [out, retval] long* plResult );
  [helpstring("Subtract Method")] HRESULT
      Subtract( [in] long l0p1, [in] long l0p2,
               [out, retval] long* plResult );
  [helpstring("Multiply Method")] HRESULT
      Multiply( [in] long l0p1, [in] long l0p2,
               [out, retval] long* plResult );
  [helpstring("Divide Method")] HRESULT
      Divide( [in] long l0p1, [in] long l0p2,
             [out, retval] long* plResult );
};

[
   uuid("FA5FEDA3-7900-11d2-BDC6-000000000000"),
   helpstring("IAdvanced Interface"),
]
interface IAdvancedMath : IUnknown
{
   HRESULT Factorial( [in] short, [out,retval] long* );
   HRESULT Fibonacci( [in] short, [out,retval] long* );
};

[
   coclass,
   progid("TechPreview.Math.1"),
   uuid("FA5FEDA4-7900-11d2-BDC6-000000000000"),
   helpstring("Math Class")
]
class CMath : public IMath,
              public IAdvancedMath
{
```

```
public:
    CMath();

// IMath
public:
    HRESULT Add( [in] long, [in] long, [out,retval] long* );
    HRESULT Subtract( [in] long, [in] long, [out,retval] long* );
    HRESULT Multiply( [in] long, [in] long, [out,retval] long* );
    HRESULT Divide( [in] long, [in] long, [out,retval] long* );

// IAdvancedMath
public:
    HRESULT Factorial( [in] short, [out,retval] long* );
    HRESULT Fibonacci( [in] short, [out,retval] long* );
};
```

When the compiler encounters an attribute, it passes it to the ATL provider. The provider passes back ATL-based C++ code for compilation. By using attributes, you're writing a COM component using ATL without knowing it! The header file contains most of the interesting attribute syntax. The only thing worthwhile in the CPP file is the module attribute, which specifies the DLL name, GUID, and version number. It looks like this:

```
//
// Math.cpp
//
...
[
    module( dll, name="MathLib",
    uuid="21091112-7A3F-11d2-81D6-0060081AEB5F",
    version="1.0"
]
...
```

If you go back and read Kirtland's MSJ articles, you can see that this move to attribute-based development was a major focus of her articles. However, at that time, a unified COM+ run time was going to provide these features. Instead, the attribute features were added via the attribute provider architecture. While this is a cool technique, it does not provide for a long-term solution to the problem that various languages and tools have their own view of how to develop COM components. Of course, in the future, the attribute features could be moved into the run time as originally planned.

Moving Toward the COM+ Environment

Microsoft has promised (and demonstrated) that legacy COM and MTS components will work just fine in the new COM+ environment. Today, you should continue to invest in the COM and MTS programming models. If you are building COM and MTS applications, continue to do so. However, you should start looking into the component features provided by Windows 2000 because they are broad and will have a significant impact on the development and delivery of applications.

Summary

In this chapter, you learned about the new COM+ features provided with the release of Windows 2000. In particular, you learned:

- ◆ COM+ merges all of the current COM programming models into a coherent, distributed development platform.

- ◆ Several new services are provided that make developing multi-tier applications easier.

- ◆ COM+ Queued Components provide asynchronous capabilities to standard COM components.

- ◆ The new COM+ Events service substantially changes the existing COM event model by providing a rich, publish-subscribe environment.

- ◆ The COM+ security infrastructure builds on the existing MTS environment and adds several new features.

Appendix

Visual C++ Native COM Support

BEGINNING WITH VERSION 5.0 and continuing with version 6.0 of Visual C++, the C++ compiler provides intrinsic support for COM-based development. This makes it easier for developers to use COM-based components in their applications. In many ways, native COM support is a preview of some of the capabilities that COM+ offers; a new version of COM that moves many of the details of COM development into the operating system. See Chapter 13 for more details.

Today, native COM support provides wrapper classes for the basic COM entities, such as interface pointers, BSTRs, and variants. The compiler provides this support with help from a number of header files — COMUTIL.H, COMIP.H, and COMDEF.H — and the new #import compiler directive.

Smart Pointers: _com_ptr_t

Chapter 4 briefly discusses smart pointers. Smart pointers act as wrappers to COM interface pointers and are an attempt to hide some of the tedium — such as having to explicitly release pointers — of working with straight COM interfaces. ATL provides a basic smart pointer class in CComPtr and CComQIPtr.

The Visual C++ smart pointer class _com_ptr_t implements additional smart pointer functionality. _com_ptr_t encapsulates CoCreateInstance functionality and uses C++ exceptions to indicate error conditions. The _COM_SMARTPTR_TYPEDEF macro creates a smart pointer for any COM interface:

```
_COM_SMARTPTR_TYPEDEF(IMyInterface, __uuidof(IMyInterface));
```

This macro produces a smart pointer class (using the _com_ptr_t template class) named IMyInterfacePtr. You then use an instance of the smart pointer class to instantiate a component that implements it; from there, you access the component's functionality just as you do through a COM interface pointer. The difference with smart pointers is that when they go out of scope, an implicit IUnknown::Release is called. Here's a simple example:

```
// From CHAPTER4_SERVER.TLI
...
//
```

```
// Smart pointer typedef declarations
//
_COM_SMARTPTR_TYPEDEF(IMath, __uuidof(IMath));
_COM_SMARTPTR_TYPEDEF(IMath2, __uuidof(IMath2));
_COM_SMARTPTR_TYPEDEF(IAdvancedMath, __uuidof(IAdvancedMath));
_COM_SMARTPTR_TYPEDEF(IComponentInfo, __uuidof(IComponentInfo));
...
IMathPtr ptrMath;

// Create an instance of the server
try
{
   HRESULT hr;
   hr = ptrMath.CreateInstance( CLSID_Math );
   if ( FAILED( hr ))
      _com_issue_error( hr );
}
catch( _com_error& e )
{
...
}
// Access the IMath interface
try
{
   long lResult;
   lResult = ptrMath->Add( 134, 353 );
   cout << "134 + 353 = " << lResult << endl;
}
catch( _com_error& e )
{
...
}
```

Notice that you use the dot (.) operator to access the smart pointer's function-ality and the pointer operator (->) to access the underlying interface pointer meth-ods. A smart pointer overloads the pointer operator to provide most of its functionality.

BSTRs (_bstr_t)

The _bstr_t type encapsulates COM's primary string type, the BSTR. As described in Chapter 4, a BSTR is a length-prefixed Unicode string. The _bstr_t type pro-vides constructors, methods, and operators that make it easier to work with BSTRs.

Primarily, these constructs include ways of moving among ANSI strings, Unicode strings, and BSTRs:

```
_bstr_t name( pInfo->bstrName );
cout << "Component name is " << name << endl;
```

Variants (_variant_t)

The _variant_t class encapsulates COM's VARIANT data type. Chapter 6 discusses the variant type. _variant_t provides constructs, methods, and operators to make working with variants easier. To demonstrate the use of the _variant_t type, the downloadable examples include a simple client application (Chapter6_Native Client) to access the Chapter 6 math component. Here's a glimpse at some of the code:

```
_variant_t result;
_variant_t Op1( long( 100 ));
_variant_t Op2( long( 200 ));
result = ptrMath->Add( Op1, Op2 );
cout << "100 + 200 = " << long( result ) << endl;
```

You construct three variant_t objects to pass to your Add method. By casting the types, you initialize the variant to the correct type (for example, VT_I4). The default constructor creates an initialized VT_EMPTY variant. The extraction operators work just like casting, as the previous example demonstrates.

Handling COM Errors (_com_error)

In most cases, the native COM wrapper classes handle COM errors through exceptions. When an error occurs (for example, an underlying CoCreateInstance fails), an exception of type _com_error is thrown. _com_error encapsulates an HRESULT and any associated IErrorInfo objects. The IErrorInfo methods are available only if the component supports rich error handling. The Error method returns an HRESULT, Description returns the string message associated with an HRESULT (such as Interface not registered for 0x80040155), and the ErrorInfo method returns an IErrorInfo object if one exists. Here's an example:

```
// Create an instance of the server
try
{
   HRESULT hr;
   hr = ptrMath.CreateInstance( CLSID_Math );
   if ( FAILED( hr ))
```

```
      _com_issue_error( hr );
}
catch( _com_error& e )
{
   cout << "Error creating instance" << endl;
   cout << "HRESULT message is " << e.ErrorMessage() << endl;
   // If rich error info is supported, display the description
   if ( e.ErrorInfo() )
      cout << e.Description() << endl;
   return -1;
}
```

Here you use the smart pointer's capability to create an instance of a component. The CreateInstance method, however, does not throw an exception, so check the HRESULT and use the _com_issue_error function to throw a _com_error. If any problems arise in the creation, catch the error and display the message associated with the returned HRESULT. Next, you determine whether rich error information is supported; if it is, you display its description.

The #import Directive

The wrapper classes provide intrinsic compiler support for the basic COM types. The real power provided by Visual C++'s native support is through the use of the new #import directive. When the compiler encounters the #import directive, it produces wrapper classes for each interface described in the referenced component's type library. The type library can be read directly (for example, from a TLB file), or the compiler can locate it in an executable's (DLL, EXE) attached resources. The #import statement uses the LoadTypeLib API to load the type information for the module. Here's a brief example:

```
//
// Chapter4_NativeClient.cpp
//
#include <windows.h>

#import "Chapter4_Server.exe" no_namespace named_guids

int main( int argc, char *argv[] )
{
...
}
```

In the previous example, #import has a number of optional attributes that affect its behavior. You specify that the classes created by #import should not be defined within a namespace and that the GUIDs should be defined using the named format (for example, CLSID_Math) with which you are familiar.

The TLI and TLH Files

The wrapper classes created by #import are placed in the output directory (such as \DEBUG) for the project. Two files are produced: a header file (project.tlh) and an implementation file (projectname.tli). Here's a glimpse of the header file for the math component:

```
// Chapter4_Server.TLH
// Created by Microsoft (R) C/C++ Compiler Version 11.00.0000
(eb20bb72).
//
// Debug/Chapter4_Server.tlh
//
// C++ source equivalent of Win32 type library Chapter4_Server.exe
// compiler-generated file created 11/25/97 at 06:47:31 - DO NOT EDIT!
#include <comdef.h>
...
//
// Smart pointer typedef declarations
//
_COM_SMARTPTR_TYPEDEF(IMath, __uuidof(IMath));
_COM_SMARTPTR_TYPEDEF(IAdvancedMath, __uuidof(IAdvancedMath));
...
struct __declspec(uuid("5fb0c22e-3343-11d1-883a-444553540000"))
IMath : IUnknown
{
    //
    // Wrapper methods for error handling
    //
    long Add ( long lOp1, long lOp2 );
    long Subtract ( long lOp1, long lOp2 );
    ...
    //
    // Raw methods provided by interface
    //
    virtual HRESULT __stdcall raw_Add (
        long lOp1,
        long lOp2,
        long * plResult ) = 0;
    virtual HRESULT __stdcall raw_Subtract (
        long lOp1,
```

```
            long lOp2,
            long * plResult ) = 0;
    ...
};
...
enum mathOPERATION
{
    mathAdd = 1,
    mathSubtract = 2,
    mathMultiply = 3,
    mathDivide = 4
};
...
//
// Named GUID constants initializations
//
extern "C" const GUID __declspec(selectany) CLSID_Math =
    {0x5fb0c22f,0x3343,0x11d1,{0x88,0x3a,0x44,0x45,0x53,0x54,0x00,
0x00}};
extern "C" const GUID __declspec(selectany) IID_IMath =
    {0x5fb0c22e,0x3343,0x11d1,{0x88,0x3a,0x44,0x45,0x53,0x54,0x00,
0x00}};
...
//
// Wrapper method implementations
//
#include "Debug/Chapter4_Server.tli"
```

Most of the preceding code should make sense. The compiler reads the type library and, using various macros and structures, it produces smart pointers for each of the interfaces. It also produces wrapper classes for both the "wrapped" and the "raw" interface methods, enumerated type declarations, and, finally, constants for the CLSID and IID GUIDs. The header file then includes the implementation file:

```
// Chapter4_Server.TLI
// Created by Microsoft (R) C/C++ Compiler Version 11.00.0000
(c4aee32c).
//
// Debug/Chapter4_Server.tli
//
// Wrapper implementations for Win32 type library
Chapter4_Server.exe
// compiler-generated file created 11/25/97 at 05:43:34 - DO NOT EDIT!
//
```

```
// Interface IMath wrapper method implementations
//
inline long IMath::Add ( long l0p1, long l0p2 ) {
    long _result;
    HRESULT _hr = raw_Add(l0p1, l0p2, &_result);
    if (FAILED(_hr)) _com_issue_errorex(_hr, this, __uuidof(this));
    return _result;
}
inline long IMath::Subtract ( long l0p1, long l0p2 ) {
    long _result;
    HRESULT _hr = raw_Subtract(l0p1, l0p2, &_result);
    if (FAILED(_hr)) _com_issue_errorex(_hr, this, __uuidof(this));
    return _result;
}
...
//
// interface IAdvancedMath wrapper method implementations
//
inline long IAdvancedMath::Factorial ( short sFact ) {
    long _result;
    HRESULT _hr = raw_Factorial(sFact, &_result);
    if (FAILED(_hr)) _com_issue_errorex(_hr, this, __uuidof(this));
    return _result;
}
...
```

The implementation file creates a series of wrapper methods for each interface implemented by the component. The methods encapsulate some of the low-level behavior of the interface. In particular, they provide a more friendly way of interacting with the interfaces. In other words, the return value is not an HRESULT, but instead is the method parameter marked as retval. This approach gives the C++ developer Visual Basic-like syntax. More important, it enables you to develop using the C++ exception model. If an error occurs, you use try/catch blocks instead of checking the HRESULT.

Which One Should I Use?

Good question. When developing components or client applications based on COM, you now have several choices. You can use interface pointers and native types (BSTR, VARIANT), or you can use ATL's wrapper classes (CComPtr, CComBSTR), or even use native Visual C++ support as well (_com_ptr_t, _bstr_t). It's nice to have so many choices, but which one should you use when developing your own applications?

The Visual C++ native COM types provide the most functionality. The smart pointer classes and COM data type wrapper classes support exceptions and operations that are not part of the ATL implementation. So, at first glance, the native COM types are the ones to use. However, if you have any hope of ever moving your components or applications to non-Microsoft compilers and platforms, you probably should not use these classes. Classes such as _bstr_t and the #import directive are Microsoft-specific and probably are not supported by other compilers (such as C++ Builder). If this isn't an issue, using the native COM support classes is the preferred technique.

If you are worried about portability, I suggest that you use ATL's wrapper classes. In some situations, though, ATL's wrapper classes don't provide much functional improvement when compared with the straight types (for example, BSTR versus CComBSTR). I expect, though, that ATL's implementations will become more functional in the future.

An Example Client Application

Native COM supports both client-side and server-side development. However, generally native support is most useful when you use components or act as a client. For example, in Chapter 4 you develop a math component that supports a number of interfaces. The #import directive makes it very easy to access the math component's functionality. The following example code shows how to access the Chapter 4 math component using Visual C++'s native COM support:

```
//
// Chapter4_NativeClient.cpp
//
#include <windows.h>
#include <tchar.h>
#include <iostream.h>

#import "..\Chapter4_Server\Debug\Chapter4_Server.exe"
                                        no_namespace named_guids
int main( int argc, char *argv[] )
{
    cout << "Initializing COM" << endl;
    if ( FAILED( CoInitialize( NULL )))
    {
        cout << "Unable to initialize COM" << endl;
        return -1;
    }
    IMathPtr ptrMath;

    // Create an instance of the server
```

```
try
{
   HRESULT hr;
   hr = ptrMath.CreateInstance( CLSID_Math );
   if ( FAILED( hr ))
      _com_issue_error( hr );
}
catch( _com_error& e )
{
   cout << "Error-creating instance" << endl;
   cout << "HRESULT message is " << e.ErrorMessage() << endl;

   // If rich error info is supported, display the description
   if ( e.ErrorInfo() )
      cout << e.Description() << endl;
   return -1;
}

// Access the IMath interface
try
{
   long lResult;
   lResult = ptrMath->Add( 134, 353 );
   cout << "134 + 353 = " << lResult << endl;

   // Try to divide by zero
   lResult = ptrMath->Divide( 0, 0 );
}
catch( _com_error& e )
{
   cout << "Error accessing IMath" << endl;
   cout << "HRESULT message is " << e.ErrorMessage() << endl;
   if ( e.ErrorInfo() )
      cout << e.Description() << endl;

   // Don't return, we forced the error with 0/0
}

// Access IMath2
try
{
   IMath2Ptr ptrMath2( ptrMath );
   long lResult;
   lResult = ptrMath2->Compute( mathAdd,
                                100,
```

```
                                         200 );
    cout << "Compute( 100 + 200 ) = " << lResult << endl;

    // Sum an array
    short sArray[3] = { 3,4,5 };
    lResult = ptrMath2->Sum( 3, sArray );
    cout << "Sum( 3,4,5 ) = " << lResult << endl;
}
catch( _com_error& e )
{
    cout << "Error accessing IMath2" << endl;
    cout << "HRESULT message is " << e.ErrorMessage() << endl;
    return -1;
}


// Access IAdvancedMath
try
{
    IAdvancedMathPtr ptrAdvancedMath( ptrMath );
    if ( ptrAdvancedMath )
    {
      long lResult;
      lResult = ptrAdvancedMath->Factorial( 12 );
      cout << "12! = " << lResult << endl;
      lResult = ptrAdvancedMath->Fibonacci( 12 );
      cout << "The Fibonacci of 12 = " << lResult << endl;
    }
}
catch( _com_error& e )
{
    cout << "Error accessing IAdvancedMath" << endl;
    cout << "HRESULT message is " << e.ErrorMessage() << endl;
    return -1;
}


// Access IComponentInfo
try
{
    IComponentInfoPtr ptrInfo( ptrMath );
    if ( ptrInfo )
    {
      COMPONENT_INFO* pInfo = 0;
      ptrInfo->get_Info( &pInfo );
      cout << "Component author is " << pInfo->pstrAuthor
                                     << endl;
```

```
            cout << "Component version is " << pInfo->sMajor <<
                                    "." << pInfo->sMinor << endl;
            _bstr_t name( pInfo->bstrName );
            cout << "Component name is " << name << endl;
            if ( pInfo->pstrAuthor )
                CoTaskMemFree( pInfo->pstrAuthor );
            if ( pInfo->bstrName )
                SysFreeString( pInfo->bstrName );
            if ( pInfo )
                CoTaskMemFree( pInfo );
        }
    }
    catch( _com_error& e )
    {
        cout << "Error accessing IComponentInfo" << endl;
        cout << "HRESULT message is " << e.ErrorMessage() << endl;
        return -1;
    }

    // We have to release the pointer here
    // because if we call CoUninitialize before
    // it goes out of scope, we'll get an exception
    ptrMath = 0;
    CoUninitialize();
    return 0;
}
```

Chapter6_NativeClient Example

The downloadable examples (http://www.widgetware.com) also contain a client
that demonstrates how to access the automation-based Chapter 6 component. It
demonstrates the use of the _variant_t class when working with variants.

Index

Symbols

A

531

Continued

Continued

Continued

Continued

Continued

Continued

Continued

Continued

Continued